4-16 (5)

DEC 1 4 2015

W9-AXG-658

HOLLYWOOD AND THE HOLOCAUST

FILM AND HISTORY

Series Editor: Cynthia J. Miller

HOLLYWOOD AND THE HOLOCAUST

Henry Gonshak

ROWMAN & LITTLEFIELD
Lanham • Boulder • New York • London

Published by Rowman & Littlefield
A wholly owned subsidiary of The Rowman & Littlefield Publishing Group,
Inc.
4501 Forbes Boulevard, Suite 200, Lanham, Maryland 20706
www.rowman.com

Unit A, Whitacre Mews, 26-34 Stannary Street, London SE11 4AB

British Library Cataloguing in Publication Information Available

Library of Congress Cataloging-in-Publication Data

Gonshak, Henry, 1958–
Hollywood and the Holocaust / Henry Gonshak. pages cm
Includes bibliographical references and index.
ISBN 978-1-4422-5223-3 (hardcover : alk. paper) — ISBN 978-1-4422-5224-0 (ebook)
1. Holocaust, Jewish (1939–1945), in motion pictures. 2. Holocaust, Jewish (1939–1945)—Influ-
ence. 3. Motion pictures—United States—History—20th century. 4. Motion pictures—United
States—History—21st century. I. Title.
PN1995.9.H53G66 2015
791.43'658—dc23
2015016263

♾™ The paper used in this publication meets the minimum requirements of
American National Standard for Information Sciences Permanence of Paper
for Printed Library Materials, ANSI/NISO Z39.48-1992.

Printed in the United States of America

CONTENTS

ACKNOWLEDGMENTS

Hollywood and the Holocaust could never have been written without the assistance of my late father, Irwin Gonshak. My father began his career as a social studies teacher at a New York City junior high school, but his real love was for educational and dramatic radio. For many years, he worked as a script writer for WNYE-FM, the official radio station of the New York City Public School System. My father read the *New York Times* every day of his adult life, and he must have read with scissors in hand, because he sent me literally thousands of articles, from the *Times* and elsewhere, which proved vital to my research. My student assistant, Pat Wright, also deserves my thanks for undertaking the laborious task of organizing and filing all those clippings.

My father also found me dozens of books on the Holocaust, many of which became sources for this work. A great supporter of locally owned bookstores, he ordered all these books through Butte's own independent store, Books & Books. Every time we talked on the phone, my father would ask if I needed new books and often had books to recommend. Although he defined himself as a "secular humanist," my father never lost his intimate connection to cultural and ethnic Judaism. Indeed, my father was a Jewish scholar in his own right. As a young man, he wrote scripts for the radio program *The Eternal Light*, a Jewish dramatic show, which happened to be the first American media outlet to broadcast the story of Anne Frank. Many of the books used for *Hollywood and the Holocaust* were simply plucked off the shelves of my father's personal library, which included an extensive collection of Judaica. My only sadness is that my father didn't live long enough to see this book in print. But my memories of him permeate every page.

I would also like to thank the institution where I've taught English for the last twenty-five years: Montana Tech in Butte. My college awarded me a sabbatical, which I spent working on this book. Let me also thank the US Fulbright Program, which allowed me to spend the 2008–2009 school year teaching Jewish-American literature as well as the Holocaust in American film at the University of Wroclaw in Poland. My light teaching load left me plenty of time to engage in on-site research about the Holocaust in Poland. As part of that endeavor, I gave a paper at a Holocaust conference at Jagiellonian University in Krakow. It was during this conference that I first visited Auschwitz.

As well, I'd like to thank the US Holocaust Memorial Museum in Washington, DC, where I not only spent many hours wandering through its information-packed exhibits but also did research for the book in the museum's extensive library for scholars. Additionally, my thanks go out to the Jentel Artist Residency Program in Sheridan, Wyoming, where I devoted a month to working on this book.

Among the editors at Rowman & Littlefield, I worked most closely with Cynthia Miller, editor of the publisher's Film and History series, in which this book appears. Throughout the lengthy process of bringing *Hollywood and the Holocaust* into print, Miller was a wonderful editor: knowledgeable, meticulous, steadfast, and kind.

Finally, thanks to my wife, Nancy Coughlin, who worked with me from start to finish. Though all errors of fact and judgment are, of course, my own, Nancy edited two full drafts of this book, sentence by sentence, word by word. Nancy has the literary equivalent of perfect pitch in music: she has a remarkable gift for revision. I dedicate this book to her, as well as to my wonderful daughter, Rebecca Gonshak, with all my heart.

Introduction

CAN HOLLYWOOD GET IT RIGHT?

This book is a study of fictionalized representations of the Jewish Holocaust in Hollywood movies from the World War II era up to the present day. Its premise is quite simple: for better or worse, the average American (as well as millions internationally) generally learns about the Holocaust not through history books, documentary films, or "serious" works of literature and cinema but rather through Hollywood portrayals (along with other examples of mass media, such as commercial television, popular fiction, and Broadway plays). What happened during the Holocaust, why it happened, whether it can happen again, what lessons should be drawn from the genocide—whatever answers ordinary people find to these vital questions have been determined predominantly by popular culture, with its primary branch being Hollywood, which both shapes and reflects public attitudes in a complex dynamic. For most Americans, *Schindler's List* isn't *about* the Holocaust; it *is* the Holocaust. In short, given mass media's huge and ever-growing influence, the issue of how adequately Hollywood portrays the Shoah (and of precisely which criteria should be used to define adequacy in such portrayals) should interest anyone concerned about public perceptions of the Holocaust.

By what standards, then, should Hollywood Holocaust films be judged? This complex question touches on myriad aesthetic, cultural, and sociopolitical issues. First, in an admittedly controversial decision, I have not assessed these depictions strictly on the basis of whether or not they adhere to historical facts. Not that I believe by any means that historical accuracy is an irrelevant criterion. On the contrary, I think that Hollywood films that grossly distort the history of the Holocaust, as many do, are extremely irresponsible, given the importance of the topic, the power of the media, and the historical amnesia permeating American society. Indeed, as this book will show, Hollywood is notorious for blithely ignoring the specific historical context in which the genocide occurred, and, instead, converting the tragedy into some free-floating emblem of cosmic evil.

Nonetheless, to judge such depictions exclusively by the standard of historical authenticity would mean denying artistic license to screenwriters and directors of Hollywood Holocaust films. This book includes chapters on two such films, which deliberately depart from the historical record: *X-Men* and *Inglourious Basterds*. *X-Men* is a science fiction film featuring a mutant villain who is a Holocaust survivor, and *Inglourious Basterds* concludes with an alternate history plot twist, in which a rugged band of Jewish-American GIs gun down Hitler, Goering, and

Figure 0.1. *Schindler's List* (1993). Oskar Schindler (Liam Neeson) and his assistant, Itzhak Stern (Ben Kingsley), pore over the list of Jews they hope to save from extermination. [Screen grab]

Goebbels at a movie premiere in Paris. I have all sorts of problems with both films, but the fact that they revise history isn't one of them. Numerous books and movies based on other historical events take liberties with the historical record yet are still considered classics. Tolstoy's *War and Peace*, for example, is hardly completely accurate about Napoleon's war with Russia, yet that hasn't hurt its standing as one of the greatest novels ever written. Shakespeare is an even better example. Shakespeare's history plays consistently take considerable license with the historical record. In *Henry IV, Part I*, for example, Shakespeare makes Prince Hal and Hotspur the same age, even though the historical Hotspur was actually a couple of decades older, in order to establish the two men as equal rivals for King Henry IV's fatherly affections. Shakespeare's altering of the historical facts for dramatic purposes, however, hasn't inspired critics to dismiss the play as worthless.

Why should the Holocaust be the one event in which, when translated into art, total fidelity to history is demanded? Such a view accords the Holocaust a kind of sacred status—a view that seems counterproductive both for artistic reproduction and as a framework for historians. One way the Holocaust is made sacred is through the figure of the "sanctified survivor" who has become a saint as a result of his or her suffering. This character type appears frequently in Holocaust movies, beginning with *The Diary of Anne Frank*, but also appears in the first *X-Men* movie, based on the popular comic strip. Making the Holocaust sacred inevitably distorts the historical event and also functions as a distancing device for the viewer, since the horror of the Holocaust becomes more bearable if it can be wrapped in this cloak of religiosity. Religiosity is encapsulated in the very root of the word "Holocaust," since the word is derived from a Greek word that means a "burnt offering," a sacrifice to God.

The sacralization of the Holocaust is brilliantly satirized in an episode of the TV sitcom *Seinfeld*, aired in 1994 and called "The Raincoats." Here, Seinfeld takes his girlfriend, with whom he's been unable to be intimate for an extended period of time, to see *Schindler's List* and is so sexually frustrated that he ends up making out with her during the screening of the film. This shocking behavior is witnessed by Seinfeld's arch-enemy, Newman, also attending the movie, who immediately rushes off to reveal Seinfeld's perfidy to Seinfeld's parents, who happen to be visiting New York. In an immortal line, Newman tells the couple, "He was moving on her like the storm troopers into Poland." Naturally, Seinfeld's parents are horrified by their son's actions. The episode's satirical point is that for American Jews, the viewing of *Schindler's List*, with its powerful evocation of the Holocaust, has become akin to attending a religious event; making out during a screening of Spielberg's movie is comparable to making out during a synagogue service. With a decline in religious practice among many American Jews and with American Jewry fractured over so many issues, such as Israel, it's no surprise that Jewish Americans have decided en masse that the Holocaust should be elevated to this sacred status, as the one event all Jews can agree is central to Jewish identity.[1] This understandable but unfortunate sacralizing of the Shoah has spread from the Jewish American community to the American public at large, as can be seen in so many Hollywood Holocaust films.

Judging Hollywood Holocaust movies purely by a standard of historical accuracy is problematic for another reason. As Aaron Kerner argues,

> Authenticity is a red herring. Narratives, whether we are speaking of conventional fictional film or documentary, are always already a construct. Historical events can only be *re*-presented; there is no transparent window through which we might render the past. This is not to say that "realistic" representations cannot, or should not, be made, but rather that authenticity, whatever that might be, or look like, should not be the criterion on which we predicate our assessments.[2]

In other words, *no* Holocaust film is totally historically accurate, however much it may strive for such accuracy; every film, even a documentary, is shaped aesthetically by its producer and conforms to certain genre conventions. Later, Kerner speculates that the imperative wielded by so many prominent critics of Holocaust film, such as Annette Insdorf and Ilan Avisar—that such films be judged on a strict standard of historical authenticity—may be partly driven by a "fear where the lack of fidelity might in some fashion embolden or otherwise lend fodder to the agenda of historical revisionists or Holocaust deniers."[3] Holocaust denial is a serious problem in our modern world, and Holocaust films whose presentation of the facts about the Shoah serve as a bulwark against the deniers are certainly performing a worthy function. But fear of Holocaust denial shouldn't inspire critics to straight-jacket filmmakers by insisting that only "realistic" cinematic depictions of the Shoah are acceptable.

In place of a rigid standard of historical accuracy, then, I have adopted another approach when considering Holocaust films: directorial intention. Is the filmmaker trying to teach some lesson, uncover some insight about the Holocaust in an attempt to leave the viewer better informed about some aspect of it? Or, on the contrary, is he or she merely exploiting this explosive subject—which at present seems so inexhaustibly fascinating to the American public—in a mercenary bid to manufacture a blockbuster or as a kind of shortcut either to "horror" or to perceived "depth" or "significance"? In other words, I think it's less important for the purveyors of Hollywood to be narrowly faithful to even the most superficial facts about the Holocaust than it is for them to strive to be true to the spirit, the essence, of the event (though, of course, opinions will differ widely as to exactly what that "essence" is).

Later in this introduction, I'll discuss in some detail Hollywood's penchant to distance viewers from the full horror of the Holocaust through myriad strategies of sentimental distortion. It's a serious problem, but the crucial qualification to keep in mind is that a certain amount of distancing is legitimate, perhaps even required, since if one presents the Holocaust in all its unadulterated tragedy, one will almost surely lose that mass audience one is hoping to educate. The general goal of such portrayals should be to strive to tread the fine line between, on the one hand, depicting the Shoah with such unmitigated horror and dauntingly complex realism as to lose the average viewer, and, on the other hand, reducing the genocide to an accessible but deeply distorted event. In the chapter on *Schindler's List*, I will argue that Spielberg's is the Hollywood Holocaust film that, to date, best treads the precarious middle ground between pure horror and schmaltz.

In any event, it's unfair to judge Hollywood Holocaust depictions by the same lofty standards used to critique less mainstream portrayals. Personally, my favorite film about the Holocaust is the documentary *Shoah*, directed by Frenchman Claude Lanzmann, which consists of nine hours of "talking head" interviews with perpetrators, witnesses, and victims and that forces viewers to confront squarely the Holocaust's most disturbing emotional and intellectual truths. (*Shoah* is also an excellent example of a "constructed" Holocaust documentary, since Lanzmann places himself *in* the movie as an interviewer and often artfully steers his subjects in certain prearranged directions.) It was watching *Shoah* on public television in the late 1980s that made me want to become a Holocaust scholar. All in all, *Shoah* is a much better film about the Holocaust than any produced by Hollywood, but it's also one that will never appeal to more than a relatively small coterie of sophisticated and informed viewers. Hollywood directors, driven as they are by pressing commercial imperatives, don't have the luxury to appeal exclusively to specialists and intellectuals, and so compromises must be made. The secret is not to compromise *too much*.

Many have contended that Hollywood trivializes and exploits the Shoah *by definition*. Even if one accepts that Hollywood must of necessity mitigate the full horror of the Holocaust in order to reach and, so, educate a mass audience, the charge of inherent trivialization still deserves close consideration. Certainly, a plausible argument exists that the intrinsic commercialism of Hollywood, its profit-driven compulsion to "entertain," dooms from the start any effort to accurately depict a historical event so, to put it mildly, *un*entertaining. Moreover, throughout its history, our nation's mass media have tended to parrot faithfully the seemingly indefatigable optimism that is the reigning ethos of American culture—the "rags to riches," "win one for the Gipper," "have a nice day" ethos that is our society's relentless creed. Simply put, perhaps because we have had a relatively peaceful history, at least compared to most other countries, and at least in regard to violence on our *own* soil, American culture largely lacks a tragic sense, and as a result Hollywood does too. There is no Hollywood cinematic genre comparable to, for example, the genre of tragedy that was a staple of both Greco-Roman and Elizabethan popular theater—a genre that, indeed, was seen as the most elevated form of drama by both cultures. A culture that supports a genre such as tragedy is a culture that recognizes an inescapably tragic dimension to human existence—an idea that is anathema to American culture.

Given Americans' manic optimism, it's no surprise that Hollywood has never displayed much fondness for moral ambiguity, abounding instead in depictions of heroes thwarting villains in Manichean dramas of good versus evil. How, then, can Hollywood faithfully depict a genocide in which most of the perpetrators, witnesses, and even victims fall into (in Primo Levi's famous phrase) an ethical "grey zone" impervious to simplistic moral judgments?

When a poster exhibit on the Holocaust (courtesy of the Simon Wiesenthal Center in Los Angeles) was displayed in the main lounge of the Student Union Building at Montana Tech, where I teach English, I witnessed firsthand a striking example of how uncomfortably the horrors of the Holocaust clash with American culture. Although this exhibit of graphic photos took up almost the whole room, many Montana Tech students refused to allow its presence to curtail their normal activities in the lounge. As a result, alongside photographs of starving children slumped on the streets of the Warsaw ghetto and emaciated camp inmates staring blankly through barbed wire stood groups of fresh-faced Montana Tech students making amiable chitchat with their friends, scarfing down a hot dog or a slice of pizza before class, even sprawled in easy chairs watching daytime TV soaps. In many ways, this juxtaposition was as chilling as the photos themselves, since it seemed unwitting confirmation of the bleak truth that humanity's self-absorbed indifference to the suffering of others can allow an atrocity like the Holocaust to occur. Both our mass media and our politics reflect this narcissistic indifference to world affairs. Take as examples the fact that our national news programs almost completely ignore international news and that in the 2012 presidential race, foreign affairs were virtually disregarded by both candidates in favor of a near exclusive focus on domestic (mostly economic) issues. Regarding the Holocaust, the near total lack of effort by Franklin Roosevelt's administration to halt (or at least mitigate) the Nazi genocide, a position that enjoyed widespread public support, is an example highly relevant to this book of American indifference to the suffering of others. In short, the reception of the poster exhibit on my campus suggested how utterly alien the Holocaust is to American culture, both past and present—especially when it is presented free of the distortions to which Hollywood has accustomed us.

Under the circumstances, it's not surprising that sentimental distancing from the Shoah's most despairing lessons has plagued Hollywood Holocaust depictions from the start. Take the most influential example from the postwar era, the play and film versions of *The Diary of Anne Frank* (discussed in greater detail in chapter 4). In both drama and movie, the veteran husband-and-wife script-writing team of Frances Goodrich and Albert Hackett (who also, tellingly, wrote the screenplay for that heartwarming Christmas classic *It's a Wonderful Life*) plucked, out of context, a sentence from Anne's diary to serve as the concluding line: "In spite of everything, I still believe that people are really good at heart." Surely, whatever lessons the Holocaust imparts, that "people are really good at heart" is not among them. However, this maudlin belief is basically the defining ethos of American culture. Indeed, sentimentalizing the Holocaust in Hollywood has almost always been synonymous with "Americanizing" it.

The sentimentalizing of the Holocaust so rampant in Hollywood is especially regrettable because of a significant yet subtle connection between fascism and kitsch—between, that is, the irrational, emotion-laden ideologies promulgated by fascist movements and the equally emotional, intellectually simplistic appeals found in most kitschy popular art. A failed artist, Hitler was deeply committed to fashioning a Nazi artistic aesthetic, which he intended for the *Ubermensch* to foist on the rest of the world during the imperial reign of "the thousand-year Reich." In *Hitler and the Power of Aesthetics*, Frederic Spotts discusses Hitler's

> conviction that the ultimate objective of political effort should be artistic achievement and his dream of creating the greatest culture state since ancient times, or perhaps of all times. "I have become a politician against my will," he said over and over. "If someone else had been found, I would never have gone into politics; I would have become an artist or philosopher."[4]

To this vastly ambitious end, Hitler not only built towering Nazi buildings, designed by his brilliant architect, Albert Speer, but also staged huge, elaborate, minutely choreographed Nazi rallies and developed a Nazi cinema, under the control of Hitler's propaganda minister, Joseph Goebbels. Finally, more than any other previous totalitarian regime, the Nazis also harnessed radio as a means of mass brainwashing, regularly broadcasting Hitler's lengthy and bombastic speeches to the German people.

The Nazis organized an infamous art exhibit titled *Entartete Kunst* ("degenerate art"), in which the expressionist paintings of Otto Dix, Max Beckman, Emil Nolde, and other avant-garde artists were hung on bleak concrete walls, beneath sneering captions that lumped the artwork with such modern "ills" as communism, capitalism, atheism, and the nefarious schemes of international Jewry. Hitler objected both to

the quasi-abstract nature of Expressionist art and also to the often subversive and anti-authoritarian nature of its content.

As an antidote to the "Degenerate Art" exhibit, the Nazis created a
House of German Art, which displayed Nazi-approved art intended to
fashion the soul of the nation. Today, much of this art appears as the
epitome of kitsch. Consider "Discus Thrower," a sculpture depicting a
muscular, nude young athlete who functions as a symbol of the physical
prowess of the Germanic superman. Another artwork, a painting, was a
portrait of Hitler himself in full medieval military garb—the essence of
the chivalric knight celebrated in Arthurian legend. All in all, absent the
veneer of Nazi racial ideology, such works represented a vapid trumpet-
ing of "old-fashioned values" such as family, patriotism, faith and self-
sacrifice, coupled with the occasional smarmy sexual subtext—not all
that different, in short, from the worst kind of Hollywood pabulum.
Jawohl, Mein Fuhrer, it *is* a wonderful life!

Both kitsch and fascism encourage the masses to trust their feelings
and mistrust the intellectual life as aridly rationalistic. Hitler regularly
derided intellectuals as emasculated eggheads and rootless cosmopoli-
tans, as opposed to the virile Aryan ideal of man's organic connection to
the blood and soil of the fatherland; moreover, the Fuhrer often linked
an effete intellectualism with Jewishness. This was an especially potent
stereotype, since Judaism, a religion based on a book, is the most cere-
bral of all the major world religions.

Hollywood kitsch, too, almost always presents intellectuals negatively. They are either harmless buffoons, as in *The Nutty Professor* (the
joke is that only when the title character secretly transforms from a
nerdy academic into a suave hipster does he get the chicks); villainous
masterminds bent on world destruction, as in the horror and science
fiction archetype of the "mad scientist"; or robotic aliens devoid of
those passions alleged to define our humanity, as in the character of Mr.
Spock on *Star Trek,* a Vulcan whose chilly hyper-rationality is regularly
lambasted by the ship's hot-blooded human doctor, "Bones."

Perhaps the quintessence of Hollywood kitsch is the "feel-good"
movie: that prepackaged concoction elaborately rigged through endless
"focus groups" and production meetings to tug at the audience's heart-
strings. I would argue that fascism and feel-good movies make one "feel
good" in roughly similar ways. Both Hitler's fiery speeches to cheering
throngs of Nazi faithful (lauded in Leni Riefenstahl's *Triumph of the*

Will, the epitome of a Nazified feel-good movie) and the typical Hollywood feel-good flick give the audience a kind of adrenalin rush, which feels in the "high" of the moment not only thrilling but also transformatively profound. But this ecstasy vanishes as soon as a viewer leaves the theater or a critic subjects Hitlerian ideology to objective scrutiny. Notably, some of Hollywood's most celebrated films openly advocate racist ideologies—such as the sanctifying of the Ku Klux Klan in *The Birth of a Nation* or the defense of Southern slavery in *Gone with the Wind*. But even feel-good movies that don't explicitly endorse racism or other bigotry still resemble fascism in the way they brainwash audiences into mistaking a calculated illusion for something truly meaningful. As Saul Friedlander argues, "Nazism's attraction lay less in any explicit ideology than in the power of emotions, images, and phantasms."[5] This is also an excellent description of the source of the power of a feel-good movie.

Despite their patent irrationality, both kitsch and fascism are so seductive because each offers a vivid escape from reality. Both allow us to remain eternal adolescents. Rather than appealing to true sentiment, as great art does, kitsch (and fascism) appeals to sentimentality—a calculated attempt by filmmakers to profit by inspiring pseudo-emotions in the audience. Let me stress that I am not absurdly extending my comparison to the point of claiming that Walt Disney was another Hitler or that the public's yen for feel-good movies means that America is teetering on the brink of a neo-Nazi takeover. True, kitsch may contribute rather ominously to political passivity or, even worse, to its fans being more susceptible to despots and despotic ideologies of any kind, since a public influenced to feel rather than think is hardly prepared to participate competently in the democratic process. However, to overstate the fascism/kitsch parallel risks indulging in the kind of knee-jerk Hitler and Holocaust comparisons that elsewhere in this introduction I lament. Nonetheless, without conflating the two, one can still discern certain disturbing parallels between the ways fascism and kitsch manipulate the masses—parallels that should deepen critical concern when pop cultural Holocaust portrayals devolve, as they often do, into feel-good sentimentality.

Given that the blackness of the Holocaust and the insipid sunniness of American culture seem diametrically opposed, it's certainly puzzling that contemporary America seems obsessed with the Holocaust, as the plethora of Hollywood depictions attests. On the surface, this obsession seems especially bizarre given that Americans are notoriously indifferent to their own history, whereas the Shoah occurred on foreign soil over half a century ago and targeted a victim group, the Jews, whose descendants compose a tiny fraction of the current American population.

Those who maintain that pop culture inevitability trivializes the Holocaust often connect America's endless fascination with the Shoah to the rise of a culture of "victimology." As Robert Hughes argues, "The all-pervasive claim to victimhood tops off America's long-cherished culture of therapeutics. . . . Complaint gives you power—even when it's only the power of emotional bribery, of creating previously unnoticed levels of social guilt."[6]

America's current enthrallment with the Holocaust, mirrored by Hollywood, can be seen as reflecting less any genuine interest in this particular genocide than as a recognition that the European Jew murdered by the Nazis can serve as an emblem of quintessential victimhood, a model that other victim groups can seek to emulate as an oxymoronic means of empowerment. In *The Holocaust in American Life*, Peter Novick explains America's fascination with the Holocaust by noting how "the cultural icon of the strong, silent hero [has been] replaced by the vulnerable and verbose antihero. . . . The voicing of pain and outrage is alleged to be 'empowering' as well as therapeutic."[7] Such an analysis would explain why some minority activists have claimed that American Jews "make too much" of the Holocaust, as if these activists hope that by quieting Jewish discourse on the Shoah they could thrust their own group's victimization more prominently into the spotlight.

Self-serving co-optation of the Holocaust is also found today in the deplorably promiscuous use of Nazi and Holocaust analogies—with, it seems, any group one wishes to attack being damned as "Nazis" or any individual one opposes being labeled another "Hitler," while any event or situation one dislikes being branded "another Holocaust." (There is an actual rule known as "Godwin's Law of Nazi Analogies" that has become an Internet adage; coined by Mike Godwin in 1990, it states, "As an online discussion grows longer, the probability of a comparison involving Nazis or Hitler approaches."[8] In other words, Godwin said that, given enough time, in *any* online discussion—regardless of topic—someone inevitably makes a comparison to Hitler or the Nazis. Thus, on the left, a popular educational comic book is titled *The Black Holocaust of Slavery*, while gay (and Jewish) activist Larry Kramer compares Nazi anti-Semitism to America's homophobic indifference to gay AIDS victims.[9] On the right, conservative talk show host Rush Limbaugh dismisses the women's movement as being led by "feminazis";[10] the rhetoric of "pro-life" activists claims legal abortion is "another Holocaust" and abortion providers are a pack of "Nazi doctors."[11] Meanwhile, the NRA compares ATF agents to "jack-booted government thugs,"[12] while country singer Hank Williams Jr. goes on Fox News to say that Republican Speaker of the House John Boehner playing golf with President Obama is comparable to Boehner hitting the links with Adolf Hitler.[13]

Regardless of the degree to which positions taken on controversial issues such as abortion are valid, the use of tendentious Nazi and Holocaust analogies shuts down, rather than furthers, civilized, substantive debate. It attempts to clinch the argument not through facts and logic but by vilifying one's adversary and sanctifying one's own side. Even more importantly, knee-jerk Holocaust and Nazi analogies trivialize the *real* Holocaust and its *real* victims. If feminists and ATF agents are Nazis, Obama another Hitler, and legalized abortion another Holocaust, then the actual historical event couldn't have been all that important. Just as the rise of victimology can make the Jewish Holocaust victim an attractive model, so can the related rise of seemingly nonstop and often vicious feuding among groups and individuals—played out on televised political round tables, in the halls of Congress, and in the local bar—make Holocaust comparisons an increasingly sought-after weapon with which to club one's opponent.

Moreover, when trying to determine whether pop culture molds public attitudes toward the Holocaust for good or ill, it's important to remember that even when the Shoah is presented in an accurate and respectful manner, it is virtually impossible to gauge exactly how viewers or readers will respond. Indeed, there is a subjective element to the interpretative process: viewers or readers shape as well as draw meaning from a given film or book based on their particular backgrounds and belief systems.

I was forcefully reminded of this reality when I gave a presentation on the Holocaust in Hollywood to a group of troubled teenagers at an "alternative" public high school. Trying to elicit discussion after screening a harrowing clip from *Schindler's List*, I talked a bit about Nazi racial ideology, only to have one student gleefully exclaim, "Hey, I've got blond hair and blue eyes; I must be one of the Super Race!" Another described, in brutal detail and with obvious relish, various ways the Nazis had killed the Jews. Afterward, an embittered teacher (who also mentioned that he was suing one of his students for assault) informed me that I'd been "lecturing to the S.S. guards of the future." In retrospect, I think the teacher overlooked how at least some students, like Germans in the 1930s, fearful of appearing weak before their peers, may have concealed the extent of their sympathy with the Nazis' victims, but the teacher was astute to imply that people who feel like losers are the ones most often drawn to fascistic movements. In any event, given how the media desensitizes the young, in particular, to violence (as countless pundits, politicians, and parents' groups have argued), it is possible that a fair number of especially younger viewers, like some of the teens I met at that alternative school, may perceive graphic depictions of the Holocaust in pop culture as, in essence, entertaining "slasher flicks." To cite one notorious example, in 1996, when students from an urban school in Los Angeles were taken to a screening of *Schindler's List*, they responded to some of the most brutal scenes of Holocaust-oriented violence by laughing loudly.[14] In short, even when popular culture gets the Holocaust right, its efforts may be lost on a segment of the public too benumbed by mass-mediated images of violence to grasp the reality of any historical genocide.

To take this point a step further, is it possible that the American public's fascination with the Holocaust in movies and other popular representations is less noble than is customarily assumed, that this fascination may be at least partly motivated in a segment of the population by darker, more perverse emotions? In *Film and the Holocaust*, Kerner includes a fascinating chapter on Holocaust pornography—a particularly revolting subgenre of the porn industry as a whole (especially popular, intriguingly enough, in Israel)—which usually depicts scenes of sadomasochistic sex between Nazi guards and mostly Jewish prisoners. Kerner argues that Holocaust porn "turns on" audiences because viewers are erotically aroused by scenes of people, mostly women, being sexually tortured and debased. He then takes the bold step of suggesting that even in "serious" or "respectable" Holocaust movies and other representations, audiences may be sexually titillated by viewing the suffering of Jewish prisoners. Kerner's primary examples are two key scenes from *Schindler's List*, one in which a group of attractive young

Jewish women are stripped naked and herded into a chamber by the Nazis, only to discover in relief that the shower heads emit water rather than poison gas, and another in which the sadistic concentration camp commandant Amon Goeth (Ralph Fiennes) first woos and then brutalizes his beautiful, scantily clad Jewish domestic servant, Helen Hirsch (Embeth Davidtz). Kerner ends the chapter on Holocaust porn by declaring:

> This brings us to an uncomfortable conclusion: perhaps the Naziploitation genre or other pornographic representations of the Holocaust illustrate a certain truism—if amplified, or exaggerated to be sure, though—that the graphic and horrific nature of Holocaust imagery elicits from us a degree of (negative) pleasure. These films are calculated to disgust and to titillate, and we might not care to admit it, but do they in the end point to the continued morbid fascination that we have with representing the Holocaust even in more 'serious' genres?[15]

These are some of the many arguments raised by those who maintain that popular culture inevitably trivializes and exploits the Holocaust or that even when pop culture gets the Holocaust right, there is no telling what perverse reactions audiences may be experiencing. Such arguments have considerable validity. However, let me introduce the counterargument with another personal anecdote. A couple of years ago, when I gave a talk on the Holocaust in mystery and thriller novels, an elderly but spry Holocaust survivor was seated in the front row. My talk focused on two examples of Holocaust-oriented thriller novels, Robert Harris's *Fatherland* and Daniel Easterman's *The Final Judgment*, and my straightforward argument was that Harris's engrossing whodunit was an effective example of this literary genre, while Easterman's contrived potboiler was not. After I finished, the Holocaust survivor beckoned me over and asked that I repeat the title of Easterman's novel. Rather taken aback, I did so but added, "It's a pretty trashy book."

He replied, "I read anything with a swastika on the cover."

One might interpret this remark as implying an understandable obsession with the Holocaust characteristic of most survivors, but I prefer a different explanation. To me, "I read anything with a swastika on the cover" suggests that the best way to approach Holocaust movies is to go case by case, trying to keep an open mind. In fact, a defining ethos of this book might be the philosopher Edmund Husserl's injunction, "To the things themselves!" In other words, any work dealing in some way with the Holocaust, even one belonging to a genre often critically derided as pop cultural trash, has at least the potential to offer valuable insights about the Shoah, and so shouldn't be dismissed summarily.

In this book, I discuss four Hollywood Holocaust thrillers—*The Odessa File*, *Marathon Man*, *The Boys from Brazil*, and *Apt Pupil*—and give them all respectful attention. None of them are great films, but they all have their moments, at times precisely when touching on the Holocaust. In *Marathon Man*, for example, there is an electrifying scene in which an escaped Nazi dentist is recognized in Manhattan's diamond district by a group of Holocaust survivors whom he had tortured at Auschwitz. Gradually swelling in number, the group follows him down the narrow, twisting streets, crying and gesticulating like avenging wraiths. Extracting a stiletto from his sleeve, the Nazi swiftly slits one of their throats in order to make his escape. Not only is the scene gripping; it also says something about the twisted, charged relationship between Holocaust survivors and escaped Nazis. Moreover, it achieves these ends not by transcending the thriller genre but rather by employing the conventions of the genre in an edifying way.

I have tried to infuse this book with that kind of open-minded spirit. Like most Americans, especially those of the postwar generation, I am a child of popular culture and thus incapable of penning some sweeping list of anti-Hollywood attacks. Ultimately, my attitude toward Hollywood embodies both love and annoyance—a recognition of how energetic, creative, and even edifying Hollywood can be at its best, and of how vapid, predictable, and harmful it is at its worst.

Moreover, particularly with Hollywood Holocaust portrayals that appeared during or not long after the war, such as *The Diary of Anne Frank*, it is vital for critics, before they launch into outraged denunciations, to remember the importance of judging such works in historical context. If the play by Goodrich and Hackett hadn't sentimentalized and universalized Anne Frank's story (which required downplaying her Jewishness), it's inconceivable that the drama would have appealed to a Middle America still largely ignorant about the Holocaust as well as deeply suspicious of Jews. It's all a matter of perspective; one can fault the play and film for not being Jewish enough or tragic enough or applaud it for finding a way to make the American public pay attention to a European genocide against a group they disliked and that, not surprisingly, until then the public had shown almost no interest in whatsoever.

In short, Goodrich and Hackett can be credited for gauging precisely how much truth postwar America could bear to know about the Holocaust, in much the same way that Spielberg astutely assessed how much an America that was less anti-Semitic, more informed about the Shoah, but still temperamentally averse to tragedy, could bear to know about the Holocaust in the 1990s. In fact, contrasting the degree of realism found in *Anne Frank* with that found in *Schindler's List* provides a useful barometer of just how far America has come in its ability to face the Holocaust squarely—that is, quite a distance, though still not far enough. Certainly, the sorts of distortions found in *The Diary of Anne Frank* should be deemed far less acceptable in any portrayal of the Holocaust appearing more recently. So, for example, this book contains a harsh critique of Italian director Roberto Benigni's wretchedly sappy and unrealistic 1998 Oscar-winning film, *Life is Beautiful*. Finally, with works that have been remade, such as *The Diary of Anne Frank*, it is important to judge the work not only by the original version but also by more recent incarnations. In the version of the play that was revived on Broadway in the late 1990s and in the made-for-TV movie, *Anne Frank*, aired on ABC in the summer of 2001, Anne's story is told with far greater—indeed, at times quite grisly—realism.

I also claim that a certain type of *comedy* can be a valid and even insightful means of portraying the Holocaust—a stance that clashes with the common view that comic depictions of the Holocaust are invariably guilty of demeaning the Shoah. While lecturing on Augustan satire, a grad school professor of mine memorably defined the satire of Swift, Dryden, and Pope as an act of "laughing at the Devil"—an attempt to fight back against profound evil through deflating ridicule. "Laughing at the Devil" is a good definition of the effect striven for in several Hollywood Holocaust comedies. Take, for example, *The Producers*, first a Hollywood film and then a Broadway musical, about a pair of unscrupulous Broadway producers who decide to wildly oversell shares in a play so awful it is bound to fail immediately, thereby making them both rich. They pick a musical written by an unreformed Nazi and titled, unforgettably, *Springtime for Hitler*. Not surprisingly, more than a few critics have accused *The Producers* of making light of the Nazis and the Holocaust. However, in a *60 Minutes* interview, the show's creator, Mel Brooks, asserted his belief that "there's only one way to get even [with Hitler]. You have to bring him down with ridicule. Because if you stand on a soapbox and you match him with rhetoric, you're just as bad as he is. But if you can make people laugh at him, then you're one up on him."[16]

While Brooks's notion that merely arguing against Hitler reduces one to his monstrous level is absurd, his contention that the best way to bury Hitler is by making people laugh at him is a perfect example of satire as "laughing at the Devil." (The cover of the *New Yorker* issue containing John Lahr's glowing review of the play echoed Brooks's point by showing a Broadway audience laughing uproariously, save for a scowling, swastika-clad Hitler.) Indeed, there is a long tradition in Jewish Diaspora culture, both European and American, in which this powerless minority has fought back against Gentile persecution with the only weapon at its command, satire—a tradition spanning film and stand-up comedy as well as literature, and stretching from Sholem Aleichem and Isaac Bashevis Singer to Phillip Roth, Saul Bellow, Cynthia Ozick, Lenny Bruce, Jackie Mason, Woody Allen, and, of course, Brooks himself. Radu Milhaileanu, the Romanian director of *Train of Life*, a Holocaust comedy in which a band of shtetl Jews try to escape the Nazis by manufacturing a fake transport train, told an interviewer, "I wanted to tell the tragedy through the most Jewish language there is—the tradition of bittersweet comedy."[17]

Even in the camps, survivor testimony reveals, prisoners often traded jokes in an attempt to mitigate the horror of their situation, and also because, due to its utter absurdity, there *was* something funny, in a blackly comic way, in the dire circumstances in which they found themselves. According to Omer Bartov, critics who dismiss Holocaust comedy forget "the specific role humor and fantasy played in attempts to survive or at least maintain a semblance of normality and humanity during the Holocaust, and about the tradition of 'black,' 'gallows,' or 'concentration camp humor' in literary and cinematic representations of the Holocaust."[18] Thus, the best of Holocaust comedy should be seen as rooted in a long, historically explicable, at times brilliant, and potentially therapeutic Jewish literary and cultural tradition, one that didn't disappear with the arrival of the Holocaust but rather created a suitable response to this latest catastrophe for the Jewish people. As Kerner writes, since "humor is entrenched in the Jewish tradition, why shouldn't the Holocaust be treated in the comedic genre?"[19] It's noteworthy that my own book opens with chapters on two Hollywood Holocaust comedies made during the war—Charlie Chaplin's *The Great Dictator* and Ernst Lubitsch's *To Be or Not to Be*—both of which serve as brilliant examples of this satirical tradition.

The same professor who defined Augustan satire as "laughing at the Devil" praised the British man of letters Samuel Johnson as the kind of literary critic who, when you read him, makes you feel that "somebody is *home* here." I have also tried to be "at home" in my own work, and to further this end, let me note right now that, just as it is relevant to acknowledge that I am a child of popular culture, so is it germane to this study that I am an American Jew raised in New York City in a heavily Jewish neighborhood. From an early age, I was taught—by my family and my Hebrew school teachers, among others—about the horrors the Nazis had inflicted on "our people" while also being instilled with a deep love for Israel, as the Jewish homeland reclaimed out of the ashes of the Holocaust, a sanctuary created to ensure that never again would Jews have nowhere to turn when targeted for persecution. As I've grown older, this perspective has been modified—I've become, for example, increasingly sympathetic to the plight of the Palestinians and dismayed by the way Israeli settlement buildup in the Occupied Territories has thwarted the peace process—but its essence remains.

The aim of this book, then, is *not* to attempt to provide the last word on Hollywood Holocaust movies. The subject is so vast and criticism so intrinsically subjective that I could not provide an exhaustively definitive appraisal even if I tried. I have, however, attempted to touch on a wide range of representative films in a variety of cinematic genres, to trace the evolution of the Hollywood Holocaust movie over time, and to use Hollywood films as a lens through which to explore the American public's changing perspective on the Shoah.

I

THE LITTLE TRAMP BATTLES HITLER

The Great Dictator

Hollywood's depiction of Nazism and the Holocaust gets its start with Charlie Chaplin's masterful *The Great Dictator* (1940). Even before the film was made, many had noted the striking physical resemblance between Chaplin and Hitler; the German film critic, Rudolf Arnheim, for example, had written that, "looking into Hitler's face one must remember Charlie Chaplin."[1] Chaplin capitalized on the resemblance by casting himself as Adenoid Hynkel, a character transparently based on the German Führer (called in the movie "the Phooey"), the megalomaniacal dictator of the fictionalized nation of Tomania.

Indeed, Chaplin and Hitler shared more than just looks. The two men were born only four days apart, in May of 1889. Both had left home early in life in search of fame. While Chaplin's most famous recurrent character was the beloved "Little Tramp," Hitler during his early adulthood in Vienna actually *was* a tramp. After being rejected for admission to art school, he spent four years sleeping on the streets and in shelters for the indigent while struggling to make a living by selling painted postcards. By 1937, when Chaplin began work on *The Great Dictator*, he and Hitler may have been the two most famous men in the world. But, shared characteristics aside, Chaplin and Hitler were diametrically opposed in their worldviews and core beliefs. Unlike the Führer, Chaplin was an ardent advocate of democracy who aided America's battle against Germany in World War I by making speeches and selling Liberty Bonds with fellow Hollywood stars Mary Pickford and Douglas Fairbanks. Once Hitler came to power, Chaplin was an early and impassioned opponent of the Nazis, sweepingly condemning the Third Reich as being "anti-people," and thus starkly opposed to Chaplin's own liberal humanism.

Meanwhile, Hitler hated Chaplin as much as Chaplin hated Hitler. After taking the reins of the German government, the Führer, though generally a great fan of American cinema (he was especially fond of Westerns), wasted no time in banning all of Chaplin's films. The Nazis also falsely claimed that Chaplin was Jewish. An October 1938 issue of the Nazi publication *Film-Kurier* reprinted an article titled "Who's Who in Hollywood—Find the Gentile," which listed over ninety Hollywood celebrities said to have Jewish blood; Chaplin was listed second (after Jack Benny), with his real name alleged to be "Karl Tonstein." Another work of Nazi propaganda attacked Chaplin as being a "disgusting Jewish acrobat."[2] Back in 1931, when Chaplin had visited Berlin during the Weimar era, he'd been greeted by rapturous crowds. The Nazis took newsreel footage of Chaplin's visit and spliced it into their notorious film "The Eternal Jew" (1940), with narration citing the reception as proof of the comedian's pernicious influence on the German *Volk*.

Prior to *The Great Dictator*, Hollywood had almost totally ignored the threat posed by Hitler, despite the large number of Jews working in the American film industry. Germany, after all, was an enthusiastic consumer of American movies, and Hollywood had no desire to alienate these customers by making films attacking the nation's leader. In fact, Jewish MGM head Louis B. Mayer had agreed to remove parts of his studio's films that the Nazi authorities had found offensive when the movies were screened in Germany. Hollywood studio heads and producers were subjected to tangible intimidation from both German and American politicians and their agents stressing that Hollywood had better refrain from emphasizing Nazi persecution of the Jews in their movies or face the consequences. For example, the American ambassador to England, Joseph Kennedy, an avowed Nazi sympathizer, visited Hollywood in 1940 in order to convey this very message. In a letter to FDR, Douglas Fairbanks Jr. related the gist of Kennedy's words: "He apparently threw the fear of God into many of our producers and executives by telling them that the Jews were on the spot, and that they should stop making anti-Nazi pictures. . . . He continued to underline the fact

Figure 1.1. *The Great Dictator* (1940). Tyrant Adenoid Hynkel (Charles Chaplin) expresses his craving for world domination by playing with a balloon globe. [Screen grab]

that the film business was using its power to influence the public dangerously and that we all, and the Jews in particular, would be in jeopardy, if they continued to abuse that power."[3] "As a result of Kennedy's "cry for silence," popular Hollywood screenwriter Ben Hecht later wrote, "all Hollywood's top Jews went around with their grief hidden like a little Jewish fox under their gentile vests."[4] The Nazis themselves were perfectly willing to threaten reprisals if their warnings went unheeded by the Hollywood community. For example, George Gyssling, the German consul in Los Angeles, threatened that if Hollywood made anti-Nazi films, the Reich would inflict worse punishments on its country's Jews, especially the relatives of those making the films. Hitler himself participated in this blackmail. When the Führer announced the Nuremberg Laws on September 15, 1935, stripping German Jews of all their rights as citizens, Hitler warned that if "Jewish agitation both within Germany and in the international sphere" continued, he would be forced to find a "final solution."[5]

Under the circumstances, it's no surprise that before Chaplin's *The Great Dictator* dramatized in no uncertain terms that the Jews were the primary targets of Nazi persecution, the word "Jew" and Jewish subject matter were almost entirely absent from Hollywood films. (Indeed, Jews would swiftly vanish from anti-Nazi Hollywood movies made after Chaplin's, and it wouldn't be until decades later that American popular films would belatedly acknowledge that Jews had been the principle victims of the "Final Solution.") At the time, Chaplin was quoted as saying that he'd made *The Great Dictator* "for the Jews of the world."[6] The director also declared that the character of Hannah, the beautiful young ghetto orphan in the film (played by Chaplin's then wife Paulette Goddard, who was herself half-Jewish) "typifies the whole Jewish race, their strength, their resentment against senseless persecution, their hope for a better future."[7]

The seed of the idea for *The Great Dictator* may have been planted in Chaplin's mind when Ivor Montagu, a friend and associate of the great Soviet director Sergei Eisenstein, mailed Chaplin a volume of photographs of Jews issued by the Nazis, titled *Jews Are Looking at You*, which included a photo of Chaplin labeled "the little Jewish tumbler, as disgusting as he is boring."[8] Montagu hoped the book might inspire Chaplin to make an anti-Nazi movie. More encouragement came from Alexander Korda, the Hungarian-born head of London Film Productions, who suggested that Chaplin might imitate Hitler in a comedy about mistaken identity. Soon after, the screenwriter Konrad Bercovici sent Chaplin a six-page treatment that largely mirrored the film the director eventually made, casting Chaplin in the dual roles of the Tomanian dictator and a meek Jewish barber. (When, after the movie appeared, Bercovici received neither financial compensation nor a screen credit, he sued Chaplin for plagiarism; ultimately, Bercovici received an out-of-court settlement for $90,000.)

Mulling over Bercovici's story line, Chaplin realized that the film could enable him to make a smooth transition into talking motion pictures—a leap the silent-picture star had found daunting. "Then it suddenly struck me," he later recalled. "Of course! As Hitler I could harangue the crowds in jargon and talk all I wanted to. And as the tramp I could remain more or less silent. A Hitler story was an opportunity for burlesque and pantomime."[9] (The fact that Chaplin bestowed verbose speech on his film's villain, while having his hero remain relatively silent, reflects, according to Annette Insdorf, "Chaplin's own ambivalence toward sound. If Hitler aped Chaplin's image, the silent comedian got even by draining the dictator's speech of meaning.")[10]

Predictably, given the political climate, Chaplin was warned from a variety of quarters against making *The Great Dictator*. When news leaked out that Chaplin was making a satire about Hitler, isolationist and crypto-Nazi groups in America raised strenuous objections. Threatening letters were sent to the director. Even Chaplin's own studio, fearing monetary losses, tried to dissuade him from doing the film, with the heads of other studios chiming in their agreement. The consensus among Jews in Hollywood was that a Hitler-bashing movie would only make conditions worse for their coreligionists in Europe. Certain he would never be able to convince his studio to pay for the film, Chaplin decided to finance it entirely on his own. But he was sufficiently influenced by the naysayers among his colleagues that at one point he did decide to cancel the project and only changed his mind when FDR sent the architect of the New Deal, Harry Hopkins, to tell Chaplin that the film had to be made—a detail that sheds a fascinating light on Roosevelt's own attitudes regarding what messages Hollywood should communicate about the Nazis.

Still, the Hollywood community wasn't uniformly hostile to Chaplin's project. At the time, America's film capital was filled with Nazi-fleeing German émigrés, such as Fritz Lang (who after America entered the war would direct the anti-Nazi film *Hangmen Also Die!*). Lang and other like-minded émigrés helped found the popular and successful Hollywood Anti-Nazi League. Even if criticisms of Hitler hadn't yet made it to the screen, the mood in Hollywood was decidedly hostile toward the German dictator. Moreover, it would be oversimplified to say that prior to *The Great Dictator* Hollywood studios uniformly refused to broadcast their hatred of Hitler on the screen. The one studio that was willing to do so was Warner Brothers, in part because the brothers that coheaded the studio were fuming over the murder by Nazi thugs in 1934 of their main representative in Germany, Joe Kaufman, who was killed because he was a Jew. In 1939, the same year that Chaplin began work on *The Great Dictator*, Warner Brothers released *Confessions of a Nazi Spy*, a thriller about the espionage activities of the American Bund, an American Nazi group, which lightly touched on anti-Semitism. Before *Confessions*, Warner Brothers released *The Life of Emile Zola* (1937), directed by the anti-Nazi activist William Dieterle, casting the noted Jewish actor Joseph Schildkraut (who would later play Anne Frank's father in the play and film versions of the diary) in the part of Captain Alfred Dreyfus, falsely accused of treason by anti-Semitic forces in France, whose innocence Zola vociferously defended.

As for the Germans themselves, they were hardly indifferent to that "disgusting Jewish acrobat's" plan to shoot an anti-Hitler film. Responding to instructions from Berlin, Gyssling wrote a letter to Joe Breen, the head of the Production Code Association, warning that Chaplin's playing Hitler would "naturally lead to serious troubles and complications."[11] Due to such political pressures, it's no surprise that US officials told Chaplin that an anti-Hitler movie would inevitably be banned in the United States and abroad. With England still trying to appease Hitler, British authorities took a similar position concerning the work of their famous native son. On March 2, 1939, six months after Neville Chamberlain's notorious participation in the Munich Conference, through which he hoped to avert war by allowing Hitler to take over Czechoslovakia, J. Brooke Wilkinson, the secretary of the British Board of Film Censors, sent Breen a cable noting "the delicate situation that might arise in this country if personal attacks were made on any living European statesman. You are aware of our stringent rule that the representation of any living personage without their written consent is disallowed on the British screen."[12]

All things considered, it's no surprise Chaplin opted to shoot the movie under conditions of strict secrecy. (Filming began six days after England and France declared war on Germany.) In fact, when *Life Magazine* in June of 1940 published an unauthorized photo of Chaplin dressed as Hynkel, the director sued the magazine for a million dollars. According to Ilan Avisar in *Screening the Holocaust*, "The most important political goal of *The Great Dictator* was the shattering of the image of Hitler, who in 1939–40 was still venerated by many."[13] Nonetheless, Chaplin firmly denied that the film was propaganda, stating that "some people have suggested that I made this picture for propaganda purposes. This is far from the truth. I made *The Great Dictator* because I hate dictators and because I want people to laugh."[14] It seems Chaplin also made the film to end Hollywood's overwhelming silence on the evils of Nazism. If Hollywood insisted on remaining largely mute about what a bad guy Adolf Hitler was, Chaplin would break that silence.

Three years in the making, the film opened in 1940, a year before America entered the war and at the height of the Nazi blitzkrieg against

London. Despite being banned in some locales—such as Chicago, with its heavily German population—*The Great Dictator* was a smashing commercial success. In New York City, appreciative crowds packed the theater for fifteen weeks. *New York Times* critic Bosley Crowther listed the movie as one of the three biggest moneymakers among recent films. Ultimately, *The Great Dictator* would go on to make five million dollars, the largest gross of any Chaplin film to that date. It was nominated for five Oscars, though it took home no awards.

The movie was also shown at a special screening for President Roosevelt. Despite his previous private support for the film via his messenger Hopkins, at the screening Roosevelt's only comment to Chaplin was that the movie was "giving us a lot of trouble in the Argentine."[15] There was a large German population in Argentina, and resentment toward the film among this group was stirring anti-American feeling.

It appears that Roosevelt wasn't the only head of state to see *The Great Dictator* in a private screening; although naturally the film was banned in Germany, evidence suggests that Hitler himself may well have viewed the film. According to John McCabe's biography of Chaplin:

> In the fullness of time Hitler actually saw the film. Chaplin was told this by an agent who fled Germany after working in the film division of the Nazi Ministry of Culture. The man told Chaplin that Nazi agents bought a print of *The Great Dictator* in Portugal and took it to Germany. Predictably, when Goebbels saw it he raged, denounced it, and decreed it must never be shown. Hitler, however, insisted on seeing the film—alone. The next night he saw the film again, and once more alone. That is all the agent could tell Chaplin. Chaplin, in telling the story to friends, added, "I'd give anything to know what he thought of it"[16]

In a 2002 television documentary called *The Dictator and the Tramp*, novelist and Hollywood screenwriter Budd Schulberg is interviewed, and Schulberg asserts that, as an American soldier investigating Nazi documents after the fall of Berlin, he'd discovered records indicating that Hitler had indeed twice ordered the movie for private viewing.

After the film's release, Chaplin continued to publicly decry Nazism and was often sought out for speaking engagements by organizations sharing his views. But the progressive, anti-Nazi sentiments Chaplin expressed in *The Great Dictator* and in his public speeches rankled more conservative, isolationist, often anti-Semitic elements in American society. In September, 1941, Senators Bennett Clark of Missouri and Gerald Nye of North Dakota introduced a resolution calling for an investigation of what the senators claimed was pro-war propaganda emanating from Hollywood. Listing the heads of the eight major studios, Nye noted darkly that they all had "Jewish sounding names" and concluded his remarks with the "hope . . . that our Jewish people will so conduct themselves as to invite more of such spirit as ours. Unfortunately, certain of them are not doing so."[17] Questioned in the Senate about which films he found objectionable, Nye confessed that the only one he'd seen was *The Great Dictator*, the one Hollywood picture dealing directly with the threat to the Jews.

Shortly afterward, isolationism was dealt a fatal blow by the Japanese attack on Pearl Harbor, but, after the war, Chaplin's liberalism would get him in trouble with Joseph McCarthy's House Un-American Activities Committee, which accused the comedian of harboring Communist sympathies. Eventually in 1954, Chaplin returned to England, going into permanent exile from his adopted home. He would only return to America decades later to receive an honorary Oscar, finally welcomed back by the nation that had scorned him after he'd treated it to such brilliant entertainment.

Now to the movie itself. Not surprisingly, since Chaplin said he made *The Great Dictator* for "the Jews of the world," individual Jews and the Jewish community are portrayed very favorably. Chaplin plays two roles—the mad Tomanian dictator and a shy, sweet-natured Jewish barber. Having developed amnesia as the result of a wound suffered during the previous Tomanian war, the barber returns to the Jewish ghetto intending to reopen his shop, unaware that during his recovery period Adenoid Hynkel has come to power and instituted a policy of repression against the Jews. As Michael D. Richardson notes, "Chaplin's film begins with a moment of visual confusion."[18] In the movie's first scene, the barber is seen in battle, following Falstaff's injunction that "discretion is the better part of valor" by immediately surrendering to the enemy. Viewers may assume at this point that the figure on the screen is Hitler, since Hitler did serve as a soldier in World War I. It is only gradually that we come to realize the barber's true identity. Richardson interprets this initial, apparently deliberate audience confusion as "reinforc[ing] the idea that the two characters inhabit the same physical body, suggesting an interpretation of the film as a metaphor for a divided self."[19]

It's an intriguing thesis, but as the movie progresses and the two roles Chaplin plays get clarified, *The Great Dictator* establishes a clear moral opposition: Hynkel is evil, and the barber is good. And since the barber serves as a typical representative of the Jewish race, the Jews, by extension, are good, too. While some of the ghetto's Jews disagree over the extent of the threat Hynkel poses, by and large they form a warm, supportive, close-knit community. It's also a fairly realistic portrait; often played by Jewish actors, many of the Jews speak in authentic Yiddish accents. With the exception of Hannah, most of the Jews are older as well, which bestows on them the wisdom of age and also makes them appear fragile and vulnerable. Moreover, they are all working class: barbers, laundresses (like Hannah), grocers, and so forth. From Chaplin's quasisocialist, New Deal perspective, this is also to their credit; in Chaplin's previous film, the brilliant *Modern Times* (1936), the director had celebrated the nobility and perseverance of the proletariat as they struggle against the dehumanizing exploitation of the machine age. The Jewish characters' working-class backgrounds also challenge the widespread anti-Semitic stereotype of the Jew as a pernicious capitalist oppressing the workers—a stereotype promulgated by Hitler.

Only one wealthy Jew appears in *The Great Dictator*, the industrialist Epstein, who never appears on screen but to whom Hynkel appeals for a loan to help finance the Tomanian military as the dictator prepares to invade the neighboring country of Osterlich. During the brief period that Epstein considers whether to grant the loan, Hynkel opportunistically relaxes his policies against the Jews. But when, upset over the dictator's anti-Semitism, Epstein turns Hynkel down, the persecution resumes. Through the lens of historical hindsight, the Epstein subplot is disturbing, since it implies that wealthy Jews could buy their way out of danger—that the Nazis were willing to relent in their anti-Semitic actions if sufficiently bribed—when we now know that rich and poor Jews alike were targeted by Hitler's Final Solution. Contrary to what is implied in this scene in *The Great Dictator*, no matter how compliantly the Jews responded to Hitler (and they were, as a rule, remarkably compliant), nothing was going to deter the Führer's determination to exterminate the Jewish people. In another respect, however, Chaplin perfectly captures what the Jews were confronting. By showing the Jews living in a traditional ghetto and depicting the entire ghetto as threatened by Hynkel's tyranny, the film demonstrates that it wasn't individual or even groups of Jews who were threatened by the Nazis but rather the entire European Jewish community.

More troubling is the film's treatment of the issue of Jewish resistance—a vexing subject that would appear repeatedly, in myriad ways, in portrayals of the Holocaust in American popular culture. When storm troopers harass the barber for erasing the word "Jew," which had been painted on the front of his shop, the barber fights back, but his resistance seems as much a product of ignorance as heroism, since he is unaware of the political changes that have occurred during his hospitalization. The one true resister in the ghetto is Hannah; when the barber is trading blows with the storm troopers, she leans out a nearby window and conks them over the head with a frying pan. Hannah sums up the ethos of resistance when she says, "We can't fight alone, but we can lick 'em together." Hannah's behavior is realistic in the sense that it was usually the younger generation of Jews who urged violent resistance to the Nazis, while their elders often counseled a response of passive fatalism.

But when Hannah extols the viability of communal resistance, she seems to be speaking for Chaplin himself. As Annette Insdorf writes in her book *Indelible Shadows*, the movie "presents [resistance] as a constant possibility and responsibility."[20] But surely Chaplin's view underestimates the gaping power imbalance between the fearsome Nazis and the helpless Jews. When Jews did resist, most notably in the Warsaw ghetto, it wasn't because they harbored any fantasies about actually defeating the Germans but rather because they wished to die fighting instead of being led meekly to the gas chambers. In contrast to the real Nazis, the storm troopers in *The Great Dictator* are played as slapstick Keystone Cops, blundering, hapless figures of fun. The philosopher Theodor Adorno was basically right when he wrote of this scene: "*The Great Dictator* loses its satirical force and becomes offensive in the scene in which a Jewish girl hits one storm trooper after another on the head with a pan without being torn to pieces. Political reality is sold short for the sake of political commitment; that decreases the political impact as well."[21]

The issue of Jewish resistance is explored at greatest length in the subplot concerning Commander Schultz, a Tomanian officer whose life the barber had saved in the previous war, and who, initially a protégé of Hynkel's, grows disgusted with the dictator's anti-Semitic policies and tenders his resignation. Arrested, Schultz escapes and turns up in the ghetto, where he implores the Jews to combat Hynkel by blowing up a government building. The men of the ghetto assemble for dinner, where each is served a pudding for desert; one pudding contains a coin, and whichever man ends up with that pudding will be assigned the job of blowing up the building. However, unbeknownst to the men, Hannah, convinced the mission is suicidal, has placed a coin in every pudding. To avoid being chosen, each man surreptitiously slips his coin into the pudding of the barber, who, equally unwilling to risk his life, swallows each coin in turn.

The scene is hilarious, but does it also suggest that the Jews failed to resist the Nazis because they were cowards? Does it, in other words, support the widely held notion that the Jews of Europe, facing the Germans, went, in that awful phrase, "like sheep to the slaughter"? Although most critics don't think so, interpretations of the scene vary. For example, in *The Holocaust in American Film*, Judith Doneson finds the scene "sweetly humorous in its pathos" and believes it "point[s] up the absurdity of the Jews taking on the Tomanians when they had yet to figure out how to save themselves."[22] In contrast, Ilan Avisar faults the timidity of the Jewish characters but reads the scene more broadly, feeling it symbolizes

> the universal cowardice which accommodated and compromised with Hitler's imperialist ambitions. . . . Although all the characters are ghetto Jews, Chaplin points to a universal phenomenon of cowardice and duplicity. European countries and the rest of the world avoided confronting the Nazi menace by passing responsibility to one another, hoping to be individually spared by Hitler.[23]

Of the two interpretations, Doneson's is the more persuasive. While elsewhere, as noted, Chaplin seems to favor Jewish resistance, here he appears to suggest that there is something futile and self-destructive in a handful of elderly civilians tackling the Tomanian war machine. Throughout *The Great Dictator*, the Jew is presented as an everyman, and, more specifically, as a "little man," buffeted by fate and the powers-that-be, exactly the character represented by the "Little Tramp." As such, these men respond to Schultz's harebrained scheme not as Jews but as ordinary human beings, preferring life to suicide missions. Their natural pacifism is consistent with the "peace" message proclaimed in Chaplin's climactic speech that concludes the film.

If the barber in *The Great Dictator* is a pacifist, Adenoid Hynkel is, of course, his polar opposite, a bloodthirsty warmonger. As Richardson writes, "The barber, even as a soldier, is a reluctant combatant, while Hynkel is repeatedly associated with violence, in word and deed."[24] An unforgettable portrayal, hilarious and chilling at the same time, Chaplin's depiction of Hynkel may amount to the most scathing attack on a world leader in the history of film. By having Chaplin play both the barber and Hynkel, and basing the plot on a case of mistaken identity when the barber is erroneously assumed to be the dictator by Hynkel's men, *The Great Dictator* points up the absurdity of Hitler's racial theories—all that esoteric Nazi claptrap about ennobled Aryan and degraded Jewish physical features—since in the film a ghetto Jew and an Aryan leader look so alike no one can tell them apart. As Chaplin himself wrote in his autobiography, in making the film he "was determined to ridicule that mystic bilge about a pure-blooded race. As though such a thing ever existed outside of the Australian Aborigines!"[25] When the Phooey is dressed in civilian clothes and the barber in a military uniform, Hynkel's troops mistake the barber for Hynkel and vice-versa; Richardson notes how easily the role reversal is carried off: "Both these moments present the uniform, above all, as the constituent piece of the Hynkel/Hitler identity, suggesting two things: that the abstract figure of a dictator rather than a particular personality drives the fascist cause; and that members of the fascist society are incapable of anything more than surface-level engagement."[26]

The fact that Hitlerian ideology was so crazy it would appear laughable if it were not so deadly is reiterated in a subsequent scene: Garbitsch, one of Hynkel's top advisors, suggests to Hynkel that, once he's gotten rid of the Jews, he should then kill off the "brunettes," which would leave him in charge of a blond world ruled by a black-haired dictator. While Hynkel/Hitler is the primary target of Chaplin's satire, Garbitsch, based on Goebbels, Hitler's minister of propaganda, also is subjected to some satirical thrusts. An educated man, more reserved and reflective than the blustering buffoon Goering and fanatically loyal to the Führer, Goebbels was the advisor most committed to brainwashing the German people and always had Hitler's ear. Kerner writes, "If there is any devilish agent in *The Great Dictator*, it is Garbitsch, who plays Mephistopheles, promising the world to Hynkel, feeding his ego."[27] Through their relationship, Kerner argues, the film enacts "the Faustian theme—where a character is promised the world, if only they give their soul to the fascist cause."[28] Kerner's Faustian reading is intriguing, but in the end the comparison doesn't really work. In both Marlowe and Goethe's versions, Faust at the play's start is the greatest philosopher, scientist, and theologian on earth. He is a figure of enormous stature who falls precipitously when Mephistopheles seduces him with his demonic wiles into damning himself for eternity. In contrast, Hynkel is a villain at the film's start who needs no prodding from anyone else in order to do evil. He's damned from the beginning. So Garbitsch may be Mephistopheles, but Hynkel is no Faust.

No less absurd than Garbitsch's scheme to exterminate Tomania's brunets is the side-splitting speech that Hynkel delivers to his adoring people the first time we see him on screen. Chaplin closely studied newsreel footage of Hitler's speeches before making the film in order to master the dictator's wildly theatrical mannerisms and in the end creates a speech that combines pure gibberish with German words, such as "Sauerkraut" and "Wienerschnitzel," ripped out of context. Throughout this harangue, the dictator's words are not just figuratively but also *literally* nonsense. As Richardson notes, "The lack of discernible content . . . suggests that Hitler's persuasive rhetoric is devoid of actual ideas."[29] As Hynkel rants on, the off-screen English translator continually downplays the vitriol of the dictator's speech. After, for example, Hynkel has launched into a tirade about the *Juden* so venomous it wilts the microphone, the translator blandly remarks, "The Phooey has just referred to the Jewish people." The satire alludes both to the way the Nazis perpetually concealed their true motives from the rest of the world, often through the medium of duplicitous mass communication, and also to the way the outside world, reluctant to confront Hitler, perpetually mitigated the extent of the threat he posed.

Hynkel and the Jewish barber are diametrically opposed in their attitudes toward other human beings. The barber is sweet, loving, and empathetic to the pain of others, as is most evident in his shy flirtation with Hannah, as well as in his warm relations with the other members of the ghetto. Hynkel, in contrast, sees other people in purely functional terms, as objects or tools that he can use to accomplish his megalomaniacal ends. So, for example, when the dictator needs the seal on an envelope moistened, he has one of his guards stick out his tongue. In another instance, a Tomanian inventor presents the Phooey with what he assures is a "perfect" bulletproof suit. When, to test the invention, Hynkel fires a pistol, killing the man on the spot, Hynkel's only response is to mutter, "Far from perfect."

Certainly, this characterization of Hitler is spot-on. After all, the Jews were not the only race he considered expendable. As the Allies closed in and it was clear Germany couldn't win the war, Hitler, holed away in a bunker under Berlin, refused to surrender. Convinced his own people had failed him by not emerging victorious, he judged that they, too, deserved annihilation in a suicidal struggle. Under Hitler, despite his frequent protestations of love for the German *Ubermensch*, the *people* served *him*, and not the other way around. According to Kerner, this idea that Hitler despised not only the Jews but also his purported "super race," the German people, is suggested in *The Great Dictator* in Chaplin's decision to adopt as the symbol of Hynkel's regime not the swastika but the "Double Cross," represented by a pair of "x's": "Certainly, this is an apt characterization of the Nazi regime that not only betrayed European Jewry—many of whom held German citizenship . . . but the regime also betrayed all of Germany, leading the nation headlong into a catastrophic war under false pretense and brazen scapegoating."[30]

Another of Hynkel's notable traits is that the dictator is publicly forceful but privately weak. Hynkel is forever being bested by material objects. He can't extricate pens from their holders; when he goes duck hunting, with his first shot he overturns his boat and goes plunging into the lake. Indeed, Hynkel comes off as something of a figurehead. When Tomania is visited by the dictator of Bacteria, Napaloni (based on Mussolini and brilliantly portrayed by Jack Oakie), the Bacterian leader easily foils Hynkel's every attempt to display his superiority to his fellow tyrant. That night, at a ball thrown in Napaloni's honor, the corpulent Mrs. Napaloni waltzes the scrawny dictator around the dance floor as if he were a rag doll.

Is this hapless figure an accurate portrait of Hitler? It's certainly true that the Führer was hardly omniscient, especially as a military strategist;

if Hitler had not meddled so much and so incompetently in the plans of his generals, Germany might have won the war. On the other hand, it's doubtful that Hitler could have achieved the power he did as absolute ruler of Germany if he were as hapless as Adenoid Hynkel. Still, turning Hitler into a buffoon is central to Chaplin's satirical strategy. Converted into a figure of fun, Hitler—at least on screen—is stripped of his power to harm. As Richardson observes, "Chaplin methodically dismantles the elements of the Hitler myth."[31]

Perhaps the most famous scene in the entire film—and one memorably illuminating of Hynkel's personality and that of tyrants throughout the ages—is when the dictator, alone in his office, expresses his desire for world domination by caressing a globe, which turns into a balloon that Hynkel bounces off his head and hands and rear end, all to the swelling strains of Wagner's *Lohengrin*. At the scene's end, the balloon bursts and Hynkel weeps inconsolably. In his biography of Chaplin, *Charlie Chaplin and His Times*, Kenneth Lynn writes that "at bottom, all of the memorable scenes in *The Great Dictator* are built on pantomime."[32] Even though the film was Chaplin's first talking picture, the director hadn't relinquished his genius for physical comedy that transcends slapstick and turns profound—the kind of scene on which all his silent films are based.

The globe scene can be contrasted with one showing the Jewish barber shaving a customer in perfect time to the melody emanating from his radio of Brahms' rousing "Hungarian Dance No. 5." Comparing the two pieces of music used in the two scenes, it seems that Brahms's piece is a more authentic expression of folk culture than Wagner's. In her comparison of the scenes, Insdorf draws a symbolic interpretation: "The juxtaposition of these two scenes suggests that the barber's razor will be the agent of Hynkel's deflation—as, indeed, Chaplin's keen humor is to Hitler's image in the film."[33] One might also see the scenes as contrasting humble but useful labor (giving someone a shave) with a tyrant's power-mad schemes, which, should they succeed, will only leave mankind in misery.

Moreover, of course, Wagner, a notorious anti-Semite himself, was Hitler's favorite composer, and Wagner's operas were often put on by the Nazis in lavish productions at the annual Bayreuth Festival. In fact, Wagner's relatives were intimate friends of Hitler's, part of the Führer's inner circle, although these inconvenient facts were hushed up by the

Wagner family after the war. In *Twilight of the Wagners: The Unveiling of a Family's Legacy*, Wagner's great-grandson, Gottfried Wagner, who has become a champion of better relations between Germans and Jews, describes his shock at discovering an old reel of film that revealed his family's intimacy with Hitler during the war: "What I discovered left me stunned. I saw my aunts, Uncle Wieland, and my grandmother, Wini-fred, together with Hitler, who was dressed in an elegant double-breasted suit, laughing as they strolled in Wahnfried Park. Happy Fuh-rer, happy Wagner children, happy Grandmother Winifred! . . . All arms were outstretched in a '*Heil* Hitler' salute: Wagner's art and the Fuhrer's power."[34]

If *The Great Dictator* is insightful about the character of Hitler, it also sheds a penetrating light on the Nazi regime as a whole, and on the nature of fascism in general. Near the film's end, at a grandiose rally for the Party of the Double Cross, Garbitsch introduces "Hynkel" (who is really the barber) by explaining that under the present Tomanian re-gime individual human needs have been subordinated to the needs of the state, which means that the personal freedoms of ordinary citizens must be curtailed for the good of the collective. This, in a nutshell, was Chaplin's view of fascism, an ideology that violated everything he be-lieved as a liberal individualist and fervent democrat. In that same intro-ductory speech, Garbitsch also makes quite clear the persecution Hyn-kel (and, of course, Hitler) intended to wreak upon the Jews: "The rights of citizenship will be taken away from all Jews and other non-Aryans. . . . They are inferior, and therefore enemies of the State."[35] It's true that Garbitsch doesn't spell out Hynkel's exterminationist inten-tions toward the Jews, but the details of Hitler's Final Solution were not yet known to the outside world when Chaplin made *The Great Dictator* in 1939.

Chaplin also has fun with the Nazi conception of art. When the hyperactive Hynkel rushes from one task to the next, one of his regular stops is a studio where a sculptor is fashioning a bust of the dictator while a painter is doing his portrait; Hynkel pauses to pose for a few seconds, then rushes out, to the frustration of both artists. In an even funnier scene, after Hynkel has delivered his opening speech and is driving off in his motorcade past adoring throngs, we see statues of the Venus de Milo and Rodin's *The Thinker*, except that both statues have raised arms and are "Sieg Heiling" the dictator. In both cases, totalitarian art serves only to glorify the dictator and his regime. A failed artist himself, Hitler likewise strenuously sought to turn German art into propaganda touting his ideology—indeed, to turn the entire Nazi state into a kind of nightmarish "work of art," featured in the massive rallies and monumental buildings designed by his chief architect, Albert Speer. Such art was the epitome of Nazi kitsch, a point *The Great Dictator* registers.

Despite these sharp satirical hits against the Nazi regime, many, especially modern-day, critics fault *The Great Dictator* for underestimating the full horror of Hitlerian evil, especially regarding Nazi persecution of the Jews. As previously noted, the film's storm troopers are merely slapstick buffoons. Moreover, at one point Hynkel's hapless, portly henchman Herring (based on Herman Goering) gleefully informs the dictator that a Tomanian scientist has invented a "poison gas" which will "kill everybody"—a horribly inappropriate reference in light of the Nazis' later use of Zyklon B to gas prisoners. In another scene, Garbitsch advises Hynkel to step up his persecution of the Jews, since it will "keep the people's minds off their stomachs," but in reality, unlike many past anti-Semites, Hitler wasn't simply scapegoating the Jews for opportunistic reasons. He actually believed the Jewish people posed a potentially deadly threat to the Aryan race and had to be annihilated. As historian Christopher Browning tells Ron Rosenbaum in *Explaining Hitler: The Search for the Origins of His Evil*, "I think [Hitler] *was* a true believer . . . that he does believe Jews were the source of all evil in the world."[36]

The Great Dictator's underrating of the radical degree of Nazi evil, toward the Jews and any opponents of the Third Reich, is reflected even more strikingly in the scene in which the barber is briefly imprisoned in a Tomanian concentration camp. The film depicts life in the camp as only slightly more onerous than that found at a low-budget summer camp, with the prisoners comically goose-stepping across the campgrounds and the barber whimsically asking a guard to light his cigar. In these scenes, we are as far from Auschwitz as one can imagine. But however much we may cringe at these trivializing scenes today, it's important to remember, as noted earlier, that *The Great Dictator* appeared in 1940, when knowledge in the Western democracies of what the Nazis were perpetrating was far from complete and the worst atrocities of the Holocaust had yet to occur.

The introduction to this book questioned whether comedy is ever an appropriate way to depict the Nazis and the Holocaust or if it amounts to "making light" of the Holocaust in a manner as offensive as it is inadequate. This issue is relevant not only to *The Great Dictator* but also to the "Holocaust comedies" that follow it: *To Be or Not to Be* (1942), *The Producers* (1968), and *Jakob the Liar* (1999), among others. At the time *The Great Dictator* appeared, despite the overwhelming critical and popular acclaim the film received, its comic approach to the Nazis did generate controversy. A contemporary review in *The Hollywood Citizen* summed up this objection: "It's hard to be funny about war when war is ravaging humanity."[37] In *My Autobiography*, published in 1964, Chaplin himself expressed second thoughts about *The Great Dictator*'s comedic approach: "Had I known of the actual horrors of the German concentration camps," he wrote, "I could not have made fun of the homicidal insanity of the Nazis."[38] Yet, all things considered, if Chaplin indeed wouldn't have made *The Great Dictator* had he known of the horrors of the camps, then perhaps there was a silver lining to his ignorance, since without it the world would have been deprived of this marvelous film. In fact, perhaps Chaplin is too hard on his own movie, since the film serves as an effective way to "laugh at the Devil." The key is to remember the time in which *The Great Dictator* appeared, to examine the film in a historical context, and to make allowances accordingly.

If the comedy in *The Great Dictator* incites controversy, the long speech by Chaplin that concludes the film has also riled many critics, both at the time and today. Mistaken for Hynkel, the barber addresses the crowd with a long speech extolling peace and brotherhood and condemning dictators. Simultaneously, Hannah and some other Jews from the ghetto, who've escaped to Osterlich, are set on by Tomanian troops. The barber's speech concludes with the stirring exhortation: "Look up, Hannah! The soul of man has been given wings and at last is beginning to fly . . . into the light of hope." Hearing these words from a loudspeaker, Hannah, who'd been flung to the ground by a Tomanian soldier, obediently raises her tear-streaked face as sunlight breaks through the clouds—the film's final image.

Clearly, the deliverer of this speech is not the barber but Chaplin himself. At the end of the movie, Chaplin abandons any pretense of cinematic verisimilitude, breaking the so-called "fourth wall" that allows audiences to maintain the illusion that what they are viewing is reality. Tossing his narrative aside, the director addresses the audience in his own person, telling them in no uncertain terms his film's intended message. Originally, Chaplin had planned to have the soldiers in attendance respond to the speech by throwing down their weapons and breaking into folk dances, but the director decided to keep the focus firmly on the speech itself. The movie's conclusion seems to be an implicit admission by Chaplin that, ultimately, slapstick is an inadequate means to convey the dangers posed by Hitler; after a point, only straightforward didacticism will do. While the speech has a theological quality, its spirit is ecumenical; at the start, Chaplin alludes to the Christian commandment to "love thy neighbor" when he says, "I don't want to be an emperor. . . . I don't want to rule or conquer anyone. I should like to help everyone." And the speech also quotes from the New Testament: "In the seventeenth chapter of St. Luke, it is written that the kingdom of God is within man—not one man nor a group of men, but in all men!" Indeed, the speech reads rather like Chaplin's version of the Sermon on the Mount.

At the time, many critics, even those who otherwise liked *The Great Dictator*, criticized Chaplin's ending as unpersuasive and cloyingly optimistic. The critic Gerald Mast, for example, derided the speech as "a severe stylistic disruption in form—from human comedy and political burlesque to humanistic hearts and flowers."[39] Such contemporary attacks upset Chaplin, who retorted, "They had their laughs and it was fun, now I wanted them to listen. I did this picture for the return of decency and kindness."[40] In a *New York Times* interview conducted shortly after the film's release, Chaplin appeared even more embittered and perplexed by the negative response: "I had a story to tell and something I very much wanted to say. . . . The picture is two hours and three minutes in length. . . . May I not be excused for ending my comedy on a note that reflects honestly and realistically, the world in which we live, and may I not be excused in pleading for a better world?"[41] When, decades later, Chaplin published his autobiography, he reprinted the speech in its entirety—hoping, perhaps, that the passage of time would lead readers to regard his words more favorably.

Other critics have compared the speech to the mad rant by Adenoid Hynkel near the film's start (these two speeches do more or less frame the film), suggesting that in a movie condemning totalitarian propaganda, Chaplin ultimately turns, ironically enough, into a propagandist himself. This argument is made at some length and with considerable cogency by Michael D. Richardson:

> The premise of the film is undermined by the valorization of Chaplin's concluding speech. If the film began with a critique of Hynkel's oratorical prowess and persuasive ability as effective yet devoid of ideas, it ends with praise of Chaplin's own skill in this regard. The unseen masses, once so eager to cheer Hynkel, regardless of the fact that his speech was pure nonsense . . . are once again susceptible to powerful rhetoric. Moreover, the film undermines the principle opposition—fascism versus democracy—by recentering the film on a single figure. . . . Although Hynkel is no longer visible in the film and the barber has taken over his appearance, Chaplin has not fully exorcised the dictator from his representation. [42]

While it's true that these two speeches frame the movie, it makes more sense to see them not as bookends, but as polar opposites, since Hynkel's tirade explicitly condemns individual rights while Chaplin's is a plea for human freedom. If Hynkel's speech is "pure nonsense," Chaplin's certainly is not; indeed, his exhortation for human brotherhood and an end to war and tyrants seems just as relevant to our age as it was to Chaplin's own. Human nature being what it is, it will probably remain eternally relevant. After the barber's speech ends, there is a brief shot of the assembled masses cheering, just as they cheered Hynkel's speech, but, again, what we are seeing is more a contrast than a comparison; now the masses are cheering for their own individual independence, not the abdication of that independence to the will of a despot. Yes, Chaplin here is a "single figure," but that does not make him a dictator; presidents who run democracies are also single figures but stand uneasily atop a hierarchy of elected political representatives.

Other critics have faulted Chaplin's speech for placing no particular emphasis on Hitler's evil intentions toward the Jews. In this vein, Bill Krohn complains that "the barber's speech is not about the Shoah." [43] But, as has already been discussed in considerable detail, *The Great Dictator* as a whole highlights Nazi anti-Semitism in a way that dramatically sets it apart from any other Hollywood film of the time.

Still others have pointed out that, since *The Great Dictator* was only screened in the Western democracies, while banned in Germany, in

Nazi-occupied countries, and in other fascist countries such as Italy and Spain, Chaplin was preaching to the choir, while the oppressed masses who most needed to hear his words never had a chance to do so. But these critics forget that when *The Great Dictator* appeared in 1940, there was still considerable support for Hitler and the Nazis in the Western democracies. Had everyone in these nations already agreed with Chaplin's message, the film wouldn't have been so controversial, nor would so many friends and colleagues have counseled Chaplin against making the movie.

Finally, still other critics, accusing Chaplin of being a fellow-traveling supporter of the Soviet Union, have dismissed the speech as, in Mast's words, "Marxism sweetened with American idealistic clichés."[44] This is the line taken in Kenneth Lynn's eviscerating biography of Chaplin, in which Lynn blasts the speech as nothing more than Communist propaganda. "The [film's] peace [message] perfectly complimented the Communist line in the pact period," Lynn writes. "For Chaplin did not end his picture with a call to arms against Hitler. . . . Instead, he made a plea for universal 'kindness and gentleness.' Without these qualities, Chaplin warned the world [that] 'life will be violent and all will be lost.'"[45] Along these lines, Lynn notes that the speech was later issued as a pamphlet put out by the British Communist Party. The biographer also argues that Chaplin's "peace" message was agreeable to American isolationists, pointing out that the "isolationist" Daughters of the American Revolution invited Chaplin to recite the speech during the presidential inaugural festivities at Constitution Hall on January 19, 1941 (the same day Chaplin met with FDR after the president had watched a special screening of *The Great Dictator*). As for the speech's final exhortation to "Look up, Hannah," Lynn, noting that Hannah was also the name of Chaplin's mother (a mentally ill woman who was institutionalized for much of his childhood), snidely asserts that "Chaplin fused a dreamy politics with sentimental thoughts about his mother into a single ecstatic spasm"—which seems to dismiss the speech as an act of rhetorical masturbation.[46]

But I disagree that Chaplin's concluding speech places the director in the camp of American isolationists. After all, in the penultimate paragraph of the speech, Chaplin uses the word "fight" three times in as many sentences and calls his listeners (not just the troops at the rally but also the members of the audience) "soldiers": "Now let us fight to fulfill that promise! Let us fight to free the world. . . . Let us fight for a world of reason. . . . Soldiers! In the name of democracy, let us unite!" These words hardly sound pacifistic. If anything, they can be read as Chaplin calling for the Western democracies to stand up to Hitler militarily, which was precisely the message isolationist Senator Gerald Nye drew when he accused *The Great Dictator* of touting pro-war propaganda. Clearly, Nye was one American isolationist who didn't find the film's message congenial, whatever the DAR's motives for inviting Chaplin to recite the speech at their gathering. Finally, if Chaplin were merely obeying instructions from Moscow, why would he make a Hitler-bashing movie *during* the Nazi/Soviet pact? Wouldn't Stalin in 1940 have found a film *praising* his then ally Hitler much more appealing?

Like many progressives of the time, Chaplin was drawn to the Soviet Union as an allegedly "classless society" and a "worker's paradise." But the director possessed far too independent a mind ever to function as a mere Communist puppet. Indeed, the speech's sweeping condemnation of dictators can be interpreted as a denunciation of *all* undemocratic leaders, Communist as well as fascist, whether or not that was Chaplin's explicit intention:

> Don't give yourself to these brutes—who despise you—enslave you—who regiment your lives—who tell you what to do—what to think and what to feel! Who drill you . . . treat you like cattle and use you as cannon fodder. Don't give yourself to these unnatural men—machine men with machine minds and machine hearts!

It is reported that when Stalin privately watched *The Great Dictator*, it was precisely at this point that the Soviet leader ordered the projector shut off. On a more personal note, when, during a Fulbright-sponsored year in Poland, I screened this movie to my Polish students, several remarked during our discussion afterward that Chaplin's final speech had reminded them of their country's own ultimately successful struggle to throw off the yokes of Communism and Soviet oppression.

At the very least, no one can doubt the sincerity of the speech's sentiments, enhanced by Chaplin's fervent delivery, with the camera fixed on his face in close-up. Perhaps most importantly, the speech is undeniably prophetic, given the Nazi atrocities that were fully revealed at the close of the war. Had the world heeded Chaplin's warnings expeditiously, rather than waiting to act until Hitler had swallowed up much of Europe, might Auschwitz have been averted? Along these lines, Arthur Schlesinger comments in *The Tramp and the Dictator*, while Chaplin's speech might have sounded mawkish at the time the film opened, his denunciation of mass violence now resonates in light not only of Nazi crimes but also of the ever-present threat of global extinction in our nuclear age.

2

ACTORS VERSUS NAZIS

To Be or Not to Be

Given the problematic and controversial nature of anti-Nazi comedy, it's striking that 1942, only two years after *The Great Dictator* appeared in theaters, saw the opening of a second American comedy that used humor to lampoon the Nazis: *To Be or Not to Be*. The director was Ernst Lubitsch, a German Jew who had immigrated to Hollywood before Hitler's rise to power. Lubitsch left Germany in 1922 when he was invited to the United States by silent-picture star and Hollywood businesswoman Mary Pickford. In the Weimar Republic, Lubitsch had directed lavish historical epics such as *Anna Boleyn* (1920) and *The Loves of Pharaoh* (1922). In America, according to film historian Thomas Doherty, the director "was the German import who yielded the highest return on investment as the master chef behind Hollywood's most sophisticated comedies of manners."[1]

To Be or Not to Be starred Jack Benny and Carole Lombard. Lubitsch began shooting the movie in 1941, before the United States had entered the war; thus, like Chaplin, the director risked—in making a film bashing the Nazis and celebrating those who resisted them—angering the isolationists, still a potent force in America. Midway through the filming, the Japanese bombed Pearl Harbor and the United States joined the Allies. By the time the film came out in 1942, World War II was raging. Although all the facts wouldn't be revealed to the world until after the war, top Nazi officials had gathered at the Wannsee

Conference to lay out a "Final Solution" to the "Jewish Question," while poison gas had begun to be used to kill prisoners at the camps at Auschwitz, Belzec, and Sobibor. A considerable amount of information about these atrocities had begun to appear in European and American media, though it was often buried in the back pages of newspapers. Of course, none of these gruesome realities appeared in *To Be or Not to Be*, though the film, which opened with documentary footage of a devastated Poland following the Nazi invasion, was hardly oblivious to Nazi brutality. As it happened, about a month before the film's premiere, Carole Lombard, returning from a War Bond drive in the Midwest, was killed in a plane crash. Lombard's tragic death led some sympathetic critics to single out her excellent performance for praise, though a more common response was that audiences found it hard to laugh at a comedy in which the female lead was recently deceased.

Opening with the Nazi invasion of Poland, the film focuses on the consequences of the occupation on a Warsaw theater troupe led by the Polish actor Joseph Tura (Benny) and his attractive wife Maria (Lombard). Full of the zany plot twists typical of a screwball comedy, the story relates how the troupe must stop a Nazi spy, Professor Siletsky (Stanley Ridges), from passing along to the Nazi high command the names of everyone in the Polish resistance. Applying his thespian skills, Tura pretends to be a Nazi commandant, Colonel Ehrhardt, in a staged meeting with the professor, in which Tura attempts to finagle the list of Polish partisans out of Siletsky's possession. When Siletsky is killed in a shoot-out, Tura next must impersonate the Nazi spy with the actual Colonel Ehrhardt (Sig Ruman). Through a final elaborate subterfuge, the troupe manages to flee Poland and escape to England during a theatrical production in Warsaw at which Hitler, himself, is present. The actors are accompanied in their escape by an intrepid young fighter pilot in the Polish resistance, Lieutenant Sobinski (Robert Stack), who happens to be infatuated (and possibly is having an affair) with Mrs. Tura.

While there is at least one Jewish character in *To Be or Not to Be* (through whom Nazi anti-Semitism is subtly hinted), the word "Jew" is never mentioned; instead, the movie's focus remains squarely on the German persecution of the Poles. In 1943, after the movie had appeared, the American Jewish Congress (AJC) urged the leaders of the film industry to make movies dealing directly with the Nazi genocide

Figure 2.1. *To Be or Not to Be* (1942). Joseph Tura (Jack Benny) impersonates a Nazi officer as his wife Maria (Carol Lombard) plays along. [Screen grab]

against European Jewry. When these requests were rebuffed, the AJC next appealed to Lowell Mellett, then chief of the Bureau of Motion Pictures of the Office of War Information, asking him to intervene with the studios. After talking with various studio heads, Mellett approvingly passed along their consensus response to the AJC leadership: "It might be unwise from the standpoint of the Jews themselves to have a picture dealing solely with Hitler's treatment of their people, but interest has been indicated in the possibility of a picture covering various groups that have been subject to the Nazi treatment. This of course would take in the Jews."[2] This compromise describes exactly the approach taken in anti-Nazi Hollywood films made during the war, which, rather than singling out the Jews as particular targets of Nazi persecution, simply included them among a range of groups the Germans were depicted as victimizing. When Hollywood downplayed Nazi anti-Semitism, studio insiders described the move, with painful irony, as in the best interests of Jews themselves. (Not only did *To Be or Not to Be* adopt such an approach, but so did other movies made during World War II, including three films I'll be discussing: *Hitler's Children* [1943], *Hitler's Madman* [1944], and *Tomorrow, the World!* [1944].) In short, before the war, Hollywood was afraid to make films criticizing the Nazis; once America entered the war, the studios decided that the Nazis were now fair game, but not Nazi anti-Semitism.

In *Ernst Lubitsch's American Comedy*, William Paul challenges the conventional belief that *To Be or Not to Be* was uniformly savaged by critics and rejected by audiences when it first appeared, arguing that it actually received a variety of responses, with some critics reacting quite favorably, especially those outside New York City.[3] While Paul may be right, there's no question that the film generated enormous controversy and enjoyed far less praise than did *The Great Dictator*. One reason audiences may have found *The Great Dictator*'s anti-Nazi satire more palatable is simply that Lubitsch couldn't match Chaplin's superstardom. A second reason may be that Chaplin's film is set in an imaginary place, a fantasyland called Tomania, whereas *To Be or Not to Be* takes place in real-life Nazi-occupied Poland, with Hitler mentioned by name and briefly appearing on screen. William Huff writes that "the Lubitsch burlesque, laid in Nazi-invaded Warsaw, was called callous, a picture of confusing moods, lacking in taste, its subject not suitable for fun making."[4] The *Philadelphia Inquirer* called it a "tasteless effort to make fun of the bombing of Warsaw," while the National Board of Review, while favoring the film, warned that "sensitive people won't like it."[5] Another backhanded compliment was delivered by the critic for the *New York Morning Telegraph*, which wrote, "If it were set any place but Warsaw, it would be among the best things Lubitsch has done."[6]

The Polish-American community was especially irate over what it saw as Lubitsch insensitively satirizing Polish suffering under the Nazis. Along these lines, one joke in *To Be or Not to Be* especially incensed the film's critics, along with many Polish Americans. Forever fishing for compliments, Tura (disguised as Professor Siletsky) asks Colonel Ehrhardt if he's ever heard of "that great Polish actor Joseph Tura." Ehrhardt replies, "Yes, what he did to Shakespeare, we are now doing to Poland." After the film previewed, many of those closest to Lubitsch, including his own wife, begged the director to cut this line, but he adamantly refused. The joke needs to be taken in context, of course, since the line lampoons not the German attack on Poland but the egomania of even the most incompetent of actors. But this distinction tended to be lost on audiences in 1942.

While Chaplin regretted making *The Great Dictator* after the full horrors of the Nazi regime had been revealed, Lubitsch staunchly defended *To Be or Not to Be* against all criticisms—at the time the film opened and for the rest of his life. After *New York Times* critic Bosley Crowther panned *To Be or Not to Be*, Lubitsch responded by writing a full-length article that subsequently appeared in the paper. In it, he succinctly summarized the principle objections to the film: "I am accused of three major sins—of having violated every traditional form in mixing melodrama with comedy-satire or even farce, of endangering our war effort in treating the Nazi menace too lightly, and of exhibiting extremely bad taste in having chosen present-day Warsaw as a background for comedy."[7] Defending himself against the charge of "treating the Nazi menace too lightly," Lubitsch wrote:

> I admit that I have not resorted to the methods usually employed in pictures, novels, and plays to signify Nazi terror. No actual torture chamber is photographed, no flogging is shown, no close-up of excited Nazis using their whips and rolling their eyes in lust. My Nazis are different: they passed that stage long ago. They talk about it the same way as a salesman referring to the sale of a handbag. Their humor is built around concentration camps, around the suffering of their victims.[8]

Applying Lubitsch's defense to Colonel Ehrhardt's controversial line, "What he did to Shakespeare, we are now doing to Poland," one can infer that for the Nazi colonel brutality and carnage has become so routinized, so matter-of-fact, that it's an appropriate subject for a clever bon mot. This view of the horribly desensitized Nazi is reinforced when the colonel chuckles with glee when Tura tells him that his nickname among the Poles is "Concentration Camp Ehrhardt." Actually, this attitude makes Ehrhardt *more* frightening than if he were a crazed killer foaming at the mouth. Such a take on the Nazis accords with the views of many modern-day Holocaust historians, who focus on the Nazis' bureaucratized approach to genocide, what Hannah Arendt has famously called "the banality of evil."

Lubitsch also denied that *To Be or Not to Be* was anti-Polish:

This picture never made fun of Poles, it only satirized actors and the Nazi spirit and the foul Nazi humor. . . . When in *To Be Or Not To Be* I have referred to the destruction of Warsaw, I have shown it in all seriousness; the commentary under the shots of the devastated Warsaw speaks for itself and cannot leave any doubt in the spectator's mind what my point of view and attitude are toward these acts of horror. What I have satirized in this picture are the Nazis and their ridiculous ideology. I have also satirized the attitude of actors who always remain actors regardless of how dangerous the situation might be, which I believe is a true observation.[9]

But one reason the humor in *To Be or Not to Be* aroused such ire is that popular American audiences in the 1940s were unfamiliar with the genre of black comedy, which finds absurdist humor in the horrific—in war and death and persecution. William Paul insightfully compares *To Be or Not to Be* with such acclaimed antiwar comedies as *M*A*S*H* and *Catch-22*, both appearing in 1970, by which time, confronted by the quagmire in Vietnam, disillusioned audiences were ready for nihilistically black comic takes on war.

Another reason audiences may have been baffled and offended by *To Be or Not to Be* is that, unlike *The Great Dictator*, Lubitsch's film deliberately fails to establish a crystal clear distinction between heroes and villains. Lubitsch admitted as much himself when he acknowledged that one of his aims was to satirize "the attitude of actors," who are, after all, the presumed heroes of the movie. As Michael D. Richardson writes, "What distinguishes Lubitsch's film from Chaplin's is its refusal to posit the binaries that guided *The Great Dictator*. The Turas are not paragons of virtue—Joseph is an egotistical ham, given to self-promotion and prone to cowardice, and his wife, Maria, enjoys entertaining young men from the audience when her husband is safely onstage," though he acknowledges that "the sins of the Turas are certainly venal in comparison to those of Hitler."[10] Moreover, the film commends the numerous deceptions practiced by the Warsaw troupe in the course of manipulating the Nazis, upholding, in Richardson's words, "the principle of the ends justifying the means. . . . Here it is trickery and deceit that become desirable virtues. . . . What makes Lubitsch's film compelling—and what caused the most consternation—is that he made no apology for this lack of moral certainty."[11] Today, audiences are used to films that blur the distinction between good and evil, but that was certainly not true of audiences in the 1940s; indeed, Hollywood of that era made its living portraying utterly clear-cut moral distinctions.

Like *The Great Dictator, To Be or Not to Be* takes a potshot at Hitler in its opening scene. A voice-over narrator breathlessly announces that none other than Adolf Hitler himself has been spotted in downtown Warsaw while we are treated to a shot of Hitler standing nonchalantly in front of a sign that reads "Maslowski's Delicatessen," surrounded by a crowd of curious Polish civilians. It turns out that the figure is not actually Hitler but an actor from Tura's troupe named Bronski (Tom Dugan). Informed by his fellow thespians that his performance as the Führer in an anti-Nazi play the troupe is currently performing is unconvincing, Bronski has donned his Hitler costume and taken to the streets to test his credibility as the German leader. The charade is exploded when a small girl approaches "Hitler" and asks, "Can I have your autograph, Mr. Bronski?" Even though the word "Jew" is never mentioned, surely there is something subversively philo-Semitic in having an actor playing Hitler posed in front of a delicatessen. Even more importantly, the scene satirically demystifies Hitler; removed from the ennobling backdrop of the Third Reich, Hitler is revealed for what he actually is— in the narrator's words, "a little man with a moustache."

In the very next scene, the line between reality and theatrical illusion blurs even further. We see Jack Benny in a Nazi uniform and wearing a swastika armband, encircled by other Nazi officers; when a figure presumed to be Hitler enters the office and all the officers greet him with "Heil Hitler!" the Hitler-figure replies with the immortal line, "Heil me." It is only when a director breaks in at this point, incensed at "Hitler's" unauthorized ad-libbing, that we realize we are watching a play-within-a-film, the anti-Nazi play Tura's troupe is performing before the Germans invade—the same play in which Bronski has been cast in the role of the Führer. Before this realization dawns, the audience assumes it is going to be asked to endure a film in which Jack Benny plays a Nazi. In fact, this was precisely the assumption drawn by Benny's father, Meyer Kubelsky, the first time he saw the film. On that occasion, Kubelsky walked out on the movie in the opening minutes, incensed at seeing his son playing a Nazi and saying, "Heil Hitler!" Benny wrote to his father, but the old man refused to respond, more or less disowning his son. Finally, when Benny phoned, his father answered, and Benny was able to explain that if Meyer watched *To Be or*

Not to Be in its entirety, he'd discover that the movie was *against* the Nazis. Placated, Kubelsky went on to see the film forty-six times.[12]

In truth, Kubelsky's confusion was understandable, since in this early scene Lubitsch is deliberately trying to baffle the audience regarding Benny's relationship to the Nazis and the movie's relationship to Nazism in general. No doubt, it was this strategy of calculated audience disorientation that got the film in trouble when it first appeared. By having our first glimpse be of stage "Nazis," Lubitsch slyly suggests that the real Nazis were similarly poseurs—artificial, illusory, full of theatrical but empty gestures, devoid of substance. As Richardson astutely notes, "Lubitsch makes acting, that is, impersonation—the central motif of the film—a direct attack on the excessive theatricality of the Nazi regime. Instead of countering fiction with truth, he answers theater with more theater."[13] Because the Nazis' entire regime is based on theatrical artifice, it's no surprise than none of the Nazis catch on to the deception when Tura impersonates Colonel Ehrhardt or, later, when Bronski impersonates Hitler; as Gerd Gemunden writes, "Those who have been taught to obey the Fuhrer by respecting his metonymic representations—his portrait, the Hitler salute, etc.—relinquish the ability to question the authenticity of representations."[14] Chaplin makes a similar satirical point in *The Great Dictator* about the essential hollowness at the center of the Third Reich when he depicts Adenoid Hynkel as a man who in public, thundering from the podium, comes across as a fearsome leader but who in private is such a hapless incompetent he can't shoot a duck or even remove a pen from its holder.

This theme of theatrics versus reality reappears in the film's central plot, in which Tura and his troupe must impersonate various Nazis in order to undertake a very real act of resistance against actual Nazis. In this respect, the film makes literal the idea that play-acting can be a form of resistance and that art can effect social change—two highly idealistic notions that refute any view of the movie as cynical or nihilistic. (The idea of acting-as-resistance is also found in two more recent Holocaust films that I'll discuss: *Life Is Beautiful* [1997] and *Jakob the Liar* [1999].) When Professor Siletsky is shot by members of the troupe, his death occurs on stage. His protracted demise has all the appearances of a schlocky stage death (Siletsky feebly attempts a final "Heil Hitler!" before toppling to the boards); but, in truth, fatal reality has penetrated the world of the theater, and the real-life risks the actors have accepted as the potential consequence of their "theatrical" resistance are reiterated.

This embrace of heroism seems to explain one meaning of the film's title, *To Be or Not to Be*. The phrase, of course, is from *Hamlet* and translates roughly as "Should I live or die?" The film's most prominent running gag is that the rather promiscuous Mrs. Tura and her paramour, the dashing young Polish airman Lieutenant Sobinski, have an arrangement whereby at each nightly performance, when Tura launches into his dreadful special performance of Hamlet's "To be or not to be" soliloquy, Sobinski will slip out of the audience and down to Maria's dressing room. But the line has other implications. Like the melancholy Dane contemplating suicide, the actors are considering risking their lives, by courting death for the sake of their country. In a sense, the actors are asking themselves, "To be or not to be heroic?" (Interestingly, Hamlet himself was a revenger who loved the theater and used a play-within-a-play to further his own plot.)

At bottom, the troupe members in *To Be or Not to Be* are such charming and memorable heroes precisely because they are all such unlikely candidates for heroism. Moreover, however heroically the actors behave, they're never idealized, in good part because they never lose that egotism that Lubitsch (echoing the feelings of many other directors, one imagines) whimsically implies is a professional hazard of the acting trade. Benny's character, for example, may be risking his life for Polish freedom by playing the roles of Professor Siletsky and Colonel Ehrhardt, but that doesn't stop him from asking every Nazi he meets, "I assume you've heard of that great Polish actor Joseph Tura?" Although the two films are otherwise worlds apart, the focus on unlikely heroes in *To Be or Not to Be* foreshadows the even less likely hero, Oskar Schindler, a Nazi war profiteer turned Righteous Gentile, featured in *Schindler's List*.

If *To Be or Not to Be* plays rather profoundly with the ambiguous relationship between the theatrical and the real, it also explores the no-less-fraught relationship between the theatrical and the political—in particular, Nazi politics. Because we see actors portray Nazis early in the film, the actual Nazis we subsequently encounter have a similarly theatrical, unreal air. Because Tura impersonates first Professor Siletsky and then Colonel Ehrhardt, when we meet the real Siletsky and Ehrhardt they seem to be actors playing themselves. Even the invasion of

Poland has a theatrical ambience. When the invasion starts, one troupe member says, "The Nazis are putting on the show now, and it's a much bigger one than ours," to which the servant Maria replies, "And there's no censor to stop them"—a reference to how Polish censors had closed the troupe's anti-Nazi play to appease the Germans. At the invasion's conclusion, the voice-over narrator says, "The curtain has fallen on the Polish drama, a tragedy with no relief in sight."

What is Lubitsch suggesting with this interweaving of the theatrical and political worlds? On one level, we see some more gentle ridicule of the self-involvement and insularity of actors, so smitten with their profession that they perceive even a military invasion through the lens of their trade. But, more importantly, the implication is that both theater and politics (especially fascist politics) are obsessed with appearances, with deliberately fostering illusions in order to sway the public. *To Be or Not to Be*'s opening scene, in a sense, turns Hitler into a ham actor—surely not an entirely inaccurate take on the Führer, since Hitler, in fact, meticulously rehearsed his speeches before delivering them to his followers, focusing not only on his words but also on his gestures, his dress, and the look of his hair. Even Hitler's decision to grow a well-trimmed moustache was a carefully calculated political move.

But if *To Be or Not to Be* implies commonalities between the theatrical and the political—all comparisons unflattering to the political realm—the film also suggests some sharp differences between the two worlds. The actual Nazis play their brutal roles with strict adherence to authority. Colonel Ehrhardt is terrified that Tura (playing Siletsky) will repeat to the Führer the joke that Ehrhardt has ill-advisedly shared, whose punch line is that Hitler is "a piece of cheese." In the Nazi world, unlike that of the theater, there is no room for comedy, especially where the absolute leader is concerned. Near the film's end, another moment vividly illuminates the Nazis' embrace of blind obedience. As part of their scheme, Tura and his troupe have hijacked a Nazi plane to fly them safely to England, but this leaves them with the problem of how to dispose of the German pilots. The solution is that Bronski, impersonating Hitler, orders the two pilots to jump (sans parachutes) out of the airborne plane, an order they both immediately, mindlessly obey, leaping to their deaths—another example of the black comedy that gives *To Be or Not to Be* such a modern ring.

The film's theatrical troupe, in contrast, is (in Paul's words) "an anarchic collection of messily uncontrolled egos."[15] When Bronski ad-libs, "Heil me," to the consternation of his director, Dubosch, another actor, Greenberg, asks Dubosch if he'd like to hear Greenberg's opinion of Bronski's improvisation. When the director replies, "No, Mr. Greenberg, I do not want to hear your opinion," Greenberg responds, "All right, then, let me give you my reaction." The implication is that Greenberg intends to share his views regardless of whether those in authority approve or not. Actors, the film implies, are temperamentally unsuited to live in totalitarian cultures, which is very much to their credit. In that respect, they are, perhaps, ideal resisters against fascism. Moreover, the actors are always acutely aware of the division between reality and the roles they are playing—from which they often maintain an ironic distance. The Nazis, in contrast, have been forced by the complete conformity of their totalitarian society to *become* their roles. Stripped of any distance between themselves and the parts they play, they have been deprived of an inner life, a private self. Indeed, this evisceration of the private realm is one of the cruelest sufferings a fascist state imposes on its citizens. Insdorf dislikes the equivalency *To Be or Not to Be* draws between actors and Nazis, with each group displaying the "same childish narcissism," which she suggests makes the Nazis look less evil than they actually were.[16] But she ignores how the film sees Nazis and actors as both equivalent and *antithetical*; in the latter sense, the acting troupe represents a kind of anarchic utopia, the polar opposite of Nazi society.

Perhaps the most interesting Nazi in *To Be or Not to Be* is the short-lived Professor Siletsky. A Nazi spy, Siletsky also does his share of acting. At the film's start, he pretends to be a member of the Polish resistance exiled in England in order to uncover the names of all the partisans, which he plans to hand over to the Germans. Siletsky also behaves duplicitously in the hilarious scene in which, at Nazi headquarters, the professor tries to seduce the lovely Maria Tura, who plays along in an attempt to gain access to Siletsky's list of Polish partisans. In this scene, Siletsky tries both to woo Mrs. Tura and to convert her to Nazism while Lombard wittily parries his every thrust in a brilliant performance that is, itself, a parody of her public image as a screen sex goddess. The scene cleverly exposes the connection (especially for Nazis) between military and sexual conquest. When Siletsky asks, "Shall we drink to a blitzkrieg?" Maria replies, "I prefer a slow encirclement." "In the final analysis," Siletsky continues, "all [we Nazis] are trying to do is create a happy world." Mrs. Tura responds, "And people who don't want to be happy have no place in this happy world." "We're just like other people," Siletsky insists. "We love to sing. We love to dance. We admire beautiful women. We are human [touching her hand]—and sometimes very human." Siletsky concludes: "Why don't you stay for dinner? I couldn't think of anything more charming, and before the evening is over, I'm sure you'll say 'Heil Hitler'!" This line must represent the ultimate eroticizing of fascism—a woman's orgasmic cry turns into the Nazi salute. One wonders how that joke ever passed the censors. While it was the erotic dimension inherent in Nazism that inspired the revolting genre of Holocaust porn, in *To Be or Not to Be*, Nazi eroticism is hilariously parodied rather than exploited for sexual titillation.

In this scene with Maria, Professor Siletsky also appears as an example of a cinematic type common among Hollywood Nazis—the Nazi as lecher. *The Great Dictator*'s Hynkel is also a sexual predator, attempting, in one scene, to rape one of his secretaries before more pressing duties call. In *Schindler's List* as well, Nazi commandant Amon Goeth is about to rape a beautiful Jewess prisoner with whom he's infatuated, before, as a good Nazi, he decides to beat her up instead. This lecherous Nazi is also a staple of Holocaust porn. For example, in the softcore exploitation flick *Ilsa, She Wolf of the SS*, the title character is a female version of this type, a brutal wife of a camp commandant who beds male prisoners and then has them tortured and killed when they fail to quench her insatiable lusts. Likewise, in *The Reader*, we find a slightly modified variant of this character, when a female former Nazi camp guard—who, though less purely villainous, is sexually voracious—has a torrid affair with an underage boy after the war (who's unaware at the time of her notorious past). Of course, by depicting Nazis as lechers, Hollywood is able to firmly distance these villains from Americans, with their presumably straight-laced values and wholesome sexual habits.

One wonders if Hitler's own rather mysterious sexual proclivities helped fashion the Hollywood type of the lecherous Nazi. Hitler, while living in Munich before becoming Chancellor, may have had a sadomasochistic, incestuous sexual relationship with his beautiful young niece, Geli Raubal, which could have been what drove the girl to suicide.[17]

Even during the Führer's lifetime, journalists and others apprised of the Raubal scandal were speculating that Hitler was some kind of pervert. As Ron Rosenbaum reports in *Explaining Hitler: The Search for the Origins of His Evil*, a remarkable essay appeared in London's *Spectator* in 1934. Titled "Hitlerism as a Sex Problem," it made the sweeping claim that Hitler's own sexual deviance had turned the entire German people into a nation of perverts, characterized by "distorted sex show[ing] itself in Jew-baiting, persecution and ultrapuritanism."[18] The myth was even widely circulated that Hitler's sexual abnormalities were caused by the fact that he had only one testicle, the other having been bitten off by a goat. The Soviet leadership took this theory seriously enough that, when the Russian army found Hitler's body in the bunker under Berlin, they had it transported to Moscow, where Soviet doctors could examine Hitler's genitalia. (It turned out that, like most men, he had two testicles.)

If Professor Siletsky is not only a deviant lecher but also a truly dangerous Nazi who possesses the power to destroy the entire Polish underground, the film's other main Nazi, Colonel Ehrhardt, is far less menacing. Although it's casually suggested that the colonel has had untold numbers of Polish partisans shot, he comes across as a complete idiot. When it appears that Tura, playing Siletsky, will be exposed by Ehrhardt as an imposter (since the body of the real professor has been delivered to Nazi headquarters), Tura is easily able to foil Ehrardt's plan through a hastily improvised scheme that involves pasting a fake beard on the professor's corpse.

Ehrhardt's greatest terror is that news of one of his blunders will be passed along to his bosses. As was true of the Tomanian policemen in *The Great Dictator*, Ehrhardt is troubling as a screen Nazi because his haplessness makes the Nazis appear much less threatening then they really were. Insdorf justly complains that "in 1942 it might have seemed a cop-out to show that the Nazis' most powerful motivation was fear of their own superiors."[19] Indeed, Ehrhardt represents another common Hollywood depiction of Nazism—not the lecherous Nazi but the cartoon Nazi, most widely popularized by the 1960s TV sitcom *Hogan's Heroes*, about a plucky band of American POWs who run roughshod over their incompetent Nazi captors. (In fact, Sig Ruman, who plays Ehrhardt, bears a striking resemblance, with his popping eyeballs and rotund physique, to the actor John Banner, who played the bumbling

Sergeant Schultz on *Hogan's Heroes*.) As Richardson observes, in *Hogan's Heroes*, "it is difficult to even speak of the German officers and soldiers as enemies"; Schultz "and the Prussian *Kommandant* Klink are as ineffectual as they are likeable. The social structure of the camp is almost like that of an extended family in a contemporary sitcom, where Klink and Schultz represent the ostensible parental authority figures constantly undermined by their precocious children."[20] On one hand, Hollywood's cartoon Nazi is—like the progenitor of the type, Adenoid Hynkel in *The Great Dictator*—an example of the aforementioned satirical strategy of "laughing at the devil," disarming villainy through ridicule. But the problem inherent in this approach is that by making Nazi "devils" figures of fun, one obviously diminishes their true evil. No doubt that is a large part of the appeal of the cartoon Nazi—no one as hapless as Colonel Ehrhardt or Sergeant Schultz could ever be a cause for concern.

Like almost all anti-Nazi Hollywood films made during the war, *To Be or Not to Be* "closets" Jews by turning them into just one victim group among many targeted by Hitler. However, I sense the movie has a philo-Semitic subtext. The acting troupe itself seems a kind of surrogate for the Jews—plausibly enough, since Jews have played such a prominent role in the entertainment industry both in Europe and America. (Moreover, whether the troupe is simply seen as a group of actors or interpreted as surrogate Jews or representatives of the "Common Man," there is a delightful poetic justice in watching German *Übermenschen* outwitted by a motley group of *Untermenschen*, thus upending Nazi ideology.) As well, one troupe member is clearly designated as Jewish—Greenberg (Felix Bressart). No, no one calls Greenberg Jewish, nor does he ever identify himself as a member of the faith. But early in the film Greenberg snidely remarks about another member of the troupe, "What you are, I wouldn't eat." The other actor retorts, "How dare you call me a ham." For Hollywood in 1942, this amounted to signaling that a character was Jewish in neon lights.

One can justly complain that, as a Jew in Nazi-occupied Poland, Greenberg surely wouldn't have been left unmolested by the Germans, who would, instead, have deported him to a ghetto or a camp. Still, by keeping Greenberg around, however unrealistically, Lubitsch is able to feature him in perhaps the film's most fascinating scene—the only one alluding at all to the Holocaust. Greenberg is depicted as a second-rate actor relegated to bit parts who is convinced that he can win lasting fame if he is only permitted to play, of all things, the role of Shylock in a production of Shakespeare's *The Merchant of Venice*. As with the other actors in the troupe, Greenberg is no saint; his desire to play Shylock seems based not on a wish to portray a character who arguably depicts the humanity of the Jews but rather simply on a yen to finally get a major role; as Krohn writes, "Shylock's sense of racial victimization is elided by Greenberg's rancor over the professional slight that condemns him to be a spear carrier."[21]

To Be or Not to Be is structured on the familiar cinematic technique of comic repetition, most notably in Tura's repeated performances of Hamlet's "To be or not to be" soliloquy. Greenberg repeats Shylock's famous speech about the Jews ("If you prick us, do we not bleed?") three times through the course of the film, in each instance in a very different context, which casts the same words in quite a different light. The first time, Greenberg's delivery comes off as purely comic, as this bit actor grandiosely imagines himself in a lead role. The second time comes when Greenberg and another actor are surveying a Warsaw devastated by the Nazis, and Shylock's words now transform into a eulogy for a defeated Poland: "If you poison us, do we not die?"

Greenberg's final rendering of the speech is the lynchpin in the troupe's elaborate plot to spirit themselves out of Poland. Hitler has arrived to attend a gala performance at Warsaw's main theater. Greenberg's role is to create a commotion in the hall outside the theater, whereupon several members of the troupe posing as German soldiers will arrest him. Then another group of stage "Nazis," including Bronski in the role of Hitler himself, will appear on the scene and insist that, for the sake of the Führer's safety, Hitler must leave immediately, which will allow the troupe to commandeer some Nazi automobiles to convey them to the nearest airport. (Admittedly, the troupe might have found a simpler method of escaping from Poland, but this scheme no doubt appealed to their—and our—love of the theatrical and to the plethora of zany plot twists characteristic of screwball comedy.) When the fake Hitler and his entourage approach the captured Greenberg, he delivers his Shylock speech directly to the Führer. The speech begins, "Hath not a Jew eyes?"—although, tellingly, the filmmakers removed the word "Jew" from the script. Instead, the line becomes, "Have I not eyes?" which may partly be a reflection of Greenberg's egomania. However, the speech is uttered with an angry intensity Greenberg hasn't conveyed in his previous performances. When he gets to the last line, the actor glares straight at the camera and cries, "And if you wrong us, shall we not revenge?"

To Be or Not to Be was directed by a German Jewish director and headlined by a Jewish star. Given that background, for the filmmakers to have an identifiably Jewish character recite Shylock's speech about the Jews to Adolf Hitler must be an allusion to the Holocaust. And, in this context, the speech's final reference to "revenge" has to convey the message that the Jews, however helpless they may seem in 1942, will one day have revenge on their Nazi persecutors. As Krohn observes, "In no version of the speech is the word *Jew* ever uttered. It doesn't have to be—Greenberg's name, nose and Shylock obsession identify his cultural heritage. Lubitsch's solution to the taboo on references to the Shoah is not to use the taboo word at all—it is never spoken in *To Be or Not to Be*—while having Greenberg ring all the changes on the most famous denunciation of anti-Semitism ever written."[22]

Indeed, this moment in the film is fascinating. For one, it shows that the largely Jewish cast and crew who made *To Be or Not to Be* clearly had some idea about the ongoing genocide against European Jewry in 1942—the worst year of the Holocaust. This shouldn't surprise us. As is discussed in Deborah Lipstadt's *Beyond Belief: The American Press and the Coming of the Holocaust, 1933–1945* and David Wyman's *The Abandonment of the Jews: America and the Holocaust, 1941–1945*, by 1942 there were news stories in the *New York Times* and other national publications about the Nazis' persecution and mass murder of the Jews—on rare occasions even on the front page.[23] Meanwhile, individual American Jews along with American Jewish organizations had organized rallies, circulated petitions, lobbied members of Congress, and collected money on behalf of imperiled European Jewry. We should consider Yehuda Bauer's valuable distinction in this regard between "information" and "knowledge"; in other words, American Jews might have had "information" about the Holocaust without truly "knowing" its full scope. But clearly the Jews behind *To Be or Not to Be* had at least an inkling of the Holocaust and desired revenge—even if they were only able to express these feelings in this one subtle and fleeting scene in the film. Since the powers-that-be in Hollywood were insistent that anti-Nazi films should *not* stress the Nazi persecution of the Jews, to do precisely that in a Hollywood movie, no matter how allusively, displayed real courage and conviction.

Nonetheless, what is so problematic about the way *To Be or Not to Be* turns Shylock's speech about the Jews into a philo-Semitic call for the Jewish people to revenge themselves against the Nazis is that Shylock is himself an anti-Semitic stereotype. Critics have argued this point, with many bardologists (some Jewish, like Harry Levin) denying the charge, but for me the debate is largely closed. Shylock fits neatly into the ancient anti-Semitic stereotype of the Jew as a devious, greedy moneylender; indeed, over the centuries his name has become synonymous with this type. Moreover, Shakespeare establishes Shylock as the play's villain, demanding a "pound of flesh" from the virtuous (and Christian) Antonio—a demand that recalls those Christian allegations against the Jews known today as "blood libel." As in all Shakespearean comedy, the villain is ultimately thwarted by the saintly Portia, who conveys the play's message about Christian spirituality and forgiveness, as contrasted with Jewish materialism and vengefulness, and who, through some clever legal wrangling at Antonio's trial, not only denies Shylock his gruesome revenge but forces him as well to convert to Christianity. The evil Jew isn't even around for Act V.

On the other hand, whatever his personal feelings may be have been about Jews (and one suspects he largely shared the anti-Semitic views then common in England, which had evicted the Jews several centuries before), Shakespeare was a dramatist who seemed congenitally incapable of ever reducing a character to a pure stereotype. While in most of the rest of the play Shylock comes off as an anti-Semitic caricature, in the speech Greenberg recites Shakespeare morally complicates his villain. Taken out of context, as it is in *To Be or Not to Be*, Shylock's speech is a plea to the Christian world to recognize the shared humanity of the Jews and to acknowledge that Jews suffer just as much when they're persecuted as any human beings would under similar circumstances. In fact, on its own Shylock's speech comports perfectly with contemporary teachings about tolerance. Put in current academic terms, the moneylender's words deny the "otherness" of the "Other." In the film's context, Shylock's speech about the humanity of the Jews comes across as a forceful rebuttal to Hitler's core belief that the Jews were *sub*human, sharing no common bonds with the Aryan race.

It's no surprise that Mel Brooks long wanted to remake *To Be or Not to Be*, which he finally did in 1984, as a film directed by Alan Johnson but produced by Brooks and starring himself in the Jack Benny role, along with a talented cast including Anne Bancroft (Brooks's wife), Charles Durning, Tim Matheson, and José Ferrer. After all, in his very first film in 1968, the controversial but hilarious *The Producers*, Brooks had made a movie in the tradition of both *To Be or Not to Be* and *The Great Dictator* that combats Nazism by lampooning it.

Brooks's remake of *To Be or Not to Be* isn't nearly as good a film as either *The Producers* or Lubitsch's original version. It is mildly entertaining, but by the 1980s, the film's plot no longer packed the punch it had originally in the 1940s, when it appeared at the same time as the Nazis were ravaging Europe and when Hitlerian anti-Semitism was a taboo topic in Hollywood. Moreover, the hyperactive Brooks lacks Benny's deadpan humor, and Bancroft shows little of Lombard's inimitable sex appeal. Brooks's remake is also lacking in originality, since he tends to follow Lubitsch's version scene-by-scene, and often even line-by-line. However, Brooks has added two excellent elements to the original story, both of which foreground the Holocaust in a way absent from the first version. One is that the of Mrs. Tura's dresser, a woman in the 1942 version, is now a flamboyantly gay man, who is forced by the Nazis to wear a pink triangle and who's brutally taken off and beaten by the Gestapo until the Turas are able to secure his release. Thus, the movie highlights the Nazi persecution of homosexuals—a proscribed subject for decades after the Holocaust, virtually invisible in American popular culture until Martin Sherman's play *Bent* appeared on Broadway in 1979. (Given the homophobia evident in many of Brooks's earlier films, including *The Producers*, the sympathetic gay character in *To Be or Not to Be* represents something of a moral advance for the director.) Second, Brooks has added to his remake a group of bedraggled Polish Jewish refugees, all wearing yellow stars, whom Tura grudgingly agrees to hide in the basement of his theater. These additions reflect how public awareness of the Holocaust had been steadily growing in American culture in the decades since the war.

These two Holocaust-oriented subplots come together in an original scene that is the best moment of the remake of *To Be or Not to Be*. Tura and his confederates decide to smuggle the Jewish refugees out of Poland by disguising them as clowns performing for a full house of Nazi officers and then having them exit the stage and the theater in the middle of the show. However, as they are descending into the audience, one Jewish refugee, confronted by row after row of uniformed Nazis, becomes petrified with fear, which risks exposing all the Jews to the Germans. Thinking fast, the gay dresser, also in a clown costume, slaps a yellow star on the paralyzed Jew and pretends to arrest her, drawing a pistol out of which pops a Nazi flag—thus turning a potentially deadly situation into a part of the play. The audience of Nazi officers roars its approval. The scene neatly complements the theme at the heart of the 1942 version of *To Be or Not to Be*: namely, that theatrics and play-acting (even as here of a farcical kind), which display the capacity of the human imagination, can, under certain circumstances, constitute a form of anti-Nazi resistance.

3

HOLLYWOOD FIGHTS WORLD WAR II

Hitler's Madman; Hitler's Children; Tomorrow, the World!

Although Nazism was a taboo subject for Hollywood films when Chaplin began *The Great Dictator* in 1937, the climate changed dramatically in 1941 when the United States entered World War II and Germany became America's enemy. Now, in contrast, the US government and the public in general *encouraged* Hollywood to make anti-Nazi movies, and the film industry (which had always been more anti-Nazi than the country at large, given the large number of Jews and refugees from Hitler within the Hollywood community) responded by churning out a plethora of what were essentially propaganda films backing the war effort by bashing the Nazis and celebrating American values. This chapter looks at three films in this propagandistic genre: *Hitler's Madman* (1943), *Hitler's Children* (1943), and *Tomorrow, the World!* (1944).

Hitler's Madman is loosely based on the 1942 assassination in Czechoslovakia of Reinhard Heydrich, head of the SD (*Sicherheitsdienst*, or Security Service), which operated as an auxiliary of the SS. Heydrich was a ruthless, brilliant leader and the consummate technocrat. Earlier the same year he was killed, he had chaired the Wannsee Conference, a meeting of top Nazi officials at which a comprehensive plan for the Final Solution of the Jewish Question was first laid out. At the time of his death, Heydrich's official title was, ironically enough, "protector" of Nazi-occupied Czechoslovakia. The assassins who tossed hand grenades under Heydrich's speeding car were thought at the time to be Czech resistance fighters, though contemporary historians suspect they may, instead, have been British commandos. In a furious retaliation, Hitler and Himmler razed the entire Czech village of Lidice, killing 860 Czechs in the process, based on the unproven charge that the villagers had sheltered the assassins. The atrocity roused widespread outrage in the Allied countries combating the Nazis, including the United States.

The next year, Hollywood was inspired to make two films based on Heydrich's assassination and the destruction of Lidice. *Hitler's Madman* was the first American movie directed by Douglas Sirk.[1] Although born in Denmark, Sirk worked as a young man in Germany as a director, first in the theater and then in films. Disturbed by the Nazi regime, he immigrated to Hollywood. MGM Studios gave Sirk only one week to make *Hitler's Madman*, which starred John Carradine and Patricia Morison and was cowritten by Jewish American playwright Peretz Hirschbein. Ultimately, MGM head Louis Mayer liked the film and helped spread its distribution. Sirk would go on to make his name in Hollywood as the popular director of lush domestic melodramas such as *Magnificent Obsession* (1954) and *Imitation of Life* (1959), but he retained a lifelong fascination with Hitler's inner circle. In 1983, as an old man, he told an interviewer, "I think in the future there will be many plays—tragedies—about Hitler, Goering and Goebbels. They are definitely great dramatic figures."[2]

At the start of *Hitler's Madman*, a member of the Czech underground (Alan Curtis) fails to convince fearful local villagers to help him engage in acts of sabotage against the German occupation. The scene soon shifts to Heydrich, played by Carradine. The actor, whose best-known role was in *The Grapes of Wrath* but who appeared mostly in horror and noir detective flicks, might seem an odd choice to play Heydrich. Carradine's performance is memorable, if rather over the top. (While living in Germany, Sirk had actually met Heydrich and said later that Carradine shared with Heydrich a kind of "showy, Shakespearian personality" that made the actor right for the role.) Carradine plays Heydrich as a psychopath with glimmers of decadent sophistication who relishes doing evil. In a scene late in the film, in which the wounded Heydrich dies with Himmler at his bedside, the "Hangman of Prague" (as he was known to the Czechs) comes across both as a coward, fearing his own imminent death, and a homicidal maniac, insisting that the only policy the Nazis should follow is to "kill them all." Discussing this scene, Krohn writes, "The émigrés who made *Hitler's Madman* knew about Heydrich's role overseeing the *Einsatzgruppen* and his close relationship with Himmler. The strongest scene in the movie portrays Heydrich's last moments. . . . The makers of *Hitler's Madman* are attempting to portray something like the primal scene of the Final Solution in this sequence: 'Kill them if you want to be safe, every day. All of them.'"[3]

Heydrich also fits the Hollywood Nazi stereotype by being, like Adenoid Hynkel and Professor Siletsky, a vile lecher. In a scene between Heydrich and a group of Czech young women (including a young Ava Gardner in a minor role), it's clearly implied that the Czech nation's "protector" plans to force the most attractive among them to serve as sex slaves for the German military. After Heydrich has spent some time drooling over the terrified beauties, one of them, refusing to be prostituted by the Reich, leaps out a window to her death. The suicide of this girl so traumatizes the village elders that they overcome their timidity and join the Czech resistance.

Heydrich is also depicted as virulently anti-Christian. In one scene, Heydrich and his motorcade run into a Czech Christian folk festival in progress. When a local priest in attendance expresses to the Nazi leader his commitment to the Christian teaching of "turning the other cheek," Heydrich puts the priest's beliefs to the test by savagely striking him. After wiping his boots with a sacred cloth draping one of the icons, Heydrich orders a soldier to shoot the priest. Later, in the film's climactic scene, the village of Lidice is destroyed in punishment for Heydrich's death. The men of the town are shot, while the women are shipped off to concentration camps. Sirk fills the screen with Christian imagery; the male villagers recite Christian prayers as they are lined up before the firing squad while the camera keeps returning to a shot of a statue of an angel, shot at odd angles and juxtaposed with images of the burning town. One would never know from the way *Hitler's Madman* pits Nazism against Christianity in a Manichean struggle between a violent and a pacific creed, that the Church in many Nazi-occupied countries collaborated with the Germans. It wouldn't be until the miniseries *Holocaust* appeared on millions of American television screens in the late 1970s that American pop culture would begin to address that disturbing reality.

There is only one reference to the Jews in all of *Hitler's Madman*. After Heydrich is killed, a group of high-level Nazi officials convenes to decide what to tell the press about who is responsible for the assassination. One official recommends blaming it on the Jews. "That's always good," agrees another. It's not much of an allusion, considering that by 1943 the crematoria were going full blast at Auschwitz, Treblinka, and Sobibor. What *Hitler's Madman* focuses on, in lavishly Gothic detail, is the slaughter of the people of Lidice. (Himmler decides to destroy Lidice in the first place because a neighboring village, more strongly suspected of harboring the assassins, contains a munitions plant.)

At the film's conclusion, the shimmering spirits of the dead men of Lidice appear on-screen—backed by the wavering flames rising from the burning village—and tell the audience directly to preserve the memory of the slaughter at Lidice by fighting Hitler, reciting the words

Figure 3.1. *Hitler's Madman* (1943). A German soldier maintains order in the Czech village of Lidice, whose citizens will soon be massacred as collective punishment for the assassination of Reinhard Heydrich. [Screen grab]

of the poem that inspired the film, Edna St. Vincent Millay's "The Murder of Lidice." Lest any audience member be so dense as to miss the movie's message that the dead of Lidice were martyrs, the film's final image is of a statue of Saint Sebastian pierced by arrows, a glowing halo above his head.

Hitler's Madman has many of the markings of a modern-day Holocaust film, with its images of innocent civilians being shot or dragged off to concentration camps and its concluding message to the audience to "never forget"—except, of course, that the victims of the Nazis here are not Jews but Gentile Czechs. The film's choice of emphasis reflects, to some extent, that Americans in 1943 still were unaware of the full dimensions of the Holocaust. But it also reflects, even more strongly, Hollywood's craven refusal during the war years to acknowledge that Hitler's primary target was European Jewry. Nazi-murdered Christian civilians were a safe topic for Hollywood in 1943; Nazi-murdered Jewish civilians were not, even though the former were an anomaly, while the latter were not. A few critics at the time recognized and denounced this omission. For example, in 1941, Eliot Paul and Luis Quintanilla published a satirical book called *With a Hays Nonny Nonny*, which imagined how Hollywood would treat various Biblical stories. In one section, they surmise that if Hollywood had filmed the Biblical story of Esther, it would have been changed into a tale of the Nazi oppression of the Czechs. Paul and Quintanilla write, "It would be bad for the public to get the idea that the Nazis are persecuting Jews. . . . The solution is not to show [the Jew] at all. He becomes a Czech or some kind of Central European the 40,000 [moviegoers] can view impersonally."[4]

The same year *Hitler's Madman* appeared in American movie theaters, Hollywood produced another anti-Nazi propaganda film: *Hitler's Children*—a lurid melodrama that dwells, in gory detail, on various Nazi abominations. Although it never mentions the Holocaust, *Hitler's Children* exemplifies a trend that will continue to be discernible when US films do decide to foreground the Shoah (such as in the movie I'll consider in the next chapter, *The Diary of Anne Frank*), namely, the "Americanization" of this European story, as US directors strove to make these foreign events seem relevant to an American mass audience. In the case of *Hitler's Children*, the desire to Americanize the plot led the filmmakers to produce what is, from a modern perspective, a bizarre story.

The director of *Hitler's Children* was Edward Dmytryk. In 1947, three years after the film appeared and not long after the end of World War II, Dmytryk also made *Crossfire*, a film about an insanely anti-Semitic American veteran just back from the war who murders a Jew. *Crossfire* was the first American film to deal directly with the subject of anti-Semitism (appearing just a few months before *Gentleman's Agreement*, a better film about American anti-Semitism produced by a rival Hollywood studio, which would go on to win a Best Picture Oscar). Thus, it seems fair to say that if the Nazis' persecution of the Jews is absent from *Hitler's Children*, it wasn't because the director was indifferent to the plight of the Jewish people but, on the contrary, was simply toeing the studio line regarding the censoring of Nazi anti-Semitism.

Hitler's Children is loosely based on a nonfiction book, Gregor Ziemer's *Education for Death: The Making of the Nazi*. The film stresses its origins in this work in the opening credits, as if to emphasize that what will transpire is based in fact rather than fiction—a kind of forerunner to the Hollywood docudrama. The movie opens during the early years of the Nazi regime in an American school located in Berlin that is presided over by a handsome, avuncular American teacher, Professor Nichols (Tim Holt), who is fond of cardigan sweaters and smoking pipes. The school happens to be next door to a Nazi institution that indoctrinates members of the Hitler Youth. In the first scene, we see that a fight has broken out between pupils from the respective institutions of learning. The two schools are a study in contrasts—a point the film emphasizes by crosscutting from one to the other. In the American school, discipline is loose, both teachers and pupils crack jokes, the curriculum is open ended, students have a say in what they will study, time is set aside for games, and classes are coed and often held outside in the fresh air. In the Nazi school, in contrast, the all-male members of the Hitler Youth sit stiffly in chairs arranged in orderly rows in the classroom, speaking only when spoken to by their teacher, who regales his charges with such stirring exhortations as, "Tomorrow, we will rule the world!" Of course, the two schools are presented as microcosms of the two societies—American democracy versus Nazi fascism. In a subplot reminiscent of *Romeo and Juliet*, one Hitler Youth member, Carl (Otto Kruger), falls in love with a girl at the American school, Anna (Bonita Granville, a young actress so all-American she went on to play the lead in a series of Hollywood films based on the *Nancy Drew* mysteries). Charmed by Anna, Carl ends up spending time with both her and Professor Nichols, which exposes him to American influences.

When the Nazis begin to cement their grip on power, a contingent of German soldiers turns up at the American school and demands that its ranks be purged of students belonging to various groups, including Poles, Jews, and Lithuanians. Thus, Jews are listed as just one among several groups targeted by the Nazis, in accord with studio policy at the time. The German soldiers also demand that Professor Nichols turn over any of his students who are of German ancestry, since such students properly belong to the Reich. This group, it so happens, includes Anna, who was born of American parents in Germany. Anna is promptly relocated to a Nazi labor camp, where her German overseers strive to transform her into a docile daughter of the fatherland. Professor Nichols wastes no time in launching a vigorous campaign with the Nazi authorities to have Anna released, which sets him at loggerheads with Carl, who in the meantime has become an SS officer thrilled to see his beloved Anna brought into the Aryan fold. If *Hitler's Madman* implies that the main victims of the Nazis were Czechs (rather than Jews), *Hitler's Children* implies, even more incongruously, that Hitler's primary target, trapped in a Nazi concentration camp, is a fresh-faced American teenager. Only if the Nazis are imperiling an American, presumably, can the interest of American audiences be roused.

By pretending to be an American educator conducting a study on the Nazi educational system, Nichols convinces the German authorities to allow him to visit the labor camp where Anna is being held. In the course of these scenes, the film seizes an opportunity to express (through the perspective of the good professor) American disapproval over a particular Nazi policy: the acceptance of Aryan illegitimacy. One inmate at the labor camp Nichols meets is an unmarried, pregnant German woman who, rather than being banished from respectable society, is being lovingly cared for by the Nazis, since her bastard child will swell the ranks of the *Übermensch*. Whatever their motives, the Nazis' acceptance of illegitimacy among pureblood Germans (which the film describes accurately) hardly seems one of their graver sins. However, just as with the Hollywood type of the Nazi lecher in *Hitler's Madman*, focusing on this particular Nazi policy enables *Hitler's Children* to distance the allegedly depraved Nazis from America, with its wholesome family values, one of which is the stigmatizing of unmarried, pregnant women. In the camp, Nichols also discovers that the Germans are sterilizing women who are considered, for various reasons (including the holding of dissident views against the state), unfit to have children. The scene also has some basis in fact, since the Nazis did activate a plan as part of their "euthanasia" campaign to sterilize those Germans judged too defective to bear offspring.

Like *Hitler's Madman*, *Hitler's Children* presents the Church as fiercely anti-Nazi. Here the depiction seems even less accurate, since the Church in question is that of Germany, which, with a few noble exceptions,[5] directly backed the Nazi regime. When Anna escapes from the labor camp, she stumbles into a church where an elderly German minister is delivering a fiery anti-Nazi sermon to his congregation. His congregants, the minister insists, must choose between the "Gospel of Christ" and the "Gospel of Hitler." When German soldiers enter the church in search of Anna, they notice the minister denouncing the Führer and detain him as well. Landing in Gestapo headquarters doesn't even momentarily deter the old minister from continuing his Nazi-bashing fulminations. Before long, he is lecturing Gestapo agents about how the "inalienable rights" of human beings are bestowed by God, thus fusing religious and democratic values while comparing Hitler to Attila the Hun. Astoundingly, the Gestapo do *not* punish this avowed enemy of the state, instead releasing him, because, one agent explains, they don't want to turn the old man into a "martyr."

Meanwhile, Anna is arrested and condemned to public whipping before the assembled labor camp inmates. Attending the punishment in his capacity as an SS officer, Carl initially just looks on as his beloved is flogged, but then his better self takes over and he rushes in to put a stop to the violence. For this treasonous act, Carl is himself arrested. In prison, he recants his disobedience, and the Nazi high command decides to have his trial broadcast via radio to the entire German nation in a propaganda move designed to prove that even the most recalcitrant of its citizens eventually see the light. Called on to speak in his defense, Carl seems at first to be obediently touting the party line, but then he abruptly changes tack, telling the youth of Germany that they are receiving an "education of death" and, while brandishing his fist in the air, crying, "Long live the enemies of Nazi Germany!" For this dramatic deviation from the approved script, Carl is shot dead on the spot by a

Nazi guard, as is Anna, who had leapt to her feet in the courtroom to applaud Carl's words. Carl's climactic address somewhat recalls Chaplin's longer speech at the end of *The Great Dictator*, although in *Hitler's Children*, the anti-Nazi oration is woven more organically into the narrative.

In the character of Carl, we see a basically decent young man who has the misfortune of being brainwashed by the Hitler Youth but who, because he is fortuitously exposed to the influence of some good-hearted Americans (not to mention swept up by the power of romantic love), eventually comes to his senses and denounces his Nazi overlords, even though it costs him his life. In this rewriting of history, it's not that the Germans elected, worshipped, and died for Hitler but, instead, that the German people were just *another* group of innocent victims of the Führer's machinations.

Here, at the height of World War II, Hollywood not only was reluctant to cast aspersions on the German people but actually sympathized with them. Did the film industry suspect as early as 1943 that America was destined to win the war, whereupon Germany would become an ally of the United States in its new war with former US ally the Soviet Union? Perhaps. But a more likely explanation is that Hollywood was still smarting from the prewar attacks of American isolationists who accused the film industry of being run by perfidious Jews, which made the Jews in question reluctant to make movies attacking Christians, even if these Christians belonged to a nation with which America was officially at war. Moreover, Hollywood's prewar reluctance to make movies offending Germany may have been so entrenched that it continued even *after* America entered the war. Old habits die hard. Instead, it seems the approach was to draw a sharp distinction between the Nazis, who were evil, and the German people, who were good.

There are many anti-Nazi Hollywood movies, made both before and after America's entry into the war, which, like *Hitler's Children*, exonerate the German people from any responsibility for the evils of the Third Reich and instead place blame exclusively on the Nazi leadership. *I Was a Captive of Nazi Germany* (1936) is based on the true story of Isobel Lillian Steele, a twenty-three-year-old American music student who was arrested and imprisoned in Berlin on suspicion of espionage. In defending the film against its many critics, both German and American, producer Alfred T. Mannon insisted that his film had striven to portray the German citizenry as "wholesome people."[6] Likewise, as its title implies, Sam Newfield's film *Hitler—Beast of Berlin* (1936) portrays Hitler as a homicidal maniac who has devilishly hoodwinked the decent German people into obedience. Finally, Warner Brothers' *Underground* (1940), a thriller set in Berlin, tells the story of Germans actively resisting the Nazis, even though in reality there was little organized German resistance to the Third Reich.[7]

A war-era anti-Nazi film that exonerates the German nation even more dramatically than *Hitler's Children* is *Tomorrow, the World!* (1944)—the only movie in this trio to feature a prominent Jewish character and to deal at any length (albeit unsatisfactorily) with Nazi anti-Semitism. *Tomorrow, the World!* looks at Nazi Germany exclusively through the lens of the Hitler Youth. Based on a Broadway play by James Gow and Armand D'Usseau, the film was adapted for the screen by Leopold Atlas and Ring Lardner Jr. It stars fourteen-year-old Skippy Homeier, in his first film appearance, reprising the lead role he had in the play. Homeier plays a young German teenager, Emil, a member of the Hitler Youth who is adopted by his American uncle, Michael Frame (Fredric March), and brought to the United States. Adopting a stagy German accent, Homeier plays Emil as a kind of demon child, who almost immediately plunges into a range of sinister activities that wreak havoc on the Frames' idyllic middle-American household. Much praised for his performance, Homeier would go on to play mostly juvenile delinquents.

It seems highly implausible that Emil could so easily immigrate to America at a time when the United States and Germany were at war, but *Tomorrow, the World!* is not a study in realism. Fresh from the Hitler Youth, Emil has a strict, formal, militaristic bearing; he greets everyone by clicking his heels and snapping to attention. Despite his Nazi training, Emil is a remarkably inept saboteur. Rather than hiding his Nazi leanings in order to carry out his clandestine operations more successfully, Emil appears for lunch dressed in his Hitler Youth uniform on the day he arrives. On the same day, at their very first meeting, he tries to enlist the help of the Frames' German-born maid in stealing papers from Mr. Frame's office relating to work he is doing for the military high command in Washington. Not surprisingly, the maid refuses immediately, expressing her allegiance to her host country. Because Emil is such a hapless spy, it's hard to see him as dangerous, which drains the film of drama and suspense.

Emil also doesn't hide his harsh criticisms of America from the Frame family or anyone else. A sexist as well as a Nazi, he is aghast that a woman is working in the Customs Office when he enters the United States, and he cites the fact that men do laundry in America as proof of "degeneracy." When Emil meets some classmates who are Boy Scouts, he is amazed that the Scouts, unlike the Hitler Youth, only engage in "childish" activities, such as going on campouts and roasting hotdogs, with no time spent on worthwhile endeavors like military training and racist ideological indoctrination. Giving a report to his class at school, Emil exclaims, "America is a cesspool. The only pureblood of America is the Sioux Indian."

Emil also holds his own father, who had opposed the Nazis, in contempt. When asked about him, Emil touts the Nazi line that his father, Frame's brother, had been an enemy of the Third Reich who'd contributed to Germany's defeat in World War I and who had cravenly committed suicide. Frame counters that his brother was a noble dissident scholar whose books the Nazis had burned (because, Frame explains, "the Nazis are afraid of ideas"). Rather than taking his own life, Frame insists his brother had been killed by Hitler's henchmen. Unconvinced, Emil ends up slashing a portrait of his father hanging in the Frame living room.

But the worst violence Emil wreaks is on his young American cousin, Pat (Joan Carroll), a cheerful, effusive girl who never stops loving and trying to help Emil no matter his misdeeds nor how stubbornly he rebuffs her affection. On discovering that Emil has stolen Mr. Frame's keys so that he can break into a locked desk drawer in his office and steal top-secret military papers, Pat refuses to promise Emil that she won't tell her father about the theft. In response, as they descend to the basement, where Pat has planned a birthday party for her cousin, Emil smashes her over the head with a poker, knocking her unconscious. When Mr. Frame learns of the attack, he calls the police and, giving up on his nephew, plans to send him away to a reformatory. But when Emil discovers that Pat had spent all her savings on purchasing the birthday gift he'd requested, a new watch, the boy breaks down and cries—his first sign of repentance. Next, through tears, Emil says a kind word about his father. Then he reveals that as a small child he'd been locked in a dark cellar by the Nazis. Clearly, the boy is on the road to recovery, and he has been reformed by Pat's enactment of the Christian teaching to love one's enemy.

Along with hating America and women, Emil also detests Poles (flinging some slurs at a classmate of Polish descent) as well as Christians ("Sunday school," he sneers, "is only for girls"). In this respect, *Tomorrow, the World!* conforms to the tendency we've already seen in *To Be or Not to Be*, *Hitler's Madman*, and *Hitler's Children* of insisting that the Nazis had equal contempt for a wide range of groups, rather than stressing Hitler's special animus toward the Jews. However, to its credit, *Tomorrow, the World!* does go further than these other films in addressing Nazi anti-Semitism through the character of Michael Frame's fiancée, Leona Richards (Betty Field), who is openly Jewish. We first learn of Richards's Jewishness on the day Emil arrives, when he tells her and Frame that on the plane he "was supposed to sit next to a big, fat Jew," a slur that inspires Frame to spring the news.

If the script didn't specifically note Richards's Jewishness, there is no way the audience would have known, since she is given absolutely no identifying Jewish traits. To some extent, Richards's dejudaization simply exemplifies the "melting pot" ideal that prevailed in America in this era, long before the rise of multiculturalism and identity politics. According to this philosophy, immigrant groups were supposed to gain admission to the American mainstream by divesting themselves of any particularizing ethnic or religious traits and blending smoothly into a homogenized common culture. Indeed, Richards, who has the misfortune to end up as Emil's teacher, attempts to explain to the German boy the American "melting pot" concept—unsurprisingly, to no avail, since the tenet is antithetical to Nazi ideology.

As one might expect, given how assimilated Richards is, the film presents as utterly unproblematic the fact that Leona is marrying a non-Jew. Today, however, the high rate of intermarriage is one of the most pressing issues roiling the American Jewish community. Since Judaism doesn't proselytize, every Jew who intermarries may well be another Jew lost to the Jewish community. Early in the twentieth century, the Jewish intermarriage rate was very low. But between 1940 and 1960, the rate doubled to 6 percent—not a high number, perhaps, but a harbinger of things to come. Subsequently, the intermarriage rate would continue to rise every decade, until the rate among third- or fourth-generation American Jews had soared to 52 percent by 1990. Moreover, in mixed marriages it's unlikely that children will be raised Jewish, particularly if the Jewish partner is male.[8] That same 1990 survey that found such a high intermarriage rate among American Jewry also discovered that only 28 percent of intermarried couples were raising their children as Jews, and only 13 percent were affiliated with any branch of Judaism.[9] This reality has inspired among American Jewry, in the words of J. J. Goldberg, "a nationwide panic over impending Jewish disappearance."[10]

Given the extent of anti-Semitism in America before and during World War II, pressures to assimilate may have been particularly intense for American Jews. (According to opinion polls, while in 1938 one-third of Americans believed that Jews had "too much power in the United States," during the war years, that number rose to 56 percent.)[11]

Thus, it's no surprise that Hollywood, a business run by nervously assimilated Jews, was sure to present its Jewish American characters as respectably dejudaized—that is, as "real Americans." (We'll see this kind of characterization in the film I'll be discussing next, *The Diary of Anne Frank.*) Even when Hollywood dared to touch the explosive subject of anti-Semitism—in a film such as *Gentlemen's Agreement*, in which Gregory Peck plays a reporter who pretends to be Jewish and discovers rampant anti-Semitism—none of the Jewish characters, such as an old army buddy of Peck's, possess any discernible Jewish traits. In order to persuade everyone that he's a Jew, all Gregory Peck has to do is to go on being Gregory Peck.

In *Tomorrow, the World!* when Emil discovers in horror that he's about to be related by marriage to a Jew, he wastes no time in launching a secret campaign to break up the engagement. To this end, he tells his Aunt Jesse (Agnes Moorehead), who lives with the family, that after the marriage she will be forced out of the home by this insidious Jewess. At school, Emil writes in chalk on the sidewalk that Richards is a "Jewish tramp." In response, Richards slaps Emil in the face and tells Michael they must call off the wedding because she can't bear the thought of living under the same roof as his Nazi nephew. Although Richards's brief moment of mild violence seems entirely justified, she immediately regrets losing her temper. In fact, what's most notable about her general response to Emil is that she not only seldom has a harsh word for this fanatical Hitler Youth member but even ends up taking Emil's side when Frame is inclined to think the worst about his nephew. When Emil spouts sexist and anti-Semitic bile, Richards reminds Frame, "He heard those things in his country." When Emil turns up for lunch clad in his Hitler Youth garb, Richards excuses him on the grounds that he'd no other clothes to wear. When Frame, furious that Emil has almost killed his daughter, begins to strangle his nephew, Richards comes to Emil's rescue. And when Frame is intent on incarcerating Emil in a reformatory, Richards rebukes his decision, even though getting rid of Emil would enable her to live in marital harmony with Frame. "If you can't turn one little child into a human being," she snaps at her fiancé, "Heaven help the world when the war is won and we have to deal with twelve million of them."

In short, Leona Richards is a saint. It might seem that to portray a Jewish character so sympathetically is philo-Semitic, perhaps even suggesting that American anti-Semitism during the war was less rampant than many have maintained. One might argue that Richards's kindness toward Emil is motivated by maternal sympathy and also that she is assuming her assigned role as a teacher by nurturing her student. But I am more persuaded by Ilan Avisar's argument that the movie makes Jews sympathetic by Christianizing them, since Richards's behavior follows "a turn the other cheek philosophy."[12] Of course, to Christianize Jewish characters is offensive, since Christians have been trying for centuries to convert Jews, often at the point of a sword. Moreover, the insistence that any Jew subjected to Nazi persecution must "turn the other cheek" automatically invalidates the desire for revenge and justice experienced by many Jewish victims of the Nazis, as well as rejects on moral grounds armed Jewish resistance against the Germans, as exhibited, for example, in the Warsaw ghetto.

With its focus exclusively on German children, *Tomorrow, the World!* may be seen as infantilizing the entire German people. We extend more latitude when judging children and are more inclined to see the miscreants among them as individuals who are still unformed enough to be capable of reformation—victims of forces outside their control. The film suggests that all Germans are, like Emil, helpless children who've been led down the wrong path but can be brought back to virtue by a "parental" America. As Michael Frame says to Emil, "You're a test case, and I'm an optimist about the German people. People can be changed." Once again, the villains are not the Germans but the Nazis, a handful of evil men who have managed to brainwash a credulous but basically decent nation.

Not content with defining America as everything Emil and the Nazis are not, screenwriters Atlas and Lardner have given Fredric March several didactic lines that explicitly point out the differences between a democratic and a fascist state. "You've been drugged, but we've got the antidote," Frame tells his nephew. "In the US, we don't torture little boys; we reason with them." "That's the difference between us and the Nazis," Frame remarks at the film's climax, after Emil's reformation has begun. "We want people to ask questions. It doesn't make us soft."

Granted, allowances need to be made for films produced during wartime, when the fact that the very survival of the nation is at stake naturally induces massive patriotic solidarity. Still, it's disturbing that *Hitler's Children* and *Tomorrow, the World!* so relentlessly attack Nazi propagandizing when the movies are themselves, of course, propaganda. The irony is that, even though the United States is depicted as a prejudice-free Eden, the filmmakers found it necessary to dejudaize Leona Richards in order to pander to American anti-Semitism. Moreover, by focusing on an American family on the home front rather than American soldiers fighting overseas, *Tomorrow, the World!* sends the comforting message that Americans at home can also do their part by showing Germans the error of their ideological ways. As such, the movie fulfills its function as wartime propaganda but does little to inform Americans about the Nazi persecution of the Jews.

4

HOLLYWOOD DISCOVERS
THE HOLOCAUST

The Diary of Anne Frank

The immediate postwar era produced a handful of Hollywood films that touched on the Holocaust, through rarely at any length. The year 1946 saw the appearance of *The Stranger*, directed by and starring Orson Welles, in which Welles plays an escaped Nazi hiding out, postwar, in a pastoral New England village and hunted down by a determined police detective played by Edward G. Robinson.[1] In one scene, Robinson shows Welles's fiancée, played by Loretta Young, film footage of what Krohn describes as "the first images of the death camps in a Hollywood film."[2] But Krohn continues, "Why does Robinson never mention the Jews while he narrates the projection, identifying Franz Kindler, the Nazi played by Welles, as the architect of the camps? He says that Kindler's plan was to exterminate the entire population of conquered nations—a sweeping statement that obscures the identity of the race that the camps were built to destroy."[3]

Two years later, in 1948, Fred Zinnemann (who would go on to direct such Hollywood classics as *High Noon* and *From Here to Eternity*) produced *The Search*, about children orphaned by World War II and housed in Displaced Persons' (DP) Camps in war-ravaged Europe. In Lawrence Baron's words, *The Search* "was the first mainstream American film shot on location in the shambles of heavily bombed German cities and devoted to the shattered lives of DPs."[4] The plot

focuses on an amiable American soldier (Montgomery Clift) who befriends a young Czech named Karel (Ivan Jandl), an escapee from a DP
camp whose mother, Hannah (Aline MacMahon), has been searching
for him all over Europe.

Having lost his own parents in the Holocaust, Zinnemann was drawn
to making movies about the Nazi-orchestrated genocide. (In 1977,
Zinnemann would make another anti-Nazi film, *Julia*.) With the exception of the leading roles, Zinnemann casts actual DP children as themselves, which gives the film a documentary-like authenticity. Although
Karel and Hannah are not Jewish, the Jewish dimension of the DP crisis
isn't ignored. One of the children is a Jew who has escaped the Nazis by
pretending to be Catholic. And many of the other children are young
Jewish Zionists preparing to depart for Palestine. Unfortunately, the
ultimate reunion between Karel and Hannah is maudlin and sentimental, which mars the film as a whole. As *Variety* aptly remarked, "By
putting a saccharine finale on a single case, there's an undue submer-
gence of the fact that other millions of these pitiable youngsters are still
in camps and have still failed to find their mothers and security."[5] But
in an interview, Zinnemann defended his formulaic happy ending: "All
of us realized, of course, that it would be necessary to soften the truth to
a certain extent, because to show things as they really were would have
meant—at least in our sincere opinion—that the American audience
would have lost any desire to face it, used as they have been to seeing a
sentimentalized world."[6]

Another postwar Holocaust-oriented film is 1953's *The Juggler*, starring Kirk Douglas and Milly Vitale and directed by Edward Dmytryk
(who, back in 1947, had made *Crossfire*, about a rabidly anti-Semitic
American soldier who murders a Jew). Douglas plays a Jewish refugee,
Hans Müller, who immigrates to Israel in an attempt to overcome the
bitterness left by his experiences in a concentration camp. The movie
was filmed in Israel. Like the Holocaust survivors in *The Pawnbroker*
and *Sophie's Choice* (films discussed later in this book), Müller is
plagued by "survivor's guilt." His erratic behavior sets a police detective
named Karni (Paul Stewart) on his trail. Later, he meets a teenaged,
orphaned Sabra, Yehoushau "Josh" Bresler (Joey Walsh), whom he
teaches to juggle, drawing on the skills he had perfected as a professional juggler in Germany. Unfortunately, Josh wanders into an abandoned

minefield, breaking his leg. He recovers from his injury at a nearby kibbutz, where Müller meets a kibbutznik named Ya' El (Vitale).

Eventually, Karni succeeds in tracking Müller down, which leads the refugee to barricade himself in Ya' El's room with a rifle. But Ya' El and Karni convince Müller to give himself up and seek help. The movie ends with the implication that now Müller is on the road to recovery. The film's producer was Stanley Kramer, who would go on to direct *Judgment at Nuremberg* (1961). Lawrence Baron applauds the movie for being "fixated on the mental instability of survivors forever scarred by their experiences of deprivation, dehumanization, and loss."[7] But in general, the critics dismissed *The Juggler* as sappy and contrived.

The postwar Hollywood Holocaust film that by far exerted the greatest influence on audiences and critics was *The Diary of Anne Frank* (1959). The movie version of Anne Frank's story was closely based on the play that had appeared on Broadway only three years before (the movie retained the play's plot structure, all its scenes, and most of its dialogue), and its screenwriters, the husband-and-wife team of Frances Goodrich and Albert Hackett, had penned the original play. Hollywood and Broadway veterans, by the time they took on the *Diary* assignment, Goodrich and Hackett had authored scores of plays and thirty-one films, including such screen classics as *The Thin Man* (1934), *It's a Wonderful Life* (1946), and *Easter Parade* (1948). Because of the close connection between film and play, and because the theatrical version of *The Diary of Anne Frank*, which won the Pulitzer Prize, was the most critically acclaimed and financially successful dramatization of the Holocaust ever to appear on Broadway, it seems worthwhile to introduce the movie by discussing the play in some detail.

Goodrich and Hackett's version will forever be linked with the strange story of the Jewish American writer Meyer Levin. Levin played an important role in getting the diary itself translated into English. He brought it to the attention of the American public through his glowing review on the front page of the *New York Times Book Review* and then got permission from Anne's father, Otto Frank (the only member of the group in the secret annex to survive the Holocaust), to write a theatrical adaptation of the diary. However, when Levin's version was rejected by the play's producers—because, Levin alleged, it was considered "too Jewish"—he grew so enraged that he ended up suing not only the producers but Otto Frank as well and nursed a lifelong grudge. Levin was convinced that his (more faithful) adaptation of Anne Frank's diary had been denied its rightful place on the American stage. Levin's own story is fascinating in itself—at times tragic, and at other times inadvertently comic—because of the extreme behavior of its protagonist and provides a unique perspective from which to tackle the central question of whether the play is guilty of dejudaizing and romanticizing Anne Frank's narrative in a way that fundamentally distorts both the diary and the nature of the Holocaust.

After Anne Frank's diary had been published, first in its original Dutch and then in French and German translations, Otto Frank tried without success to see that an English version appeared in Britain and the United States. In America, nine major publishers rejected the book. When Levin attempted to help Frank get the book published, he encountered resistance from publishers certain that the American public had no interest in dredging up the horrors of World War II by reading the story of a Dutch Jewish girl who came to a horrific end. As Levin wrote Frank, "I sent the diary to a half dozen editors whom I knew. The reactions were uniform: they were personally touched, but professionally they were convinced that the public shied away from such material."[8] The diary was finally accepted by Doubleday, due less to Levin's influence than to the endorsement of several young editors at the publishing house, who were enthusiastic enough to take a chance on a book of dubious profitability.

Levin's charges that his theatrical version was rejected because it was "too Jewish" were probably valid, because it appears that most of those involved with *The Diary of Anne Frank* were concerned with downplaying both Anne's Jewishness and Nazi anti-Semitism. This group included Otto Frank, as became clear when the play's coproducer, Cheryl Crawford, contacted the popular Southern novelist and playwright Carson McCullers about the possibility of writing the adaptation.[9] Levin was appalled that Crawford was not only considering a playwright other than himself for the job but that he'd chosen a non-Jew. In protest, Levin wrote to Otto Frank (then residing in Switzerland), insisting that "no stranger can as well express the soul of a people as someone from that people."[10] In reply, Frank disagreed, claiming that his daughter's diary "is not a Jewish book . . . though Jewish sphere, sentiment, and surrounding is the background. . . . It is (at least here) read and understood more by Gentiles than in Jewish circles. . . . So do not make a Jewish play out of it!"[11]

While it may seem incredible that a Holocaust survivor would fail to understand the centrality of his daughter's Jewishness to any understanding of her story, Otto Frank's attitude reflected his highly assimilated German Jewish background, which had inculcated habits of mind that somehow remained unshaken by his experiences in Auschwitz. Frank was so assimilated that he had once proposed giving Anne a Bible as a Chanukah gift so that his daughter could learn something about the New Testament, only backing off in response to the consternation of his other daughter, Margot, who harbored Zionist leanings.[12]

A universalization of his daughter's experiences was precisely the message conveyed when Frank announced the establishment of the Anne Frank Foundation, intending to preserve her legacy. In a pamphlet issued by the organization in March 1960, the Holocaust was re-

Figure 4.1. *The Diary of Anne Frank* (1959). Anne (Millie Perkins) sits with her beloved father, Otto (Joseph Schildkraut), in their secret annex in Amsterdam. [Screen grab]

ferred to simply as "a period of immorality and injustice," without any reference to Jews, while the Nazis appeared purely as "enemies of humanity."[13] As for Anne's diary itself, her father called it "a demonstration . . . that in the end the powers of evil are not equal to good will and mutual understanding."[14] Clearly, by downplaying Anne's Jewishness and Nazi anti-Semitism while also drawing an affirmative message from her story, Goodrich and Hackett were conscientiously obeying the wishes of Anne's own father.

In his controversial book *The Holocaust in American Life*, Peter Novick attempts to rebut the view that the Broadway play dejudaized the diary by arguing that the diary was dejudaized to start with. Novick sees Anne as her father's daughter—a fully assimilated Jew with few ties to Jewish cultural or religious traditions. He agrees with Jewish scholar Robert Alter that "it is impossible to 'universalize' a document that is already universal."[15] If anything, Novick insists that the Goodrich and Hackett play makes Anne come off as *more* Jewish than she seems in her diary. He cites theater reviewers for two Zionist magazines, *Jewish Frontier* and *Midstream*, who both pointed out that while in her diary Anne had referred to Chanukah just once in passing, adding that "St. Nicholas Day was much more fun," the play devotes an entire extended scene to a Chanukah celebration in the annex, while omitting any reference to Christmas.[16] For Novick, the real scandal is not that Goodrich and Hackett dejudaized Anne's diary but rather that Jewish critics, to satisfy their own agendas, had turned Anne into what she never actually was: a strongly self-identified Jew. "The diary," he concludes, "was not twisted into an optimistic and universalist document by the Hacketts. . . . It *was* such a document, and it was that fact which commended it to Americans in the 1950s, including most of the organized Jewish community."[17]

Novick's argument provides a useful corrective to any simplistic outcry over the play's alleged "universalization" of Anne Frank. However, Novick's contention that Anne was uninterested in Judaism isn't sustained by a close reading of the diary. On the contrary, the evidence of her book suggests that Anne's sense of her own Jewishness and awareness of the historical suffering of the Jewish people was strengthened over time by the perils she was facing.

Consider this diary passage, inspired by Anne's alarm over an attempted break-in at the warehouse located just below the secret annex:

Who has inflicted this upon us? Who has made us Jews so different from all other people? Who has allowed us to suffer so terribly up till now? It is God that has made us as we are, but it will be God, too, who will raise us up again. If we bear all this suffering and if there are still Jews left, when it is over, then Jews, instead of being doomed, will be held up as an example. Who knows, it might even be our religion from which the world and all peoples learn good, and for that reason and that reason only do we have to suffer now. We can never become just Netherlanders . . . or representatives of any country for that matter, we will always remain Jews, but we want to, too. Be brave! Let us remain aware of our task and not grumble, a solution will come, God has never deserted our people. Right through the ages there have been Jews, through all the ages they have had to suffer, but it has made them strong too.[18]

In this remarkable passage, Anne is indeed expressing an affirmative message, but it is based on a traditionally Jewish conception of the Jews as a "chosen people" whom God will never desert and who ultimately will serve as a moral example to the world, a "light unto the nations."

Novick's related claim that there was no deliberate attempt by the creators of the play to leach the Jewish content out of Anne's story is also belied by analysis of how the drama was actually composed. The figure who seems to have had the greatest influence in dejudaizing the play was the director Garson Kanin. For instance, in Goodrich and Hackett's original version, during an argument between Anne and her would-be boyfriend in the annex, Peter van Daan, Anne snaps, "We're not the only Jews that have had to suffer. Right down through the ages there have been Jews and they've had to suffer."[19] In a letter to the playwrights dated November 8, 1954, Kanin derided the scene as "an embarrassing piece of special pleading."[20] Throughout history, he continued,

people have suffered because of being English, French, German, Italian, Ethiopian, Mohammedan, Negro, and so on. . . . The fact that in this play the symbols of persecution and oppression are Jews is incidental. . . . It is Peter here who should be . . . outraged at being persecuted because he is a Jew, and Anne, wiser, pointing out that throughout the ages, people in minorities have been oppressed. In other words, at this moment, the play has an opportunity to spread its theme into the infinite.[21]

In their revision, Goodrich and Hackett faithfully followed Kanin's instructions "to spread [the play's] theme into the infinite." Now Anne replies to Peter: "We're not the only people that have had to suffer. There've always been people that have had to . . . sometimes one race . . . sometimes another."[22]

Almost everyone involved in making the movie version of the *Diary* was just as eager to dejudaize Anne's story as had been those who had produced the play. The president of 20th Century-Fox, Spyros Skouras, was quoted by a San Francisco newspaper as saying that he didn't want to hold a benefit to raise money for the movie hosted by any particular (read "Jewish") organization, because "this isn't a Jewish picture, this is a picture for the world."[23] Hackett verified the newspaper story when he wrote to Otto Frank that "they [the management] are very anxious to make this picture have a universal appeal. And I think that is the right approach, don't you?" The studio needn't have worried. Even Jewish American spokespersons heartily approved of the universalizing of Anne's story. For example, John Stone, head of the Jewish Film Advisory Committee (whose job was to ensure that Jews were portrayed positively in the media), after reviewing a copy of the script, wrote enthusiastically to the director, George Stevens: "This screenplay is even better than the stage play. You have given the story a more 'universal' meaning and appeal. It could very easily have been an outdated Jewish tragedy by less creative or more emotional handling—even a Jewish 'Wailing Wall,' and hence regarded as mere propaganda."[24]

One way the film's producers went even further than those who had created the play in dejudaizing the diary was through their casting decisions. For example, Stevens dropped the actress who'd played Anne on Broadway, the Jewish Susan Strasberg, even though her performance had elicited rave reviews. After a much-publicized, worldwide talent search, Stevens cast in Strasberg's place a Gentile former model, Millie Perkins.[25] Not only was Perkins much too old to play the thirteen-year-old Anne, but, according to Annette Insdorf, "when she dresses up, the thin, dark-haired actress bears a striking resemblance to Audrey Hepburn, one of the most popular female stars of the fifties."[26] Indeed, as Lawrence Baron reports, "some critics felt that her performance was the film's major flaw. Bosley Crowther of the *New York Times* considered her appearance too mature and acting too amateurish to be convincing."[27] In casting the role of Peter, the teenage boy with whom

Anne enjoys a fleeting, virginal romance in the secret annex, Stevens chose another non-Jewish actor, Richard Beymer, a teen idol who later played the all-American role of Tony in the film version of *West Side Story*.

The play's producers had been committed not only to universalizing Anne's story but also to making it entertaining. Coproducer Kermit Bloomgarden declared that "the only way this play will go is if it's funny."[28] Indeed, in both the play and film there are many comic touches. In one example, the Frank girls have been told by their parents to wear, in layers, all the clothing they intend to bring so that the Nazis won't discover them carrying suitcases through the streets of Amsterdam. When Anne arrives at the annex, she immediately, in front of everyone, begins peeling off her dress. Her shocked mother exclaims, "Anne, please!" "It's all right," Anne replies, "I've got on three more."[29] *The Diary of Anne Frank* also includes moments of pure slapstick. For instance, during the Chanukah celebration, Anne surprises the group with homemade gifts for all in attendance. To the huffy, self-absorbed dentist, Mr. Dussel (with whom Anne is forced to share a bedroom), she gives a pair of earplugs "to put in your ears so you won't hear me when I thrash around at night."[30] After stuffing them in his ears, Dussel cries, "Good God! They've gone inside!"—whereupon he starts thumping his head in a frantic attempt to extricate the plugs.[31] While black comedy can certainly be an insightful means by which to explore the existential absurdity that shadows the Holocaust, in *The Diary of Anne Frank*, Goodrich and Hackett seem, instead, to be inserting fluffy light comedy as a way to divert the audience in order to render palatable what 1950s audiences might otherwise find an insufferably gloomy story. In this respect, the comedy serves the same basic function as the play and film's overall affirmative message—to distance audiences from the full horror of the Holocaust. On the other hand, the film's comedy does have the virtue of pointing out that humor exists even in the most horrific circumstances, that it's an inherent part of human existence. There are, as well, a fair number of references in the movie to the ways the Nazis have singled out the Jews for mistreatment. Baron points out:

> The opening of the film makes it unmistakably clear that the Germans have targeted the Jews for persecution. Otto returns to Amsterdam and climbs down from the lorry filled with passengers in striped concentration camp outfits. As he reads the diary Miep gives him, his

voice segues into Anne's. She explains that since her family was Jewish, they immigrated to Holland when Hitler came to power. After
the German occupation of the Netherlands, she recalls, 'things got
very bad for the Jews.' She lists activities the Nazis had prohibited
Jews from doing.[32]

Moreover, the identifying yellow star that the Nazis forced the Jews to
wear is referred to repeatedly. Shortly after arriving at the annex, Peter
angrily rips the star from his jacket and tosses it in the stove. After some
hesitation, Anne does likewise, but she notices that, because the cloth of
her coat beneath the star is less faded than the rest, an outline of the
star still remains, which leads her to exclaim, "It's still there!" One could
read this moment as a symbol of how Anne's Jewishness is something
she can never shed, precisely the point Anne herself made in her diary.
But if this was Goodrich and Hackett's intention, one wonders how
many viewers discerned this extremely subtle symbolism.

     There are also allusions to the Germans' roundup of Jews. Citing
Baron again, "Anne learns from Dussel that her best girlfriend has been
sent to a camp. . . . That night Anne has a nightmare and envisions
women inmates swaying listlessly while standing at attention. Anne recognizes her girlfriend among them. Gunshots awaken Anne, who cries
out, 'Save me! Save me! Don't take me!'"[33] The most extended reference to the fate of Dutch Jewry comes in a voice-over from the diary:
"Right here in Amsterdam every day hundreds of Jews disappear. . . .
They surround a block and search house by house. . . . Hundreds are
being deported. . . . They get their call-up notice . . . come to the Jewish
theatre on such and such a day and hour. . . . If you refuse the call-up
notice, then they come and drag you from your home and ship you off
to Mauthausen. The death camp!"[34] In the film, Anne's voice-over is
juxtaposed with a shot of a group of Jews being hustled off by German
soldiers to trucks bound for the concentration camps. The shot is initially filmed from above, to create the impression that Anne is viewing this
scene from her attic window. The principle inaccuracy in Anne's words
is the implication that only Jews who *refused* to come to the roundups
were shipped to Mauthausen and other camps, while, in truth, *all* Jews
caught in the Germans' net, whether they complied with orders or not,
were destined for the same fate.

     Readers will have to decide for themselves whether the references
cited above are sufficient to provide a clear awareness that the principle

targets of the Final Solution were Jews. In wrestling with this question, one must never ignore historical context. In the era in which the play and film opened, the word "Holocaust" had yet to be coined as a referent to the Nazi genocide against the Jews, so there was no word in common usage that defined the Final Solution. However, while, to its credit, *The Diary of Anne Frank* tells us that the Nazis hated the Jews, it doesn't tell us why or how this hatred compares to the contempt and persecution the Germans leveled against other groups. Most importantly, one would never know from the *Diary* that the aim of the Final Solution was the total annihilation of European Jewry.

As Stephen Whitfield writes in *In Search of American Jewish Culture*, "In . . . the 1950s, a vigorous and various pluralism was still subdued for the sake of a consensus that emphasized social stability."[35] With the memory of the Holocaust still fresh, American Jews weren't eager to risk antagonizing the nation that had defeated the Nazis and had made them feel relatively welcome. As well, the belief that Jews used their prominence in Broadway and Hollywood to brainwash the American public with a Semitic agenda was still widely held.[36] Finally, should a philo-Semitic *Diary* lead to a rise in anti-Semitism, McCarthy's House Un-American Activities Committee might be, it was feared, inspired to associate Jews with Communism, as Hitler had done.

As a result of this social climate, according to critic Henry Popkin in *Commentary Magazine* in 1952, the perhaps unconscious attitude of Jewish artists was "if we pretend that the Jew does not exist . . . then he will not be noticed; the anti-Semite, unable to find his victim, will simply forget about him."[37] Thus, it's entirely possible that Otto Frank, Garson Kanin, Goodrich and Hackett, George Stevens et al., were all correct: had *The Diary of Anne Frank* foregrounded Anne's Jewishness and the Nazis' anti-Semitism, it might have been rejected by the American public. Still, there was something self-defeating about this counterstrategy, since the less directly Jewish victimization is depicted by popular culture, the less likely Americans are to feel sympathetic to the survivors and their offspring.

Through one character, Mrs. Van Daan, *The Diary of Anne Frank* flirts with an anti-Semitic stereotype. The woman is depicted as shallow and lascivious. At one point, she actually kisses the straight-laced Otto Frank on the lips, in the presence of both her husband and his wife. The woman's most prized possession is her fur coat. When Mr. Van

Daan insists on handing over the coat to one of their Dutch protectors, Miep, to sell, she bemoans the loss as if her husband had stolen her child. In the play and film's defense, Goodrich and Hackett have based their portrayal on the way the actual Mrs. Van Daan is depicted in Anne's diary. She is also juxtaposed with other Jewish characters who are quite different, especially the almost saintly Otto Frank. (In the movie, Mrs. Van Daan is brilliantly played by the Jewish Shelley Winters—a performance that earned her an Oscar for Best Supporting Actress.)

Toward the end of both play and film, the gluttonous Mr. Van Daan is caught stealing food at night, which inspires such a rift among the group that Mrs. Frank demands that the Van Daans find another hiding place. The food-stealing scene is memorable and insightful. Mr. Van Daan doesn't come across as a villain; he's just gnawed by hunger. One imagines that many of us in the same situation would act the same way. And yet, by the same token, his theft is indefensible, especially since, as Mrs. Frank angrily points out, the group has children to feed. When, a moment later, Peter bursts in to announce that he's heard on his radio that the Allies have invaded Normandy, which means a German defeat may be imminent, Mr. Van Daan, spurred by this good news to regain his humanity, drops his head in his hands and moans, "I'm so ashamed."[38] In this scene, the agonizing dilemmas facing Holocaust victims are presented without evasion or sentimentality. The scene seems a milder version of what, according to survivor testimony, transpired regularly among prisoners in the camps, where selfishness was nearly mandatory for survival, while altruism could be suicidal. Indeed, since, as the audience knows, everyone hidden in the annex will end up in the camps, the scene seems to foreshadow the horrors that await them.

No such praise can be given to a lengthy scene midway through the play and film in which the Franks and the others celebrate Chanukah. Baron defends the scene, insisting that "the Chanukah celebration in the play and movie is far more elaborate than Anne's diary entry about it. . . . [Moreover,] the text is quite specific about the Jewish meaning of the holiday: 'We kindle the Chanukah light to celebrate the great and wonderful deeds wrought through the zeal with which God filled the hearts of the heroic Maccabees, two thousand years ago.'"[39] Nonetheless, as the only reference to Jewish religious observance in the *Diary*, the scene leaves a lot to be desired. For one, the celebrants sing the song "Chanukah" in English rather than, as they surely would have actually done, in Hebrew. During the writing of the play, Hackett justified this change to Otto Frank, explaining that, had the group sung in Hebrew, it "would set the characters in the play apart from the people watching them. . . . The majority of our audience is not Jewish. And the thing we have striven for . . . is to make the audience understand and identify themselves."[40] But surely a better scene would have educated Christian viewers about Jewish ritual, rather than turning Jews into mirror images of the Gentile audience. Such dejudaizing can also be discerned in Goodrich and Hackett's very decision to have Chanukah be the Jewish holiday the group celebrates rather than a more important date on the Jewish calendar, such as Yom Kippur, Rosh Hashanah, or Passover. Chanukah is, after all, the most Christianized of Jewish holidays, a minor celebration whose status has been elevated, especially in America, because it happens to coincide with the Christmas season, as a way of making Jewish children feel less deprived. (On the other hand, the Chanukah story might be inspiring to the Jews in the secret annex, since it is a tale about the Israelites casting off foreign domination and reestablishing their ancestral homeland.)

But surely the most objectionable line in *The Diary of Anne Frank* is Anne's saccharine assurance that, "In spite of everything, I still believe that people are really good at heart"—words plucked out of context from the diary. In both play and film, Anne repeats this line twice. The first time the line is preceded by Anne, in response to Peter's avowed atheism, expressing at length the nature of her religious faith: "I don't mean you have to be Orthodox . . . or believe in heaven and hell and purgatory and things. . . . I just mean some religion . . . just to believe in something! When I think of all that's out there . . . the trees . . . and flowers . . . and the goodness of people we know . . . Mr. Kraler, Miep, Dirk . . . all risking their lives for us every day . . . when I think of these good things, I'm not afraid anymore. . . . I find myself, and God."[41]

Predictably, Anne's faith has nothing to do with being a Jew; in fact, she explicitly disavows the doctrines of any specific religion. Instead, what she expresses is a kind of squishy, ecumenical theology, precisely the sort of religious belief that well-intentioned 1950s American liberals like Goodrich and Hackett would endorse. It's an expression of belief so vaporous that no one (except perhaps the most cantankerous atheist) could possibly object to. How, after all, can anyone be against a God manifested in trees and flowers and human goodness? On the other hand, one might ask, why has such a benevolent deity sanctioned the Holocaust? But this question exposes dangerous theological issues that Goodrich and Hackett have no desire to explore.

The second time Anne says, "In spite of everything, I still believe people are really good at heart" is at the very end. In the play, the line appears in voice-over when Otto Frank is revisiting the annex after the war and poring over his daughter's diary, as if Anne is now speaking from beyond the grave, less a human being than an angelic presence. In reply, Frank murmurs, "She puts me to shame," as the lights fade and the curtain falls.

As for the movie, director George Stevens had been one of the American filmmakers who'd been embedded with the US military when it liberated the concentration camps and had taken reams of documentary footage of the horrors revealed. Perhaps with that experience in mind, Stevens originally shot an ending to the film that showed a numbly swaying Anne in a concentration camp uniform, encircled by fog. But this conclusion so disturbed a preview audience in San Francisco that it was dropped. Instead, the film ended as had the play, with Anne's voice-over intoning: "In spite of everything, I still believe that people are really good at heart." If anything, the movie placed even *more* emphasis on this schmaltzy finale. In the film, Anne's line is punctuated by the camera soaring up into the cloudy sky, while the strings on the musical soundtrack throb dramatically.

As Bruno Bettelheim points out, Anne's famous words amount to a kind of Holocaust denial. "If all men are good," he writes, "there was never an Auschwitz."[42] Bettelheim argues that Anne Frank's diary, and even more the play and film based on it, became popular not because the American public wanted to learn about the Holocaust but for just the opposite reason—because it wanted to pretend that the Holocaust never happened.

"People are really good at heart" comes across as an apt expression of traditional American optimism. When studied in the diary in the context of the passages that immediately precede and follow it, Anne's words look quite different. Just before the line, Anne writes, "That's the difficulty in these times: ideals, dreams and cherished hopes rise up within us, only to meet the horrible truth and be shattered."[43] And right after insisting that "people are really good at heart," Anne returns to her previous gloom, summoning up an apocalyptic vision of "the ever-approaching thunder, destruction, and the suffering of millions."[44] Most tellingly, in the same passage Anne confesses: "I simply can't build up my hopes on a foundation consisting of confusion, misery, and death."[45]

Evaluating "people are really good at heart" in the context of the diary suggests that Anne's vaunted optimism actually exists in painful tension with an equally powerful pessimism. In the full passage, she is torn between two emotional poles, as her natural desire to hope for the best, to retain the innocence she has preserved since childhood, clashes with the reality of what the Nazis are doing to the Jews. Perhaps most importantly, Anne, as she admits, seems to cling to the idea that human kindness is fundamental not because this is the most persuasive proposition under the circumstances but rather because to accept the alternative, that people are capable of incalculable evil, which the facts of the Holocaust demonstrate, is so emotionally shattering as to be unbearable, depriving her of the hope she believes she needs if she is to have any chance of psychological survival. Basically, Anne is taking a leap of faith that transcends the rational. An actress playing Anne might suggest this spin on the statement if she stressed, "In spite of *everything*, I still believe that people are really good at heart." But it's hard to imagine that most audiences at the time interpreted the line in this manner. Instead, most probably responded as Goodrich and Hackett intended—with a surge of emotional uplift that dispensed the gloom of the Holocaust through words that sounded great so long as one didn't think about them too much. In its last lines, *The Diary of Anne Frank* turns into a Hollywood "feel-good" movie.

In both play and movie, Anne's final actions accord with her last words. When German soldiers burst into the annex and its occupants gather up their few belongings in preparation for their departure, the play's stage directions read, "Mr. and Mrs. Frank look over at Anne. She stands, holding her school satchel, looking back at them with a soft, reassuring smile. She is no longer a child, but a woman to meet whatever lies ahead."[46] Anne's pose in the movie is identical. Along with being a woman, Anne seems distinctly like a martyr, more reminiscent of Christian than Jewish tradition. Christianity's central event, after all, is an act of martyrdom, Jesus's crucifixion; while Jewish history also extolls its martyrs (for example, the warriors at Masada, who, rather than surrender to the Roman legions, committed mass suicide), martyrdom has nowhere near the centrality in Judaism that it does in Christianity. In the close of *The Diary of Anne Frank*, Anne appears to be on her way to transforming from a human being into an angel, a transformation completed, as noted, when her final words thunder posthumously.

In his concluding soliloquy in both play and film, Otto Frank informs the audience that Anne's tranquility was not altered by her imprisonment: "It seems strange to say this, that anyone could be happy in a concentration camp. But Anne was happy in the camp in Holland where they first took us. After two years of being shut up in these rooms, she could be out . . . out in the sunshine and the fresh air that she loved."[47] But Frank neglects to tell us the conditions under which Anne subsequently died at Bergen-Belsen. Concerning this event, we have the testimony of Hanneli Goslar—a childhood friend of Anne's who was imprisoned with her in the camp but survived the Holocaust—who briefly saw Anne in her final days. In *Anne Frank: The Biography*, Melissa Müller paraphrases Goslar's recollection of the meeting: "She was freezing and couldn't bear the lice any longer. Anne's voice was barely recognizable, and her words were despairing. She had suffered too much already. Her father was dead [she thought], and, she told Hanneli, she did not want to live any longer."[48] This image of Anne in her final days has all but been effaced from popular consciousness, thanks in large part to the play and film versions of *The Diary of Anne Frank*. As Alvin Rosenfeld observes, "This image of the emaciated, lice-ridden girl lying dead amidst the human waste of the camp latrine, then dumped into a huge hole that served as a mass grave, forms no part of the cherished 'legacy' of Anne Frank."[49]

Similarly, Aaron Kerner argues that the budding but ultimately thwarted romance between Anne and Peter subscribes to the standard formula for the Hollywood melodrama:

> The love story that develops—the amorous relationship that grows between Peter and Anne is also figured within the melodramatic pretense of being "too late." In the closing moments of the film Peter and Anne, alone, stare outside through the broken skylight, shattered earlier during a bombing raid. They try to cheer each other up, imagining what they'll do when they get out of their secret hideaway. Sirens close in on them. . . . The Germans are closing in on them. As the sirens continue the young couple embrace and kiss, the music

swells on cue, embellishing the melodrama. But the consummation is interrupted; it is too late as the Germans arrive, shouting, whistling, and banging on the door. The *coitus interruptus*, the disruption of the formation of a familial unit—as embodied in the budding relationship between Peter and Anne—is indicative of the formulaic "unhappy ending."[50]

In Kerner's reading, *The Diary of Anne Frank* is less about the Holocaust than it is, true to the standards of Hollywood melodrama, about Anne becoming a woman—or almost becoming a woman, balancing on the cusp of womanhood before that process is interrupted by the invading Nazis: "The profound grief that we feel for Anne is that she is blocked from occupying her 'proper' place, and is left instead in an abject state, somewhere between daughter and wife."[51] This foiled metamorphosis, Kerner maintains, is central to the film: "One of the most striking features of the Anne Frank narrative is that we witness the transition of her character—she enters the attic a girl and becomes a young woman. Her sexuality, and her desire for Peter, are key features of the melodramatic form."[52] Such a change in Anne is emphasized in the stage directions, quoted earlier, in which Goodrich and Hackett describe Anne's appearance as she waits to be taken away by the Germans: "She is no longer a child, but a woman to meet whatever lies ahead."

This subplot presents a significant weakness in the film, largely because it adheres too neatly to the formula of Hollywood melodrama. It's true that in the diary Anne speculates about her incipient womanhood, her pubescent sexuality (for example, after she menstruates for the first time), and also makes no attempt to hide the depth of her feelings for Peter, rendered even more intense by the cloistered environment of the secret annex. There is poignancy in the fact that, because of the Holocaust, this romance will never be able to bear fruit. But the movie transforms what was really a very unusual relationship into a stock Hollywood romance—played by two matinee idols, who, when they kiss, are rendered draped in shadows, a pair of silhouettes, while the music throbs. When I show *The Diary of Anne Frank* in class, this scene invariably elicits groans from my students. Just like the inclusion of slapstick humor and the ending of the film with Anne's saccharine optimism, the Anne/Peter romance seems yet one more way *The Diary of Anne Frank* distances audiences from the horror of the Nazi persecution of the Jews and replaces that horror with comforting, familiar Hollywood conventions.

A distinguished crew of actors, director, and screenwriters were assembled to produce the movie version of *The Diary of Anne Frank*. Director Stevens had an impressive oeuvre of previous films, including *Gunga Din* (1939), *Woman of the Year* (1942), *Shane* (1953), and *Giant* (1956). In the role of Otto Frank, Joseph Schildkraut was retained from the play. A veteran theater actor, Schildkraut had also appeared often on the screen, where, as noted earlier, he'd once played Captain Alfred Dreyfus in *The Life of Emile Zola* (1937). Schildkraut said that playing Otto Frank on stage and screen was "the culmination of my professional career."[53]

The filmmakers did make some changes when *The Diary of Anne Frank* moved to the big screen. Although, like the play, the film remains almost entirely set in the secret annex where the Franks hide, Goodrich, Hackett, and Stevens did make some attempts to "open up" what on the screen could easily turn into a stifling chamber drama. To this end, some exterior shots were added, such as German troops marching down the streets of Amsterdam. There are also repeated shots of chirping, flying seagulls—symbols of the freedom denied those stowed away in the annex. Goodrich and Hackett also added the dream sequence, in which Anne imagines her best friend lined up with other prisoners in a camp. As well, the movie was shot in CinemaScope, which gave it an open, sweeping look that mitigated against the feeling of claustrophobia that must have been experienced by the actual inhabitants of 263 Prinsengracht.

As with the play, care was taken to make the film look historically accurate. The outdoor shots were all filmed on location in Amsterdam, including shots of the exterior of the actual building where the Frank family had hidden. As for the attic itself, it was a studio replica reconstructed to look more or less identical to the apartment in which the Franks were sequestered.

The film was a hit with both critics and audiences, just as the play had been, and for the same basic reasons. *The Hollywood Reporter*, for example, exulted in the film's "glowing promise of universal sisterhood and brotherhood" and proclaimed that the movie amplified "Anne's final philosophy [as] expressed in her diary—that other peoples have always suffered persecution but there have always been some people . . . who have taken a stand for decency. This proved to her that the world is fundamentally and enduringly good."[54]

Meyer Levin's lifelong concerns achieved some posthumous validation in 1997 when *The Diary of Anne Frank* was revived on Broadway in a new adaptation by Wendy Kesselman, a Jewish American author who had written previously about the Holocaust. In Kesselman's version, the Chanukah song, "Maoz Tzur," is sung in Hebrew. When the bitter Peter expresses a desire to convert to Christianity, Anne replies, "You'll always be Jewish in your soul."[55] Most importantly, the new version ends not with Anne intoning in voice-over that "people are really good at heart" but instead with an epilogue in which Otto Frank explains to the audience that all those in the annex save him died in the camps, concluding with a stark description of Anne's death in Bergen-Belsen, the details of which weren't widely known until 1988.

In an article in the *New York Times*, Kesselman explained the reasons behind her changes in the original script: "It seems absolutely necessary to do it this way, because we know so much more now, and we're ready to hear it. We have to hear it. . . . I don't think in the '50s we were ready for it. People didn't want to . . . know. But it's crucial now that we know as much as we possibly can. Because it's the truth."[56]

The revised play suggests that popular culture is capable of rewriting Holocaust narratives in response to the way our society has gradually come to a fuller reckoning with the Shoah. Still, perhaps it's time to call a moratorium on the story of Anne Frank. It's often repeated that *The Diary of Anne Frank* is the second-most-popular book in the world, after the Bible. But how many people today who have a copy on their shelves are actually reading it (unless they are forced to in class)? Increasingly, *The Diary of Anne Frank* seems a product of the immediate postwar era, for whom it told exactly as much about the Holocaust as that era was willing to hear—clearly something, but not nearly enough. There are many other Holocaust stories to tell—most of them edgier, darker, more disturbing than the tale told by Anne Frank—and perhaps the American public is finally ready to hear them. Still, I doubt *The Diary of Anne Frank*, in all its various incarnations, will ever disappear entirely from popular consciousness, because the book, play, and movie all raise some profound questions. What would a girl as talented as Anne Frank have accomplished if she had been allowed to grow to adulthood? And what about the approximately 1.5 million other Jewish children also murdered by the Nazis? What might they have done if their lives hadn't been cut short?

5

HOLLYWOOD JUDGES THE GERMANS

Judgment at Nuremberg

Three years after *The Diary of Anne Frank* appeared in American theaters, another Hollywood blockbuster that addressed the Holocaust, but had a much broader sweep, was released: *Judgment at Nuremberg* (1961), directed by Stanley Kramer. During the Nuremberg war crimes trials, the victorious Allies prosecuted high officials in the Nazi regime for what were labeled "crimes against humanity." Discussing the significance of the trials, Bradley F. Smith writes in *Reaching Judgment at Nuremberg*: "A moment's reflection suggests that many of the significant forces that shaped the European and American transition from war to peace and then to cold war appeared in microcosm during the trial. . . . The trial deserves our attention even more because it was a crucial episode in modern man's effort to grapple with the responsibility of leaders for unleashing war and causing mass atrocities."[1]

Rather than depicting the most prominent of these trials, which prosecuted members of Hitler's inner circle, such as Hermann Goering, *Judgment at Nuremberg* focuses on a later trial—one transpiring after these more sensational prosecutions were over—which indicted German judges because their courtroom verdicts furthered the Third Reich's aims by upholding Nazi law. Such a focus is a mixed blessing. On the one hand, the film misses a chance to explore the guilt of those directly responsible for the creation and implementation of the Holocaust. On the other hand, it succeeds in dramatizing how responsibility for the Shoah and other Nazi atrocities extends far beyond the Führer's chief advisors into the social institutions, civil as well as military, which composed the fabric of German society under Hitler.

Judgment at Nuremberg was not American pop culture's first attempt to address the trials. That distinction belonged to a 1959 television program of the same name broadcast on the distinguished dramatic series *Playhouse 90*. Based on a script by Abby Mann (who would also compose the film's screenplay), it featured a stellar cast, including Claude Rains, Paul Lukas, and the German actor Maximilian Schell. The program was produced by Herbert Brodkin, who would later produce the influential 1970s TV miniseries *Holocaust: The Story of the Family Weiss*. The program covered much the same ground as the movie would later, including identical judges, prosecutors, defendants, and witnesses, but at roughly one-third the length of the cinematic version. As a result, writes Gavin Lambert in a contemporary review in *Film Quarterly*, "not surprisingly, in a program of less than ninety minutes, some of the characterizations seemed a bit thin; but for much of the time the show worked as dramatic journalism."[2] Whether due to these characterization problems or because the program appeared on the small screen at a time when television was still in its infancy, the show, despite its strengths, had nowhere near the influence of Kramer's film. Nor, as with many television shows before and after, was it immune to commercial pressures; as Insdorf reports, "Commerce clearly got in the way of authenticity" because "the sponsor of the show, the American Gas Association, objected to the use of the word 'gas' in reference to the concentration camp death chambers."[3]

By the time he turned to *Judgment at Nuremberg*, the maverick director Stanley Kramer already had a reputation in Hollywood as the "king of the message movie." His previous films—*The Defiant Ones* (1958), touching on racial intolerance through the story of two escaped convicts; *On the Beach* (1959), imagining a post-nuclear-holocaust world; and *Inherit the Wind* (1960), dramatizing the 1925 Scopes "Monkey" Trial over the teaching of evolution in public schools—had tackled controversial social and political topics in a way that exhibited a willingness to challenge the ingrained timidity of the major studios when it came to dramatizing contentious subject matter. Although he made "message movies," Kramer denied that he was a didactic filmmaker, explaining in an interview that the purpose of his films was simply "to provoke an audience into thought. . . . That's about as much as I can accomplish, but that's a great deal. It isn't necessary for people to agree with me. It is enough to open up the gate of thought and controversy."[4] Certainly, *Judgment at Nuremberg* is a film that inspired, at the time it appeared (and has continued to inspire), differing, even clashing, opinions as to what its real "message" is.

A film about the Nuremberg trials faces an obvious problem: How do you interest the general public in such a ghastly subject? Before embarking on the project, Kramer was acutely aware of this dilemma, telling another interviewer, "Do you think United Artists wanted to make that thing about the trial? They weren't interested at all in war guilt and those people in the ovens and crooked judges."[5] The director's savvy solution, demonstrating his knowledge of Hollywood's inner workings, was to fill the cast of *Judgment at Nuremberg* with big-name stars, explaining, "I studded it with people to get it made as a film . . . that . . would reach out to a mass audience."[6] The gambit paid off; *Judgment at Nuremberg* was a box office smash. But the move aroused the cynicism of some more mandarin critics; when Lambert, for example, quipped that the director had made "an All-Star Concentration Camp Drama, with Special Guest Appearances,"[7] he had a point: Kramer risked distracting his audience from the movie's higher purpose by peopling it with celebrities, and, indeed, it's nearly impossible to take stars who appear as secondary characters in the movie, such as Montgomery Clift and Judy Garland, seriously in their roles. Kramer's casting strategy established a trend of featuring big-name stars in Hollywood's subsequent Holocaust films, whether it was Rod Steiger in *The Pawnbroker* (1965), Liza Minnelli in *Cabaret* (1972), or Robin Williams in *Jakob the Liar* (1999). In fact, it took a director of Steven Spielberg's stature in Hollywood to buck this trend by casting a relative unknown, the Irish actor Liam Neeson, as the lead in *Schindler's List* (1993).

In *Judgment at Nuremberg*, the trial's presiding justice, Judge Haywood, portrayed as a humble, impeccably virtuous small-town American jurist, is played by Spencer Tracy. Kramer chose Marlene Dietrich to fill the role of Mrs. Bertholt, the aristocratic widow of a Nazi general executed by the Allies who strikes up an ambiguous friendship with Haywood. Both were naturals for their roles. Few actors embody homespun American values better than Tracy, and Dietrich was a German-born actress who—hailed in her native land as a sex goddess following her sensational appearance in 1929 in the hit film *The Blue Angel*—had immigrated to America before the Nazi era. During the war, she openly sided with her new country by entertaining US troops in Europe, which led many Germans to label her a "traitor." In 1939, Dietrich officially became an American citizen, telling reporters, "I am doggone glad to be a niece of Uncle Sam. The United States is the most glorious and wonderful country in the whole wide world."[8] Thus, even though she played a Nazi general's wife, no one could accuse Dietrich of harboring sympathies for the Third Reich. Kramer shrewdly recast the mesmerizing Maximilian Schell, a relative newcomer to Hollywood, as the German attorney defending the Nazi judges, and Schell rewarded Kramer's confidence by turning in the best performance in the film.

In other instances, Kramer cast famous actors in parts that played against type. For the volatile, self-righteous American prosecutor at the trial, the director picked Richard Widmark, who previously had played mostly gangsters and other lowlifes in hard-boiled crime films. True to form, Widmark plays the prosecutor's role with bombastic dyspepsia. Perhaps the oddest castings of all were the three famous American actors Kramer chose to play German characters. Two were given fairly minor roles. Montgomery Clift plays a feebleminded German baker with alleged Communist sympathies, sterilized by the Nazis on the order of one of the justices on trial. According to studio insiders, at this point in his life Clift was so battered by drug and alcohol addiction that it was a challenge for the filmmakers to get him to perform at all. But these problems almost seem to work to Clift's advantage in this particular role, informing the baker's permanently bewildered, semicomatose expression. Another American star, Judy Garland, appearing in her first film in six years, plays a shy, dumpy German Fräulein whom the Nazis prosecuted for befriending a Jewish merchant, thus violating their racial laws. Garland exhibits her trademark gift for on-screen vulnerability, and she competently manages her German accent. But it's confusing that some of the German characters are played by Americans, while others are played by actual Germans. Some German viewers may even have found Kramer's decision to cast Americans as Germans offensive.

Kramer's worst casting decision was to choose Burt Lancaster, usually a virile leading man, to play the most important of the Nazi defendants—Ernst Janning, an internationally renowned German jurist who had helped fashion the Weimar Era's democratic constitution. Lancaster was Kramer's second choice, after Laurence Olivier turned down the part. (In 1976, however, Olivier would brilliantly play an escaped Nazi doctor in the thriller *Marathon Man*.) Many years later, Kramer would lament that his failure to land Olivier for the role was one of his two biggest disappointments about the making of *Judgment at Nuremberg* (the other being his inability to get permission to film in the actual courtrooms where the Nuremberg trials took place, resulting in a recreation of the courtroom on a sound stage in Southern California). Kramer had grounds to be regretful. Of his performance, reviewer Arthur B. Clarke wrote at the time: "His bearing through the trial is almost catatonic; and, when he finally comes to life and speaks a piece for which the audience has not been prepared, he is unbelievable and embarrassing to watch."[9] In another contemporary review, Ronald Steel complained that Lancaster "gives a somnambulistic, clench-jaw rendition," adding, "A glimpse of those gorgeous choppers might have helped."[10]

In making *Judgment at Nuremberg*, Kramer and his crew generally tried to stick to the facts, but the filmmakers never saw themselves as producing a documentary. Telford Taylor, US chief counsel for war

Figure 5.1. *Judgment at Nuremburg* (1961). A major Nazi defendant, Ernst Janning (Burt Lancaster), testifies at his war crimes trial. [Screen grab]

crimes at the Nuremberg trials, rejected an offer to serve as an advisor on the set, because of what Taylor regarded as excessive dramatic license in the script (particularly concerning the character based on Taylor himself, the trial's chief prosecutor). In response, attorney Gunther Schiff, one of the studio's lawyers, wrote Taylor, "I know . . . you will realize . . . that the script is not meant to portray with historical accuracy . . . the persons or events who were involved in . . . the Nuremberg Trial. Rather it was Abby [Mann's] desire . . . to depict in a fictional manner the essence of what occurred at Nuremberg."[11] Schiff's letter provides a succinct definition of the "docudrama." *Judgment at Nuremberg* may now be seen as a pioneering effort in the genre—one whose portrayal of the Shoah would reach an apex of sorts with *Holocaust* but would also be exemplified, with mixed success, in other TV miniseries such as the equally protracted *War and Remembrance* (1989). Schiff's letter inadvertently reveals problems inherent in the genre of Holocaust docudramas. One is that the form's reliance on composite characters may induce the audience to mistake these fictitious figures for actual historical individuals. Even more problematically, Schiff skirts the difficulty of discerning precisely what is the "essence" of a historical event.

Judgment at Nuremberg premiered in America on December 16, 1961, the same day that Adolf Eichmann was sentenced to death in Jerusalem for being a chief architect of the Holocaust. This striking parallel was noted by the press at the time. Some reporters cynically wondered if Kramer had deliberately scheduled his film's opening to coincide with the trial's verdict. Others found the juxtaposition more edifying: Murray Schumach wrote in the *New York Times*, "In a somber courtroom set in Hollywood, genocide is as current these days as it is in the Beit Ha'am in Jerusalem, where Adolf Eichmann is being tried for responsibility for the deaths of six million Jews."[12]

Soon after its American premiere, *Judgment at Nuremberg* also opened in West Berlin, where the screening was treated as a major cultural event. Held in the Berlin Kongresshalle, the guest list included members of the West German Senate, along with Allied commanders, and the showing was introduced by the West Berlin mayor (later the West German prime minister), Willy Brandt, who hailed it as "an important political event" showing what happens when a nation abandons justice and calling such abandonment "the greatest problem in the world."[13] Germans in the audience, however, were generally unresponsive, and when *Judgment at Nuremberg* subsequently appeared in theaters throughout West Germany, it played to largely empty houses. Germany, it seems, was not yet ready to confront its Nazi past. That wouldn't happen until a decade later, sparked in good part by the miniseries *Holocaust*, which, despite (or perhaps because of) its reliance on melodrama and kitsch, provided the impetus many Germans needed for that reckoning. It's not true, however, that *Judgment at Nuremberg* had no effect on West Germany at the time of its release there. One subplot in the movie concerned the Feldenstein case (based on the actual Katzenberg case), which hinged on Nazi laws prohibiting contact between Aryans and Jews. This did inspire West German student demonstrators to force the early retirement of the judge who had heard the Katzenberg case.

Back in America, *Judgment at Nuremberg* was nominated for eleven Academy Awards. Schell took Best Actor honors, while Abby Mann won for Best Screenplay Adaptation. Kramer, who'd never received an Oscar, was given an Irving Thalberg Lifetime Achievement Award, which surely implied a favorable nod toward *Judgment at Nuremberg*. The overwhelmingly laudatory reviews tended to stress the film's moral worth rather than its entertainment value (a response that echoed the reception several decades later to *Schindler's List*). One critic effused, "To evade this film is a weakness in courage . . . This picture is a . . . clarion call for peace, fair dealing, mercy, and absolute justice."[14]

Politicians also weighed in. New York Senator Jacob Javits, apparently forgetting that the movie was fictionalized, called *Judgment at Nuremberg* one of the most "eloquent documentaries of our time."[15] Perhaps the most distinguished political figure to endorse the film was Eleanor Roosevelt, who opined: "It must have taken courage to produce this film at this time—a time when most of us have forgotten what went on in Germany before and during World War II."[16] As one of the lone voices in her husband's administration urging Roosevelt to try to stop the Nazi genocide against the Jews, the former First Lady's judgment carried real moral authority.

However, while audiences today are probably most interested in what *Judgment at Nuremberg* has to say about the Holocaust, most critics at the time did not engage with the topic. Instead, they tended to focus on two large themes. One was to see the movie as using the Nuremberg trials as a means to address general philosophical issues that transcended the historical circumstances of the trials themselves. This tack was taken by Brendan Gill in the *New Yorker*: "The questions are among the biggest that can be asked and are no less thrilling for being thousands of years old. . . . They concern nothing less than the degree of accountability, individually and collectively, as members of the human race, for the life and well-being of every other member of the race."[17]

Another critical response was to interpret *Judgment at Nuremberg* as only ostensibly about World War II, while implicitly addressing issues urgently relevant to our contemporary world. Jason Epstein wrote in this vein in *Commentary*: "It seems to me that we are being asked. . . to think of ourselves at the end of World War II in a position similar to that of the defendants—ordinary men . . . who under the stress of a national crisis are acquiescing in crimes beside which Hitler's seem small. . . . We too may one day be called to account for decisions we failed to make, for opportunities we overlooked, for alternatives we were too blind to know were there."[18]

In other words, Epstein saw *Judgment at Nuremberg* as suggesting that contemporary American leaders who pursued the arms race with the Soviet Union were just as guilty as (if not *more* guilty than) the Nazi leaders who plunged Europe into World War II, while those ordinary Americans who acquiesced in our government's destructive and suicidal actions were as responsible as those German citizens who did nothing to halt Hitler's crimes. Even if one accepts that US leaders made mistakes during the Cold War (as they surely did), it's still an outrageous comparison, demonstrating how even sensitive intellectuals like Epstein were often misled by the passions aroused by the Cold War while remaining blind to the full evil perpetrated by the Nazis. Ironically, as I'll discuss, American blindness to the depth of Nazi evil is one of the messages presented by *Judgment at Nuremberg*.

Does *Judgment at Nuremberg* see the Holocaust as, on the one hand, an occasion to ponder abstract moral issues while, on the other, turning the genocide into a covert allegory about contemporary America? Is the absence of contemporary critical commentary about the film's treatment of the "Final Solution" due to the fact that *Judgment at Nuremberg*, like almost all the anti-Nazi Hollywood films that preceded it, largely effaces the reality that the Jews were Hitler's primary targets? Or is this silence attributable to the fact that American critics in the early 1960s were, like society at large, so oblivious to the Holocaust that they failed to see that the film was actually a groundbreaking treatment of the Nazis' persecution of the Jews?

Clearly, one of Kramer's intentions in *Judgment at Nuremberg* was to universalize the Holocaust: "Who among us may judge others?" he told an interviewer at the time. "Who among us is so innocent that we are . . . sure of the guilty?"[19] The implication of Kramer's remark is that when the Nazis perpetrated their crimes they were acting on dark thoughts and emotions residing in all of us, even if they usually remain latent. Lawrence Langer had *Judgment at Nuremberg's* universalizing tendencies in mind when he wrote that the film deals more with principles than individuals.[20] Indeed, the primary principle the film addresses is that of justice. What does it mean to act unjustly? Are human beings even capable of acting justly? If so, how must we think and live in order to qualify as just men and women?

Judgment at Nuremberg explores the issue of justice most acutely through the character of Ernst Janning. How did this brilliant architect of Weimar democracy end up as a Nazi functionary? Throughout most of the trial, Janning remains stonily silent, but eventually, while defense attorney Rolfe is viciously interrogating a prosecution witness, Janning erupts, dismissing his own attorney's attempts to defend him, and delivers a long speech in which he flatly condemns himself and his fellow Germans. By going along with the Nazis, the ex-judge declares, "I made my life excrement." He concludes, "If there is to be any salvation for Germany, those of us who know our guilt must admit it no matter what the cost in pain and humiliation." When delivering his verdict, Judge Haywood calls Janning "a tragic figure" whose "fate illuminates the trial's most shattering truth: the defendants aren't monsters. Under national crises, even extraordinary men can commit vast crimes." Clearly, *Judgment at Nuremberg* presents Janning's story as a cautionary tale of what awaits even the best leaders when, out of misguided patriotism, they act during national emergencies in ways that violate their own consciences.

But there's a muddle here. At the film's end, in a final confrontation between Janning and Haywood after the verdict, Janning implores the American jurist, "I did not know it would come to that. You must believe it. You must believe it." Why does the German defendant condemn himself in public and then seek to palliate his guilt privately with

Haywood? Is it because Janning, despite his courtroom utterances, has not confronted his full culpability? Or does Janning's later remark simply imply his acknowledgment that he didn't realize the full extent of his crimes at the time he committed them? This confusion weakens Janning's characterization, a serious flaw in the film. As Langer writes, "Janning's declaration of guilt is not enough, psychologically or artistically: not enough for himself, because he has not penetrated his motives, and not enough for us, because we still do not know how such a decent man came to lend his judicial prestige to the Nazi cause."[21]

As exemplified by *The Diary of Anne Frank*, universalizing the Holocaust raises clear dangers. One danger is that such an approach will end up mitigating the guilt of the perpetrators. Should we, say, blame Ernst Janning when, under similar circumstances, most of us probably would have acted the same way? The second danger is that if one moves too quickly from the particular to the universal, one may downplay or simply ignore the specific historical circumstances in which the Holocaust occurred.

On the other hand, forbidding the raising of universal questions when studying the Holocaust poses its own problems. The most evident risk is that one might comfortably distance oneself from the Nazis, insisting that the Germans acted as they did because of some unique evil in their national character, thus avoiding any troubling questions about human nature, including one's own. This danger is lamentably exemplified by Daniel Jonah Goldhagen's best-selling *Hitler's Willing Executioners: Ordinary Germans and the Holocaust*, in which the historian insists that every last German, and Germans alone, fully and knowingly embraced all facets of what Goldhagen calls Hitler's "eliminationist anti-Semitism."[22] In a forum about the book held at the US Holocaust Memorial Museum in Washington, DC, historian Christopher Browning insightfully condemned Goldhagen's thesis as "curiously comforting" because it exempts from blame for the Holocaust everyone *except* the Germans. The ideal, then, is a balanced approach that both scrutinizes the historical particulars of the Nazi genocide and explores the larger moral and philosophical issues that genocide itself raises. The problem with *Judgment at Nuremberg* is not that it raises universal questions but that it does so at the expense of a close examination of the historical details regarding Nazi persecution, especially of the Jews. However, unlike in *The Diary of Anne Frank*, in *Judgment at Nurem-*

berg the intent of these universalizing tendencies is not to dejudaize the characters in order to appeal to anti-Semitic American audiences and, hence, seems less insidious.

Exploring the way *Judgment at Nuremberg* portrays the relationship between America and the Third Reich, one must distinguish among three different topics, all examined by the film. One is the degree to which the United States abetted the rise of the Nazis, or at least failed to try to halt that rise.[23] The second is the extent to which, after the war, the United States, for a variety of self-interested reasons, failed to prosecute the Nazis with sufficient zeal.[24] The final topic is whether it's valid to draw parallels between the Nazi regime and contemporary America.[25] That Kramer had America in mind while making the film is implied by his remark in a *New York Times* profile that ran on the eve of the movie's premiere: "I am interested in . . . what we in America stand for. This interest is what attracted me to 'Judgment at Nuremberg.' . . . It is not the attitude of the Germans that I have tried to emphasize in the film. It is the attitude of the Americans—the judge and the prosecuting attorney and all the others who participate in this . . . representation of the momentous judgments at Nuremberg."[26]

What's troubling about Kramer's remarks is his professed *lack* of interest in what the *Germans* "stood for," surely a central issue in the Nuremberg trials. In *Popular Culture and the Shaping of Holocaust Memory in America*, Alan Mintz argues that Kramer's remark should be seen as the director's attempt to "spin" the American reception to his film, since "Kramer's call for a self-examination of our national fiber . . . expresses an anxiety about whether, in the eyes of American viewers, a film about foreign crimes will escape being off-putting."[27] As we've seen, Kramer was a director with one eye firmly on the box office; still, the fact remains that *Judgment at Nuremberg* has a lot to say about America, little of it flattering.

Consider the first topic: the degree to which the United States abetted the Nazis' rise. In the course of his defense, Rolfe insists that the rest of the world also bears guilt for Nazi crimes, because they knew of Hitler's intentions and either did nothing or actually helped further the Führer's aims. As an example, Rolfe cites American industrialists who profited by rearming the German state. The defense attorney doesn't name names, but an informed viewer can fill in the blanks; both the openly anti-Semitic auto manufacturer, Henry Ford (who published

The Protocols of the Learned Elders of Zion and *The International Jew*, along with venomous essays in his company newspaper, *The Dearborn Independent*), and the avaricious CEOs at IBM (who aided the Nazis in developing a primitive computer system that allowed them to keep track of prisoners in the camps), for example, helped empower the Third Reich through extensive business dealings.[28]

On the second issue—whether justice was served by the Allies at Nuremberg—at one point during the trial a US senator counsels Haywood to go easy on the defendants so as not to rile an important Cold War ally (arm-twisting that increases in urgency when, during the course of the film, the Soviets move their troops into East Berlin and the Berlin Wall is erected). The issue of Cold War anti-Communism is raised by one of the defendants himself, Emil Hahn (Werner Klemperer)—the least repentant of the bunch—who during the trial justifies his continued allegiance to the Nazis by insisting that the Nazi state provided a vital bulwark against Soviet Communism.

In his verdict, Haywood resists such pressures from American politicians to be lenient by handing down life sentences to all the defendants, which might suggest that American justice has prevailed, except that a note at the film's end reveals that of the ninety-five defendants sentenced to prison terms in the Nuremberg trials, not one was still serving his sentence.

As for the film's implicit parallels between the United States and Hitler's regime, most of these parallels are drawn by Rolfe in the course of his defense. When Colonel Lawson calls to the stand a witness who was ordered sterilized by one of the defendants during the Nazi era, because, Lawson alleges, of his Communist allegiances, Rolfe seeks to prove that it was, rather, the man's feeblemindedness that motivated the sterilization. Then Rolfe reads a judicial opinion penned by the distinguished American Supreme Court Justice Oliver Wendell Holmes approving the sterilization of the mentally incompetent. When Lawson shows horrifying footage from the Allied liberation of the concentration camps, Rolfe retorts by noting the Allies' firebombing of Dresden, which killed untold scores of civilians and seemed to lack any military purpose. Later, when meeting with Janning in prison, Rolfe implies that the dropping of atomic bombs on Hiroshima and Nagasaki was just as ethically repugnant as the Holocaust: "Thousands and thousands of burnt bodies! Women and children! Is that their superior morality?"

No character in the film ever *refutes* these comparisons Rolfe makes between the Americans and the Nazis, though his arguments are hardly irrefutable. One might, for example, point out that the dropping of the atomic bomb on Hiroshima had an unassailable military objective: namely, to terrorize the Japanese into surrendering, thus obviating the need for a bloody American land attack on Japan. Nonetheless, Rolfe's comparisons between Hiroshima and the Holocaust may have resonated with American audiences in 1961. By then, the Cold War was reaching its zenith, with the Cuban Missile Crisis only a year away. Many Americans viewed Hiroshima as the first blow (even if it was aimed at Japan rather than Russia) in a nuclear struggle that could literally result in mankind's extermination. Under the circumstances, Rolfe's comparison may not have sounded far-fetched.

When *Judgment at Nuremberg* opened, the civil rights movement was squarely in the public eye, with the Supreme Court decision in *Brown v. Board of Education* only a few years old and Martin Luther King Jr.'s nonviolent opposition to Southern segregation attracting national attention. It's hard to imagine that the film's comparisons between Nazi anti-Semitism and American racism, however subtle, went unnoticed by attentive viewers. While Lawson is showing ghastly footage of the camp liberations, the camera cuts deliberately to the face of a black American GI providing security in the courtroom. Does this slaughter of innocents remind the GI of the lynchings of equally innocent blacks in the American South? The trial also covers the Feldenstein Case, where a German Jew was executed for allegedly romancing an Aryan girl, which may have reminded viewers of the way Southern blacks were beaten, arrested, or killed for supposed dalliances with white women. Just as enlightened Germans reflected on their political and judicial morals during the Nuremberg trials, progressive Americans were, perhaps, also wondering if the US system of justice would act morally and effectively, in this case to ensure equal rights for African Americans.

I don't think *Judgment at Nuremberg* intends to draw a direct comparison between the United States and the Nazis. Rather, the film seems to suggest that there are enough similarities to temper American self-righteousness. Instead of haughtily condemning the Nazis, the movie implies, Americans would be better off using an exploration of the consequences of Nazi racism as a spur toward rectifying the injustices plaguing our own nation.

Clearly, the most problematic aspect of *Judgment at Nuremberg* is the way in which it presents the Nazi genocide against the Jews. Because the defendants were exclusively justices in the Nazi government, the film excludes from the docket any Germans who directly participated in the Holocaust. Moreover, the trial focuses on only two cases adjudicated during the Nazi era: one of a German gentile man accused of being a Communist, the second of a German Jew accused of violating the Nazis' racial laws. By pairing the cases, the film seems fallaciously to imply, deliberately or not, that Communists and Jews were persecuted equally by the Nazis.

Moreover, in the Feldenstein case, the focus is not on the deceased Feldenstein but rather on the German girl he supposedly seduced, Irene Wallner (who insists on the stand that their relationship was purely platonic). So, as with the sterilization case, the film's focus is on a suffering Gentile German, not a Jew. Indeed, not only are no Jewish characters called to testify—in fact, there are no Jews in the entire film. The absence of Jewish witnesses makes the trial dramatically different from the Eichmann trial, where the Israeli prosecutor's strategy was to put scores of Jewish Holocaust survivors on the stand (including those with whom Eichmann had had no dealings at all) to tell their stories to the Jerusalem courtroom and, via television, to the world, as a means of broadly educating viewers about the Shoah. Under Rolfe's brutal interrogation, Wallner admits that, though she was underage at the time, Feldenstein had kissed her. Thus, the viewer is left with the impression that Feldenstein may have been guilty, which echoes the anti-Semitic stereotype of the Jew as a lecherous violator of Aryan maidenhood, either as a seducer or a rapist.[29]

But the larger problem is that *Judgment at Nuremberg* implies that it *matters*, both ethically and historically, whether Rudolf Petersen was sterilized by the Nazi judges because he was a Communist or mentally retarded and whether Feldenstein really did conduct an underage affair with Irene Wallner. The film fails to portray the fact that the Nazi system was so polluted that such fine points of law were irrelevant. As a result, *Judgment at Nuremberg* fails to get to the root of the Third Reich's evil, never explaining how this regime was capable of perpetrating the Holocaust.

When the filmmakers sent a copy of the script to James Brand, one of the American judges during the actual Nuremberg trials, Brand advised Abby Mann to include the fact (which arose during the actual Katzenberg case) that under Nazi law proof of an Aryan girl simply sitting on the lap of a Jew warranted the death penalty.[30] Mann ignored Brand's advice, but had he accepted it, *Judgment at Nuremberg* might have made clear that—given the draconian nature of Nazi anti-Semitic legislation—it was irrelevant whether or not Feldenstein and Wallner had actually consummated an affair. Merely showing Wallner any affection at all signed Feldenstein's death warrant.

By far the most shocking, and memorable, moment in *Judgment at Nuremberg* is one in which Colonel Lawson plays seven minutes of actual documentary footage of the liberation of the camps. Such footage had never before been inserted into a fictional Hollywood movie, though in the future it would be used in countless popular films and television programs.[31] Camp liberation footage had been aired immediately after the war in newsreels, but by 1961 such images had long vanished from the screen and from the consciousness of most Americans, especially now that West Germany was a staunch Cold War ally. The footage is exceedingly graphic: lampshades made from human skin; corpses of children; boxcars stuffed with doomed prisoners; hideous camp medical experiments; interiors of gas chambers; gold fillings wrenched from the teeth of gassed bodies; canisters of Zyklon B; naked, emaciated bodies being bulldozed into open graves. The camera cuts from these gruesome images to the defendants, who look annoyed and uncomfortable, as well as to Haywood's stunned face as this mature and worldly man beholds an unimaginable atrocity. After the film is over, the prosecutor concludes, "Who were the bodies? Members of every occupied country of Europe. Two thirds of the Jews of Europe were exterminated. More than six million, according to the Nazis' own figures."

Very few critics, at the time and especially now, consider this scene a satisfactory means of educating audiences about the Holocaust. Judith Doneson, for example, complains that "nothing is said of [the Nazis] planned systematic destruction [of the Jews]. We are never enlightened as to what policy caused their death."[32] Alan Mintz concurs: "The footage is used as a sensational move to shock us into acknowledging the moral enormity of the crimes, but we are not asked to investigate their nature and genesis or to inquire about the identity of the victims. Nor are we given a framework in which to locate what we are watching."[33]

Doneson and Mintz agree that *Judgment at Nuremberg* fails to clarify its documentation of the Nazi genocide by explaining the systematic policy, rooted in Nazi ideology, that drove the slaughter. If this were a contemporary film, appearing at a time when a basic understanding of the Holocaust pervades American society, this failure would be completely unacceptable. However, it is crucial to evaluate *Judgment at Nuremberg* in the context of its times. For one thing, as a portrayal of the Holocaust, the film represents a marked advance on *The Diary of Anne Frank*, which, as discussed in chapter 4, ends with Anne's treacly invocation of the essential goodness of mankind. In contrast, *Judgment at Nuremberg* foregrounds the horror of the camps. It's doubtful that many viewers, after seeing Lawson's screening at the trial, would agree with the fictionalized Anne Frank that "people are really good at heart." Moreover, many viewing the footage may have been so shocked by what they saw that they were inspired to learn more about the genocide, thus discovering the context the film omits.

As well, one can't forget the pressures on Kramer not to be too specific about the crimes perpetrated by a nation that had become a key US ally. Shortly after it opened, the film inspired a photo feature in *Life* magazine in which the writer reflected: "Some who see the film will question the sense of reopening old wounds now, perhaps tending to estrange a free world ally and giving a propaganda wedge to the enemy."[34]

According to Mintz, most in the Jewish American community at the time applauded *Judgment at Nuremberg*, just as they had approved of *The Diary of Anne Frank*. Even though Jewish victims of the Nazis are largely absent from the screen, most Jewish Americans, Mintz argues, chose to see the film as being about the Holocaust: "American Jews . . . assumed that there were many subjects that Hollywood studios would not put on the big screen. That the fact of the Holocaust was presented in *Judgment at Nuremberg* and documentary footage shown was taken as a source of wonderment; that the Holocaust as a 'parochial' tragedy should be represented was considered beyond all expectation. Jewish viewers therefore saw themselves as receptors of an encoded communication; they picked up and discreetly unscrambled signals of what could not be said."[35] It's tempting, from a modern perspective, when Holocaust consciousness has saturated American culture, to view this Jewish American response as timid or benighted. But given the silence about the Holocaust that pervaded American society in the early 1960s, there's a compelling argument for taking that response at face value.

Moreover, even though Kramer claimed to be more interested in America than Germany, *Judgment at Nuremberg* is, in fact, a damning portrait of the behavior of America's cherished Cold War ally during the Nazi era. In a scene that immediately follows Lawson's presentation of his camp footage, the defendants, now sequestered and furious at Lawson's tactics, are all busily denying that the genocide ever happened, until one of their number, who served with Eichmann, casually acknowledges the truth of what the prosecutor has presented. The implication is that the Nazi bureaucracy was much better informed about the Holocaust than it claimed after the war.

In an earlier scene, when Mrs. Bertholt (Dietrich) similarly insists that no one other than the SS knew of the genocide, Haywood replies, "As far as I can make out, no one in this country knew." This exchange occurs in a Nuremberg café, where Bertholt and Haywood converse surrounded by ordinary Germans singing rousing German folk songs and keeping time by banging their beer steins on the tables. In his *New York Times* review, Bosley Crowther maintained that all this carousing immediately following Lawson's footage is meant to present a cozy ambience that is "created for the benefit of the audience which is thus made to feel a warm compassion for the people of Germany," still able to celebrate despite the depredations they suffered during and after World War II.[36] Crowther sees these celebrating Germans as representing the "real" Germany, which is distinguished from the Nazi regime. In contrast, I find the scene far more sinister, especially when, in an arresting trick of cinematography, a thumping beer stein dissolves into the judge's gavel banging his table to recommence the trial the following day. The linking of festive Germans with the Nuremberg trials implies that Nazism may be deeply rooted in German common culture. Moreover, it is surely disturbing to witness ordinary Germans drinking and singing right after we have viewed the horrors of the Holocaust. Indeed, Ernst Janning, in his self-excoriating speech toward the end of the trial, explicitly implicates ordinary Germans in the Holocaust when he insists that they "*were* aware of the camps. We saw our neighbors dragged away. Maybe we didn't know the details, but, if so, it's because we didn't want to know."

In short, *Judgment at Nuremberg* casts a net of blame widely over the entire German nation. True, the film establishes a hierarchy of guilt. Those who ran the gas chambers and manned the firing squads and their superiors who ordered them to do so were most guilty. But those judges who, obeying Nazi law, sentenced innocent people were also to blame. And so were the ordinary Germans who did nothing when their neighbors were hauled off to the camps. No wonder the German masses were so lukewarm when the film was first screened in West Germany. All in all, *Judgment at Nuremberg* is a bolder, more daring movie than contemporary critics who analyze it exclusively through the lens of the present recognize. In fact, the film laid the foundation for subsequent Hollywood cinema to be discussed in future chapters—such as *The Pawnbroker*, *Sophie's Choice*, and *Schindler's List*—which deal more adequately with Nazi war crimes and the Holocaust.

6

HOLLYWOOD'S HOLOCAUST SURVIVOR

The Pawnbroker

In his 1965 film *The Pawnbroker*, Sydney Lumet was one of the first US filmmakers to introduce a character who would in time become a staple of American Holocaust cinema: the survivor. Focusing on Holocaust survivors rather than Holocaust victims offers advantages to directors, both because one can trace the impact of the genocide on the survivor, even many years after it occurred, and because one can set the film in modern times, thus avoiding the arduous task of trying to re-create the world of the Shoah. Fascinating, if problematic, *The Pawnbroker* is based on a 1961 novel by Edward Lewis Wallant, a young Jewish American writer of great promise who died at the age of thirty-six. Originally, MGM was slated to produce the film, but after the studio demanded too many script changes, including an upbeat ending, the movie was taken over by a more agreeable independent producer, Ely Landau.

Like Stanley Kramer, Lumet was a maverick Hollywood director whose movies often dealt with issues of individual responsibility in the face of social injustice. His 1957 film *Twelve Angry Men*, about a juror who must persuade eleven others of the innocence of a young Puerto Rican man, was called by critics "a rebuttal to the lynch-mob hysteria of the McCarthy era" and an "anti-conformist tract and a plea for social justice."[1] Two movies Lumet made after *The Pawnbroker—Serpico* (1973) and *Prince of the City* (1981)—both deal with a lone honest cop battling rampant police corruption in New York City. And in *Book of Daniel* (1980), based on E. L. Doctorow's novel, the director revisited the Old Left and the controversy surrounding the execution of the Rosenbergs for allegedly smuggling nuclear secrets to the Soviets.

Lumet filmed *The Pawnbroker* entirely on location in New York City, and the gritty black-and-white shots of inner-city poverty greatly enhance the film's power and realism. *The Pawnbroker* stars Rod Steiger, who would later play a Hassidic rabbi in the Holocaust-oriented film *The Chosen* (1981). In Lumet's film, Steiger plays Sol Nazerman, a Holocaust survivor who now, two decades after the war, lives on Long Island with relatives and owns a pawnshop in Spanish Harlem. Steiger gives a remarkably subtle performance, depicting Nazerman as haunted, isolated, nihilistic, and catatonic. Even though, for most of the action, Steiger is made up to resemble a man much older than his actual age at the time, the subterfuge is never apparent, so fully does the actor inhabit the role. The brilliance of Steiger's performance was recognized; in 1964, he won Best Actor honors at the Berlin International Film Festival, and, in 1965, he was nominated for an Academy Award. Indeed, at the time, critics almost universally acclaimed the film as a penetrating exploration of the life of a Holocaust survivor.

In the opening scene, we see Nazerman, who has lost his wife and children in the Holocaust, living in a relatively affluent, but characterless, suburb. Nazerman's relatives are a vapid, materialistic clan who flatter him because he supports them with the profits from his pawnshop. They are so indifferent to the pain he has suffered that they are planning to take him along on a family trip to Europe, blithely oblivious to the fact that returning to Europe might be traumatic for a Holocaust survivor. Nazerman, in turn, barely tolerates his relatives. In a scene shot from above, we see Nazerman supine on a lawn chair in a backyard identical to a seemingly endless row of others. He looks utterly alone, despite being surrounded by family, and entirely out of place. Nazerman's loveless family is contrasted with that of his assistant in the pawnshop, Jesus Ortiz (Jaime Sánchez), a young, handsome, idealistic Puerto Rican from Spanish Harlem. Ortiz is committed to putting his gang-related past behind him and bettering himself by acquiring his employer's business acumen in order to pull himself out of poverty. Ortiz lives with his doting mother, and the pair, despite living in a cramped ghetto apartment, have a loving relationship.

Figure 6.1. *The Pawnbroker* (1964). Holocaust survivor Sol Nazerman (Rod Steiger) sits in his Harlem pawnshop, the shadow of the bars covering his window resembling the bars in a concentration camp. [Screen grab]

In another sharp contrast between Nazerman and his employee, Ortiz enjoys an infinitely better love life. Sol is trapped in a frigid relationship with Tessie (Marketa Kimbrell), the widow of a friend murdered in an escape attempt from the same camp where Nazerman was imprisoned, while Nazerman helplessly watched. As Nazerman lies limply in Tessie's arms, her dying father, Mandel (Baruch Lumet, the director's father), another Holocaust survivor, shrieks curses at the couple from his bed in the next room. In contrast, Ortiz is plunged in an ebullient romance with a pretty young black woman (Thelma Oliver), who, though a prostitute, loves him dearly and is eager to help him financially to fulfill his dream of owning a pawnshop. The problematic nature of the film's portrayal of Jews and Judaism is evident early on in the way Ortiz's Latino family is portrayed so much more positively than Nazerman's Jewish counterparts, as if the film is saying that Latinos are vibrant, passionate, and full of life, while Jews are joyless, ineffectual, and neurotic.

The Pawnbroker has nothing to say about the Holocaust as a historical event. We learn nothing about the Nazis' policies toward the Jews or how these policies metastasized into a systematic scheme of mass murder. Indeed, the film is really not about the Holocaust but about a Holocaust survivor. It is clear that Nazerman's current life has been wrecked by his experiences during the Shoah. Joshua Hirsch sees Nazerman as a sort of poster child for post-traumatic stress disorder (PTSD): "The film presents Sol as a kind of PTSD case study, complete with symptoms of emotional deadening, avoidance of trauma-associated stimuli, difficulty with anniversaries of traumatic events, and feelings of helplessness and shame."[2] Nazerman suffers constantly from brief but vivid flashbacks to his days before the Holocaust as well as in the camps, usually triggered by some apparently innocuous event. Near the movie's start, in a scene shot in dreamlike slow motion, we see Nazerman with his wife, children, and parents before the war, enjoying a picnic on a riverbank. It's an idyllic scene, with the man twirling his daughter in his arms—before, that is, the Nazis arrive in trucks to take them all away. Of this scene, Hirsch writes, "At the end of the sequence, the family members' gazes are torn away from one another and directed toward the horrifying onscreen sight of the Nazis. In his dream, Sol thus represents his trauma as the breaking of the family gaze by the Nazis."[3] The contrast between the virile, happy young man in the flashback and the decrepit shell of a human being Nazerman has become could not be sharper. Equally sharp is the disjunction between the obviously loving bond Nazerman shared with the family who was murdered by the Nazis and the utter estrangement he feels toward the relatives with whom he lives in America. The flashback suggests how Nazerman carries the memory of his murdered family inside him, which makes it impossible for him to start a new life.

Later, Nazerman is riding on the subway when he suddenly flashes back to a memory of traveling in a boxcar stuffed with prisoners en route to the concentration camp. In another gripping scene, a desperate prostitute offers her body (along with her jewelry) to Nazerman in the pawnshop, baring her breasts and imploring, "Look!" The sight of her naked breasts inspires Nazerman to recall a moment when the camp's Nazis smashed his head through a window and forced him to watch a guard raping his wife. Hirsch points out that during this brief scene Nazerman is able to see his wife but she can't see him, and, during the scene, Nazerman's gaze is blocked by an approaching soldier. "Thus," Hirsch writes, "Sol's gaze, once a sign of mutual possession, has been broken and inverted into a sign of a loss of mutuality, his isolated possession by others—his trauma."[4]

The way these jolting memories flash for just seconds in Nazerman's mind as the camera rapidly crosscuts between present and past is utterly compelling and elicited considerable praise from critics when the film appeared. In *Commonweal*, for example, Philip T. Hartung asserted that the flashbacks "are as startling in their past-is-present implications as those in *Wild Strawberries* and *Hiroshima, Mon Amour*."[5] And psychiatrist Ernst Becker wrote that Nazerman's "mind is continually prey to obtrusive flashbacks, flashbacks to a world he has left, but which still claims him. Physically and externally he is here; inwardly and emotionally he is elsewhere. . . . Nazerman's story is one my generation has lived vicariously so many times, we would rather be spared the details. We almost are—the thing is handled with such perfect economy; we see only a few heart-rending and soul-rending flashbacks."[6] Hirsch notes that Nazerman's flashbacks are so brief that the audience almost experiences them subliminally, which increases the intensity of our identification with Nazerman. He also points out that, unlike the traditional flashback, a character does not introduce the memory to an interlocutor, as the screen then blurs into the event from the past; instead, Nazerman's flashbacks jump at us out of nowhere, often when he is alone. In this respect, the flashbacks in *The Pawnbroker* are very different from the more classic ones, such as those found in *Sophie's Choice*, and represent an example of how *The Pawnbroker* imports techniques widely used in experimental, avant-garde cinema into a mainstream movie.

Hirsch concludes, "Formal disruption in *The Pawnbroker* is no mere aesthetic experiment; it is a cinematic symptom of a disruption in history."[7] In other words, Hirsch suggests that the way Nazerman's memories erupt seemingly out of nowhere into his consciousness functions in the film as a symbol of how the Holocaust erupted into world history with comparable abruptness, an event that seemed to have no historical precedent. While in Wallant's novel Nazerman's memories of the camps appear only in nightmarish dreams, Lumet made the decision to have the man's recollections explode into his waking awareness. (As we will see in future movies, not only in *Sophie's Choice* but also in *Ene-*

mies: A Love Story, other Holocaust survivors will also be emotionally crippled by memories that invade their present lives.)

Another way *The Pawnbroker* suggests that Nazerman hasn't really "survived" the Holocaust is through the similarities implied between his past and present life. "The shop with its bars and fences," writes Annette Insdorf, "replicates the storerooms of the concentration camp."[8] At his desk behind a metal grill, which throws a checkerboard of shadows on his face and shoulders, Nazerman is a man in a metaphoric prison, divided literally and figuratively from everyone who enters the shop. Perhaps Nazerman has reconstructed the camp around him out of a guilt-ridden desire to punish himself for having survived. Or perhaps, even though Nazerman is a Holocaust survivor himself, his guilt is meant to allude to the guilt of American Jews who certainly could have done more to help their coreligionists in Europe during the war; as Haskel Lookstein concludes: "In general, the Jewish community of the Holocaust period has been accused of being too timid in responding to the indifference of America and its Allies and, consequently, of being unequal to the unprecedented human challenge with which it was confronted."[9]

Moreover, in a controversial twist, Nazerman has become disturbingly like the Nazis who victimized him in the camps. Even Nazerman's name may be a play on "Nazi-man." As a pawnbroker, Nazerman is someone who takes away not lives but dreams by purchasing treasured heirlooms—bronzed baby shoes, a framed certificate won at a high school debating contest. These keepsakes are sold to him by the ghetto residents who stumble into his shop, desperate for some quick cash with which to buy alcohol, drugs, or simply food for the table. In one scene, when Nazerman is handed a wedding band by a mousey young woman whose marriage has ended, he flashes on a memory of the Nazis removing rings from the fingers of young women bound for the gas chambers, jewelry that would ultimately end up in the Nazis' coffers.

We eventually learn that Nazerman is being paid to maintain his shop by a ghetto crime baron, the African American Rodriguez (Brock Peters). Rodriguez uses the shop as a front for the two businesses from which he really derives his wealth: as a slum landlord and as owner of a string of local brothels. Thus, in another instance of the former victim turned victimizer, Nazerman is indirectly living off the money made through the exploitation of poor ghetto residents and prostitutes. In an arresting analogy, Insdorf calls Sol "a contemporary *Kapo*, controlling the poor clients who barter with him, but also controlled—and imprisoned—by his superiors."[10] Clearly, if Nazerman is a kind of "*Kapo*," then Rodriguez is placed in the position of "commandant." Once again, Nazerman remains, symbolically and emotionally, trapped in the camps.

When *The Pawnbroker* opened, several critics suggested that the film implied a comparison between Nazerman's present behavior and the way the German people acted during the Nazi era. For example, Penelope Gilliatt wrote that "the shame of surviving the concentration camps where his wife and family died has numbed him to present reality, including the fact that he takes money for his relatives from a Negro who lives off tenement rents. The analogy between the German in the war who didn't want to know and the Jew now who doesn't want to know is made with fair crassness."[11] *New York Times* critic Bosley Crowther made a similar observation: "By counterpointing the memories of the hero against the withdrawn and sterile life he lives amid the wretchedness of Harlem, it brings him—and us—to the realization that his unwillingness to commit himself to helping others is, in a sense, comparable to the unwillingness of the German people to involve themselves in trying to stop Hitler's rise."[12] In this respect, Nazerman is similar to the ordinary Germans in *Judgment at Nuremberg* who guzzle beer and sing folk songs in local taverns while their compatriots are being tried for war crimes by an American judge.

Eventually, in response to Ortiz constantly begging his boss to explain the secret of Jewish success in business, Nazerman launches into a tirade that offers his own embittered explanation:

> You begin with several thousand years during which you have nothing but a great, bearded legend. . . . You have no land to grow food on . . . to hunt, not enough time in one place to have a geography or an army or a land-myth. Only you have a little brain in your head and this bearded legend to . . . convince you that there *is* something special about you, no matter your poverty. With it you obtain a small piece of cloth—wool, silk, cotton. . . . You take this cloth and you cut it in two and . . . sell the two pieces for a penny or two more than you paid for the cloth. With this money . . . you buy a slightly bigger piece of cloth, which . . . may be cut into three pieces and sold for *three* pennies profit. You must never succumb to buying an extra piece of

bread . . . a luxury like a toy for your child. . . . And so you continue
until there is no longer any temptation to . . . grow food . . . [or] to
gaze at limitless land which is in your name. You repeat this process
over and over for approximately twenty centuries. And then, *voila*—
you have a mercantile heritage, you are known as a merchant, a man
with secret resources, usurer, pawnbroker, witch, and what have
you.[13]

While some critics have argued that Nazerman is blaming the Jews for
turning into greedy usurers and pawnbrokers, Nazerman clearly recognizes that this transformation was a survival mechanism in response to
oppressive circumstances. The underlying issue is whether Nazerman's
portrait of European Jewry is accurate. Of course, religious Jews would
deny that the Jewish God is nothing more than a "bearded legend." But,
while we're never told if Nazerman was a man of faith before entering
the camps, one can surely see how the Holocaust might have turned
him into a nonbeliever, as it did many other Jewish survivors, such as
Elie Wiesel (as he depicts in his memoir, *Night*).[14]

Moreover, it isn't as if Nazerman has invented the Jewish type he
analyzes. Jews were overrepresented in the moneylending profession,
not because of any innate greed in the Jewish soul but rather because
moneylending had been a despised profession to Christians ever since
Jesus threw the usurers out of the temple and was therefore one of the
few occupations the hated Jews were permitted. (Of course, not only
Christians loathe moneylenders; on the contrary, moneylenders are universally suspect—among Muslims as well, even among atheists.) One
can argue that being relegated in such numbers to this stigmatized
profession had a dysfunctional effect on the Jewish community. Clearly,
the Jews' status as moneylenders (and also often as tax collectors for the
local aristocracy) made them targets of abuse for centuries from their
Christian neighbors, both those in high and low places; for example, in
his notorious pamphlet *About the Jews and Their Lies*, Martin Luther
declared, "They [the Jews] have captured us and our goods through
their accursed usury."[15] How could such constant opprobrium not take
its toll?

Crammed into filthy ghettos, European Jewry was bowed and
scarred by these draconian prohibitions. As Rita Steinhardt Botwinick
writes, "Many Jews forgot how to play, how to enjoy the beauty of
nature, and how to take pleasure from physical activity."[16] The Zionist

movement—which created the institution of the kibbutz in order to return Jews to the land—originated in the belief that its mission was to create a "New Jew," contrasted with the allegedly warped Jews of Europe. As Tom Segev reports in *The Seventh Million: The Israelis and the Holocaust*, when Zionists first encountered Jewish Holocaust survivors in the DP (displaced persons) camps, they attributed the "cynicism, nihilism and lawlessness" of the refugees "not only to the survivors' experience in the camps . . . but also to their life in . . . exile, before the Holocaust. . . . As proud Zionists, [they] had always detested . . . the 'Exile mentality.'"[17] Under the circumstances, is Nazerman a self-hating Jew because he concludes that the European Jew was "a man with secret resources, usurer, pawnbroker, witch, and what have you"?

In short, rather than reinforcing "cheap Jew" stereotypes, Nazerman is participating in a painful but necessary discussion about the nature of European Jewry in which Jews and others have been long engaged. Moreover, every view Nazerman expresses must be weighed in the context of his traumatization as a Holocaust survivor. Finally, it's important to emphasize that from a contemporary perspective there is nothing demeaning or immoral about being a moneylender or a merchant. Today, banks lend money and are not vilified for it.

At the climax of *The Pawnbroker*, Ortiz reneges on his newfound principles by succumbing to the constant pressure exerted by his former gang members to help them rob Nazerman's pawnshop. Ortiz's motives for this disloyalty aren't clarified, but it seems he is devastated when, late in the film, the always acerbic Nazerman tells his assistant, "You're nothing to me." Since Ortiz sees Nazerman as a mentor and perhaps even a father figure (as far as we know, Ortiz is fatherless), Nazerman's rejection crushes him. Thus, the film suggests that Nazerman himself bears some responsibility for the robbery—that the crime is, in a sense, a consequence of the way Nazerman pushes anyone away who tries to reach out to him. When the three thieves arrive to rob his shop, Nazerman is plunged in a memory of three Nazis arriving to round up his family, thus, linking these two events in the viewer's mind.

When Nazerman, who by now seems almost eager to die, refuses to hand over his cash, one thief threatens him with a gun. This gesture prompts Ortiz to have a change of heart. As Ortiz rushes to save his employer, he is fatally shot. Crouching over Ortiz's body, his assistant's blood on his hands (literally and perhaps figuratively), Nazerman finally breaks down, but the gut-wrenching scream he emits is silent. Then, in an unforgettable gesture, Nazerman presses his palm on the spike that holds the pawnshop tickets until he draws blood. He then stumbles through the crowd that's gathered around Ortiz's body, and the film's final image (shot from above) is of Nazerman wandering aimlessly through the streets of Spanish Harlem.

What are we to make of this dramatic conclusion? When, triggered by Ortiz's death, all Nazerman's repressed emotions finally explode, it is significant that his scream is silent. The silence of that scream seems emblematic of the tragic situation of the Holocaust survivor, who has witnessed horrors so awful they can't be communicated. It may also suggest that the outside world is not interested in hearing this Ancient Mariner's disturbing truths (at least in 1965). Finally, the silent scream may imply Nazerman's helplessness at dealing with continued anti-Semitism even after the Holocaust; earlier in the movie—for example, one client calls Nazerman a "money-grubbing kike." Through Nazerman's arresting gesture of impaling his hand on the shop's ticket spike, we see that Nazerman has devolved into a being who barely exists apart from his disreputable profession—a kind of living ticket stub. (That Nazerman doesn't exist apart from his job may also be implied by titling the film *The Pawnbroker*.)

As well, Nazerman punishes himself because he recognizes that he bears indirect responsibility for Ortiz's death, since it was Nazerman's rejection of Ortiz that pushed his assistant into allying himself with the gang. Nazerman recognizes that in a sense Ortiz has died in his place. Through Ortiz's death, the movie suggests a parallel between post-Holocaust anti-Semitism and racism in contemporary America.

Many critics have found *The Pawnbroker*'s climax abundant in Christian symbolism. Ilan Avisar, for example, noting that Ortiz's first name is Jesus, argues that "Ortiz is the sacrificial martyr whose death saves Nazerman's life."[18] Avisar also sees the film as rife with heavy-handed religious puns on Nazerman's name. Through his salvation, Avisar argues, Nazerman goes from being a "Nazi-man" to being another "man of Nazareth." In other words, Ortiz's blood on his hands represents a kind of baptism; Nazerman becomes saved and Christianized at the same time in a moment of symbolic crucifixion. One might take Avisar's reading a step further and interpret the wound Nazerman

draws when he impales his hand on the ticket spike as a kind of stigma-
ta.

If true, Avisar's Christian reading of the film's conclusion is damning. While it may be valid to portray a Jewish Holocaust survivor as
loveless and exploitive, to reward him with a Christianized salvation
seems unacceptable. After all, Christian theology believes that Christ's
Second Coming will be preceded by the "conversion of the Jews." In
her analysis of the book version of *The Pawnbroker*, Dorothy Bilik
found that Wallant expressed "unease with Jewish materials, ancient
and modern," and perhaps some of that "unease" has been transferred
to the screen.[19]

However, there is a problem with Avisar's interpretation: it's by no
means clear that Nazerman *is* saved at the film's conclusion. In Wallant's novel, Nazerman's salvation is made manifest. Earlier in the story,
Nazerman's sometime girlfriend, Tessie, phoned to inform him that her
father had died, and Nazerman had responded with callous indifference. Now, after Ortiz's death, the book ends: "Then he began walking
to the subway to take the long underground journey to Tessie's house,
to help her mourn." In the film, in sharp contrast, Nazerman simply
wanders off into Spanish Harlem, directionless and alone. Thus, while
the book ends with Nazerman connecting with another human being,
Lumet's version does the opposite: it deepens Nazerman's already profound isolation. If the director's intention, like Wallant's, is to suggest
that Nazerman has been "saved" by Ortiz's death, why doesn't he end
the film with a scene in which Nazerman says kaddish with Tessie?
(Indeed, including such a scene in the original script might have satisfied MGM's desire for an upbeat ending.) The film's ambiguous, open-
ended conclusion is another way, like its original use of flashbacks, in
which *The Pawnbroker* has more in common with experimental, avant-
garde cinema than it does with Hollywood movies, which almost invariably wrap up with a neat, unequivocal finale. Clearly, in rejecting this
ending, Lumet intends not to save Nazerman but rather to exacerbate
his alienation. And, if Nazerman hasn't been "saved," it becomes much
less likely he's been "Christianized" in the ways that Avisar suggests.

Just as *Judgment at Nuremberg* used the Holocaust to allude to
contemporary American conflicts regarding civil rights and class exploitation, some critics see Lumet as suggesting a parallel between the
Nazis' persecution of the Jews and America's persecution of the largely

black and Hispanic urban poor in 1960s Harlem. As film critic Andrew Sarris quipped at the time: "The idea behind the production seems to be that by combining the Jewish Problem with the Negro Problem the picture would be twice as profound because the audience would be twice as depressed."[20] If such a combination was indeed Lumet's intent, he may have been influenced in this direction by the fact that he was married at the time to the civil rights activist (as well as singer and actress) Lena Horne.

If, indeed, *The Pawnbroker* is implying a direct comparison between Nazi Germany and contemporary Spanish Harlem, then such a comparison is clearly facile. However riven with racial and economic conflict, 1960s America was no Nazi Germany. However, if a director sees resemblances between two different societies, does that necessarily imply that he thinks the societies identical? Can't an analogy with the Holocaust be used to shed light on injustices in other societies, not because these societies are mirror images but rather because the Holocaust was such an ultimate atrocity that it illuminates other events in ways less extreme catastrophes cannot? Lumet himself stated that in *The Pawnbroker* "there certainly was no attempt to show Harlem as a modern concentration camp."[21] Why not take the director at his word? Searching for a way to express his agony at America's racial injustice, the socially conscious Lumet must have found comparison with the Holocaust inexact but useful. Moreover, especially in the postwar period, a comparison can be drawn between the conditions in America for both Jews and other ethnic minorities, since all these groups were outsiders to the WASP establishment that controlled the country. Given this parallel, it's no surprise that American Jews took such an active role in the black civil rights struggle, far out of proportion to their numbers in the population at large.[22] Thus, it makes sense that in making a Holocaust-oriented film, a Jewish director like Lumet might draw comparisons with the plight of Latinos and African Americans.

To its credit, *The Pawnbroker* dares to present us with a resolutely *un*ennobled Holocaust survivor. When the film appeared, many critics felt Nazerman's character displayed what was often termed the "survivor syndrome." Writing in the Zionist journal *Midstream*, Albert Bermel credits both Lumet and Wallant, in their depiction of the "psychopathology of Nazerman," with having researched this syndrome, which he claims is characterized by "morose behavior, withdrawal, general

apathy alternating with occasional short-lived angry outbursts . . . perva-
sive guilt . . . and spells of confusion with the past—when every building
looks to them like the Auschwitz blockhouse, every policeman like an
S.S. guard."23

A few critics, however, questioned the consensus that most survivors, like Nazerman, were broken men and women. The *New Republic's* Stanley Kaufmann wrote at the time:

> Why is Sol still so much in the grip of the past? Why is this particular
> survivor so specially paralyzed? Many of us have known people who
> have . . . suffered so grossly that the fact of life thereafter seems (to
> us) incredible; yet there they are living—working, quarreling, remar-
> rying, propagating deliberately . . . to refute the ovens. They are
> certainly not unmarked or forgetful; yet they are certainly not numb
> like Sol. I do not argue that all people must respond similarly to
> experience, only that because Sol is such a remarkable exception, we
> miss an explanation.24

What film was Kaufmann watching? As discussed, in one flashback
Nazerman watches helplessly as a friend and fellow prisoner tries to
scale the camp fence and escape, only to be shot dead by a guard. In
another flashback, even more traumatic, Nazerman has his head
smashed through a window so that he can be forced to watch a guard
raping his wife. Why aren't these memories "explanation" enough for
Nazerman's present emotional paralysis?

In truth, in American culture at large, it is Kaufmann's sunny view
about survivors happily working and propagating that has tended to win
out over Bermel's more pessimistic diagnosis of the "survivor syndrome," because many Americans need to believe that Holocaust survivors have been ennobled by their suffering. We see that need in the
affirmative ending to *The Diary of Anne Frank*. We see it in the need to
"convert" survivors who've lost their faith—a plot motif found in a sci-
ence-fiction film I'll discuss, *X-Men*. We see it in Americans' adulation
of the Italian film *Life Is Beautiful*—in which the experience of the
camps enables a father to demonstrate his indestructible love for his
young son.

Nazerman's catatonia may be extreme, but it's unlikely that most
other Holocaust survivors escaped unscathed. Moreover, to insist that
all survivors can transcend their suffering is a way to deny the disturb-

ing reality that most, whatever recovery they achieve, retain permanent scars. Holocaust scholar Lawrence Langer, for one, has argued that any talk of ennobled suffering falsifies the very essence of the Holocaust experience: "Among the leading ideas we are forced to surrender as we read [Holocaust testimonies and literature] is the comforting notion that suffering has meaning—that it strengthens, ennobles, or redeems the human soul. The anguish of the victims in ghettos and camps, in hiding or in flight, in brave if futile rebellion, can be neither soothed nor diminished by a vocabulary of consolation."[25] For recognizing this reality, *The Pawnbroker* deserves praise.

7

THE HOLOCAUST ON THE HORIZON
Cabaret

Cabaret had a long history before it arrived on the screen in 1972. The film originated as two short novels, *Mr. Norris Changes Trains* and *Goodbye to Berlin*, both published in the 1930s by the British writer Christopher Isherwood. A homosexual, Isherwood had gone to Berlin in the early 1930s with his friend, the poet W. H. Auden, looking to indulge in the city's vaunted gay subculture, so different from Edwardian England, where homosexuality was criminalized. As Isherwood relates in a memoir published decades later, *Christopher and His Kind*, both men indulged fairly indiscriminately, and Isherwood wound up in a serious relationship with a young German named Heinz, who during World War II was imprisoned by the Nazis for draft evasion. It was Isherwood's relationship with Heinz, and his boyfriend's German nationality, that turned Isherwood into a pacifist during the war. *Goodbye to Berlin*, in particular, is more a series of beautifully drawn sketches than a developed novel, displaying Isherwood's trademark gift for dialogue (which he'd later exploit as a Hollywood screenwriter). Eventually, the narrator meets the unforgettable Sally Bowles—a young, bohemian English expatriate trying to succeed as an actress, with little talent and less success but possessed of an irrepressible zest for life. Not only is Sally the most memorable character in Isherwood's novel, but she'd go on to be the star of both the play and film versions of *Cabaret*. In

Goodbye to Berlin, Sally and the novel's male protagonist (based on Isherwood himself) form a platonic but intimate friendship.

The books are autobiographical; Isherwood even uses his own name for the narrator. But the author announces in the famous opening to *Goodbye to Berlin* that "I am a camera with its shutter open"; that is, he will be present in the action more as a witness than as a participant. One senses that Isherwood felt compelled to adopt this perspective because he was a naturally autobiographical writer who, due to the era's homophobia, couldn't reveal that he was gay. However, in his two Berlin novels, Isherwood did feel free to write frankly about the Nazi rise he witnessed firsthand, and he proved to be an astute observer of the threat it posed at a time when many in the West remained oblivious.

The first stage version of Isherwood's Berlin stories was as a 1951 dramatic play by John Van Druten called *I Am a Camera*, starring Julie Harris as Sally Bowles. *I Am a Camera*, however, downplayed Isherwood's Nazi material in a way that recalls Hollywood's timid reluctance to anger Hitler in the films it made before America's entry into the war. *New York Times* reviewer Michiko Kakutani has described Van Druten's play as "less a story about pre-World War II Germany than a gently comic portrait of a Holly Golightly who happened to find herself in Hitler's Berlin."[1]

The stories were next transformed into a far more risk-taking Broadway musical. *Cabaret* opened at the Broadhurst Theater on October 20, 1966, under the direction of Hal Prince, with a book by Joe Masteroff and songs by John Kander and Fred Ebb—all Broadway veterans. Joel Grey played the cabaret's Master of Ceremonies (a role he reprised for the film); Bert Convy played the Isherwood character, cast as an American named Bradshaw; Jill Haworth was Sally Bowles; and the famed Austrian-born actress Lotte Lenya played Fräulein Schneider, the landlady of the Berlin boarding house where Bradshaw and Bowles reside. Dealing with such controversial material as sexual decadence and the rise of Hitler, *Cabaret* represented a radical departure from the traditional Broadway musical of the time, such as *Hello Dolly* and *The Music Man*, which had offered audiences far more wholesome fare. The gamble paid off; the play was a smash, drawing large, appreciative crowds and winning eight Tony Awards, including Best Musical. According to Grey, *Cabaret*'s success shocked everyone involved in the production. Because of its unorthodox approach and subject matter, they had all expected it to bomb.

The play's male lead is the bright, reserved, young American writer Clifford Bradshaw, who, arriving in Berlin for reasons that are never clear, plans to support himself by giving English lessons. Bradshaw is the Jamesian innocent American abroad—straightforward, honest, and no match for the decadent European world he will encounter. Bradshaw meets Sally when he watches her in the Kit Kat Club singing a tune that reflects her licentious lifestyle, with the refrain, "Don't tell Mama, whatever you do." True to character, Sally makes the first move. The two are mismatched in countless ways, including politically. When Sally discovers a copy of *Mein Kampf* atop Bradshaw's desk, he explains, "I thought I should know *something* about German politics." "Why?" Sally replies. "You're an American!"

There is one main Jewish character in the play, Herr Schultz, a middle-aged rooming-house border who owns a fruit store. Perpetually warm and cheerful, Schultz becomes first the lover and then the fiancé of the house's middle-aged proprietress, Fräulein Schneider—a touching relationship between two lonely older people who are thrilled to have found one another. However, the engagement proves ill fated, due to the long reach of Nazi anti-Semitism. Schneider worries that if she marries a Jew she will lose her license to rent rooms. As if to confirm her fears, soon after she voices this concern, a brick crashes through the window of Schultz's shop. Schultz dismisses the idea that the vandalism is politically motivated, displaying a credulity that characterizes all of Schultz's responses to the rise of the Nazis.

Just as *Cabaret* depicts one principle Jewish character, so also, serving as his antithesis in this well-structured play, it provides us with one central Nazi, who proves to be Bradshaw's seemingly genial pupil, Ernst Ludwig. While Herr Schultz and Fräulein Schneider are celebrating their engagement at a party at the boarding house, Ludwig arrives sporting a swastika armband. Bradshaw expresses his indignation. "Our party will be the builders of a new Germany," Ludwig retorts. Their argument is temporarily halted when Herr Schultz offers to serenade the revelers with an ersatz Yiddish folk song, supplied by Ebb and Kander. It's a sentimental tune about a *meeskite*, the Yiddish word for "ugly" or "funny-looking." The song concludes with a cloying moral:

"Anyone responsible for loveliness, large or small / Is not a meeskite at all!"

The relevance of this song is unclear. Why should a German Jew, on the eve of Hitler's seizure of power, sing this particular song to an audience that includes an ardent Nazi? Indeed, the song conjures up uncomfortable echoes of the common anti-Semitic stereotype that Jews are physically ugly. More benignly, the song recalls the archetypal shtetl Jew, who is a "little man," stoically weathering the buffets of fate, a recurrent figure in Yiddish literature. On a literal level, the tune implies that the "meeskite," Herr Schultz, has found beauty and been rendered beautiful through his love for another meeskite, Fräulein Schneider. Both the film version of *Cabaret* and the play's 1997 Broadway revival wisely dropped this treacly and problematic number from the repertoire.

Ultimately, Fräulein Schneider breaks off the engagement. "I have battled alone," she tells Bradshaw, "and I have survived. . . . For, in the end, what other choice have I? This is my world!" Although one might criticize Schneider for bowing to Nazi anti-Semitism, the play suggests she has no choice and presents her as somewhat admirable in her indefatigable ability to carry on.

Cabaret fails to explain why Ernst Ludwig has become a devout Nazi, other than suggesting (again without explanation) that Ludwig is anti-Semitic. The character remains a cipher. Thus, an opportunity is missed to explore why the German people fell under Hitler's spell. True, *Cabaret*'s depiction of Nazism sets it apart from any previous Broadway musical, but the investigation only goes so far. Like *Judgment at Nuremberg* and *The Pawnbroker*, however, the stage version of *Cabaret* does imply something about the 1960s era in America in which it was created and performed. It was a time of violent social unrest and growing opposition to the Vietnam War that bore more than a passing resemblance to Weimar-era Germany.

The film version of *Cabaret* was directed by Bob Fosse, whose previous career had been primarily not in Hollywood but on Broadway, as the choreographer of such lavish musicals as *Damn Yankees* and *How to Succeed in Business without Really Trying*. Fosse strove to make *Cabaret* authentic, shooting the film on location in West Berlin and Munich and filling the German roles with German actors, such as Helmut Griem, who plays decadent German aristocrat Maximilian von Heune.

Fosse related that he tried to base his version of *Cabaret* less on the musical than on Isherwood's novel. To that end, the director didn't want to use any members of the Broadway cast (and cast Joel Grey only reluctantly, after being urged to do so by the movie's producer). Fosse did, however, bring back Kander and Ebb to write three new songs for the film: "Maybe This Time," "Mein Herr," and "The Money Song." As Sally, Fosse chose Liza Minnelli, who had already been performing songs from the musical *Cabaret* in her traveling stage show. For the role of Brian (named Cliff in the play), Fosse picked the young British actor Michael York.

Thus, the director reversed the nationalities of the two principles, with Brian now British, while Sally is an American. Because Sally is the film's most captivating character, Fosse may have concluded that an American Sally would have more appeal to an American audience. But Sally seems more appropriate as an American in other respects as well. With her insistence on remaining upbeat in the face of the many vicissitudes of her life, even to the point of willful self-delusion, Sally symbolizes classic American optimism, both its irrepressibility and its frequent self-deception. By the same token, Brian seems more suitable as an Englishman, with his concern for propriety and the "stiff upper lip" he manifests when problems arise.

Every bit as successful as the play, the film might have won the 1972 Best Picture Oscar if it hadn't had the misfortune of competing against *The Godfather*. Even so, the movie was nominated for ten Oscars and won eight: Minnelli for Best Actress; Grey for Best Supporting Actor; Fosse for Best Director; Geoffrey Unsworth for Best Cinematography; David Bretherton for Best Editing; Ralph Burns for Best Music, Scoring Original Song Score, and/or Adaptation; Robert Knudson and David Hildyard for Best Sound; and Rolf Zehetbauer, Hans Jürgen Keibach, and Herbert Strabel for Best Art Direction/Set Decoration.

Like the play, the film opens in and repeatedly returns to the Kit Kat Club, where all Sally's musical numbers are performed. The cabaret itself has multiple thematic and symbolic connotations. On the one hand, the club represents an escape for the drunken, rowdy crowds from the frightening social and political realities transpiring outside as Nazi power swells. As he introduces the performances, the emcee croons to the audience, "Leave your troubles outside! So—life is disappointing? Forget it! In here life is beautiful—the girls are beautiful—

even the orchestra is beautiful." Alcohol, half-naked girls, raucous music, transvestites, slapstick routines, salacious double entendres—the cabaret offers a plethora of opiates for weary, worried souls.

At the same time, it is a microcosm of the Weimar Era in its death throes. Not only an escape from the outside world, it also *is* that world, in which the German people have given themselves up to mindless hedonism, oblivious to the looming specter of totalitarianism. Or perhaps the German people are aware but frantically sublimating their fears; *Cabaret* suggests that Weimar-era Germany, sensing the end was near, plunged into a kind of desperate decadence, a final fling before the curtain came down forever. Apparently, the film's depiction of Weimar Germany as a cesspool of depravity was historically accurate. American actress Louise Brooks lived in Berlin during this period and later recalled, "Sex was the business of the town. At the Eden Hotel, where I lived . . . the café bar was lined with the higher priced trollops. The economy girls walked the street outside. On the corner stood the girls in boots, advertising flagellation. Actors' agents pimped for the ladies in luxury apartments in the Bavarian quarter. Race-track touts at the Hoppegarten arranged orgies for groups of sportsmen. The nightclub Eldorado displayed an enticing line of homosexuals dressed as women. At the Maly, there was a choice of feminine or collar-and-tie lesbians. Collective lust roared unashamed at the theater."[2]

Of all the cabaret's disturbing characters, perhaps the most disturbing is the mysterious, androgynous, vaguely sinister Master of Ceremonies, who is never given a name and is never seen outside the club. Clad in a tight black tuxedo jacket, sporting lipstick and rouge, his dark hair slicked back, the Emcee is a decadent figure, mildly sadistic and utterly without pity, but he also seems a blank—almost a kind of doll or robot. Without an inner life, he seems willing and able to adapt himself to any conditions, to follow any master who comes along. In that respect, he may represent the paradigmatic German in the early days of the Nazi rise to power.

Like Fräulein Schneider, the Emcee is an inveterate survivor, but of a far more menacing kind. His chameleon-like adaptations to fascism are implied late in the film in a short scene in which he and his chorus girls engage in a spirited, high-kicking dance that abruptly transforms into martial music backed by military-sounding drums, which prompt the Emcee and the girls to halt their dancing and goose-step off the stage. The Emcee is in drag in this scene, having donned a blonde wig and fishnet stockings, and it's only gradually that we realize he isn't merely one of the chorus girls. The scene's disturbing blend of Nazism and transvestitism suggests how Hitler's regime was a reaction to the decadent murk that infected Weimar Germany but perhaps also alludes to the perversity of the Nazi regime itself.

In one song the Emcee performs, "If You Could See Her," *Cabaret* subtly examines Nazi anti-Semitism. In this number, the Emcee appears hand-in-hand with a gorilla clad in a chic dress and bonnet and clutching a handbag. The Emcee warbles a ditty in which he laments how a callously judgmental society refuses to try to understand what has attracted him to his simian beloved: "When we're in public together / I hear society groan / But if they could see her through my eyes / Maybe they'd leave us alone." The singer enumerates his darling's manifold virtues: "She's clever, she's smart, she reads music / She doesn't smoke or drink gin like I do." But what elevates "If You Could See Her" beyond farce is its punch line. After the Emcee has beseeched one last

Figure 7.1. *Cabaret* (1972). Nightclub singer Sally Bowles (Liza Minnelli) performs with the club's leering emcee (Joel Grey). [Screen grab]

time, "If you could see her through my eyes," he leans toward the audience, cups his hand to his mouth, and mutters, sotto voce, "She wouldn't look *Jewish* at all!"

Lamentably, in the 1966 play, although this line was listed in the script as an "alternate," what Joel Grey actually sang was, "She isn't a *meeskite* at all!" Apparently, the Broadway *Cabaret* was willing to address sexual decadence, abortion, transvestitism, prostitution, promiscuity, and so on, but didn't dare to include a frank allusion to Nazi anti-Semitism, which was deemed too dicey for the Great White Way. Did Broadway audiences catch on that *"meeskite"* was actually a coded reference to Jews? Perhaps, but more obtuse audience members may have assumed that "If You Could See Her" was merely a schmaltzy song, like *"Meeskite,"* about how the ugly are also deserving of love, albeit with a more sardonic spin on the theme.

In the PBS documentary *Broadway Musicals: A Jewish Legacy*, Hal Prince, the producer of the play version of *Cabaret*, argues that using "Jewish" at the end of the song would have been viewed as "special pleading." We heard these same arguments made a decade earlier in regard to *The Diary of Anne Frank*. Fortunately, the creators of the film version of *Cabaret* were more daring than their predecessors.

Concluded properly, "If You Could See Her" is an incisive look at the nature of Nazi anti-Semitism. Indeed, Hitler explicitly viewed Jews as subhuman. From a Darwinian perspective, gorillas are often seen as less evolved ancestors of human beings, especially notable for their physical ugliness. As noted, one commonplace of anti-Semitic iconography was to depict the Jews as physically repulsive. As well, the Nuremberg Laws officially and quite severely proscribed marriages or any sexual (or merely affectionate) relations between Aryans and Jews, which the Nazis almost literally considered as being between creatures of different species—a proscription relevant to the Feldenstein case in *Judgment at Nuremberg*. These specific slurs against the stereotypical Jewess were a subgenre of anti-Semitic ideology. Like her male coreligionist, the Jewess was often portrayed as homely, but she was also frequently depicted as nefariously seducing the Aryan male, usually with her wealth, which was indicated by her lavish attire, the kind of finery that also adorns the gorilla in the song. As noted, even in *The Diary of Anne Frank*, Mrs. Van Daan can be seen as adhering to the stereotype of the shallow, materialistic Jewess. Finally, in using slapstick to make a

deadly serious point about Nazism, the scene recalls similar moments in
The Great Dictator and *To Be or Not to Be*.

In composing the screenplay of *Cabaret*, Jay Presson Allen went
further than the play in foregrounding Nazi evil. For example, Fosse
and Allen add an early scene in which the owner of the Kit Kat Club
evicts a Brown Shirt from his establishment for distributing Nazi literature to the patrons, only to be subsequently beaten to a pulp in an alley
outside the club by a gang of *Sturmabteilung* (or SA) thugs. The scene
underscores the degree to which the Nazis are now so powerful that
they can no longer be safely dismissed by those Germans revolted by
their politics.

In another new scene, Brian is disgusted to find the other lodgers in
the boarding house gathered in the parlor listening to a Hitler speech
on the radio and earnestly discussing among themselves the danger
posed to the German economy by the "International Jewish Conspira-
cy." The scene serves a similar function to one in the play in which the
celebrants at Schultz and Schneider's engagement party burst into a
Nazi anthem. In both instances, we see that Nazism doesn't appeal only
to fringe elements of the German population; on the contrary, ordinary
Germans are being duped. But the scene in the film is more effective in
this regard, because it deals more specifically with the allegations Hitler
leveled against the Jews: namely, in this case, that greedy, powerful
Jewish financiers were bankrupting Germany. It's a canard with obvious
appeal to the German public, since it strikes in the pocketbook, always
the ideal target for political demagoguery, especially in a time, like the
era of the Weimar Republic, when the German economy was in shambles. Indeed, in only one respect does the film fall short of the play in
terms of spotlighting the Nazi threat—since the character of Ernst
Ludwig is dropped, the movie lacks a central figure who represents a
purely Nazi frame of mind.

Perhaps the film's most penetrating insight into the reasons behind
the Nazi ascension is garnered through the addition of the memorable
character Baron Maximilian von Heune, an aristocratic German playboy. In the course of his carousing, Max turns up at the Kit Kat Club,
where he quickly adopts Sally and Brian as his latest playthings—buying
them luxuries, treating them to a weekend as guests at his lavish estate,
having sex with each of them in turn, promising them an exotic safari to
the wilds of Africa. But then, just when Sally is convinced that Max will

provide both her and Brian with a permanent meal ticket, he grows bored with their company and drops the couple precipitously. The baron symbolizes the decadent German aristocracy whose irresponsibility, the film suggests, allowed Hitler to come to power.

In one scene, Max, Sally, and Brian, tooling around Berlin in Max's limousine, see the draped body of a victim of the Nazis. "The Nazis are thugs," Max remarks complacently. "But let the Nazis get rid of the Communists. Then we'll control them." Max's words are historically accurate; when the Nazis first appeared on the scene, German conservatives, viewing them as a bunch of rubes, did think they could manipulate the Nazis into vanquishing a political group they saw as a much greater threat, the Communists, who they believed had the potential to take over Germany in the same way they subverted the Russian empire.[3] The delusion underlying Max's view of the Nazis is highlighted in one of the film's most significant scenes, suggesting the way Hitler was able to brainwash Germany. In this scene, Max's limo stops at a rural German beer garden. While Sally sleeps off a full night of partying in the car, Max and Brian pause for refreshment. A blond-haired, blue-eyed adolescent with delicate, handsome features begins serenading the crowd with "Tomorrow Belongs to Me" (a song that appeared in the musical during the engagement party). As the camera slowly pulls back from the boy's face, we perceive that he is clad in the uniform of the Hitler Youth, including a swastika armband, and realize that the song is not some harmless folk ballad but rather a Nazi anthem. Gradually, more and more of the beer garden's customers start singing along, until the entire assembly has joined in, except for one old German peasant, who scratches his head and frowns, presumably confused and perturbed at the direction in which his country is heading. When the boy finishes the song, he extends his right arm in a disciplined Nazi salute, whereupon the entire crowd salutes back. As Max and Brian return to the car, Brian asks rhetorically, "Do you still think you can control them?" Max doesn't reply, and as the limo pulls off down the country road, "Tomorrow Belongs to Me" continues to sound in the background. It's such a catchy tune that we, the audience, almost feel compelled to sing along. As a result, we understand on a visceral level how seductive the Nazi movement could be.

While dropping the doomed Herr Schultz, the film adds two new well-developed German Jewish characters, Fritz Wendel (Fritz Wepper) and Natalia Landauer (Marisa Berenson). One of Brian's English-language pupils, Fritz is an impecunious young man who, originally for financial reasons, decides to woo the wealthy Natalia, an heiress whose father owns a famous Berlin department store. The decorous Natalia, while equally attracted to Fritz, repels his hapless attempts at seduction. When Fritz asks Natalia to marry him, she declines, in part because she fears he's a gigolo after her fortune but primarily because she thinks Fritz isn't Jewish. Ironically, however, it turns out that Fritz, as he confesses to Brian, *is* a Jew and has been pretending to be Protestant to escape anti-Semitic persecution. By now Fritz is wildly enamored of Natalia. Reclaiming his Jewish identity at the very moment when Hitler is poised to seize power, Fritz weds Natalia in a traditional Jewish ceremony. In an artful juxtaposition, the wedding scene immediately follows the one in which the Emcee performs "If You Could See Her." Thus, Fritz traverses a long moral trajectory—from a selfish fortune hunter to a man who places himself in mortal danger to be with the woman he loves.

Both Fritz and Natalia are highly sympathetic Jewish characters. Natalia, in particular, comes across as an exceedingly fragile flower, childlike, all delicacy and sensitivity; one is hard-pressed to imagine anyone more vulnerable to the Nazi threat. When a pair of Brown Shirts slit the throat of her beloved dog, leaving its carcass on her doorstep, the act seems to foreshadow her own demise in the Holocaust, since she is just as helpless as her lapdog.

Of Fritz and Natasha, Judith Doneson writes, "Perhaps they serve as counterpoints to the decadence of their friends. . . . This accords with one commonly held stereotype of Jews as sober and steadfast types. . . . The Jew becomes . . . a figure of continuity and stability in a world where everything is in flux and chaos—indeed a positive statement about the Jew and his miraculous ability to survive the Holocaust to come."[4] I agree with Doneson (Natasha is another example, like the fictionalized Anne Frank, of the sanctified Jewish Holocaust victim), except for her odd insistence that Fritz and Natasha represent the Jews' "ability to *survive* the Holocaust." On the contrary, the salient feature of both characters is that they are doomed. Their wedding ceremony might as well be their funeral. Natasha seems largely oblivious to the Nazi threat, until her own possessions are destroyed, but Fritz assuredly is not; he reclaims his Jewishness fully aware of the doom into which he has plunged—a sacrifice he is willing to make for the woman he loves.

The insertion of homosexuality into the story is another way the film differs from the musical. In the play, Sally and Cliff have a straightforward heterosexual affair. In the movie, in contrast, the sexually forward Sally makes a pass at Brian, only to intuit, based on his inert response, that Brian is gay. Turning Sally's lover into a homosexual makes their relationship infinitely more interesting. Brian's homosexuality erects an added obstacle impeding the progress of this doomed romance, a second hurdle that must be cleared along with Sally's pronounced aversion to monogamy. When the couple decide to wed, after Sally learns she is pregnant (though unsure who the father is), we wonder not only how Sally can possibly turn into a dutiful wife and mother but also how Brian can act straight, even as we understand fully why the two outcasts could be drawn to this traditional family arrangement.

Of course, since Christopher Isherwood himself was gay, this plot twist seems one way Fosse has fulfilled his professed ambition to return the story to its original source. (Even so, when Isherwood himself saw a screening of the movie, at the end he reportedly leapt to his feet and exclaimed, "I never slept with any damn woman!") Finally, since the Nazis targeted gays as well as Jews, there's an implicit parallel between these homosexual allusions and the film's depiction of Nazi anti-Semitism. *Cabaret*'s inclusion of homosexual material foreshadows the play and film versions of *Bent*, about the Nazi persecution of German gays.

As in the play, Sally aborts her baby, selling the fur coat Max had bought her to pay for the operation—a decision that destroys not only her engagement to Brian but their entire relationship. After this heartbreaking scene, which leads to Brian returning to England, while Sally remains in Berlin, Sally offers a musical explanation for her life choices via the play's title song, which tells the story of a hooker named Elsie, who died young of "too much pills and liquor." A few stanzas later, Sally spells out the personal relevance of Elsie's story: "And as for me / I made up my mind back in Chelsea / When I go, I'm going like Elsie." In other words, Sally, like Elsie, has unapologetically chosen a life of pure hedonism, knowing full well it will lead to her own destruction. One wonders what will happen to Sally under the Nazi regime; it's hard to imagine that she'll fare well, especially once Hitler declares war on America. But perhaps it doesn't matter. Before the Nazis have a chance

to destroy Sally, there's an excellent chance she'll already have destroyed herself. This is the pathos underlying the surface gaiety of the
song's famous refrain: "Life is a cabaret, old chum / Come to the cabaret."

Cabaret ends as it begins, with the Emcee and the rest of the company singing "*Willkommen,*" welcoming the crowd in several languages
to the endless joys proffered by the Kit Kat Club. In the play, large
mirrors on stage reflect the audience back to itself, implicating viewers
in the narrative. In the movie, at both start and finish, the camera
lingers on a reflection of the crowd, grotesquely distorted as in a fun
house mirror—except that in the closing shot several uniformed Nazis
are glimpsed in the audience, their swastika armbands prominent. No
longer looming on the horizon, the Nazis have attained power. Rather
than being outside the escapist world of the cabaret, they are now
thronging the tables.

In an interview, Fosse explained his film in terms that suggest the
director may have intended an implied parallel (as the play did as well)
between Weimar-era Germany and America in the 1960s and 1970s: "I
was not out to make a factual film, a documentary. . . . All I wanted to
present and remind people of was the impending doom."[5] Picking up
on this suggestion in a contemporary review, film critic Stephen Farber
opined, "*Cabaret* may even be read as a warning that contemporary
America, because of its new sexual freedom, is a sick society, comparable to Weimar Germany."[6] To extend the comparison, does *Cabaret*
imply that just as the Weimar era led to Nazism, so in America the
1960s counterculture has produced the backlash of the Nixon presiden-
cy, with perhaps far worse reactions to come?

The idea that decadence leads to totalitarianism is undeniably intriguing. If Fosse intended such contemporary parallels in *Cabaret*, that
seems another example (also found, as we've seen, in *Judgment at Nuremberg* and *The Pawnbroker*) of the way this era's filmmakers seemed
addicted to the notion of using the Holocaust as a lens through which to
view current events. However, in every case, the comparison failed to
persuade while also trivializing the Shoah in the process. But *Cabaret*
needn't be interpreted as a covert allegory about 1970s America, with a
riotous counterculture inadvertently inspiring a right-wing reaction
backed by the "moral majority." The film has plenty to say simply about
Weimar Germany and how its fragility and chaos laid the groundwork

for the Nazi ascension. The movie is best appreciated if seen as speaking about that era, and that era alone.

Like Fosse's film, the 1987 Broadway revival of *Cabaret* hinted that Cliff was bisexual and dealt more directly with the Nazis' rise to power. But that revival was tame compared to the one staged in 1998 by the Roundabout Theater Company, which radically reenvisioned the 1966 production, turning an already dark play even darker. The director was Sam Mendes, who would later direct the Oscar-winning film *American Beauty* (1999), and the codirector and choreographer was Rob Marshall, who would later direct the Oscar-winning film version of *Chicago* (2002, based on the musical that was scored by the same team of Kander and Ebb). Sally Bowles was played by British film actress Natasha Richardson, whose performance won her a Tony Award for Best Actress. The Emcee was played by the young British actor Alan Cumming, who delivered a career-making performance that inaugurated a lucrative career in Hollywood. Cumming's mere appearance on stage was arresting. Bare-chested, dressed in tight-fitting black pants that were held up by straps that ran from his crotch to his shoulders, he wore bright red lipstick and dark eye shadow, sported red sequins sparkling on his nipples, and, perhaps most notably, had visible needle tracks running up and down his arms.

In the production, the entire theater was converted into a cabaret, with audience members who purchased orchestra seats sitting at actual café tables and being served cocktails before the curtain rose by ragged-looking German waiters and waitresses. The result, according to Michiko Kakutani in her glowing review in the *New York Times Magazine*, was that "it implicates the audience in the frenetic escapism, and coming horror, of 1930s Berlin."[7] In essence, Mendes and Marshall took the onstage mirror that reflected the audience in the 1966 production a step further by including theatergoers even more intimately in the performance.

The revival also made clear that Cliff is at least bisexual and possibly just gay. For example, in an early scene in the Kit Kat Club, Cliff kisses a chorus boy on the lips. (In this production, the cabaret chorus includes men as well as women.) In the song "Two Ladies," where the Emcee celebrates a gleeful ménage a trois, one of the female roles is played by a male chorus member, which led the *New York Post's* John Podhoretz to huff that "the performers run behind a sheet and simulate various sex acts, including a genuinely disgusting homosexual practice known as 'fisting.'"[8]

In the revival, the Emcee also makes more explicit his allegiance to the Nazis. If the 1966 play objectionably downplayed Nazi and anti-Semitic themes, the 1998 revival, if anything, went too far in the opposite direction, by turning the Emcee into a raving Nazi. The Emcee makes his Hitlerian affinities known when, at the end of Act I, after the celebrants at the engagement party have sung "Tomorrow Belongs to Me," he punctuates the Nazi anthem by pulling down his pants and mooning the audience, which reveals a swastika tattooed prominently on his buttocks. Theatergoers could muse over that image during inter-mission.

The most shocking addition to this version of *Cabaret*—which fore-grounds the Holocaust in a way not only the 1966 theater production but also the 1972 film never did—comes during the Emcee's last mo-ment on stage. At this point, the backdrop flies up, revealing the brick and barbed wire of a concentration camp. Simultaneously, the Emcee removes his coat, under which he wears a camp inmate's striped uni-form, sporting both a yellow star and a pink triangle. Then he marches into a gas chamber. This is the revival's final image, panned by nearly all of the New York critics. In an otherwise largely positive *Newsday* re-view, for example, Linda Winer called this moment "a cheesy final tableau that ends this exuberantly unsentimental production on an im-age of mawkish literalism."[9] Podhoretz rendered a historical objection: "By sending the emcee to the gas chambers wearing both a Jewish star and a pink triangle, he [Mendes] clearly indicates that he wants his *Cabaret* to be, as they say, 'inclusive.' (Forget for a moment that it is deeply offensive and a profound distortion to assert that Nazi homopho-bia and the systematic murder of 6 million Jews are morally or histori-cally equivalent.)"[10]

The insertion of a concentration camp image does seem a rather exploitive attempt to up the ante even further in this programmatically in-your-face production, one that doesn't present the Holocaust in any meaningful way. The scene also clashes with the production's afore-mentioned attempt to turn the Emcee into an overt Nazi sympathizer. How can the Emcee be both pro-Nazi and a camp inmate at the same time?

Podhoretz also felt that the revival's depiction of homosexual behavior—all that "fisting" and kissing of chorus boys—inadvertently worked against the show's presumably pro-gay sympathies. The message of the show, said Podhoretz, is "that Weimar was horribly depraved—and that the depravity derived largely from its openness to homosexuality. In fact, the portrait of homosexuality . . . would warm the cockles of Pat Robertson's or Jerry Falwell's heart."[11] This criticism is unfair. Historically, after all, Weimar Berlin did have a thriving gay subculture that manifested itself primarily through bars and clubs; that's what drew Isherwood to the city in the first place. The fact that homosexuality expressed itself in this rather seedy and subterranean way wasn't because German gays were any more "depraved" than straights but simply because, even in a libertine environment like 1930s Germany, the reigning powers were homophobic enough more or less to force gay life underground.

Podhoretz was equally unimpressed by Fräulein Schneider's vaunted ethos of survival: "'I lived through inflation,' she says [when ending her engagement to Herr Schultz], 'I'll live through this.' Doubtless she will, while 6 million others won't."[12] Podhoretz's sarcasm reflects the aversion many, especially Jews, still feel to the idea that Germans also suffered during World War II. But given the Allied carpet bombing of Dresden, Hitler's insistence that Germany fight to the last man, and the rape and plunder of the German population by the advancing Soviet army, it's undeniable that Germany suffered during the war, and suffered horribly. With the passage of time, this reality has become clearer both inside and outside Germany. It is underscored, for example, in Gunter Grass's 2002 novel, *Crabwalk*, about the sinking of the *Wilhelm Gustloff*, a German cruise ship turned refugee carrier, which was attacked by a Soviet submarine in 1945, causing nine thousand Germans to drown in the Baltic Sea—the deadliest maritime disaster of all time. As the Nobel Prize–winning author of *The Tin Drum*, which contained a scathing denunciation of the complicity of the German people with Hitler's regime, Grass is well positioned to dramatize in this later work how much ordinary Germans were afflicted during World War II.

In the final analysis, critical opinion about the quality of the 1998 revival of *Cabaret* differed sharply. *New York Times* theater reviewer Ben Brantley maintained that "like its heroine, Sally Bowles, [the production] wants nothing more than to shock, and as with Sally, the desire winds up seeming more naive than sophisticated. . . . Mr. Mendes and Mr. Marshall are overeager to capitalize on the anything-goes license allowed a latter-day production of 'Cabaret'."[13] But critic Linda Winer called the revival a "political and pan-sexual spectacle that could only be suggested in the musical's groundbreaking 1966 premiere and in the beloved 1971 [*sic*] movie. What a grown-up treat."[14] Clearly, any production that inspired such strong and divergent feelings must be doing something interesting.

8

HOLLYWOOD HOLOCAUST THRILLERS

The Odessa File, Marathon Man, The Boys from Brazil

As if weary of the somber themes and weighty dramas presented in the 1960s in such Holocaust films as *Judgment at Nuremberg* and *The Pawnbroker*, Hollywood decided to lighten up in the 1970s by inserting the Holocaust as a plot device into a trio of otherwise fairly conventional thrillers: *The Odessa File* (1974), *Marathon Man* (1976), and *The Boys from Brazil* (1978). Despite their formulaic nature, however, these movies all feature gripping scenes and even offer some genuine insights into the Holocaust, particularly *Marathon Man*, which, at times, proves that the tropes of the thriller genre can be manipulated to shed light on the Shoah.

Directed by Ronald Neame, *The Odessa File* is based on Frederick Forsyth's 1972 best-selling novel of the same name. The film's credits list Holocaust survivor and famed Nazi hunter Simon Wiesenthal as a "documentary advisor" on the set, and a minor character in the movie is clearly based on Wiesenthal. (Another character based on Wiesenthal will assume a major role in *The Boys from Brazil*.) Wiesenthal claimed that the filmmakers had offered him a hefty sum to play himself in the movie but he'd declined because he didn't want the public to associate his Nazi hunting with the entertainment industry. Instead, a well-known Israeli stage actor, Shmuel Rodensky, played the role.

A decade after his brilliant performance as a Nazi-defending German lawyer in *Judgment at Nuremberg*, Maximilian Schell returned to the Holocaust theme to play Eduard Roschmann, a brutal former SS commandant at the Riga concentration camp. After the war, Roschmann had escaped justice through the intervention of a top-secret organization called "Odessa," composed of ex-SS officers—an organization with clandestine power in high places in the new West Germany. Odessa used its influence to arrange for Roschmann to assume a new identity in his native land.

Roschmann was an actual person, a Nazi officer who'd been second-in-command in the ghetto of Riga, the capital of Latvia, where the Jews had called him "the Butcher of Riga." Allegedly responsible for the wartime deaths of 35,000 people, Roschmann was captured by the British after Germany's defeat and put on a train to Dachau, where the Americans were holding a war crimes trial. But en route, Roschmann had escaped by leaping out a lavatory window and fled to Argentina. Before starting his novel, Forsyth had met with Wiesenthal, who'd given the writer access to his extensive file on Roschmann, whom the Nazi hunter had said was among his "top fifty wanted men."[1] The widely viewed film version of *The Odessa File* almost helped bring about Roschmann's capture. In 1977, a man in Buenos Aires saw the movie and then reported to the police that Roschmann was living on his street under an assumed name. Roschmann was arrested by Argentine police, but within twenty-four hours he'd again escaped. However, four weeks later, it was officially reported that he'd died of a heart attack in Paraguay. All in all, the case is an example of Hollywood's power to influence current events.

The film opens with an intriguing subplot involving Israel. The year is 1963, and under General Nasser's leadership, scientists in Egypt have designed warheads loaded with bubonic plague that have the capacity to wipe out the Jewish state. To be operational, all these weapons lack are guidance systems, which are currently being created by West German scientists covertly in the employ of Odessa. The Israeli secret service is feverishly trying to infiltrate the Odessa group in order to stop the scientists before the guidance systems are completed.

The implicit view of Israel reflected here is consistent with how the Jewish state was generally seen by America in the early 1970s.[2] With Israel's 1967 war not long past and its 1973 Yom Kippur war on the horizon—both wars Israel undertook against a large coalition of Arab forces with its very survival at stake—America felt understandable concern for its close ally. Moreover, Israel's stunningly swift victory in 1967, against massive odds, won the state many admirers in America and around the world. As a result, Hollywood tended to portray the Jewish state, ancient and modern, as a heroic David battling Goliaths in thriller flicks, like *The Odessa File*, along with others such as the 1981 TV miniseries *Masada* and 1984's *The Little Drummer Girl*. This attitude was to change, of course, after Israel launched a largely unprovoked invasion of Lebanon in the early 1980s, which tarnished its halo. The American film industry responded not by demonizing Israel but by simply removing it almost entirely from the screen.

A note appearing at the start of *The Odessa File* insists that what is about to transpire is based on documented research: that is, that there really was an Odessa group that linked ex-SS officers, including Roschmann; that Nasser really did seek to perfect rockets designed to annihilate Israel; and that many of Nasser's key scientists in this project had formerly belonged to Hitler's rocket-development program. Of course, the problem with insisting on historical accuracy in a thriller that includes fictional plot twists is that the viewer is unable to divorce fact from fiction. Forsyth's novel is even more baffling in this regard. A "Publisher's Note" prefacing the book reads, "Many characters in *The Odessa File* are real people. Some will be immediately recognized by the reader; others may puzzle the reader as to whether they are true or fictional, and the publishers do not wish to elucidate further because it is in this ability to perplex the reader as to how much is true and how much false that much of the grip of the story lies."[3] The note, however, seems more plausibly intended to protect the publisher and author from any potential legal liabilities.

The film's protagonist is a freelance West German reporter, Peter Miller (Jon Voight), who, at the start of the movie, obtains a diary composed by an elderly Holocaust survivor living in Hamburg, named Salomon Tauber, who has just committed suicide by, with grisly irony, gassing himself. At the film's opening, Miller is portrayed as a rather callow young man who supports himself by penning lurid stories for the German tabloids. However, Miller's consciousness is raised when he pores over Tauber's diary and discovers the motive for the old man's suicide: a few weeks before his death, he had glimpsed the sadistic commandant who had tormented him at Riga, Eduard Roschmann, alive and free in Hamburg, thanks, Tauber is sure, to the ministrations of Odessa. Reading the diary, Miller also comes across a description of a scene Tauber had witnessed during the war in which Roschmann—arguing with a *Wehrmacht* captain over whether Roschmann's prisoners or the captain's wounded soldiers will be loaded onto a German naval vessel—shoots the man dead. This episode from the past will be crucial to the film's climax.

One line in Tauber's diary, which Miller reads in voice-over, will sound familiar to viewers of previous Hollywood Holocaust movies. The old man insists, "I bear no hatred toward the German people. People are not evil; individuals are evil." In case we missed its import, this sentence is repeated at the very end of the film in another voice-over, accompanying a scene showing Solomon's old friend Marx, another Holocaust survivor, saying the kaddish for his companion at the Holocaust museum, Yad Vashem, in Jerusalem. As we have seen, this theme is evident as far back as anti-Nazi American films made during the war, such as *Tomorrow, the World!* and *Hitler's Children*. Recalling scenes in *Judgment at Nuremberg*, one wonders if West Germany's status as a crucial anti-Soviet ally influenced Hollywood's decision to whitewash popular German support for Hitler in a film made during the Cold War.

But before we implicate Hollywood too harshly in this regard, it's important to note that not only is Tauber's line lifted from the book, but Forsyth's novel goes even further in this direction; here, Tauber writes, "I bear no hatred or bitterness toward the German people, for they are a good people. Peoples are not evil; only individuals are evil."[4] In this form, Tauber's sentiments are contradictory; if a people by definition cannot be collectively evil, then by the same token they cannot be collectively good.

After perusing Tauber's diary, Miller decides to put his investigative reportorial skills to use by tracking down Roschmann and exposing Odessa. A German newspaper editor whom Miller contacts, however, is skeptical of the story's commercial appeal. "Dead Jews don't sell papers," he bluntly tells the reporter. "People don't want to know." Like *Judgment at Nuremberg*, this scene in *The Odessa File* suggests that the German people are eager to forget their Nazi past and also that, despite the Holocaust, anti-Semitism remains a problem in the country.

Unfazed by the editor's dismissal, Miller zealously commences his investigation. Gradually, he discovers that the Odessa group has penetrated many of the top levels of the German government; an esteemed military veterans' group teems with Odessa personnel, and both a high-ranking law enforcement official and the minister of justice appear to be agents of the organization. In search of information, Miller travels to Vienna to meet with Wiesenthal, who is given his own name and who has also been on Odessa's trail for years. Wiesenthal informs the reporter that Odessa was originally formed to help SS personnel escape after the war. The group, rich from all the Nazi money and treasure it was able to smuggle out and deposit in Swiss bank accounts after the war, has branches in Latin America but is based in Germany and has infiltrated all facets of German life.

Eventually, Miller is kidnapped by Israeli secret agents who are also after Odessa. Although Miller's and the Israelis' motives for wanting to penetrate Odessa differ, the agents recruit Miller to pose as an ex-SS officer in order to infiltrate the group. Because Odessa is already aware that the reporter is after them, Miller seems a poor choice to act as spy, but this plot glitch is ignored as the story hurtles on.

After various life-threatening adventures, Miller succeeds in locating Roschmann, now an electricity magnate living on an ample estate outside a provincial German town. Although the local police protect the mansion, Miller is able to sneak in and confront Roschmann. Despite the burden of makeup designed to make him look elderly, Schell gives a marvelously understated performance as the villainous Roschmann. While Miller points a revolver at his chest, an unrepentant Roschmann defends his actions both during and after the war: "We Germans ruled the world. The SS were the elite. Today they want to crush us. That's what's dividing this country. We created the new generation by weeding out the sickly. . . . Germany is rising again." Noting Miller's own blond, blue-eyed Aryan looks, Roschmann continues: "We're on the same side. Why should it matter to you what happened to a few miserable Jews?"

Here *The Odessa File* fatally falters in conveying any significant message about the Holocaust. Miller reveals that his father happened to be that Wehrmacht captain whom Roschmann shot dead during the war. At this revelation, a crestfallen Roschmann replies, reasonably enough, "So, you didn't come about the Jews after all." Miller lamely responds: "What you and your kind did to those people sickened all of mankind. But I'm here about my father." Recognizing now that his protestations are useless, Roschmann grabs for a concealed revolver, whereupon Miller fatally shoots him. Not long after, the film ends.

When *The Odessa File* appeared, the real Roschmann was still at large, and mirroring that, Roschmann escapes at the end of Forsyth's novel. But director Ronald Neame considered this conclusion too depressing for a Hollywood movie. Informed of the director's decision, Wiesenthal wrote a friend, "He [Neame] explained to me that it was impossible to present moviegoers with a despicable Nazi criminal for two hours and then let him get away. At a film's end, people want satisfaction and to see justice triumph."[5] Thus, Hollywood's need for emotional closure had once again trumped the historical record.

But there are other distortions of Holocaust history here as well. One of the lesser sins of the concluding scene is that it implies a clear moral division between the Wehrmacht (represented by good men like Miller's father) and the SS (represented by the evil Roschmann). When Miller accuses Roschmann of "war crimes," the ex-Nazi dismisses the allegation as "sentimental claptrap," insisting that "soldiers obey orders." Miller snaps, "Don't compare yourself to a soldier. You were a mass murderer." But contemporary historians have questioned the assumption that the German army was blameless for the Holocaust, that there was an unbridged divide between the Wehrmacht and the SS. When the Germans invaded the Soviet Union, the Einsatzgruppe followed in the wake of the Wehrmacht, marching into areas the German military had pacified and murdering millions of Jewish civilians. How could the Wehrmacht have had no idea what the Einsatzgruppe was doing?

However, the biggest statement about the significance of the Holocaust is found in Miller's final scene with Roschmann. From the film's start, the audience has been assuming that Miller is risking his life to find Roschmann because Tauber's diary has alerted the young German to the Holocaust, and he is seeking retribution for those six million murdered Jews by bringing a Nazi war criminal to justice. Yet now we discover that Miller's true motives have been nothing more than a desire for personal family revenge. This ending nullifies what had seemed, until now, the film's praiseworthy theme: how the postwar German generation, discovering their forebears' perpetration of the Holocaust, are demanding that the wartime generation account for its past. Instead, we find another example of Hollywood dejudaizing the Holocaust.

In 1976, two years after *The Odessa File*, another Holocaust-themed Hollywood thriller, *Marathon Man*, opened. Directed by John Schlesinger and starring Dustin Hoffman, the movie was the first time the pair had worked together since collaborating on the brilliant *Midnight Cowboy* (1969). Like *The Odessa File*, *Marathon Man* was based on a best-selling novel—William Goldman's 1974 book of the same name. Goldman also wrote the screenplay. In fact, almost all American Holocaust-related films made in the 1960s and 1970s were based either on novels (*Exodus*, *Ship of Fools*, *The Odessa File*, *Boys from Brazil*, *Sophie's Choice*) or plays (*The Diary of Anne Frank*, *Cabaret*). It seems that Hollywood, unsure about the box office appeal of the Holocaust, took advantage of Shoah-based stories that had been successful in another form first. By the same token, in all of these films, with the exception of *The Diary of Anne Frank*, the Holocaust appears as a subplot, again suggesting the film industry's reluctance to tackle directly such an explosive and potentially unprofitable topic.

Marathon Man adopts the plot device made famous by Alfred Hitchcock in such films as *The Thirty-Nine Steps*, *The Man Who Knew Too Much*, and *North by Northwest*: an everyman is drawn accidentally into a deadly web of intrigue and must discover heroic abilities within himself he never knew existed in order to survive. In *Marathon Man*, the everyman in question is a young, bookish history graduate student at Columbia named Thomas "Babe" Levy (Hoffman), an aspiring marathon runner who lives in a cramped Manhattan apartment and has, intriguingly, a German girlfriend. Levy's father was a renowned left-wing history professor who—apparently because he was blacklisted during the McCarthy era—took his own life. Levy's doctoral dissertation on McCarthyism is, in part, an attempt to exonerate his father. Thus, like so many other Holocaust-oriented movies we've discussed, *Marathon Man* draws implicit parallels between the Holocaust and contemporary American problems, in this case the McCarthy era. Comparing Nazism to McCarthyism has a certain validity, which points up the danger of the latter, since in both cases demagogues scapegoated their political opponents by falsely claiming that they posed a threat to the security of the nation. And Hollywood knew a lot about McCarthyism, since McCarthy and his minions had pressured the industry into "blacklisting" many members of its community, thus destroying their careers.

Levy has a conflicted relationship with his older brother, who goes by the nickname of "Doc" (Roy Scheider). Doc has led his kid brother to believe that he is a successful Washington businessman, but, in fact, he's immersed in a vaguely defined covert operation with the federal government, which puts him in contact with an escaped Nazi named Christian Szell (Laurence Olivier). Loosely based on Josef Mengele, Szell is a dentist by trade who during the war had conducted sadistic medical experiments at Auschwitz. Believed to have died at the end of the war, Szell had actually fled to South America, where he'd assumed a false identity. In fleeing, Szell had taken with him a fortune in diamonds that he had stolen from his victims and that is now stored in a safety deposit box in a Manhattan bank. When Szell's brother, en route to withdraw the diamonds, is killed in a car accident, Szell is forced to risk exposure by entering the United States in order to claim the loot. However, when Szell and Doc meet secretly in Manhattan, the exchange sours and the ex-Nazi ends up murdering the American agent. Fatally wounded, Doc stumbles back to his brother's apartment and dies in his arms, after first whispering some cryptic last words, which lead everyone—both the American agents and Szell and his henchmen—to assume that Levy possesses secret knowledge that he must be forced to reveal.

The most confusing aspect of this convoluted plot concerns the central question of why the American government is conspiring with escaped Nazis. Though all the facts will probably never be revealed, we do know that the American government recruited some former Nazis to help fight the Soviet Union in the Cold War, some for service in the US space and weapons programs. We also know that American officials briefly held Mengele in US custody before letting him slip away.[6] *Marathon Man* appeared in 1976, at a time when public suspicion of the American government ran high, thanks to Watergate and the covert expansion of the Vietnam War. Therefore, a thriller that implied a secret relationship between hidden Nazis and the American government held great resonance. It is through this subplot that *Marathon Man* appears to be trying to draw connections between Nazi Germany and America during the McCarthy era, but the connections remain tenuous.

But, again, this aspect of the story—US officials and escaped Nazis potentially in cahoots—remains muddled. The closest we get to a full explanation is when Levy is spirited away from Szell's clutches by an

American associate of Doc's, Peter Janeway (William Devane), who explains that Szell was known by the prisoners in Auschwitz as the "White Angel," because of his abundance of white hair and because he'd helped Jews escape if they were willing to bribe him with diamonds. Janeway claims that the American government has been protecting Szell in exchange for the ex-Nazi revealing the whereabouts of his former comrades, now also in hiding. This explanation appears to clear up the mystery, until the car containing Janeway and Levy returns to Szell's lair. Janeway, it turns out, has been working for Szell all along and had only pretended to rescue Levy in an attempt to get the young man to disclose whatever secrets he'd discovered from his dying brother. Therefore, we don't know if what Janeway has shared with Levy is the truth or if he's simply fabricated this story as a means of tricking the young man into opening up. We're not even sure if Janeway is actually working for the American government.

Two scenes are especially memorable. In one, Szell tortures Levy by strapping him into a dentist's chair and drilling into a nerve in Levy's teeth. The scene recalls the horrific medical experiments conducted in the camps by Nazi doctors—a historical detail beloved of countless thriller writers and filmmakers adapting Nazi material because it's precisely the sort of ghoulish act perfectly suited to the genre. On a more mundane level, the scene appeals to the common human fear of going to the dentist. In *Film and the Holocaust*, Aaron Kerner identifies the scene as an example of "torture porn" and sees *Marathon Man* as a forerunner of Eli Roth's series of *Hostel* films, in which a psychopath entraps a collection of attractive young people and then subjects them to a variety of sadistic tortures that often partake of a sadomasochistic erotic element. Although the comparison seems a bit hyperbolic, Kerner notes that "Szell is clinical in manner and speech, never once losing his temper, or letting his emotions get the better of him"—classic traits of the clinical sadist, who always keeps his violent tendencies firmly in check.[7] "True to the sadist disposition," Kerner continues, "everything is meticulously planned."[8] Kerner explicitly connects Levy to a camp inmate when he observes that "Babe is wearing a robe and white and grey striped pajama bottoms, evoking the attire associated with concentration camp internees."[9] Like camp prisoners, Babe Levy is completely helpless in the face of Szell's torture.

A second unforgettable scene involving Szell occurs when the ex-Nazi travels to the diamond district in lower Manhattan in an attempt to sell his jewels. The New York City diamond industry has long been run by Jews (especially the Hasidic), and as Szell walks through the streets of the district, he is recognized by several elderly Holocaust survivors who'd been imprisoned at Auschwitz. One old woman points at him frantically, screaming in German, "The White Angel!" Another, a clerk at a store where Szell had inquired about his diamonds, trails him down the street. Other elderly Jews, on hearing Szell's notorious name, begin to surround him, their fixed stares and almost zombie-like movements giving the impression that they have returned from the grave to stalk their former persecutor. When the clerk finally catches up with Szell, the Nazi unclasps a stiletto hidden in his sleeve and slits the man's throat, before escaping in a taxi. The scene is both tautly exciting, fulfilling the demands of the thriller genre, and reflective both of the obsessive desire of Holocaust survivors to see their captors receive a measure of justice and, on a symbolic level, of how the Shoah is an event so horrific it is inescapable, permanently fixed in Jewish consciousness.

Szell doesn't elude capture for long. In the climax of *Marathon Man*, an armed Levy traps Szell in a sewage treatment facility in Central Park. As Levy points his revolver, Szell sneers, "You won't shoot me. You're too weak." Szell's taunt, like Roschmann's speech to Miller at the conclusion of *The Odessa File*, reflects the Nazi obsession with brutal machismo and perhaps, since Levy is Jewish, alludes as well to the Nazis' stereotyping of the Jew as a cowardly *Untermensch*. (Unfortunately, other than giving him a Jewish last name, the film makes nothing of Levy's Jewishness, and we can only vaguely infer how it impacts his confrontation with an ex-Nazi.) When the two grapple, Szell ends up stabbing himself with his own stiletto, and then his wounded body plunges over a railing, landing atop a rotating metal wheel. The symbolism is potent if rather obvious: this piece of human sewage has justly met his end in a sewage treatment plant.

Despite exciting scenes that touch on the Holocaust, *Marathon Man* reveals no deep insights about the Shoah or Nazism. Szell's character never transcends the type of the Hollywood Nazi, a cartoon monster, although it's easy to forget Szell's one-dimensionality because of Olivier's quietly intense performance. We never learn why Szell joined the Nazis in the first place, what motivated him to participate in the medical experiments at Auschwitz, how he feels about Hitler's defeat and his subsequent life in hiding, or even what he thinks of Jews. All we're ever told is that he's an evil sadist. By all accounts, Mengele enjoyed his time at Auschwitz—the prestige in which he was held by his fellow Nazis, the absolute power of life and death he exerted over the prisoners, the scientific information he gleaned from his horrific experiments on twins and dwarves. But we never discover if Szell derived a comparable pleasure from the events comprising his infamous past. Even in the aforementioned scene where Szell tortures Levy with his dentist's drill, it's unclear, particularly since Oliver's acting is so understated, if Szell is getting any sadistic satisfaction from tormenting this young Jew or if his aim is the purely pragmatic one of extracting information from Levy about the whereabouts of the jewels.

Perhaps the most original (if also most outrageous) of the three Holocaust-themed Hollywood thrillers discussed here is *The Boys from Brazil* (1978). Like *The Odessa File* and *Marathon Man*, *The Boys from Brazil* was originally a best-selling novel, in this case by Ira Levin, published in 1976. Like *Marathon Man*, the film is set in the present and features an escaped Nazi explicitly based on Josef Mengele, prob-

Figure 8.1. *Marathon Man* (1976). Exiled war criminal Szell (Laurence Olivier) returns to the torture techniques he inflicted on prisoners in Auschwitz. [Screen grab]

ably the most notorious Nazi who successfully escaped justice after the war. In *The Boys from Brazil*, Mengele is played by that screen icon of American integrity, Gregory Peck, who, though sporting a Hitler-like moustache and a semi-believable German accent, is woefully miscast— one of the film's main flaws. Also like *Marathon Man*, *The Boys from Brazil* features in its other leading role Laurence Olivier, except that here Olivier is playing the opposite part—not a Nazi but a Nazi *hunter*, a Holocaust-surviving Jew named Liebermann, clearly based on Simon Wiesenthal.

Even more so than with *The Odessa File*, Wiesenthal himself worried that having a character based on him appear in a Hollywood movie would damage the Nazi hunter's reputation. Wiesenthal's concerns were heightened by the fact that he'd disliked the novel, which he'd called "an insane fiction."[10] But when Olivier met with Wiesenthal in Vienna to discuss the role, Wiesenthal was flattered and helped Olivier prepare for the part. It seems that Wiesenthal hoped that *The Boys from Brazil* might help facilitate Mengele's capture in the same way that *The Odessa File* had inspired the discovery of Roschmann. However, when the film appeared, Wiesenthal was unhappy with the characterization of Liebermann (his distress no doubt exacerbated by the poor reviews the movie had received). Wiesenthal wrote to a friend, "Laurence Olivier portrays an imaginary Lieberman who is not Wiesenthal. The way Lieberman acts is neither my style nor my way of acting. Lieberman is a scared ghetto Jew. Ira Levin probably did not know any other type."[11] There is a touch of macho pique in Wiesenthal's complaint, as if the Nazi hunter believed that by portraying the character based on himself as a "scared ghetto Jew," Levin was somehow impugning Wiesenthal's manhood.

In the film, although Liebermann is aware that Mengele is hiding in Paraguay, he has not been able to capture him. Mengele makes little attempt to conceal his whereabouts. In fact, in one scene Mengele and his cohorts attend a local party that openly celebrates the Nazis, and the implication is that Mengele is being protected by the Paraguayan government. Indeed, it's hard to believe that the real Mengele would have been able to hide successfully for decades in Paraguay unless he was under the protection of top officials.[12] It's not surprising that Paraguay's right-wing dictatorship would be enamored of Nazis, although the film never investigates the role played postwar by South American governments in protecting escaped Nazis. Unfortunately, *The Boys from Brazil* also never explores how the hardly clandestine Mengele is able to elude capture with such ease. A partial explanation, however, is offered; at one point, an imprisoned former Nazi guard yells at Liebermann, "Thirty years [since the Holocaust]: the world has forgotten; nobody cares!" She seems to speak for the filmmakers, suggesting that because the world has forgotten the Holocaust, escaped Nazis are able to live freely.

What has Mengele been up to all these years in the Paraguayan jungle? The answer constitutes the film's central premise, which is both original and problematic. Apparently, when Hitler was holed up in a Berlin bunker as the Allies closed in, Mengele convinced the Führer to donate blood. Having already experimented in Auschwitz with cloning and in vitro fertilization, Mengele later used the DNA found in Hitler's blood to clone several dozen fertilized eggs, which were implanted in women around the world, selected because their lives most resembled the circumstances of Hitler's own upbringing. The goal of Mengele's scheme should, by now, be obvious: by spawning an entire horde of Hitler clones spanning the globe, he plans nothing less than to engender a *Fourth* Reich that will dominate the world, masterminded by a cloned Führer. Stumbling onto the doctor's plot, Liebermann rushes to thwart it, which inspires a climactic confrontation between Nazi and Nazi hunter at the home of one of the young Hitler clones.

What is one to make of *The Boys from Brazil*'s wild premise? Presumably, Levin intended the main plot twist of his novel to carry some weight, since it does touch on the public's well-documented fears about cloning. Despite the potential that the technology appears to offer for medical breakthroughs, cloning's less savory possibilities haunt us on a deeply human and personal level. On the other hand, one might argue that it's simply unfair to take the film's premise seriously, since we're dealing with a Hollywood thriller that makes no claims to realism.

However, when thriller writers and filmmakers turn to the Holocaust, they are assuming ethical responsibilities that don't pertain to more frivolous subjects. Indeed, the main problem with *The Boys from Brazil* for those considering its representation of Holocaust issues is that its central premise is far-fetched. This would not be a problem, except that it implies that escaped Nazis are of interest and concern only if they are concocting some ludicrous but deadly scheme, which ignores the real shame posed by actual escaped Nazis who have not been brought to justice. By all accounts, the actual Mengele spent his time in Paraguay leading a harmless and anonymous life (before he apparently drowned in a swimming accident), but that didn't make his ability to elude capture any less of a travesty. Reviewing the film in the *New Yorker*, Pauline Kael made a similar point: "Nazism has become comic-book mythology, a consumer product. Movies like this aren't making the subject more important, they're making it a joke. They're cloning Hitler to death."[13]

9

THE HOLOCAUST'S NON-JEWISH VICTIMS

Sophie's Choice

Critics were also sharply divided in their response to *Sophie's Choice* (1982), the story of a tortured romance in postwar Brooklyn between a Polish Gentile Holocaust survivor, Sophie (Meryl Streep), and a brilliant but schizophrenic American Jew, Nathan (Kevin Kline). The novel's narrator—and the movie's ever-observant and increasingly helpless witness—is the young, innocent aspiring Southern writer Stingo (Peter MacNicol), who enters both their lives when he moves into the boarding house where the couple live together.

Sophie's Choice was directed by Alan Pakula (who also made *All the Presidents' Men*, the 1976 film about Woodward and Bernstein's reportage of Watergate). Similar to Sydney Lumet's choices in filming *The Pawnbroker*, Pakula resisted studio pressures to rewrite Styron's novel to give the film a happy ending, which would surely have destroyed the picture. Pakula spent over two years casting the movie and considered many other actresses for the part of Sophie before finally choosing Streep. She had played a somewhat similar role a few years earlier in the immensely popular television miniseries *Holocaust*, as a Gentile German who marries a Jew and then insists on joining him at Theresienstadt. But *Sophie's Choice* is a superior film to the soap-opera-ish *Holocaust*, and, perhaps as a result, Streep's performance, though good in the miniseries, is even better in the movie—subtle, vivid, haunting, poignant—winning Streep the Academy Award for Best Actress in 1982. Impressively, the actress spent months studying German and Polish before shooting began in order to speak the languages in flashback scenes set in Nazi-occupied Warsaw and at Auschwitz.[1] As for Pakula, the film's Holocaust story clearly held personal meaning. "My father was a Polish Jew," the director told the *New York Times*. "If he hadn't come to this country, Sophie's story could have been my own."[2]

Pakula faced a daunting challenge in trying to convert Styron's six-hundred-plus-page novel into a film of manageable length. As Andrew Sarris pointed out in his review at the time, "William Styron's 200,000 word meditation on guilt and shame in the aftermath of the Holocaust is a more copious novel than most, which is to say that if writer-director Alan J. Pakula had really wanted to be faithful to the novel, he would have had to stop the narrative in mid-stream for a feature-length documentary on the Nazi death camps."[3] Sarris was referring to the mini-essays on the Holocaust that Styron intersperses through the novel, which Pakula wisely decided couldn't possibly be transferred to the screen. Even so, *New York Times* reviewer Janet Maslin felt Pakula did a superb job turning the book into a movie, maintaining that the film "follows the lengthy novel closely enough to capture it with amazing comprehensiveness in a little more than two-and-a-half hours."[4] In fact, the movie is much *better* than Styron's swollen, overblown novel, in which the author's desire to achieve an exhaustiveness commensurate with his weighty subject leads to verbosity, redundancy, and a penchant for style over substance; Pakula has lifted out a great basic story buried in a bombastic text.

The film's realism is enhanced by dialogue in which all the characters speak their native languages, with translations in subtitles, rather than, as so often in American Holocaust films, the characters speaking stagy English inflected by thick accents. *Sophie's Choice* is also strengthened by a haunting score by Marvin Hamlisch; I defy anyone to be unmoved by the movie's melancholy theme song, reprised throughout the film.

Sophie's Choice includes long flashbacks to Sophie's experiences in both Nazi-occupied Warsaw and at Auschwitz, narrated by Sophie herself as she gradually reveals her past to the entranced Stingo, sometimes correcting lies that she'd told him previously. The main flashback to

Sophie's experience in the camp lasts about twenty minutes and almost constitutes a minifilm in itself. The danger of such a technique is obvious: either that viewers will become so engrossed by the story-within-a-story that they will forget or lose interest in the frame story or that viewers will resent being taken away from the main narrative for such an extended period of time. In *Sophie's Choice*, the present story is comparatively more engaging than the flashbacks, largely because the present action focuses on Sophie's fascinatingly complex romance with Nathan as well as on her hardly less entrancing triangle with Nathan and Stingo. Still, had the flashbacks been deleted, with Sophie simply relating this material in lengthy monologues, the film would have been weaker. We can't fully grasp the nature of the impact the Holocaust has had on Sophie unless we *see* her persecution.

In the flashback depicting Sophie's life in Auschwitz, there is a brilliant dramatization of Hannah Arendt's famous theory about "the banality of evil."[5] Because of her fluency in German, Sophie is chosen to serve as a secretary for the camp commandant, Rudolf Hoess (Stephen Newman). The scenes in Auschwitz, along with a brief scene in which Sophie visits the Warsaw ghetto, are shot in a sepia tint by cinematogra-

Figure 9.1. *Sophie's Choice* (1982). In a flashback, an Auschwitz guard forces Sophie (Meryl Streep) to "choose" between her children. [Screen grab]

pher Nestor Almendros. However, when Sophie crosses from the camp through a wall into the lush garden surrounding the Hoess family home, the screen abruptly bursts into what seems, in contrast, almost cartoon-ishly vivid color. This is fitting, because the Hoess family, living literally next door to Auschwitz, is portrayed as a kind of Nazi version of *Leave It to Beaver*. Because SS Chief Heinrich Himmler is expected that night for dinner, Mrs. Hoess burbles to her husband, "I baked Himm-ler's favorite cake." And, later, one of Hoess's cherubic, flaxen-haired daughters says to Sophie, "Dachau was so much nicer than Auschwitz." Annette Insdorf writes of "the paradoxical nature of this domicile's in-habitants: in a different time and place they might have been a sympa-thetic bourgeois family."[6] But she misses the point. Uttered in a normal context, the family members' remarks *would* be bourgeois banalities, but the fact that they are spouting such commonplaces when just next door innocent people are being gassed turns the family into monsters. Moreover, there is more of a connection between the gas chambers and the Hoess family's home than might at first appear. In reality, the Hoess clan is *benefitting* from the murder of the Jews, since it's the machinery of mass extermination that has placed Hoess in his comfortable and powerful position as the absolute master of the death camp.

Alvin Rosenfeld makes a point similar to Insdorf's, though in his case it's meant as criticism, when he complains that the film "makes Rudolf Hoess, the Commandant of Auschwitz, seem almost a decent man."[7] It's true that, with his wife and children, Hoess is the consummate family man. But this merely reflects Hoess's atrocious ability, which many Nazis shared, to morally compartmentalize his life; Hoess can be the good family man at home, and then he can go to work and calmly supervise the murder of millions. Of course, central to this compart-mentalization is Hoess's staunch belief that the prisoners are subhuman as well as his equally fervent adherence to the central Nazi tenet that the Jews posed an existential threat to the German race. Moreover, Hoess hardly acts as a "decent man" when he's about to force himself on Sophie, attracted by her Aryan features. When the commandant learns he's being transferred to another camp, he decides that raping Sophie isn't worth the effort because he hasn't time for an extended "affair."

While Sophie escapes being raped at the hands of Hoess, her post-war relationship with Nathan is in many respects clearly abusive as well.

What are we to make of Sophie's romance with the charismatic but psychotic Nathan? Rosenfeld sees *Sophie's Choice* as a pop cultural example of the Jew being equated with a Nazi:

> In the character of Nathan Landau it becomes unambiguously clear that homicidal mania has been transferred from the Nazi to the Jew. Nathan . . . recalls no one so much as Svengali, and abuses his blonde and beautiful woman so constantly and with so much relish as to revive the wildest anti-Semitic fantasies of the Jew as sexual predator. Inasmuch as Sophie is not only a Polish Catholic but a Holocaust survivor to boot, she stands as an especially poignant victim of the Jewish penchant for despoiling helpless Christian women.[8]

Later, Rosenfeld expands his allegation: "Sophie represents a new and singularly perverse type of sex object that is beginning to emerge in the writings of certain authors drawn to the most unseemly side of the Holocaust—namely, she represents in her abused and broken body, the desirability of the Mutilated Woman."[9]

Avisar launches similar charges with similarly supercharged rhetoric: "Nathan . . . embodies many of the stereotypical notions of the successful Jew in American society. He is a musician, a scientist, a connoisseur of the arts and literature, and seems to have unlimited sources of money. . . . Given the demonic control that Nathan exercised over her, he is certainly the clear cause of her death."[10]

It's true that Nathan, tormented by his maniacal conviction that Sophie is cheating on him with Stingo, berates her mercilessly, calling her a "Polish whore" and other obscenities and demanding to know why *she* survived Auschwitz when so many millions died. However, it is worth noting that Pakula deliberately downplayed the brutal aspects that Styron had woven into their relationship, to such an extent that the author complained that "the movie slighted the sadomasochistic eroticism of the book."[11] Moreover, in his relationship with Sophie, Nathan is neither a "Svengali" nor a "demonic character." First, remember that Nathan is responsible for saving Sophie's life, when he finds her a malnourished refugee, fainted on the floor of the New York Public Library. Surely Nathan's life-saving role must be considered when judging his treatment of Sophie. In fact, Sophie's loyalty to Nathan, even when he abuses her, probably derives more from her gratitude than from any Svengali-like powers Nathan allegedly possesses (though there is an undeniably mesmerizing, charismatic side to this character).

Rosenfeld and Avisar are able to turn Nathan into a "demon" because they don't deal with his mental illness. Far from being an emblem of "the successful Jew in American society," Nathan is so crazy that his brother (who *is* a successful American Jew) finds him a bogus job at a laboratory to keep him out of trouble. Moreover, Nathan is addicted to hard drugs, and his schizophrenia ultimately drives him to suicide. In truth, Nathan is far too debilitated to have "demonic control" over anyone. The tragedy of Nathan's life, as his brother tells Stingo, is that he was a childhood wunderkind who grew up to be a lunatic. Rosenfeld and Avisar, in claiming that Nathan is demonic, ascribe a degree of calculation to Nathan's behavior that simply doesn't exist. Nathan may behave sadistically toward Sophie, but he is never intentionally sadistic. In the throes of his paranoid fits, Nathan honestly *believes* that Sophie has cheated on him with Stingo. The tragic irony is that Nathan loves Sophie deeply. If he didn't, her imagined infidelities wouldn't madden him. In another tragic irony, when Nathan baselessly accuses Sophie of infidelity, he's driving away a woman who fully reciprocates his love. Nathan and Sophie are magnetically drawn to one another because they are both emotionally crippled—he by mental illness; she by the Holocaust. As Stingo says in voice-over as he gazes at the couple lying dead in each other's arms, Nathan and Sophie belong to "the butchered and betrayed and martyred children of the earth."

If anything, Nathan seems less a demon than a product of Jewish self-hatred taken to a psychotic extreme. Nathan is the epitome of the Jew who has internalized anti-Semitism, which draws him to the shiksa because she's his polar opposite and appears unkeepable, because he can't imagine that she'd want to have anything to do with a kike. In Nathan's case, Jewish self-hatred may convince him that Sophie is unfaithful, because he can't believe she could ever truly love a man like himself.

For Sophie's part, her own Holocaust-induced self-hatred and self-destructiveness are better explanations for her suicide than Avisar's claim that Nathan's baleful influence is "the clear cause of [Sophie's] death." Avisar ignores how much Sophie is a product of "Holocaust survivor syndrome." Like Sol Nazerman in *The Pawnbroker*, Sophie is a survivor who hasn't *really* survived psychologically. Maybe Sophie wants to die simply because she's already (again, like Nazerman) one of the "living dead." Indeed, Kerner comments on how Sophie looks more and more ghostly as the film progresses: "Sophie's body withers before us: anemic, ashen, gaunt, self-hating, masochistic, and suicidal."[12] It's a terrible irony that so many of the Holocaust survivors who most eloquently told their stories to the world ended up killing themselves: Tadeusz Borowski, Primo Levi, Paul Celan, Jean Amery, among others. Many less famous Holocaust survivors did as well. While the motive of every suicide ultimately remains a mystery, it appears that, in these cases, guilt at having survived the Holocaust, while so many perished, finally drove these survivors to take their own lives.

The scene in which Sophie makes her agonizing "choice" immediately on her arrival at Auschwitz may be the most powerful in the whole film. After exiting the boxcar, Sophie and her two children, a girl and a boy, are standing by the tracks in a long line of just-arrived prisoners awaiting the "selections," which will decide who will be allowed to be a slave laborer and who will be sent at once to the gas chamber. A supervising Nazi officer is struck by Sophie's beauty. Sophie tries to seize this chance by insisting to the officer that she's been sent to the camp by mistake, since she's not a Jew but a Catholic. The Nazi replies that, because Sophie is a Christian, he will privilege her with a choice: she can pick either her son or daughter to live, while the other child will be taken at once to the gas chamber. When Sophie responds hysterically, the officer insists that unless she makes this choice, *both* her children will be killed. In agony, Sophie picks her son to live, whereupon her daughter is hauled off, screaming.

In *Holocaust Testimonies: The Ruins of Memory*, Lawrence Langer discusses how Jews and others in the ghettos and the camps were often confronted by their captors with a "choiceless choice"—one they were forced to make, though either alternative was catastrophic. Sophie's "choice" in this scene is a perfect example of a "choiceless choice." Why would the Nazis inflict this kind of sadism on prisoners they were planning to kill anyway? Goldhagen argues that the Nazis, in a perfect example of circular reasoning, often humiliated their Jewish victims because it was deemed necessary to dehumanize them in order to "justify" the Nazi belief that the Jews were subhuman. Although Sophie isn't Jewish, the Nazi officer in this scene may have a similar motive. If he forces Sophie to degrade herself by "choosing" one of her children to die, then, by some twisted logic, she seems to deserve the treatment she is receiving. A simpler explanation for the officer's behavior is that there's a dark side in human nature that derives pleasure from dominating and brutalizing other people. Living in a civilized society, most of us are normally forced by legal and cultural restraints to repress this side of ourselves, but during the Holocaust such behavior was granted official sanction and even reward. Finally, the psychological torture inflicted on Sophie was a common practice in the camps because emotionally "broken" prisoners were less likely to resist.

That said, there is a problem with the way Sophie's "choiceless choice" is depicted. No one hearing Sophie's story could blame her for what she did. If she didn't pick her daughter to die, both her children would have been killed. However, there were instances in which female prisoners voluntarily denied their maternal instinct in an attempt to save themselves. This sometimes happened during the "selections," because single women had a chance to be chosen as slave laborers, while mothers were almost always sent immediately with their children to the gas chambers. In, for example, Holocaust survivor Tadeusz Borowski's extraordinary story, "This Way to the Gas, Ladies and Gentlemen," an anguished mother refuses to acknowledge her crying child as her own. Calling her a "degenerate mother," a drunken Russian sailor flings both mother and child onto the transport carrying prisoners to the gas chambers.[13]

Arguably, this scene from Borowski is even more shocking than the one in *Sophie's Choice*. If the woman had survived the Holocaust, how would she feel knowing she'd sacrificed her child's life for her own? Yet how many of us, in her excruciating situation, would have acted the same way? If Sophie had been asked by the Nazi officer to choose between her children's lives and her own, and had chosen to live, the scene would have been an even better example of "choiceless choice." As Langer writes, "An axiom of this [camp] universe . . . is that one's own survival *almost never could be severed from someone else's death*" (italics in original).[14] To demand that this pivotal scene in *Sophie's Choice* be even *grimmer* than it already is may sound extreme; however, it not only would be more realistic but also would make the movie more psychologically complex. Indeed, that Sophie's choice in this scene renders her blameless is tied to a larger problem with her characterization. Sophie is portrayed as *too* good, literally without flaws, beyond her understandable self-destructiveness. In the moments in which we see her pale, haunted, beautiful face enveloping the screen, supernaturally illuminated, it's as if we're seeing the countenance of a saint.

Aaron Kerner argues, on the other hand, that the movie *blames* Sophie for becoming a Holocaust victim and that she actually does bear some responsibility for the death of her children. (Her son is sent to a children's camp at Birkenau, where he ultimately perishes as well.) Kerner claims that

> among the "poor" choices was Sophie's decision to leave her husband for another man. At the heart of the matter is Sophie's sexual agency; her desire for a man other than her husband—the father of her two children—breaks the family unit. Viewed from this perspective, the Holocaust has very little to do with the film; rather, it functions as mere hyperbole: there is hell to pay if a woman expresses sexual desire, becomes a sexual agent. On the surface of things the film portrays Sophie as innocent and enduring grave injustices, but on closer inspection the subtext of the film suggests otherwise; it is all Sophie's fault. And, finally, it is precisely because of her "poor" judgment that her children are swallowed up in the Nazis' machinery of death.[15]

But Kerner's feminist reading that the film punishes Sophie for her emancipated "sexual agency" is belied by a careful examination of the details of Sophie's affair. Although Sophie initially claims to Nathan and Stingo that her father, a Polish professor, had been an opponent of the Nazis, the truth, as she eventually confesses, was the opposite; her father was actually a Nazi sympathizer who delivered virulently anti-Semitic lectures in his classes and participated in the removal of all Jewish students and faculty from his university following the German occupation of Poland. It was while Sophie was typing up her father's anti-Semitic diatribes that she first began to have doubts about the wisdom of his hatred of the Jews. Sophie's husband was her father's principle disciple, every bit as much a Jew hater as he was. It is proof of how far Sophie has strayed from the philosophy shared by her husband and father that when she picks a lover she chooses a member of the Polish resistance. Sophie even aids her lover in his resistance activities. Under the circumstances, it's absurd to claim that Sophie has made an immoral choice in picking her lover over her husband or that her only

motive for indulging in the affair stems from a desire for erotic exploration denied most women in a patriarchal society. Moreover, the reason
Sophie is arrested by the Nazis and sent to Auschwitz has nothing to do
with her affair. On the contrary, she is caught attempting to smuggle a
ham to feed her starving family. Contrary to Kerner's claims, *Sophie's
Choice* does not blame Sophie for her imprisonment in Auschwitz or for
the death of her children; she is presented as virtually a paradigm of the
purely innocent victim.

Some critics have objected that, because Sophie is a Gentile, she is
not a typical Holocaust survivor and that the film thus obscures the fact
that the primary targets of the Final Solution were Jews. As we have
seen in such films as *Hitler's Madman* and *Judgment at Nuremberg*,
Hollywood's Holocaust-themed movies often focus on Christians rather
than Jews, and Styron here seems to fall into that lamentable tradition.
However, it's important to remember that Nathan is an American Jew
and obsessed with the Holocaust—his cramped study packed with
books and maps on the subject. Certainly, Nathan's Holocaust mania is
a major reason he is so profoundly drawn to Sophie. Nathan agonizes
over the number of ex-Nazis who have eluded justice. Clearly, a key
explanation for Nathan's obsession is that the main victims of the genocide were Jews.

Moreover, Sophie's Christianity is not the reason she's a psychologically interesting Holocaust survivor. More intriguing is the fact that
Sophie's father—whom she had revered, though he never returned her
affections—is a Nazi-sympathizing Polish professor. Given that Sophie
is a Gentile Christian with Aryan features and a pro-Nazi father, there is
a kind of cosmic irony in her ending up a prisoner at Auschwitz.

As fascinating as the love affair between Sophie and Nathan is the
relationship between Sophie and Stingo. Near the end of the film, Stingo and Sophie attempt to escape Nathan's paranoid threats by fleeing
south. In love with Sophie, Stingo wants to marry and have children
with her on a farm owned by his family. As a way of explaining to Stingo
why she is in no condition to be a wife and mother, Sophie relates the
horrific story from her camp experience that explains the film's title and
which is depicted in flashback. Stingo and Sophie make love, and Stingo
not only loses his virginity but also has all his lavish erotic fantasies
fulfilled. However, when he awakes the next morning, he discovers a
note from Sophie explaining that she'd felt compelled to go back to

Nathan. When Stingo returns to the Brooklyn boarding house, he finds that Sophie and Nathan have committed suicide. The film concludes with Stingo's voice-over, recited as the music swells and the camera pans the Brooklyn Bridge and taken verbatim from the end of the novel: "This was not judgment day—only morning. Morning excellent and fair."

This ending is troubling. Because Sophie tells her Holocaust story only to Stingo, it's as if the Holocaust is meaningless outside of its effect on the impressionable young artist, that it functions only to facilitate Stingo's coming-of-age as a man and a writer. Why, exactly, is the day on which Stingo discovers that the woman he loves and his best friend have killed themselves "excellent and fair"? The reference to "morning," tied to an image of the sun rising over the Brooklyn Bridge, seems to draw on the conventional symbolism of the dawn as the start of a new life. The Brooklyn Bridge, too, seems a rather pat symbol of "crossing over" to new worlds, a new way of life. Kerner suggests as much when he asks if "by finding catharsis through an identification with Stingo, does this leave the Holocaust survivor in the gaping void of melancholia and utter hopelessness?"[16] If the experience of having known Sophie is going to inspire Stingo to journey to adulthood, does that mean he (and we, the audience) will leave the Holocaust victim behind?

On the other hand, if Stingo has, in fact, "grown up" as a result of seeing what psychosis and the Holocaust can wreak on two decent human beings, is that such a minor thing? Perhaps Stingo's new state is somewhat like that of the wedding guest in Coleridge's "The Rime of the Ancient Mariner," who, after hearing the Mariner's harrowing tale, "a sadder and a wiser man, he rose the following morn." Assuming he's narrating the film's events as a much older man, Stingo has been haunted by Sophie's story all his life. In Styron's novel, Stingo functions as an authorial alter-ego; in the film, he serves as a surrogate for the audience. As Stingo learns about the Holocaust from Sophie, we viewers do too, and with luck we bring some of the same empathy to bear on the horrors we are discovering.

10

CHOICELESS CHOICE

Enemies, a Love Story and *Triumph of the Spirit*

The head of the Jewish Council in the Warsaw ghetto, Adam Czerniakow, was a decent man trapped in an impossible dilemma. When Czerniakow was ordered by the Nazis to turn over all the children in the ghetto to be deported to Treblinka, he poisoned himself rather than carry out the command. Commenting on Czerniakow's suicide, Lawrence Langer notes that the Nazis had placed the ghetto leader in a situation in which there were no good options, one Langer labels "choiceless choice," which he defines as "a choice between impossibilities—no meaningful choice at all."[1] Langer sees many Holocaust victims as faced with this dreadful situation of "choiceless choice." The two films discussed in this chapter, both appearing in 1989—*Enemies: A Love Story* and *Triumph of the Spirit*—each exemplify the condition. In *Enemies*, the Holocaust survivors in postwar America seem entirely driven by the traumatization they've suffered in the Shoah, which renders them incapable of making meaningful choices in their lives. *Triumph of the Spirit* tells the story of a prisoner in Auschwitz, Salamo Arouch, who, back in his home country of Greece, was a boxing champion, which inspired the Nazi officers in the camp to force him to fight in matches against other prisoners. Arouch could either defeat his opponents, who were then sent to the gas chambers, or he could lose, in which case he went to death himself—another example of a "choice between impossibilities." "Choiceless choice" is a particularly disturbing aspect of the Holocaust, because it suggests that in times of crisis human beings can be denied free will, buffeted by circumstances outside their control.

Though hailed by the cognoscenti, *Enemies: A Love Story* never received the wide audience it deserved. At the New York Film Critics Circle Awards the year it appeared, Paul Mazursky won as Best Director, while Lena Olin received a Best Supporting Actress award. That same year, the National Society of Film Critics also chose Angelica Huston as Best Supporting Actress.

The film is based on the novel of the same name, by the Nobel Prize–winning Yiddish writer Isaac Bashevis Singer. In dealing with the Holocaust, *Enemies* is unusual in Singer's oeuvre. Singer emigrated from Poland to America before World War II, and while the hurly-burly world of Jewish immigrants in New York is a frequent setting for his work, as is the equally vibrant life of the shetl before the Holocaust, the Shoah itself appears far less frequently. Like *The Great Dictator* and *To Be or Not to Be*, *Enemies: A Love Story* takes a tragicomic approach to the Holocaust—though the comedy, unlike those other two films, is more situational, less a collection of one-liners.

Like *The Pawnbroker* and *Sophie's Choice*, *Enemies* is less about the Holocaust than about Holocaust survivors, though here we have not one survivor but three. The movie opens in Coney Island in 1949. Its protagonist, Herman Broder (Ron Silver), is a Polish Jew who survived the Holocaust by hiding in a barn on the farm of one of his family's Gentile servants, Yadwiga (Margaret Sophie Stein). Out of gratitude to the sweet-natured but rather simpleminded Yadwiga, Herman has married her, believing that his first wife, Tamara, was killed in the Holocaust, along with their children.

While Yadwiga loves Herman devoutly, the philandering Herman treats her like dirt. He is carrying on a torrid affair with the beautiful, tempestuous Masha (Lena Olin), another Holocaust survivor who lives in the Bronx with her chronically ill mother (Judith Malina). Herman pays the bills by working as a ghost writer for a big-shot New York rabbi (played with brio by the comedian Alan King), who has hired Herman less because he's impressed by his literary abilities than because he wants to give a break to a Holocaust survivor. In the emotional divide between the can-do rabbi and the feckless, melancholic Herman, one can see the mutual incomprehension existing between European Jews

Figure 10.1. *Enemies: A Love Story* (1989). Holocaust survivor Herman Broder (Ron Silver) tries to engage with his mentally unstable mistress, Masha (Lena Olin). [Screen grab]

who survived the Holocaust and American Jews who spent the war safe from the Nazi onslaught.

Meanwhile, the unstable Masha threatens to leave Herman unless he marries her, which turns the hapless adulterer into an unenthusiastic bigamist. As if life weren't complicated enough, who should turn up from the grave, so to speak, but Tamara (Angelica Huston)? It turns out that Tamara and their children were shot by the Nazis in a mass round-up of Jews. Though the children died, Tamara survived by crawling over a pile of corpses (though she still has a bullet lodged in her hip). So now Herman has *three* wives.

The primary function of the Holocaust in *Enemies: A Love Story* is to explain why survivors act as they do. In the case of the dim-witted Yadwiga, what the Nazis did to the Jews has left her with a passionate desire to convert to Judaism. Meanwhile, Tamara's horrific near-death experience has turned her into, as she tells Herman when they first reunite, a "ghost." "I'm dead," she says simply, and thereafter she is content to serve as a counselor rather than a wife to Herman, offering him sensible advice that he consistently ignores. Tamara's condition of living death recalls Sophie's comparable state in *Sophie's Choice*. In Herman's case, the Holocaust seems to have left him paralyzed, less acting than acted *on* by the three women in his life, unable to break free from any of them. As all Herman's mistakes start to push him over the edge, he ruefully reflects, "I can't decide on anything." (The film's best joke is that, while Herman appears to be living every man's dream by having relationships with three women, the actual result is a nightmare, with Herman's freedom not enhanced but severely restricted, as he hurtles joylessly from one woman to the next, exhausting himself in striving to keep all the women in his little harem, save Tamara, unaware of the others' existences.)

The affair between Herman and Masha possesses a frantic, bestial carnality that also seems a product of their mutual Holocaust experiences. In a post-Holocaust world in which all civilized values have been exposed as fraudulent, what is left, after all, but hedonism? Rather like Sophie in *Sophie's Choice*, Masha seems like a woman trying to exorcize her Holocaust demons by plunging into what she hopes will be mindless sex (as well as equally numbing binge drinking). Unfortunately, the desperation underlying her erotic appetites serves to unearth, rather than negate, her Holocaust nightmares. "Would you still want me," she asks Herman at one point, "if I came to you in your grave?" For Herman, too, his frenetic sexual carousing with Masha never pushes the Holocaust out of the picture. Once, after they've made love, he asks her, "Did you ever do it with a guard?"

Clearly, in Herman, Masha, and Tamara we have—to the film's great credit—three very human, unheroicized Holocaust survivors. None of the trio is another Anne Frank. When Herman and Tamara meet, after her relatives place an ad in the Jewish press seeking Herman's whereabouts, the pair are arguing within minutes of reuniting, as all the petty conflicts that plagued their marriage before the war immediately resurface. In Herman and Tamara's relationship, and also his affair with Masha, we see the meaning of the film's title; these people both love each other and are simultaneously one another's "enemies," making themselves and their lovers miserable. The Holocaust may not be the only reason for this love/hate dynamic, but it certainly hasn't helped.

Near the film's end, Masha commits suicide. There's a haunting image when, after Masha has downed a bottle of pills, she looks at herself in a mirror in the crepuscular darkness of her bedroom. Her beautiful features ravaged, she is laughing and crying at the same time. Again like Sophie, Masha is a belated casualty of the Holocaust.

Like a lot of Singer's fiction, *Enemies* also has an extremely unusual ending. Earlier in the film, Masha had told Herman that she was pregnant, using the news as additional leverage to force him to marry her. Masha's pregnancy proves to be fraudulent, but, in an ironic twist, Yadwiga ends up pregnant. Rejecting Masha's offer that they commit suicide together, Herman abruptly decides to overcome inertia by simply leaving town, thus breaking ties with *all* the women in his life. In his absence, Yadwiga and Tamara opt to raise Herman's child together, while Herman helps out by regularly sending them money. The women name the baby "Masha."

Thus, in a way neither sentimental nor formulaic, *Enemies: A Love Story* has a quasi-happy ending. The dead Masha lives on through her namesake. Tamara receives compensation for her own dead children by raising an infant whose father is her sometime husband. Yadwiga gets a devoted partner to help her bring up her baby. The emotional turmoil that had bound these four people together is broken. If anyone loses under this new dispensation, it seems to be Herman, divorced from his own child and estranged from two of his three wives. Still, at least for some Holocaust survivors, the film suggests, a measure of genuine survival is possible.

In order to stake a claim on critical attention amid the plethora of Hollywood Holocaust films, such movies must offer a fresh perspective. The best Holocaust films do so. *Sophie's Choice* features a Holocaust survivor who is a Polish Catholic with a pro-Nazi father. *Schindler's List* stars a Righteous Gentile who starts out as a Nazi war profiteer. *Enemies: A Love Story* depicts promiscuity among Holocaust survivors. *Triumph of the Spirit* (1989), though paling in comparison, does provide an original angle on the Holocaust by focusing on a championship boxer who, after being imprisoned at Auschwitz, continues to fight boxing matches in the camp in order to entertain his Nazi captors. The film accurately notes how the German officers in the camps had a tendency to single out individual prisoners for special treatment if these prisoners had skills the Nazis considered useful or entertaining. For example, prisoners with musical talent were often enlisted to play in the camp bands that serenaded inmates as they debarked from the boxcars—a ploy intended to calm prisoners so they could be herded more efficiently into the gas chambers. (The story of a woman's orchestra at Auschwitz is retold in the made-for-television movie *Playing for Time* [1980], starring Vanessa Redgrave.)

Directed by Robert M. Young, *Triumph of the Spirit* is based on the true story of Salamo Arouch (Willem Dafoe), a young Greek Jewish boxer who fought for the Greek team at the 1936 Berlin Olympics and was the 1928 middleweight champion of the Balkans. Arrested by the Nazis when they occupy Greece, Arouch is shipped off to Auschwitz along with his parents, siblings, and girlfriend. Still alive in 1989 when the film appeared, Arouch served as a consultant on the film. (He also has a bit part as a trainer in the boxer's corner during his matches.)

Young exercised some artistic license in retelling Arouch's story. For example, in the movie, Young has a relationship with his girlfriend Allegra (played, interestingly, by a Palestinian actress, Wendy Gazelle) before the Nazis arrive. There is a memorable early scene set in Greece where Arouch and Allegra are kissing in a movie theater while on the screen a newsreel reports on the Nazis conquering Poland. In the film, the lovers try desperately to maintain contact when both are interned at Auschwitz; in one powerful scene, Arouch searches frantically for Allegra after an air raid. In reality, while Arouch and Allegra were both imprisoned at Auschwitz, they didn't actually meet until the day the camp was liberated by the Russians. Soon after, the couple married and immigrated to Israel, where Arouch made a fortune in the shipping business. By reimagining the romance as having originated before rather than after their camp experiences, Young gives Arouch a potent motive for struggling to survive at Auschwitz; he wants to live so that he can reunite with his girlfriend after the war is over. Commenting on this subplot, Young told *New York Times* reporter John Tagliabue, "It seemed practical enough, since in many personal accounts people often desire to survive by the desire to see people again, and their desire to live is thus enhanced."[2]

Young's last film before making *Triumph of the Spirit* was the critically acclaimed *Dominick and Eugene* (1988), about a young doctor's devotion to a childlike twin brother. According to press accounts, when Young was shown the script for *Triumph of the Spirit* he was initially reluctant to make the film, because he felt the Holocaust was too momentous a subject to be conveyed in a fictionalized movie. But he changed his mind when he realized that the film was only focusing on a relatively small story within the narrative of the Holocaust as a whole, "like a cork, bubbling on the surface of the sea." This perspective was shared by the movie's producer, Arnold Kopelson, who stated, "We aren't dealing with the death of 11 million people (six million of them Jews); we're dealing with the lives of a man, his family, and the woman he loved."[3]

Like Schindler's List, *Triumph of the Spirit* was shot on location at Auschwitz/Birkenau, the first film to be shot on the site of the concentration camp. To gain access to this location, the filmmakers had to get the permission of the Polish government, and they worked in collaboration with Polish television. Since the Nazis had destroyed the main crematorium before fleeing the Allies, however, the filmmakers had to reconstruct a crematorium for use in the movie. This crematorium is then blown up when the film stages the inmate revolt (based on a historical event), which is brutally suppressed by the Germans.

While filming at Auschwitz, the members of the cast and crew were, by their own accounts, suitably awed. Dafoe told Tagliabue: "There are chilling moments. Standing at the courtyard of Cell Block 11, where they were all executed, you look up, you see a tree. That may well have been the last visual image many people saw." Director Young related a comparable story to *Los Angeles Times* film critic Pat H. Broesky; while wandering through Birkenau (the camp that adjoined Auschwitz), Young stumbled on a huge trove of silverware that had apparently been left behind by prisoners sent to the gas chambers. "There were rusted plates and thousands of utensils," the director related. "People came here thinking they were starting a new life."[4]

The film deserves credit for bringing attention to the Sephardic Holocaust—the Nazi murder of Jews living in Mediterranean and Middle Eastern countries. In the past, Holocaust historians tended to focus on the deaths of Ashkenazi Jews living in Eastern and Western Europe, perhaps because many of these historians are themselves descended from Ashkenazi Jews, but the genocide was certainly not limited to these groups. In Greece, 80 percent of the Jewish population was wiped out by Hitler, as large a percentage of Jews as lost their lives in Germany. As Lawrence Baron points out,

Figure 10.2. *Triumph of the Spirit* (1989). Jewish Greek boxing champ Salamo Arouch (Willem Dafoe) talks with a fellow Auschwitz inmate. [Screen grab]

The Sephardic looks of the leading actors do not resemble those of actors usually typecast as Ashkenazi Jews in movies about the Holocaust. . . . The musical score of *Triumph of the Spirit* expresses this cultural difference by using traditional Sephardic instrumentation and melodies. The ominous choral odes accompanying the scenes of Jews being separated, slaughtered, and incinerated are sung in Ladino, the Sephardic language that evolved from medieval Spanish. As the credits roll at the end of the film, images of Salamo, his brother, and father performing Greek folk dances emphasize their Sephardic heritage and the destruction of their culture.[5]

In the film, not long after his arrival at Auschwitz, Arouch is tormented by an especially brutal *Kapo*. Fed up, Arouch fights back against his muscled persecutor and ends up knocking him out. The fight is observed by an SS officer, who (after first putting a bullet in the brain of the unconscious *Kapo*) enlists Arouch to fight in the prisoner-on-prisoner boxing matches, which are staged for the amusement of their captors. These bouts, however, do not follow Marquess of Queensberry rules (more precisely recalling the gladiatorial combats relished by the ancient Romans, where the warriors battled to the death). There are no rounds; the boxers just keep fighting until one of them is unable to stand, whereupon the loser is hauled off to the gas chambers. Although knocked down at the start of his first bout, the scrappy, quick-fisted Arouch goes on to win, and thereafter he's undefeated in over two hundred matches.

But the bouts pose both practical and emotional problems for Arouch. The cruel irony of the matches is that the boxer experiences sympathy for his opponent, a fellow prisoner, while his true enemies, the SS officers in the audience, are the ones he has to entertain. Baron sees Arouch in his boxing matches as another character confronted by Langer's "choiceless choice": "A closer scrutiny of the movie reveals that it is not about the triumph of the spirit but rather about 'choiceless choices.' . . . The synopsis on the back of the video box succinctly describes this quandary: 'For every time Salamo wins, his opponent dies in the gas chambers.'"6

Meanwhile, as he grows progressively weaker due to the harsh conditions in the camp, Arouch must keep summoning new strength to best his opponents. While Arouch receives perks for his victories, such as extra rations of bread, even that creates problems. When Arouch brings the bread back to the barracks to share with his father (Robert Loggia), the other prisoners demand a portion, which Arouch grudgingly provides.

Boxing serves as both the main narrative of *Triumph of the Spirit* and its central symbol. In the world of the camps, one is indeed locked in a fight for survival with fellow prisoners. Baron locates *Triumph of the Spirit* within the popular Hollywood genre of the prison movie and argues that such films often display such themes: "Prison and concentration camp movies often have used athletic competition between inmates or against guards as a metaphor for the Darwinian struggle for existence within such institutions."7 In *Triumph of the Spirit*, other subplots substantiate this theme. Allegra steals food from a dying fellow inmate, for which she's flogged. Two female prisoners fight in the barracks over a pair of shoes. Another woman feigns pregnancy in order to get added food rations, until her imposture is exposed by other prisoners. In the men's camp, Arouch's brother joins the infamous Sonderkommando unit, which flings the corpses of gassed victims into the crematoria so as to attain a relatively easier life, before his unit, like all the others, is liquidated by the Germans.

Arouch's survival is initially a consequence of his boxing prowess, but ultimately it results from pure good luck. Eventually, the Sonderkom-

mandos, after elaborate planning and the meticulous gathering of explosives, succeed in blowing up one of the camp crematoria. (This historical event is also dramatized in *The Grey Zone*.) Because he happens
to be in the vicinity of the revolt, Arouch is accused by the SS of being a
coconspirator. Refusing to confess, Arouch is brutally beaten by the
Germans and left to languish in his jail cell, awaiting execution. However, before he can be shot, the Germans flee the camp in anticipation of
the liberating Soviet army. The last scene shows Arouch staggering half-
dead through the camp gates, wrapped in a ragged blanket, bound for
an unknown destination. In a voice-over during this scene, Arouch pon-
ders his fate: "All those I love are gone. Their faces and what happened
here are forever burned in my mind. How can we do this to our brothers?" Since he lost his parents, three younger sisters, and a brother at
Auschwitz, Arouch is indeed alone.

Annette Insdorf praises Dafoe's performance as Arouch, noting that
the actor "provided *Triumph of the Spirit* with additional resonance, as
his previous role was the lead in *The Last Temptation of Christ*: in both
films he plays a victim—with the difference that Salamo does not turn
the other cheek."[8] But while Dafoe was memorable as a humanized
Jesus in Martin Scorsese's controversial film, made the same year, his
performance in *Triumph of the Spirit* is curiously flat. Baron, however,
finds the listlessness of Dafoe's acting a virtue rather than a defect: "His
lack of affect models how inmates suppressed their despair, fears, and
rage."[9]

But a main point of controversy in *Triumph of the Spirit* concerns
the film's incongruous title. Like *Life Is Beautiful* (a title that is also
meant unironically), *Triumph of the Spirit* would fit as the title of any
number of sentimentally optimistic Holocaust movies. It would make a
perfect title, for example, for *The Diary of Anne Frank*, given Anne's
concluding exhortation that "people are really good at heart." However,
fortunately for the film itself, there is much less stereotypically noble
uplift in this movie than its title would imply. The film's final image of
Arouch staggering out of Auschwitz half-naked and near death hardly
looks like a moment of triumph (unless one sees the mere fact that
Arouch has, literally, survived as a triumph, which is possible). Noting
the film's many graphically brutal scenes, Leonard Maltin calls the movie "sometimes too grim."[10] Maltin's negative assessment was shared by
a reviewer for a Christian website who wrote that the film has no

"Christian [or Jewish] moral content and it is not particularly uplifting even at the end."[11] Insdorf writes that, "this harrowing drama ends—much like *Sophie's Choice*—with camp survival as a testament to endurance rather than nobility."[12] All that can be said in defense of the film's title is that it seems intended to serve as a sharp retort to the pro-Nazi movie made during the war by Hitler's favorite director Leni Riefenstahl, *Triumph of the Will* (1935), a documentary that celebrated, in lavish detail, the huge Nazi rallies staged by the Führer and Albert Speer.

While Dafoe himself believed that his character had "triumphed" at Auschwitz over the Nazis, his fellow actor in the movie, Edward James Olmos—who plays a gypsy prisoner who functions as a "fixer," running an elaborate black market—disagreed, asking, "What does the film project? The moral decay needed to survive in the camp." Thus, Olmos goes even further than Insdorf in denying that the film provides moral uplift; according to the actor, not only has Arouch not "triumphed" in any ethical or existential sense, but he has actually morally degenerated as a result of contributing to the deaths of the innocent prisoners he defeats in the ring. His remark echoes Primo Levi's famous comment that the "worst" survived Auschwitz, because the prisoners had to compete with one another for survival. Whose "spirit," then, has "triumphed" in the film? The despairing theme at the heart of the movie was missed by Roger Ebert, who carped in his negative review: "The audience is enlisted to cheer for Salamo against his enemies. We are presumably supposed to be relieved when he wins. Does this feeling not place us with the Nazis in his audience?" Ebert seems to have been fooled by the film's saccharine title into discerning a message of sentimental cheer that doesn't exist in the movie itself.

Was the film's title demanded by some studio head in an attempt to increase its box office appeal? Such speculation seems supported by the way the film was advertised. As Baron observes,

> The ad campaign and title for . . . *Triumph of the Spirit* misled viewers into believing the film was primarily about how the Jewish boxer Salamo Arouch "triumphed" over the system designed to destroy him by winning the boxing matches he fought to entertain and enrich the SS officers who attended and bet on them. The cover of the video box shows Salamo . . . standing in the ring, gazing down at an opponent he has knocked out. . . . The film's trailer consists

mostly of shots from Salamo's bouts. The narrator claims that "this is the true story of one man's fight for survival and victory in the face of death." One frame evokes the signature scene from *Rocky* (1976) with a close-up of Salamo raising his gloved fists above his head. [13]

But the studio's attempt to advertise *Triumph of the Spirit* as a Holocaust version of *Rocky*, complete with a duplicitously upbeat title, was undermined by the grim, nihilistic content of the film itself, and the movie, despite garnering some good reviews, was a commercial flop. Made for $12 million by an independent studio, Nova International Films (after the project was rejected by all the major American studios Young pitched it to), *Triumph of the Spirit* garnered only $400,000 in the United States in its box-office earnings.

11

SPIELBERG REINVENTS THE HOLOCAUST

Schindler's List

The impact that *Schindler's List* has had on public perceptions of the Holocaust is far greater than that of any other film to date. The movie is the consummate example of how for the vast majority of Americans, for better or worse, history is taught by popular culture. Unlike the television miniseries *Holocaust*—which enjoyed record-setting audiences but was panned by many in the media, and particularly among Holocaust scholars like Elie Wiesel, for its soap-operatic traits—*Schindler's List* received overwhelming praise from across the social spectrum: reviewers in mass-market newspapers and magazines, national Jewish and Christian organizations, the Hollywood establishment (the film won seven Oscars in 1993, including Best Picture, Best Director, and Best Screenplay Adaptation), educators, civic leaders, even politicians. Even more than *Judgment at Nuremberg*, most of these groups and individuals saw *Schindler's List* as more than just a movie—as, rather, a morally uplifting experience as well as a bulwark against Holocaust-denial in America and worldwide.

Yet the film was also sharply criticized by a number of Holocaust scholars and more highbrow critics—although these attacks, because they were leveled largely by ivory-towered intellectuals, never reached a wide audience. As Alan Mintz writes, "Ordinary viewers, the popular media, and communal organizations saw . . . the film [as] capable of imparting an awareness of the Holocaust to millions of people who would otherwise remain ignorant of the event. . . . The detractors were intellectuals and academics who argued that . . . *Schindler's List* had absorbed the catastrophe into the sentimental and melodramatic conventions of popular entertainment and in so doing had betrayed the event."[1]

Schindler's List is based on the true story of Oskar Schindler, a German businessman and Nazi party member who, while his factories, run by Jewish slave labor, were ostensibly producing munitions and other supplies for the Wehrmacht in Poland and Czechoslovakia, was actually risking his life to save more than one thousand Jews from the SS through a range of energetic and ingenious machinations. How Schindler transforms from a Nazi war profiteer to a "Righteous Gentile" is at the heart of the movie. Thus, through Schindler's amazing story, the movie addresses the vital issue of why some Germans (admittedly, a small minority), as well as other Gentiles living in Nazi-occupied countries, risked their lives to save Jews, while the majority of ordinary Germans either did nothing or actively participated while their Jewish neighbors were hauled off to the camps. The film also explores the fascinating relationship that develops between Schindler and Amon Goeth (brilliantly played by Ralph Fiennes), the brutal commandant of the Plaszow concentration camp with whom Schindler cleverly negotiates in order to obtain Jews for his nearby factory.

There are, however, significant differences between the real Schindler and the title character played by the Irish actor Liam Neeson. The changes Spielberg made from the actual Schindler and other historical figures who appear in the film reveal much about the director's intentions.[2] For example, after her husband's factory was moved to their native Czechoslovakia, the real Mrs. Schindler played a key role in helping those who came to be known as the *Schindlerjuden*. In the film, however, Mrs. Schindler is largely absent as her husband is saving Jews, only appearing at the end when she and her spouse must flee the oncoming Soviet army after the war is lost. As well, the historical Itzhak Stern (played by Ben Kingsley in the film) was actually a fervent Zionist, an ideology that placed him in automatic opposition both to Nazi policies and to the more conciliatory actions and attitudes of the *Judenrat*. But Stern's Zionism is omitted, as the Polish Jew, Schindler's right-hand man in the factory, is turned into someone who barely exists apart from his strenuous efforts on his employer's behalf. Moreover, the cinematic character of Stern is a composite figure composed of the historical Stern and another member of the Schindlerjuden, Mietek Pemper, who actually acted more like the Stern in the film than did the real Stern himself; it was Pemper who typed the famous list as well as worked directly under Goeth as the commandant's secretary. Pemper, however, appears to have been modest about his legacy, not publishing his memoirs until 2005 (although he served as a consultant on the film.) As a whole, the Schindlerjuden, depicted in the film as consistently pacifist, were, in actuality, capable of pragmatic violence when necessary. When, for example, Schindler's Jews were being harassed by an especially brutal Nazi guard, the Schindlerjuden conspired to murder him and then (in an eerie echo of the camp crematoria) incinerated his body in one of the factory's industrial ovens.

As for Schindler himself, it seems that the real Schindler was interested all along in helping Jews, and in Judaism and Jewish culture in general. When Schindler first met Stern, he expressed an interest in Yiddish writers and warned Stern that the next day the Germans planned to confiscate all Jewish property. Not only was the historical Schindler pro-Jewish from the start, but he may also have been anti-Nazi all along, maintaining numerous contacts from early in the Nazi era to the *Abwehr* (the German military intelligence group that involved itself in resistance to Hitler.)

In contrast, the cinematic Schindler originally seems little more than a vacuous playboy, happily enlisted in the Nazi party, with no interest in Jews other than exploiting them as slave labor in order to get rich quick. It is only gradually, especially after Schindler witnesses the Germans' horrific liquidation of the Krakow ghetto, that he transforms into a Righteous Gentile. Finally, while the movie ends with a note saying that, after the war, Schindler's marriage failed along with all his business ventures, there is no reference to the pathetic circumstances of Schindler's death. He died alone, broke except for the money he was able to save through his meager pension and handouts from the Schindlerjuden, and nearly forgotten in his hometown of Frankfurt, whose residents, like the German people in general, had no interest in paying tribute to a fellow German whose heroism cast their own inaction or collaboration in stark relief.

At the end of an article about the historical Schindler, Herbert Steinhouse, a Canadian Jewish journalist who befriended Schindler after the war, speculates about what may have motivated Schindler to save all those Jews. After considering several unsatisfying possibilities, Steinhouse eventually throws up his hands and admits that "the only possible conclusion seems to be that Oscar Schindler's exceptional deeds stemmed from just that elementary sense of decency and humanity that our sophisticated age seldom sincerely believes in."[3] For Steinhouse, the real Schindler remains an enigma, and that is precisely how Spielberg portrays him in the film.

If Schindler died largely forgotten, how was his story brought to world attention? The Australian novelist Thomas Keneally heard about Schindler through pure serendipity. Keneally happened to be in a Los Angeles leather-goods store waiting for his credit card to be authorized. The clerk, Leopold Page, turned out to be a member of the Schindlerjuden who, like most of the Jews Schindler saved, had continued to publicize the actions of his savior, especially to well-known writers and filmmakers who might be interested in retelling the story. Keneally decided Page's story could make a good novel.

After the movie appeared, many critics, while praising *Schindler's List*, expressed shock that it should be Steven Spielberg who made what seemed to be the definitive Hollywood movie on the Holocaust. Spielberg, after all, appeared to be the consummate commercial Hollywood director. He'd directed four of the ten top-grossing films of all time: *Jaws* (1975), *E.T.* (1982), *Indiana Jones and the Last Crusade* (1989), and *Jurassic Park* (1993), the last made more or less concurrently with *Schindler's List*. His films were widely hailed as slick, suspenseful, and stunning in their special effects, but few considered them to be profound. If anything, Spielberg was generally seen as a director with the sensibility of a precocious adolescent who understood children and their fantasies better than he did the adult world. Spielberg's one "deep" film up to that point, *The Color Purple* (1985), based on Alice Walker's African American novel, was generally panned as melodramatic schlock.[4]

At first glance, Spielberg certainly did not seem to be an obvious choice. His Jewish family was nominally religious, though not devout. But Spielberg's grandmother did teach English to a number of Holocaust survivors, so the topic had a presence during his childhood. While he was still young, the family moved to Scottsdale, Arizona, where Spielberg grew up as one of the few Jews in his neighborhood, and as a result, by his own admission, grew ashamed of his Jewishness. "It was a *shondeh* [Yiddish for "shame"] for me when I was growing up," he told a *San Francisco Chronicle* reporter. "I just felt like I was on the outside. . . . And I blamed a lot of it on my Jewishness and my Semitic looks and attitudes."[5] The situation became even worse when, in Spielberg's last year of high school, the family moved again, to Saratoga, California: "It was the only time I've experienced active and hostile anti-Semitism. I was beaten up and had pennies tossed at me in study hall. My mom . . . would pick me up and take me home from school, which was well within walking distance. . . . Nobody held back and nobody apologized, which really opened my eyes."[6] In a 1993 interview with *Newsweek*, Spielberg added, "It was my six months of personal horror. And to this day I haven't gotten over it nor have I forgiven any of them."[7] It seems that, on some level, the director sublimated his childhood pain into *Schindler's List*. Moreover, an awareness of his Jewish identity was impressed on him from an early age, albeit mostly negatively.

Schindler's List had a long gestation period before it made it to the screen. Back in the 1960s, Leopold Page, many years before he encountered Thomas Keneally, convinced MGM to make a movie based on Schindler's life. The studio hired *Casablanca* screenwriter Howard Koch to write the screenplay, but because Koch was disturbed by Schindler's dubious character—his boozing, womanizing, Nazi Party affiliations, and war profiteering—the project was eventually dropped. Two decades later, just after Spielberg had finished *E.T.*, MCA president Sidney Sheinberg showed him Keneally's novel and asked him to consider a screen adaptation. Spielberg said he was "drawn to it because of the paradoxical nature of the character. It wasn't about a Jew saving Jews, or a neutral person from Sweden or Switzerland saving Jews. It was about a Nazi saving Jews."[8]

After Spielberg expressed interest, the first person to attempt a screenplay was Keneally himself, but his version was so long it was more suited to a miniseries. Spielberg decided he wasn't ready to tackle the project, so he handed it over, at different times, to two seasoned Hollywood directors—Sydney Pollack and Martin Scorsese. It was Scorsese who brought in screenwriter Steven Zaillian (writer/director of *Searching for Bobby Fischer*), who penned the adaptation of Keneally's novel that was ultimately used in the film. By then Spielberg wanted to reclaim his project. "The minute I gave it to Marty, I missed it," he told

Entertainment Weekly. "I'd given away a chance to do something for my children and family about the Holocaust."[9] So Spielberg and Scorsese made a deal; Scorsese would give back *Schindler's List*, and, in return, Spielberg would hand over the project he was developing at the time, a remake of the 1950s thriller *Cape Fear.*

By his own account, *Schindler's List* was a transformative experience for Spielberg. "I'm recovering from this movie," he told an interviewer afterward. "And my wife [actress Kate Capshaw] thinks the recovery is going to go on for a long time. I'm not myself. And I'm glad I'm not myself."[10]

Perhaps most importantly, Spielberg describes filming *Schindler's List* as an experience that returned him to Judaism. "I've never identified more as a Jew as I have in the process of researching and producing and directing this film. I mean, the best thing that probably happened to me because of this film is that I've reconnected as a Jew."[11] Before making the film, Spielberg had decided to raise his children Jewish. When Capshaw agreed to convert, Spielberg studied alongside her during the long process of education Jewish converts are required to undergo, and he said that as a result he "learned more in one year than I had learned through all my formal Jewish training. I don't think I was really trained properly. I think it would have stuck with me a lot longer had the training been less like going to the dentist."[12]

Spielberg's path back to Judaism parallels that taken by many more or less secular, contemporary American Jews. That is, as children they attend Hebrew school for the amount of time needed to prepare for their bar or bat mitzvah and hate every minute of it. This "coming of age" ceremony usually signals their exit from organized Judaism rather than, as it's supposed to do, usher them into the adult Jewish community. Then, later in life, particularly after they marry and have children, these Jews abruptly discover a connection to the Jewish religion and Jewish life. In that respect, Spielberg can be seen as representing an archetypal contemporary American Jew. Of course, in Spielberg's case, his return to Judaism did not originate with but was greatly influenced by his making of *Schindler's List.*

However, it's not true that Spielberg had displayed no interest as a director in Nazism or Judaism prior to making *Schindler's List.* In the mega-hit *Raiders of the Lost Ark* (1981), the first film in the "Indiana Jones" series, Nazis (relocated to the Middle East) are the principle villains, and the grail both the good and bad guys are pursuing turns out to be the Ark of the Covenant, granted by God to the biblical Israelites as a sign of his special bond with his "chosen people," which in the movie's climax wipes out all the evil Nazis immediately on being opened. But no one could claim that Spielberg deals with these subjects with anywhere near the depth and sophistication he employs in *Schindler's List*; instead, these weighty references function merely as a means to drive forward the film's propulsive thriller plot.

After deciding to direct *Schindler's List*, Spielberg visited Auschwitz for the first time, which infuriated, rather than saddened, him. "I was deeply pissed off. I was all ready to cry in front of strangers, and I didn't shed a tear. . . . I felt so helpless. . . . And yet I thought, well, there is something I can do about it. I can make 'Schindler's List.' . . . It's not going to bring anyone back alive, but maybe it will remind people that another Holocaust is a sad possibility."[13] Spielberg's fears of "another Holocaust" were triggered by various atrocities happening at the time. "It was a combination of things: my interest in the Holocaust and my horror at the symptoms of the Shoah again happening in Bosnia. And again happening with Saddam Hussein's attempt to eradicate the Kurdish race. We were racing over these moments in world history that were exactly like what happened in 1943."[14] Spielberg might have added that the civilized world in his day was doing little more to help the victimized Bosnians and Kurds than the Allies had done to try to save the Jews during World War II.

Spielberg claimed to find a level of truth-telling in *Schindler's List* that set the film apart from his previous escapist fare:

> The reason I came to make the movie, is that I have never in my life told the truth in a movie. My effort as a moviemaker has been to create something that couldn't possibly happen. So people could leave their lives and have an adventure and then come back to earth and drive home. That was one of the things I thought: if I'm going to tell the truth for the first time, it should be about this subject. Not about divorce or parents and children, but about this.[15]

He told *New Yorker* writer Stephen Schiff, "I made 'Schindler's List' thinking that if it did entertain, then I would have failed. It was important to me not to set out to please. Because I always had."[16]

Schiff shrewdly comments in the article, "Of course, the almost un-mentionable secret of 'Schindler's List' is that it does entertain . . . that it has storytelling confidence and flair . . . that it is not, in short, a lecture but a work of art."[17]

Because, by making *Schindler's List*, Spielberg had abandoned pop-ular entertainment for a nobler calling, several critics saw parallels be-tween the director and Schindler himself. In his glowing *New Yorker* review, Terrence Rafferty wrote, "The sheer unexpectedness of Spiel-berg's rigorous refusal to simplify his protagonist's motives seems to connect him, in a minor but distinct way, to Schindler himself; this character is, after all, a man whose dedication and commitment to right-eous action simply could not have been predicted from the evidence of his prewar life."[18]

Spielberg made some major changes in Zaillian's screenplay. While the director liked the script, he found that it lacked, as he put it, "Jewish faces." "I didn't tell the story from the survivors' point-of-view," Zaillian has said, "but from Schindler's"—an approach that closely follows Ke-neally's novel.[19] Looking to broaden that perspective, Spielberg tried to make the film not just tell Schindler's story but also grapple with the Holocaust as a whole. In particular, the director wanted Zaillian to expand the extraordinary scene where the Nazis brutally liquidate the Krakow ghetto—which Schindler witnesses on horseback on a hill over-looking the city and inspires his decision to save Jews. A mere two pages in Zaillian's original script, the expanded scene, which runs for over twenty minutes, took Spielberg three weeks to film. "I wanted it to be almost unwatchable," the director said.[20] As Lawrence Baron points out, "Spielberg heightens the revulsion of the audience by turning his lens on the most vulnerable victims—children, women, and the elder-ly—who scurry to find a nook or cranny where they can hide. . . . Most of the scene is shot by a shaky hand-held camera simulating how the perpetrators and victims perceived this homicidal rampage."[21] With the inclusion of Spielberg's revisions, the script ballooned from 115 to 195 pages. As a result, the film's first cut ran to a commercially untenable four hours, and Spielberg felt compelled to reduce the movie to its final length—three hours and fourteen minutes.

Like Stanley Kramer with *Judgment at Nuremberg* and Sydney Lumet with *The Pawnbroker*, Spielberg had to battle the studio in order to get *Schindler's List* made *his* way. In Spielberg's case, Universal Studios wanted the director to shoot the picture in color, while Spielberg insisted that, in order to give the movie a documentary feel, he wanted it predominantly in black and white. Universal also wanted Spielberg to clarify what motivated Schindler's heroism. "The studio, of course, wanted me to spell everything out," the director told *Entertainment Weekly*. "I got into a lot of arguments with people saying we need that big Hollywood catharsis where Schindler falls to his knees and says, 'Yes, I know what I'm doing—now I must do it!' and goes full steam ahead. That was the last thing I wanted."[22] Ultimately, the studio agreed to green-light the project only if Spielberg first shot *Jurassic Park*. As a result, Spielberg shot *Schindler's List* by day, then retired every night to do postproduction editing on *Jurassic Park*, leaping from Nazis to dinosaurs.

In *Judgment at Nuremberg*, Stanley Kramer commercialized his film about Nazi war crime trials by packing his cast with box-office stars. In the early days of Spielberg's project, rumors circulated that the director had similar intentions. Kevin Costner was bandied about as a possibility for Schindler, as was Mel Gibson. Ultimately, however, the director chose the relatively unknown Liam Neeson, whose performance would earn him a Best Actor Oscar nomination. The rest of the cast was equally international. In the roles of Itzhak Stern and of the film's principle villain, Amon Goeth, Spielberg picked two superb British actors—Ben Kingsley and Ralph Fiennes, respectively, both better known at the time than was Neeson. As Helen Hirsch, a Jewish prisoner at Plaszow who attracts Goeth, the director chose a South African actress, Embeth Davidtz. In other Jewish-speaking roles, Spielberg cast Israelis, several the children of survivors, while he used local Catholic Poles for many of the smaller Gentile parts. As his cinematographer, the director picked a Pole, Janusz Kaminski.

On the set of the film were a considerable number of Schindlerjuden, as well as other Holocaust survivors, all of whom advised Spielberg, several relating experiences that the director worked into the movie. The scene in which a young Jewish boy saves his life during the Krakow ghetto's annihilation by pretending to German soldiers that he's been ordered to clear away corpses; the moment in the same scene in which a wealthy Jewish family hides its diamonds in pieces of bread that they swallow; another scene at Plaszow in which female prisoners prick their fingers and smear blood on their cheeks in an attempt to look healthy and so escape the "selections"—all these scenes were based on survivor recollections offered to Spielberg on the set. For the movie's unforgettable final sequence, in which the actual Jews saved by Schindler, standing alongside the actors who portray them in the film, lay stones at Schindler's grave in Jerusalem (a traditional Jewish funereal practice), Spielberg flew 128 of the surviving Schindlerjuden to Israel. Given the contribution of Holocaust survivors to its creation, it's no surprise that *Schindler's List* has been almost universally praised by survivors.

To add to its quasi-documentary ambience, Spielberg filmed almost entirely on location. The ghetto liquidation scene was shot in what remains of Krakow's Jewish ghetto. The Krakow apartment that the Nazis give Schindler after a Jewish family is evicted and Schindler's factory in the same city were the actual sites where those events transpired. Even the hilltop where Schindler must have stood in order to have a full view of the ghetto was located by one of the Schindlerjuden. Originally Spielberg had wanted to film inside Auschwitz itself, but that plan was opposed by the World Jewish Congress, which argued that such filming would "disturb the dignity of a site that . . . requires solemnity."[23] In response, Spielberg compromised, constructing a set just outside the fence bordering the camp.

Before *Schindler's List* appeared, many Holocaust scholars understandably feared that a large percentage of Americans had forgotten about the Holocaust, if they had ever known anything about it in the first place. According to a survey conducted by the reputable Roper Organization around the time of the movie's release, more than 50 percent of high school students didn't know what the word "Holocaust" meant, and a quarter of all adults were unaware that Germany was the country in which the Nazis came to power. Moreover, the Roper survey heightened growing concerns about the Holocaust-denial movement in America and Europe, whose influence might reasonably be expected to spread as the last Holocaust survivors died off. The survey found that 22 percent of respondents felt it was "possible" that "the Nazi extermination of the Jews never happened," while 12 percent said they didn't know.[24]

Many supporters of *Schindler's List* felt the film would serve as a permanent bulwark against both ignorance of the Holocaust and denial of its existence. In a *New York Times* review, Janet Maslin expressed confidence that the movie would achieve "a permanent place in memory."[25] In the *New York Review of Books*, John Gross elaborated the point: "As a contribution to popular culture, it can only do good. Holocaust denial may or may not be a major problem in the future, but Holocaust ignorance, Holocaust forgetfulness, and Holocaust indifference are bound to be, and *Schindler's List* is likely to do as much as any single work can to dispel them."[26]

Additionally, the appearance of *Schindler's List* should be situated within a constellation of events occurring from 1993 to 1994, all of which helped to preserve Holocaust memory—events that added up to what Frank Rich aptly called "the Holocaust boom." Perhaps the most important was the opening of the US Holocaust Memorial Museum in Washington, DC, in April 1993, a museum that would become the most widely visited on the Mall and would develop nationwide curricula used to teach about the Holocaust in public schools. (Aptly, the year the film appeared, Spielberg and his actors were feted at the museum at a ceremony to honor Schindler.)

On the international scene that same year, Pope John Paul II, as part of his ongoing campaign to heal the historical rift between Catholics and Jews, officially honored on "Holocaust Remembrance Day" the Nazis' Jewish victims. John Paul was also the first pope to invite Rome's chief rabbi to a Vatican ceremony. (During his papacy, John Paul would also have the Vatican establish diplomatic relations with Israel for the first time, pray at the "Wailing Wall" during a trip to the Jewish state, and sponsor the publication of a Vatican document, "We Remember: A Reflection on the Shoah," which blamed individual Catholics for pro-Nazi collaboration, though it exonerated the Church as a whole.)

At times, praise of *Schindler's List* grew so effusive as to border on the absurd. Jeffrey Katzenberg, at the time head of Disney Studios, told *New Yorker* reporter Schiff, "I think 'Schindler's List' will . . . affect how people on this planet think and act. At a moment in time, it is going to remind us about the dark side, and do it in a way in which, whenever that little green monster is lurking somewhere, this movie is going to press it down again. I don't want to burden the movie too much, but I think it will bring peace on earth, good will to men. Enough of the right people will see it that it will actually set the course of world affairs."[27] Noting that even leading politicians—President Clinton, Senator Bill Bradley, California Governor Pete Wilson—had praised the movie,

Philip Gourevitch argued in *Commentary* that *Schindler's List* was benefitting from "a kind of cultural grade inflation," which deemed criticism of the film nothing short of sacrilege.[28]

What initially drew Spielberg to Schindler's story was its central paradox of a Nazi who saves Jews. In the film itself, when Schindler is dressing for a night of hobnobbing with Nazi big shots in order to make business connections, the camera focuses briefly on the swastika pinned to his lapel. Early on, Schindler announces, with what proves to be considerable dramatic irony, "They won't soon forget the name of Schindler here. He did something no one else did. He left with two steamer trunks full of money." Later, Schindler asks his wife, "You know what makes all the difference between success and failure?" "Luck?" she replies. "No," he answers, "war." By stressing at the start Schindler's greed and unabashed Nazi ties, Spielberg makes Schindler's eventual transformation into a savior of Jews even more surprising than it was in the case of the historical Schindler.

In this moral ambiguity, Schindler contrasts sharply with the best-known prior "rescuer," the Swedish diplomat Raoul Wallenberg, who, among other exploits, managed to convince the SS commandant in Budapest to ignore an order from his superiors to murder Hungary's remaining 70,000 Jews. Soon after the Russians invaded Hungary, Wallenberg disappeared into the Soviet Gulag, never to be seen again. In 1985, a television docudrama was produced: *Wallenberg: A Hero's Story*, which, as its title implies, portrayed the Swedish diplomat as a figure of absolute, unimpeachable virtue, with none of the complexities of Schindler's character. Contrasting Wallenberg with Schindler, Lawrence Baron argues that "the shift from idealized characterizations of rescuers to less flattering ones is a hallmark of Holocaust cinema in the 1990s," a shift he approves of, since it "reduce[s] the rescuers to their human dimensions and thereby enable[s] the average American to realize that they were plausible and relevant role models of moral activism."[29]

There are, however, early hints in the film that Schindler is no passionate supporter of Hitler. In the aforementioned scene in which Schindler wines and dines the Nazi brass in a Krakow nightclub, the *New Yorker's* Terrence Rafferty notes "a handful of close-ups of Schindler's watchful face in the moment just before he moves in on the Nazis. He gazes at them coldly, clinically."[30] In general, Schindler seems too interested in money to be bothered with *any* ideological affinities—for the Nazis or any other political group.

The irony is that as Schindler changes into a Righteous Gentile, he draws on these same talents as a wheeler-dealer, except now these skills are used to save Jewish lives. When Schindler convinces Itzhak Stern to work as his assistant, Stern notes that their arrangement seems to mean that Stern will do all the work and asks, quite reasonably, just what Schindler's job will be. "Presentation," Schindler replies. Such quick-witted, charismatic savvy is equally evident in the way Schindler handles Amon Goeth, bribing and cajoling the manipulable commandant, playing on his weaknesses and vanities, until Goeth agrees to allow Schindler to move all his Jewish laborers out of the camp and have them live on the factory premises. Later, when Schindler establishes a new factory in Czechoslovakia, he convinces Goeth to permit Schindler to purchase all his Jewish workers and relocate them to his new facility.

In the novel, Keneally stresses that Schindler is a natural confidence man: "It was Oskar's nature to believe that you could drink with the

Figure 11.1. *Schindler's List* (1993). Amon Goeth (Ralph Fiennes), brutal commandant of the Plaszow concentration camp, surveys his domain from his balcony, rifle in hand. [Screen grab]

devil and adjust the balance of evil over a snifter of cognac. It was not that he found more radical methods more frightening. It was that they did not occur to him. He'd always been a man of transactions."[31] Holocaust scholar Omer Bartov argues that the moral ambiguity of Schindler's character makes the film *less* like a product of Tinsel Town, since the movie thus "subtly . . . undermines the Hollywood convention of a cinematic world neatly divided between good and evil."[32] Like the Polish acting troupe in *To Be or Not to Be*, Schindler has a genius for resisting the Nazis through perpetual improvisation and theatricality. However, when Schindler buys his Jews from Goeth, he stops acting like a capitalist because the decision bankrupts him. Ultimately, Schindler must reject his business career in order to become a Righteous Gentile—a plot twist that refutes Art Spiegelman's claim that *Schindler's List* glorifies "the benign aspects of capitalism."[33]

In leaving his protagonist an enigma, Spielberg remained true to Keneally's novel. "One of the commonest sentiments of Schindler Jews is still 'I don't know why he did it,'" Keneally writes.

> It can be said that Oskar was a gambler, was a sentimentalist who loved . . . the simplicity of doing good; that Oskar was by temperament an anarchist who loved to ridicule the system; and that beneath the hearty sensuality lay a capacity to be outraged by human savagery. . . . But none of this . . . explains the doggedness with which, in the autumn of 1944, he prepared a final haven for [the Jews who worked in the Krakow factory].[34]

Most critics applauded Spielberg's decision to leave Schindler's motives obscure. "Spielberg's artistic triumph here is that he refuses to explicate," wrote Stanley Kaufmann, "to interfere with what is actually known. He leaves the mystery of Schindler's goodness as finally inexplicable as the mystery of the human savagery around him. This, for me, is the true subject of the film."[35] Annette Insdorf notes that Schindler's mysteriousness is conveyed even by the film's cinematography.[36] Often we are just shown parts of Schindler's body (for example, as he's dressing for his night with the Nazi officers), or he is shot from behind (in the subsequent nightclub scene), or, in several instances, Schindler's form is cast half in light and half in shadow.

But a minority of critical voices resented Spielberg's lack of clarity regarding Schindler's character. For example, Philip Gourevitch noted that in the novel, unlike in the movie, when Schindler witnesses the liquidation of the Krakow ghetto, he explicitly renounces to himself his Nazi allegiances. "By robbing us of Schindler's renunciation of Nazism," Gourevitch argues, "Spielberg gives us a simply enigmatic creation, the Good Nazi," which strips Schindler of his "human complexity and replaces it with—nothing."[37]

Contrary to Gourevitch's claim, however, the film does imply that Schindler's observation of the ghetto's destruction represents a turning point. Shortly afterward, Schindler performs his first purely altruistic act when he agrees to employ the elderly parents of one of his female workers, both clearly unfit for strenuous labor. The ghetto scene features repeated shots of Schindler's anguished face. Rather than overt renunciation, Spielberg's method is to depict that scene so vividly that the audience is devastated, and assumes that Schindler is, too.

Moreover, one can't discuss this scene without noting the extraordinary image of the little girl in the red coat. Other than the frame scenes, this is the one instance where Spielberg uses color, reddening the coat of a little Jewish girl shown wandering alone through the destroyed ghetto. We sense Schindler's gaze fixated on the girl. Much later, when Goeth is burning his victims' bodies, Schindler walks past a pile of corpses that includes the girl in the red coat. While Schindler never makes this point explicitly, it seems that in witnessing the red-coated girl, Schindler sees for the first time the Nazis' Jewish victims as individuals rather than viewing them en masse, and it is this revelation that completes his transformation into a rescuer.

Other scenes highlighting Schindler's Holocaust morality are conflicting. When a female contingent within the Schindlerjuden is mistakenly routed to Auschwitz, Schindler hastens to retrieve them. In the course of Schindler's bargaining with the Auschwitz commandant, the Nazi head offers to give Schindler a new shipload of female prisoners to replace his own workers, but Schindler refuses the trade, instead lavishly bribing the commandant to get his own Jews back. This may remind readers of Lawrence Langer's point that, in the Holocaust, saving one potential victim almost always ensured the death of another. Schindler's tenacity in saving his own Jews still means that others will die in their place.

Many critics have argued that, in his role as savior of Jews, Schindler is implicitly ascribed Christ-like attributes. Because Schindler fits so neatly into the Christian archetype of the sinner turned saint, argues critic Richard Wolin, he "is a figure with whom a mass audience could readily . . . sympathize."[38] Notably, there are two scenes, one early in the film and one late, in which we see Schindler in church. In the first, he is huddled in a back pew, negotiating with black marketeers to acquire luxury items with which to bribe his Nazi contacts. In the second, in sharp contrast, Schindler apologizes to his wife for his philandering and vows to rededicate himself to their marriage. Because this second scene is set in a church, and because Schindler expresses his repentance, it appears that he's undergone a spiritual transformation.

Perhaps the biggest criticism that may be launched against *Schindler's List* is that, while Spielberg presents Schindler's story as a representative tale of the Shoah, it is, in fact, a highly anomalous Holocaust narrative. In the *New York Review of Books*, Jason Epstein argues that Schindler's behavior is "so different from the behavior of countless others at the time as to suggest that he might have come from a different planet, like another famous Spielberg character. . . . Does the film mean to suggest that, if only there had been enough Schindlers, the problem of evil which the Holocaust raises would have been solved?"[39] Indeed, Schindler's story can be seen as questioning the consensus view of historians that heroic individuals, no matter their number, might have slowed the Holocaust's progress, but certainly couldn't stop it entirely. In contrast, the film can be seen as implying that, had more people behaved like Schindler, the Holocaust might never have occurred, or at least would have been much less devastating than it was.

However, if Spielberg had focused on death rather than rescue, the results might have pleased the intelligentsia, but the movie never would have reached a mass audience. And reaching a mass audience, of course, is what a Hollywood director has to do if he seeks to inscribe the Holocaust permanently into American culture. Commercial success is impossible without compromises. The real question to ask about *Schindler's List* is not whether it makes compromises but whether it makes too many.

The character of Itzhak Stern—Schindler's right-hand man, a Jewish accountant who supervises the daily working of the factory—inspired lively critical debate among reviewers at the time. Few questioned that Ben Kingsley gives a brilliant performance as Stern. In fact, many praised the fact that Stern's relationship with Schindler evolves over time. Initially, Stern is clearly wary of the German and seems to assist him either out of desperation or because he thinks he can manipulate Schindler on behalf of his fellow Jews. Only gradually does Stern come to admire his employer as he witnesses Schindler's repeated acts of courage and self-sacrifice. *Seattle Times* reviewer John Hartl sees Stern as a surrogate for the audience: "Powerless as his character is, he becomes a kind of touchstone, the one person who tries to make sense of ongoing, unmanageable disaster. When his life is endangered, the audience feels threatened."[40]

But critics who disliked Stern's characterization pointed out how timid he appears, especially in contrast to Schindler's manly heroics. In her panning of the movie in the Jewish newspaper *The Forward*, Ilene Rosenzweig calls Stern the "king of the Jewish wimps."[41] Tim Cole agrees: "Stern . . . is portrayed as a slightly effeminate and bookish character who needs the protection of Schindler."[42] This depiction of Stern, it's worth noting, differs from Keneally's novel, where the accountant takes a much more active role in saving the Schindlerjuden.

The most extended attack on Stern's character is provided by Judith Doneson, who sees the relationship between Schindler and Stern as a symbolic "marriage," with Schindler in the role of the traditional domineering, though doting, "husband," while Stern is the subservient "wife." In helping Schindler attain greatness, Stern "evolves into the woman behind the successful man."[43] Doneson argues that Stern only questions Schindler's judgment when they are alone—as, for example, when Stern is interned briefly at Plaszow and meets privately with Schindler in order to implore his boss not to let things fall apart in his absence. Doneson concludes that Stern helps Schindler in a traditionally womanly way, by helping bring out "feminine" aspects of Schindler's character, such as kindness and compassion.

Doneson's reading is persuasive, and troublingly so, since, although Doneson doesn't make the point explicitly, the "feminized" Stern plays into anti-Semitic stereotypes about the alleged weakness and effeminacy of, especially, Ashkenazic Jewish men. Among his other canards against the Jews, Hitler insisted they were cowardly in battle, which was why Germany lost World War I.

But the larger problem with Stern's characterization is less that he's effeminate than that he's such a nonentity. Just as Laurence Olivier's performance as the escaped Nazi in *Marathon Man* is so good that one tends to overlook that the character is really a cartoon villain, so Kingsley's portrayal of Stern makes it easy to forget that the figure found in the script is so one-dimensional. Indeed, Stern is portrayed as having no life outside of his relationship with Schindler. And within the relationship there are only a few moments when Stern displays any individuality or force of character.

At first it's understandable that Stern is so deferential to Schindler, since Schindler holds Stern's life in his hands. But, as Stern's trust in Schindler grows, this dynamic would naturally have evolved. There also is no reason Spielberg couldn't have provided Stern with some life outside of his service as Schindler's assistant, especially considering that Stern is the most prominent Jewish figure in the film. Notably, the historical Stern was not only an ardent Zionist, as noted earlier, but also had a wife who stood by him throughout the Holocaust.

Critics have often pointed out how, just as with Itzhak Stern, the film's Jews in general take a back seat to Schindler's exploits. In a feisty piece in the *New York Times*, Frank Rich wrote that the movie's "emotional power is muted by the anonymity of the film's Jews."[44] Aside from Stern, "the other [Jews], who have the generic feel of composites, are as forgettable as the chorus in a touring company of 'Fiddler on the Roof' or, for that matter, the human dino-fodder in 'Jurassic Park.'"[45] Trying to explain why the film was nonetheless such a hit among American Jews, Rich speculated that these Jews were "automatically flesh[ing] out the human ciphers in 'Schindler's List' with characters and associations of [their] own."[46]

To the extent that the film's Jews are portrayed at all, claims Holocaust scholar Sara Horowitz, the movie almost exclusively associates them with money. In the aforementioned scene in which the Jewish black marketeers meet with Schindler in a church, Horowitz notes how these Jews first dip their fingers into the holy water to create the illusion that they are Christians come to worship. Horowitz concludes: "The film's reproduction of anti-Semitic stereotypes—the greedy, crafty, ugly Jew—may be the image they [the audience] retain."[47]

But Horowitz ignores the fact that *no* Jewish characters in the film are unsympathetically portrayed. Stern may be subservient, but he's smart, hard working, and dedicated as well, and without him Schindler's accomplishments would have been impossible. As Baron notes, in Stern "Spielberg fashions a character whose patient goodness slowly converts

Schindler from a boss driven only by profit motives to an unlikely hero devoted to saving as many Jews as he can."[48] The rest of the Schindlerjuden are all depicted in favorable, if not glowing, terms. As for the Jewish black marketeers, they dip their fingers in the holy water not because they wish to blaspheme the Christian religion but because they need to "pass" as Christians in order to conduct their business safely. Moreover, given Nazi anti-Semitic persecution, dealing in the black market was necessary for Jewish survival. Indeed, their selling bootleg caviar, cigars, and cognac to Schindler actually helps him in his efforts to bribe the Nazi brass and thus safeguard his Schindlerjuden.

If the Schindlerjuden are saints, their moral opposite is Amon Goeth, brutal Plaszow commandant and the film's principle villain. Thomas Doherty argues that Goeth is the most interesting figure in *Schindler's List*: "As in *Paradise Lost*, it is the devil who is the most magnetic character in the epic . . . Goeth . . . confirms again the fascination with fascism, the way evil outperforms good as a focus for narrative interest. . . . A dutiful true believer, Goeth may muster a certain weariness and distaste about his . . . work, but never any qualms. With the Krakow ghetto an inferno in backframe, he mutters, exhausted but satisfied, that he'll be happy when the night is over."[49] Indeed, with the Jews in the film relegated to the background and Schindler left an enigma, one might argue that the stage is set for Goeth to steal the show.

Critics at the time tended to see the relationship between Goeth and Schindler as consisting of two Germans who are in certain respects very similar, and in others, polar opposites. Reviewer and literary scholar Bryan Cheyette argues that Spielberg, following Keneally, presents Goeth as Schindler's "dark brother": "Goeth and Schindler are both convivial womanizers, drunkards, and war profiteers, ride horses and, in their different ways, have the lives of Jews in their hands."[50] Baron observes that "the film is filled with parallel images of the two men admiring themselves in the mirror, kissing lovers, shaving, or talking to Goeth's maid Helen."[51] It's true that Schindler couldn't so effectively manipulate Goeth if he didn't acutely understand him and perhaps, on some level, feel attracted to him. Of course, Goeth and Schindler are also diametrically opposed because one devotes his life to killing Jews while the other is equally devoted to saving them. Alvin Rosenfeld sees the central drama of the movie as the battle between a "good German" and a "bad German" and believes the combat is constructed in such

Manichean terms that the viewer is never forced to wrestle with any troubling moral complexities.

Gallons of critical ink have been spilled over Goeth's bizarre relationship with Helen Hirsch. Doherty describes the face-off between Goeth and "his nubile Jewish houseservant" in the commandant's wine cellar as "the film's strangest scene": "She stands forescreen, moist chemise clinging to her breasts. Goeth circles and delivers a seductive, sinister monologue, threat and courtship, the pure Aryan contemplating a liaison with this 'rat-faced' *Untermensch*, who is, of course, a beautiful, tempting woman. Is he becoming human? Will his rape of the girl humanize him?"[52] Film critic Roger Ebert focuses on Goeth's hypocrisy in participating in the Final Solution while slavering over a Jewess: "Goeth is one of those weak hypocrites who upholds an ideal but makes himself an exception to it. . . . He does not find it monstrous that [Helen's] people are being exterminated, and she is spared on his affectionate whim."[53] Neither Doherty nor Ebert mentions the end of this scene, in which, rather than raping Hirsch, Goeth pulls a shelf of wine bottles down on top of her. Clearly, he has resolved his inner conflict over whether to have sex with this "degenerate" Jewess by sublimating his lust into violence.

Indeed, it does seem odd that when Goeth arrives Hirsch just happens to be in a wet slip that clings to her breasts. Perhaps she's in a state of deshabille because she is preparing for bed, but that seems rather convenient for the director. Sara Horowitz argues that the scene is blatantly pornographic: "The audience participates in Goeth's erotic gaze. Like Goeth, the viewer is meant to desire Helen's body, visually sexualized by the wet clothing. As Goeth's desire resolves into a physical beating, the audience participates in a voyeurism which encompasses both sex and brutality, with the victimized Jewish woman as its object."[54] While Horowitz's charge has validity, it's worth noting that presenting Helen half-naked underscores how conflicted Goeth is between Nazi ideology and his libido. Moreover, Goeth seems not only sexually but also emotionally attracted to Hirsch. Such inner conflict makes his character more complex, less a cartoon Nazi. Is Goeth somewhat less evil because he's attracted to a Jewess, which violates every principle he lives by?

Given his ambiguous attraction to a Jewess, his random brutality, his strange friendship with Schindler, how accurate is the movie's implicit presentation of Goeth as a representative Nazi? Several critics objected that Goeth's characterization amounts to a pathologizing of Nazism— that is, reducing the Nazis to a band of violent madmen like Goeth in a way that comfortably distances the audience from any connection with Nazi behavior. Cole, for example, notes that there is nothing in Goeth's portrait that resonates with Hannah Arendt's comment about the "banality of evil" as represented in Adolf Eichmann—a bureaucrat who sat at his desk and sentenced Jews to die with a stroke of his pen. In contrast, Cole maintains, Goeth "is a psychopath who murders indiscriminately, rather than an example of a mediocrity such as Eichmann. He is not at all like us."[55]

Indeed, with Schindler so good and Goeth so evil, the film risks becoming a simple morality play. The Manichean divide between the two men is seen most clearly when they play a game of cards to decide the fate of Helen Hirsch. Moreover, by dropping from the script Keneally's reference to the fact that by the time Schindler had moved his operations to the Brinnlitz factory, Goeth had been imprisoned by his superiors for black marketeering, Spielberg is able to retain Goeth's status as the evil embodiment of absolute power.

Thus, when at the film's end, Goeth is hanged by the Allies as punishment for his crimes, the implication seems to be that the radical evil that the Nazis represent has been totally defeated, that everything associated with the Holocaust is now safely in the past. Even the film's use of color can also be seen as implying that all traces of the Holocaust are over. As noted, the contemporary action that frames the film is in color, while the middle sequence, set during the war, is in black and white. Whether intentionally or not, the apparent implication is that the Holocaust is an event that is out of time, bearing no relationship to what came either before or after.

Ultimately, what's at stake in the debate over the validity of presenting Goeth as a typical Nazi is the question of the nature of Nazi evil. Were most Nazis paper-pushers like Eichmann, who drew no distinction between sending supplies or human beings to Auschwitz? Or were they generally blood-drenched sadists like Goeth, who reveled in killing Jews? This complex question can't be answered definitively, but I agree with Cole that it's more comforting for American audiences to think that the Nazis were like Goeth rather than like Eichmann. Few of us yearn to kill people with our own hands, but many of us suffer from blind obedience to authority and a refusal to take personal moral responsibility for our actions. If the aim of Holocaust cinema is to *dis*comfort us, then Eichmann seems a better model.

A particularly problematic scene is one in which the female Schindlerjuden, having been mistakenly sent to Auschwitz, are herded naked into what appears to be a gas chamber, only to have the spouts drench them with water rather than gas. Most critics (even those who generally praised the film) found this disturbing. Cole sees this scene as another way Spielberg is distancing the audience from the Holocaust's full horror: "We sit terrified that [Spielberg] is actually going to show us this room of women being gassed. . . . But of course he doesn't. This is Hollywood. The showers produce hot water, not Zyklon B. We feel the immense sense of relief that these women felt."[56]

The scene is historically accurate, as the testimony of the women involved has revealed. But such accuracy doesn't redeem the scene for Omar Bartov:

> The fact that this "actually" happened is . . . wholly beside the point, since in most cases it did not, and even when it did, the only eyes which might have derived any . . . pleasure from watching such scenes belonged to the SS. Hence . . . Spielberg makes the viewer complicit with the SS, both sharing in their voyeurism and blocking out the reality of the gas chambers.[57]

Echoing Horowitz's interpretation of the scene in which Goeth brutalizes Helen Hirsch, Aaron Kerner sees the shower scene as profoundly sexist in its treatment of the female body:

> The sequence invites the sadistic and fetishistic gaze of the spectator. . . . Lines of women get undressed; now the humiliated female body is transformed into fetish object. . . . Surely the Marquis de Sade would marvel at Spielberg's narrative craft.[58]

But Spielberg is no Marquis de Sade. Rather, he is dramatizing what victims of the gas chambers, male *and* female, underwent in their final moments on Earth. Spielberg, however, has crafted a scene that appears to confirm the Holocaust-deniers' crazed contention that the gas chambers never existed, that such facilities were only used for what the Nazis claimed: to clean and delouse recently arrived prisoners.

After Schindler has departed and the Soviet liberators arrive, a Soviet officer tells the Schindlerjuden that there is nowhere for them to go. In the next scene, now in color, we see these same Jews flocking across a Jerusalem hillside, while the soundtrack plays "Jerusalem of Gold," a popular Israeli song. Many contemporary critics saw this scene as implying a Zionist message, suggesting that while nowhere in Europe is safe for the Jews, Israel provides a haven as the Jewish homeland. "Jerusalem of Gold" was popular in Israel during the Six-Day War, when it was taken to refer to Israel's quest to recapture East Jerusalem and so recover the Jewish holy places.

Interestingly, when *Schindler's List* was screened in Israel, "Jerusalem of Gold" was dropped, after its inclusion was heavily criticized in Israel—something that occurred in no other country where the movie was shown.[59] In its place was substituted the tune "Eli, Eli"—a musical version of a 1941 poem by Hannah Senesh, who parachuted into occupied Hungary in 1944 in an attempt to establish a Jewish underground, was captured by the Germans and executed, and became for Israelis a symbol of heroic martyrdom.

Apparently, the Israelis concluded that it was inappropriate to associate a Holocaust film with the Six-Day War, since a consequence of that war was Israel's acquisition of the occupied territories, with its population of resentful Palestinians. "Jerusalem of Gold" was the Israelis' unofficial victory hymn after the Six-Day War. When *Schindler's List* was screened in Israel for preview audiences, with "Jerusalem of Gold" on the soundtrack, Israeli viewers were generally disturbed by the inclusion of the song, and it was at this point that Spielberg inserted instead "Eli Eli." In contrast to "Jerusalem of Gold," "Eli, Eli" alludes to a person and event actually related to the Holocaust. The Israelis may also have seen Senesh, a Palestinian Jew, as an example of the "normalized" Jew Zionists lionized, in contrast to the diaspora Jew, who had rejected the Zionist appeal. A simpler explanation for the change would be that, by the time *Schindler's List* appeared, "Jerusalem of Gold" had been played so many times in Israel that it had lost its initial appeal for a majority of Israelis and been reduced to kitsch.

The implicitly Zionist conclusion to *Schindler's List* may be one reason the movie was banned in several Islamic nations. The countries' stated objections to the film ranged from concerns about its "nudity, sexual content, and violence" to complaints that it was "propaganda with the purpose of asking for sympathy for Jews."[60] Spielberg refused to cut the offending scenes in order to get the film shown in Muslim countries and publicly expressed disbelief that Muslims had failed to perceive what he considered the movie's universality: "It shocks me because I thought the Muslim nations would feel this film could be an instrument of their own issues in what was happening in Bosnia. . . . This movie speaks not only on the Jewish Holocaust, but of every Holocaust, by anyone's definition."[61]

Spielberg's insistence on the universality of *Schindler's List* seems accurate and helps explain the film's popularity. But a more problematic aspect of the film is that, by focusing on the rescue of Jews by Righteous Gentiles, the movie in a sense gives the Holocaust a "happy ending." As Alan Mintz argues, "The vast success of *Schindler's List* signifies and conforms to a kind of compact between Spielberg and his audience. . . . The Holocaust as a subject may be moved to the center of public awareness on the condition that it has a message of affirmation to offer us."[62]

Mintz is correct that had Spielberg not forged this "compact" with the American public, the film never would have enjoyed its mega-popularity. That being the case, what does Mintz want Spielberg to do? Make a film that batters the audience with Hilberg's despairing message that "there is nothing to be taken from the Holocaust that imbues anyone with hope or any thought of redemption"? Had the director taken that approach, *Schindler's List* would have forfeited the chance to educate a mass public about the Holocaust. Spielberg has framed the movie in feel-good Hollywood conventions, but on the scaffolding of these conventions, he has filled the film with countless unadulterated examples of the Holocaust's true horrors: the liquidation of the Krakow ghetto, Amon Goeth randomly shooting Jewish prisoners from his balcony in Plaszow, a Jewish boy trying to escape the gas chambers by hiding in an outhouse hole of human excrement, among many other examples. *Schindler's List* makes you feel good at some points and bad at others. It's a bargain Spielberg *had* to strike if he wanted to reach the general public with his Holocaust story.

Noting the affirmative conclusion of *Schindler's List*, Alvin Rosenfeld sees a lamentable paradigm shift in American culture in regard to the Holocaust—from a focus on victims, perpetrators, and bystanders to a focus on rescuers and survivors. But Rosenfeld is mistaken. On the contrary, if one uses Hollywood as a barometer of popular attitudes, as this book does, one notices a gradual shift toward a more honest acknowledgment of the true nature of the Shoah—from World War II anti-Nazi films that barely mention that the Jews were a target of Hitler to a film like *The Diary of Anne Frank* that focuses on Jewish victims but omits their deaths in the camps to thrillers like *The Odessa File*, *Marathon Man*, and *The Boys From Brazil* that touch on some Holocaust atrocities but use the genocide as fodder for adventure to a movie like *Schindler's List* that, despite its periodic sentimentality, does unflinchingly show us the reality of the ghettos and the camps. Admittedly, this movement is halting and incremental, but *Schindler's List* is proof that progress is being made. The affirmative aspects of *Schindler's List* are quite different from the affirmation found in, for example, *The Diary of Anne Frank*; for while the latter film concludes with the message that "people are really good at heart," such Pollyannaish optimism is not countered by depictions of the horrors of the Holocaust, as it is in Spielberg's film.

The philosopher Theodor Adorno's remark that to write poetry after Auschwitz is "barbaric" has been quoted so often as to border on cliché. But Adorno's words have struck a nerve with Holocaust scholars, because they succinctly provide a radical answer to two basic questions: Can the Holocaust be truly represented in art? And *should* it be? Several critics felt that *Schindler's List* provided a negative answer to the first question by failing, despite its strengths, to depict the Holocaust with total realism. In a generally favorable review of the film, Simon Louvish wrote that Spielberg "wishes to utilize his grand resources to show us the Shoah, no holds barred. . . . He cannot. . . . Finding a handful of thin actors to demonstrate the 'selections' of fit or unfit prisoners to be sent to work or destruction does not convey it 'as it was.' The actors cannot act this state of being which [the] Holocaust writer . . . 'Ka-tzetnik' . . . described as being on another planet, a wholly separate and different mode of being."[63]

But those critics who carp about an alleged lack of realism in *Schindler's List* ignore just how many historically accurate gruesome details about the Nazi genocide Spielberg managed to squeeze into the movie's roughly three-hour length. *Schindler's List* challenges Hollywood's axiomatic belief (reflective of American culture at large) in unfettered human free will. In contrast, the film suggests that survival during the

Holocaust was often simply a matter of luck. This reality is conveyed most powerfully in the scene in which a bare-chested Amon Goeth—swaggering on his balcony overlooking the camp after he's had sex with his mistress—hoists his rifle and randomly shoots Jewish prisoners who have the misfortune to come within his sights.

The scene in which the boxcars arrive at Auschwitz and the unloaded prisoners are subjected to the "selections," determining who will live and die, is also rendered with a meticulous fidelity to historical accuracy. We see the Nazis playing classical music to lull the prisoners into a false sense of security. Later, naked men and women run for their lives in order to persuade Nazi doctors they can still be useful as slaves. When a small boy tries to escape the Nazis by hiding in an outhouse pit, he discovers a group of children already there, who order him to leave. A moment later, the children who haven't escaped are loaded onto trucks. Unaware of their destination, they wave happily to the other prisoners, whereupon the female inmates, knowing the children are bound for the gas chambers, instinctively surge toward the trucks in alarm. The moment serves as a microcosmic portrait of the 1.5 million Jewish children murdered by the Nazis.

In exploring the question of how to represent the Holocaust in art, Mintz compares *Schindler's List* to Claude Lanzmann's *Shoah*. Precisely because he believed the Holocaust was artistically unrepresentable, Lanzmann omitted from his film any documentary footage or dramatic recreations, instead limiting the movie to interviews with victims, perpetrators, and bystanders. Basically, Lanzmann left out everything that Spielberg put in. On similar grounds, in Berel Lang's *Holocaust Representation: Art within the Limits of History and Ethics*, the philosopher argues that the more Holocaust representations stick to the historical facts of the event, the less imaginative license they employ, the more morally acceptable they will be:

> If the past serves as a guide, the Holocaust images that have the strongest claims on their viewers will be . . . closely bound to historical reference, cued on its details and imagined within its limits.[64]

Lang is right that the Holocaust is an event whose horror so defies the limits of the human imagination that it simply cannot be fully artistically represented. For this reason, documentary footage—which shows, rather than attempts to recreate, the Holocaust—is often far more powerful. In *Judgment at Nuremberg* and the miniseries *Holocaust*, the relatively brief segments of documentary footage of the Allied liberation of the camps are so devastating they threaten to dwarf the hours of fictionalized re-creation that surround them. In *Schindler's List*, too, the film's documentary coda is equally powerful, as we see the actual Schindlerjuden placing stones at Schindler's grave—the *real* human beings who have lived to an advanced age thanks to Schindler's heroism, rather than merely the actors and actresses who play them in the movie.

However, saying the Holocaust *cannot* be artistically represented with perfect realism is different from saying it *should* not be represented for moral reasons. Here is where I part company with Adorno, Bartov, Cole, Mintz, Lang, et al. The Holocaust seems to be the one historical event that critics claim it is immoral to represent artistically. When Spielberg went on to make *Saving Private Ryan* (1998), no one objected on moral grounds to the long opening scene, which graphically depicted the brutality of the D-day invasion. On the contrary, most critics praised the film for depicting combat so realistically. *Hotel Rwanda*, from 2004, which portrayed the 1994 Hutu genocide against the Tutsis, also elicited no such moral objections, even though the movie included scenes in which machete-wielding Hutu youths hacked up Tutsi civilians. Instead, critics applauded the film for casting a spotlight on a genocide that the world had ignored. Finally, if we take the long view and consider the history of Western literature, there has been for centuries a widely shared supposition that art is an appropriate mode by which to represent tragedy and atrocity aesthetically—a tradition stretching from Homer's *Iliad* to Shakespeare's *King Lear* to Toni Morrison's *Beloved*.

Why, then, do critics raise moral objections to artistic representation of the Holocaust? Why does no one say it's barbaric to write poetry after the Soviet Gulag, or after the Khmer Rouge's killing fields, or after Saddam Hussein's genocidal assaults against the Shiites and the Kurds? I think this insistence that with the Holocaust, and *only* with the Holocaust, artistic representation is immoral, is tied to the assumption that the Holocaust is unique, that any attempt to compare it to another atrocity objectionably relativizes the Shoah. However, insisting on the Holocaust's uniqueness risks removing the event from history and granting it an almost sacred status. How can we understand and learn from the Holocaust if we can't compare it to other historical events?

An outgrowth of *Schindler's List* is Spielberg's "Shoah Foundation," which has interviewed thousands of Holocaust survivors and placed their testimonies on state-of-the-art CD-ROMS for public consumption. Between 1994 and 1999, the Shoah Foundation recorded more than 51,000 survivors from around the world, including 20,000 from America. The foundation also produces Holocaust documentaries, such as the Oscar-winning *The Last Days* (1999). Just as effectively as does *Schindler's List*, the Shoah Foundation serves as a bulwark against Holocaust denial and Holocaust ignorance.

12

MORAL AMBIGUITY IN THE HOLOCAUST

Mother Night and *The Grey Zone*

Mother Night (1996) and *The Grey Zone* (2001) are two films that on the surface do not appear to have much in common. *Mother Night* is a surreal movie that relates the wild story of an American in World War II–era Germany who becomes a radio propagandist for the Nazis while secretly operating as an American spy. *The Grey Zone* focuses on the camp prisoners who served in the Sonderkommando, herding their fellow Jews into the gas chambers and then afterward burning their bodies in the crematoria—horrific work for which they received somewhat longer life spans and improved living conditions. However, despite their very different plots, both movies share the important idea that the Holocaust, rather than presenting clear-cut divisions of absolute good versus absolute evil, actually reflected what Primo Levi has defined as a "grey zone," in which captors and prisoners alike lived lives characterized by moral ambiguity. As such, both films challenge Hollywood's well-known penchant for unequivocal heroes and villains.

Mother Night approaches the Nazi era through the fun-house-mirror perspective of absurdity and paradox. Since the film is based on a novel by Kurt Vonnegut, this is not surprising. Most of the film's story is told in flashback by its protagonist, Howard W. Campbell Jr. (Nick Nolte). When the movie opens, Campbell has just been incarcerated in an Israeli prison, where he is awaiting a war crimes trial, charged with being a high-level Nazi propagandist. As part of his defense, Campbell is ordered by his jailors to write out his confession, which turns into a lengthy memoir. Although Campbell was born in America, he moved with his parents to Germany, growing up to be a popular German playwright living in Berlin with his beautiful wife Helga (Sheryl Lee). The couple is deeply in love. Even as the Nazis come to power and politics infuses German life, the pair remains resolutely apolitical, insisting that they reside in a "nation of two."

Until, that is, Campbell is approached while sitting on a park bench by Frank Wirtanen (John Goodman). An undercover agent for the American government, Major Wirtanen tells Campbell that a war between America and Germany is inevitable and tries to recruit Campbell as a spy by asking him to pose as a Nazi broadcaster. The major convinces Campbell by appealing not to his American patriotism but to his ambition as a playwright. By becoming a spy, Wirtanen says, Howard will have the chance to fulfill every playwright's dream: to create the perfect theatrical role and then get to play it himself. The major warns Campbell, however, that if he is ever exposed, the American government will deny any knowledge of him.

Campbell soon turns into a leading Nazi propagandist, rivaling Julius Streicher and Joseph Goebbels. Billing himself as "the Last Free American," he spews pro-Nazi, anti-American, and anti-Semitic bile. However, Campbell's speeches have all been carefully annotated by an American agent, who marks not only the words and syllables Howard is to stress but also the coughs and throat-clearings he is to insert—all of which amount to a code revealing Nazi secrets to the Americans.

During the war, Helga is shot and apparently killed, which leaves Campbell grief-stricken. After the war, he is briefly arrested by American troops, who force him to tour Nazi death camps. He's released when Wirtanen reappears on the scene, but the major explains that all the American government can do to reward Campbell is to find him a new identity in a squalid New York City apartment. There, drinking heavily and mourning the loss of Helga, Campbell strikes up friendships with an eccentric upstairs neighbor, a reclusive painter named George Kraft (Alan Arkin), and another neighbor, a cordial Jewish doctor named Epstein (Arye Gross), who lives with his high-strung mother. Both mother and son are Auschwitz survivors.

Eventually, Campbell is discovered by a ragtag band of American neo-Nazis, led by a punctilious dentist, Dr. Lionel Jones (Bernard Beh-

Figure 12.1. *Mother Night* (1996). Howard Campbell (Nick Nolte) is a Nazi propagandist who serves secretly as an American spy during World War II. [Screen grab]

rens), and his right-hand man, a leather-jacketed African American thug (Frankie Faison). The pair hail Campbell as a hero unjustly defamed by the Allies, and, as a gift to their idol, reunite him with a woman he first assumes to be his beloved Helga. However, after he has spent a few blissful days with his apparently resurrected wife, "Helga" reveals that she is actually Helga's younger sister, Resi, who'd had an unrequited teenage crush on Campbell in Germany.

Now the plot really thickens. Campbell's cover is blown; newspaper headlines blare that an escaped Nazi war criminal is living incognito in New York, and Campbell learns that Israeli agents are hunting him, intending to drag him back to the Jewish state to stand trial. Campbell is saved by his neo-Nazi confederates, who whisk him, Resi, and George Kraft into hiding. Soon after, Major Wirtanen reappears on the scene, informing Campbell that both Resi and Kraft are actually Russian spies planning to kidnap him and take him back to the Soviet Union, whose leaders hope Campbell will provide evidence of US/Nazi collusion during World War II. Soon after Campbell confronts Resi with what Wirtanen has told him, she commits suicide. Left alone, Campbell experiences both figurative and literal paralysis, standing unmoving on a New York City sidewalk for an entire day. Eventually, however, he makes a decision that revives him; he returns to Dr. Epstein's apartment, announces that he wishes to turn himself in to the Israelis, and asks for the doctor's aid. "Then surrender to someone who thinks about Auschwitz all the time," Epstein dismissively replies, but his mother agrees to help.

Imprisoned in Haifa, Campbell discovers that in the cell above is Adolf Eichmann (Henry Gibson), awaiting his own war crimes trial. When Campbell asks Eichmann if he believes himself guilty, the SS lieutenant replies, "No, about the six million, I don't take credit for all of them. I'm sure I could spare you a few." Just as Campbell's trial is about to begin, he receives a note from Major Wirtanen explaining that, out of loyalty to Campbell, the major has decided to testify at Campbell's trial, revealing to the world that Campbell was really an American agent. Nevertheless, just at the moment when his vindication seems secure, Campbell fashions the typewriter ribbon he's used to compose his confession into a noose and hangs himself in his cell.

What should we make of the absurdly convoluted plot of *Mother Night*? Does the film have anything interesting to say about the Nazis or the Holocaust? The story's plot twists, while often evocative, don't generally yield precise messages. Still, speculation is possible. In an intriguing black comic moment during one of Campbell's chats with Eichmann, Campbell says, "In spite of everything, I still believe that people are really good at heart." By inserting this coy allusion to the concluding line of *The Diary of Anne Frank*, *Mother Night* implicitly sets itself in opposition to everything the play and film of Frank's story were about. That is, in *Mother Night* we will find no heartwarming morals, no tales of human courage and perseverance in the face of oppression. However, while it's clear what *Mother Night* isn't saying, what it *is* saying is far less obvious.

If the story has a moral, it goes something like this: be careful who you pretend to be, because you may end up becoming it. At one point, when the war is clearly lost and Campbell is considering fleeing Germany, his father-in-law, an ardent Nazi, tells him, "Even if you *were* a spy, you could never have served the enemy as well as you served us." In Vonnegut's novel, the father-in-law elaborates: "Almost all the ideas I hold now, that make me unashamed of anything I may have felt or done as a Nazi, came not from Hitler, not from Goebbels, not from Himmler—but from you. . . . You alone kept me from concluding that Germany had gone insane."

Discussing the book, Morris Dickstein writes, "Out of pure play-acting, unhampered by any real disorderly commitment, Campbell has amusingly become the Ur-Nazi, whose work still turns up twenty years later as the staple of right-wing lunatic fringe groups."[1] Whether or not this is a fair assessment, Campbell comes to accept it, motivating him first to turn himself in to the Israelis, and then, when it appears he's going to be freed, to take his own life. Analyzing the motives for Campbell's suicide, Dickstein says, "Vonnegut is sure there are no heroes . . . and therefore that no one has the right to stand in judgment of another. By executing judgment on himself Campbell cuts through the fog of ambiguity and becomes . . . the true protagonist and center of value."[2]

In a way, *Mother Night* can be seen as a kind of black comic commentary on *Judgment at Nuremberg*, a movie that declared that Nazis could be fairly judged. *Mother Night*, in contrast, is all about the impossibility of distinguishing between appearances and reality. Was Howard Campbell a Nazi criminal or an American hero? He seems to have been both and neither. Likewise, many of the other characters in the film lead double lives. George Kraft may be a hermitic but amiable painter, or he may be a Soviet agent. When "Helga" returns, she turns out to be her sister, who, though she insists her love for Campbell is genuine, may in fact be another Soviet agent. Even the question of whether Major Wirtanen is a bona fide American agent (as opposed to a madman or deliberate villain who pointlessly destroys Campbell's life) is never entirely clear, since the major's identity is never confirmed by any outside source. Under such conditions, institutionalized justice is a chimera, and one can fairly judge only oneself, as Campbell does when he commits suicide.

Appearing in theaters in 2001, *The Grey Zone* doesn't quite fit this book's criteria, since it's more an independent than a Hollywood film. However, the movie does feature well-known Hollywood actors, such as Harvey Keitel, David Arquette, Steve Buscemi, and Mira Sorvino. As well, when the film first appeared, it was prominently reviewed in major media outlets like the *New York Times*, and currently it's readily available on DVD.

The film's title is taken from an essay by Primo Levi.[3] It refers to Levi's contention that little about the Holocaust lends itself to simple moral judgments—that, on the contrary, almost every action performed by bystanders, perpetrators, and victims alike falls not into polarized categories of good and evil but rather into a moral "grey zone" devoid of pure heroes and villains.

However, Levi recognized that those who study the Holocaust (especially those who examine it superficially) often resist its intrinsic moral ambiguity:

> In anyone who today reads (or writes) the history of the Lager [camps] is evident the tendency, indeed the need, to separate good from evil, to be able to take sides, to repeat Christ's gesture on Judgment Day: here the righteous, over there the reprobates. The young above all demand clarity, a sharp cut; their experiences of the world being meager, they do not like ambiguity. In any case, their expectation reproduces exactly that of the newcomers to the Lagers, whether young or not; all of them, with the exception of those who had already gone through an analogous experience, expected to find a terrible but decipherable world, in conformity to that simple model which we atavistically carry within us—'we' inside and the enemy outside, separated by a sharply defined geographic frontier.[4]

Citing this quote from Levi, Bryan Cheyette writes, "My contention is that the ethical uncertainty at the heart of Levi's writings is the necessary critical yardstick by which one ought to understand present-day films and novels, many of which glibly assimilate the Holocaust in a breathtakingly untroubled manner."[5]

By its very title, *The Grey Zone* signals that it plans to follow Levi's dictum by presenting a morally complex view of the Holocaust—one in which it will not be easy for the audience "to separate good from evil," "to take sides," to discern a "decipherable world." In doing so, the film adheres to Cheyette's criterion that "ethical uncertainty" must lie at the heart of any realistic Holocaust representation.

The Grey Zone opens in Auschwitz in October of 1944. A small group of Sonderkommando (prisoners who herded victims into the gas chambers, then burnt the bodies in the crematoria) is plotting an insurrection. They have amassed explosives smuggled to them by female prisoners who work in an adjoining munitions factory. When the Germans discover the clandestine activity, the women are tortured but refuse to reveal the plot. After a contingent of Hungarian Jews is gassed, a young girl (Kamelia Grigonova) is found still alive. The Sonderkommando decide to hide the girl, but she is soon discovered by SS *Oberschafführer* Eric Muhsfeldt (Keitel). The rebels succeed in blowing up two crematoria, but they are soon captured. The young girl witnesses their executions and then starts wandering toward the main gate, before she is shot by a guard. The film ends with a voice-over recitation by the young girl.

If anyone in the camps existed in a perpetual moral "grey zone," it was the members of the Sonderkommando units. These units were composed of prisoners whose job it was to perform almost unimaginably gruesome tasks. When new prisoners arrived in the transports, the Sonderkommando took their possessions, ordered them to strip naked, shaved their heads, and then deceived them into believing that they were simply going to take a shower and be deloused. After the prisoners had suffocated in the gas chambers, the Sonderkommando units removed gold fillings from the corpses' teeth and then hauled the bodies to the crematoria, where they shoveled them into the ovens. In exchange for performing these jobs, the Sonderkommando members enjoyed, by camp standards, privileged lives—being relatively well fed, clothed, and housed. They were also permitted to live for four months before they, in turn, were gassed and a new unit took their place. This was a longer life span than was afforded most camp prisoners. Most of the Sonderkommando were Jews, who thus were lying to and dispatching the bodies of their fellow Jews. Any prisoner refusing to join the Sonderkommando was killed. Suicides among its members were common.

In *The Grey Zone*, Sonderkommando Hoffman (David Arquette) says at one point, "How do you know what you'll do to stay alive until you're asked? For most of us, the answer is anything." But the film's Sonderkommando tend not to be so emotionally deadened that they are unaware of the psychological toll they will suffer for their actions if any of them do survive the Holocaust. Later, Hoffman asks, "Do you want to look anyone in the face, if any of your family is still alive, and tell them what you have done for a little more life, for vodka and bed linens?"[6] In short, the Sonderkommando are presented in all their agonizing complexity and ambiguity; as Aaron Kerner writes, the film "re-

Figure 12.2. *The Grey Zone* (2001). Prisoners in the Sonderkommando unit, assigned to herd their fellow Jews into gas chambers, face an agonizing moral dilemma. [Screen grab]

fuses to paint characters with broad strokes—good versus bad—at least insofar as the *Sonderkommando* are concerned."[7]

The Grey Zone's director, Tim Blake Nelson, told *New York Times* reporter Kristin Hohenadel, "I thought if there's ever a moral dilemma, that's it. You couldn't contrive anything more extreme—and this isn't contrived, it's true."[8] Levi had aptly said that those who worked in the Sonderkommando units were "robbed of their souls."[9] Reviewing the film in *The Jewish Week*, George Robinson writes that "the moral dilemma that hung over the *Sonderkommando* . . . is a bleaker one than those posed in conventional Hollywood narratives: they did what they did in order to stay alive another day, fully aware that their lives were forfeit anyway."[10] The tortured existences of these particular prisoners also has inspired some of the best Holocaust fiction, such as the bulk of the stories in Tadeusz Borowski's collection *This Way for the Gas, Ladies and Gentlemen*. Borowski arrived in Auschwitz only one day after the Nazis stopped gassing Gentile prisoners, witnessed the work of the Sonderkommando from his relatively privileged status as a political prisoner (which he describes in the book's title story), and then committed suicide six years after the camp's liberation.

The Grey Zone is also based on two additional principle sources. One is *Auschwitz: A Doctor's Eyewitness Account*, by Miklos Nyiszli. Nyiszli (played by Allan Corduner) is a Hungarian Jew who worked in Auschwitz with Josef Mengele, assisting the Nazi doctor with his notorious experiments on twins, attempting to find a way to increase the birth rates of German women. Nyiszli agreed to help Mengele in exchange for his wife and daughter being allowed to live in the women's camp at Birkenau. After the war, Nyiszli never practiced medicine again.

The second source for *The Grey Zone* is director Nelson's 1996 off-Broadway play of the same name. As he told *New York Times* reporter Daniel Menaker, Nelson grew up in Oklahoma in a "culturally observant but religiously skeptical" Jewish family.[11] His mother's family had fled Germany just before the Holocaust began and was sent to Tulsa by a Jewish American resettlement group trying to disperse Jews throughout the country. If the Nazi Holocaust ever came to the United States, the group reasoned, American Jews would be harder to track down. Nelson's grandfather told him as a boy, "We shouldn't be alive. . . . [We survived due to] luck and privilege. You have to earn the life that you've been given."[12] Before turning to *The Grey Zone*, Nelson had tried to write a play based on his mother's escape from Germany just before *Kristallnacht*, but he ultimately abandoned the project, convinced that his composition was just the "same old survivor's tale."[13]

The film was shot entirely in Bulgaria. Like Spielberg in *Schindler's List*, Nelson reconstructed a concentration camp, complete with gas chambers and crematoria. Nelson also employed hundreds of Bulgarian extras, some of whom were given the unenviable job of stripping naked and piling atop one another for a scene depicting a mass execution in the gas chamber. The scene is a good example of *The Grey Zone's* "relentlessly graphic" approach, in the words of *New York Times* reviewer Stephen Holden.[14] It raised a red flag for some critics—namely, that such graphic re-creations of the worst horrors of the Holocaust cross a moral line, that these are scenes that a conscientious director should leave to the viewer's imagination.

Interestingly, Nelson drew the line at depicting the gassing process itself. "That one moment felt crass," he told *Times* reporter Hohenadel. "This movie isn't about provoking people or shocking people; if that's what it ends up doing, then I've failed."[15] Nelson appears to be splitting hairs when he claims that, in his view, it is ethically acceptable for a director to show bodies piled in a gas chamber but not to depict those same prisoners actually being gassed.

Of course, this view challenges the position articulated most forcefully by Claude Lanzmann in reference to *Schindler's List*, that the Holocaust is an atrocity so horrific it is morally reprehensible to represent it fictionally and that this is particularly true of its most awful manifestation, the gas chamber. But Lanzmann's view has been persuasively rebutted. Kerner writes of *The Grey Zone*, "As forcefully and convincingly as Claude Lanzmann argues for a prohibition of such images, here we have a representation of the acts many of his interviewees from his 1985 documentary *Shoah* participated in, and as much as we might be inclined to pay deference to Lanzmann, perhaps we can appreciate the testimonies of the *Sonderkommando* all that much more with this dramatization."[16] Lawrence Baron concurs: "To extend sanctimoniously the place [the Holocaust] occupies to an area so far beyond that of other tragedies that it becomes untouchable for certain forms of artistic expression is not only self-righteous, but also self-defeating."[17] How, Baron suggests, can art truly inform the public about the Shoah if so many of the customary ways of representing it are prohibited? Those who support such prohibitions tend to see the Holocaust as unique, a position I challenge in my chapter on *Schindler's List*.

The Grey Zone was financed by an Israeli production company, Millennium/Nu Image Films, which ordinarily funds more commercial ventures. The head of the company, Avi Lerner, told the *Times*, "I wanted a happy ending. Even though the uprising was a failure, why not make a heroic story about the one who did get away? But Tim didn't want any heroes. He didn't want to compromise."[18]

Lerner here cites one of the two principle narratives entwined in *The Grey Zone*. The first, based on an actual historical event, concerns a prisoner rebellion at Auschwitz in the fall of 1944, which involved the successful dynamiting of two crematoria. As noted, the explosives were smuggled to a Sonderkommando unit by female prisoners at Birkenau, who stole the bombs while working in the I. G. Farben munitions factory. After squelching the ensuing uprising, the Nazis executed everyone involved. In the film, the ringleader among the Birkenau prisoners, Dina (Mina Sorvino), is caught and tortured but refuses to reveal to whom she passed the explosives. To try to force her to confess, the Nazis assemble all the women in her barrack and shoot them, one by one, in front of her. Eventually, Dina flings herself against the camp's electrified fence. The scene exemplifies the morally problematic nature of resistance in the camps and ghettos, since the Nazis invariably responded to such actions with collective punishment, meted out to those both involved and uninvolved. Should one, then, endanger the lives of all one's fellow prisoners by resisting the Nazis? Here is a powerful example of that moral "grey zone" intrinsic to the Holocaust.

The second narrative in the film begins when Hoffman, while hauling bodies out of a gas chamber, discovers that a young teenage girl has miraculously survived. During the gassing, the adults in the chamber, in their clambering to the top of the pile, had inadvertently shoved her down to the bottom, where she had chanced on a pocket of fresh air. Hoffman decides the girl must be saved, even at the risk of his own life, and in this endeavor he enlists the services of both another Sonderkommando member, Abramowicz (Steve Buscemi), and Dr. Nyiszli. Hoffman's heroism is surprising, because up to this point he, like almost every Sonderkommando, has come across as utterly hardened, committed above all else to his own survival, and with a decidedly violent streak. In fact, just before Hoffman finds the girl, we see him ordering the newly arrived prisoners to prepare for the "showers." When one of their number angrily insists that Hoffman is lying and that they are all really slated for extermination, Hoffman's response is to beat the man to death.

A need finally to do good, whether or not such action proves effective, has inspired the men to try to save the life of the girl. As Nyiszli uses smelling salts to revive her, Hoffman says wonderingly, "We saved her." After Nyiszli manages to revive the unconscious girl, the men hide her in a back room in the crematorium, until Captain Muhsfeldt eventually discovers her.

Soon after, the rebellion occurs and is quickly subdued. (The story about a girl surviving the gassing is true, but Nelson said he intertwined it with the narrative about the Sonderkommando rebellion in order to heighten his film's "dramatic tension.")[19] Surrounded by her Nazi captors, the girl witnesses the executions of all those resisters who have been captured alive. During the executions, she starts to wander off, almost catatonically, in a kind of slow-motion escape attempt. A Nazi officer fells her with a single pistol shot. In the final amazing moments of the film, the girl, who barely spoke while alive, relates posthumously in a poetic voice-over what happened to her own body as she was incinerated in the crematorium—how she turned to ash, how the ash settled on the straining forms of the Sonderkommando members burning more corpses, and so forth:

> I catch fire quickly. The first part of me rises in dense smoke that mingles with the smoke of others. Then there are the bones, which settle in ash, and these are swept up to be carried to the river, and the last bits of our dust, that simply float there in air around the working of the new group. These bits of dust are grey. We settle on their shoes and on their faces, and in their lungs, and they begin to get so used to us that soon they don't cough and they don't brush us away. At this point, they're just moving. Breathing, and moving, like anyone else in that place. And that is how the work continues.[20]

Through the girl's narration, Nazi mass murder takes on a kind of terrible beauty, as it turns into a process of metamorphosis. The girl's narration suggests a second meaning to the film's title; covered in the ashes of cremated Jews, the Sonderkommando exist in a perpetual "grey zone." Baron argues that "the most moving scene in *The Grey Zone* jettisons the film's graphic realism in favor of a more stylized look and poetic monologue."[21]

What motivates the Sonderkommando to undertake these two suicidal acts of resistance—to blow up a pair of crematoria, and to save the life of a young girl whom they know is doomed? Why do men who have "lost their souls" engage in such self-sacrifice? It seems these Sonderkommando have found the courage that derives from knowing one is going to die regardless of one's action or inaction. "What's the fucking difference when you're dead anyway?" one of them asks while plotting the rebellion. The remark seems a double entendre; these are men who, by virtue of their activities, are already spiritually dead; thus, literal death poses no terror. If anything, wracked by guilt over their complicity in Nazi extermination, the men *want* to die. At one point, Nyiszli says, "I don't want to be alive when all of this is over." At the same time, the men's motives are complicated by their desperate need to fight back in *some* way. Even though they know such actions are doomed, the men hope to recapture a shred of their humanity through the mere act of resistance. Their motives seem similar to those that inspired the Jews who participated in the Warsaw ghetto uprising, fully aware that their ragtag band couldn't possibly defeat the German Wehrmacht but wanting to die fighting, rather than being led meekly to the gas chambers.

As Hoffman lies face down in the mud waiting for the Nazi guard to put a bullet in his brain, he whispers fiercely to one of his comrades, "We did *something*." Just before they die, the two men discover they hail from the same village in Hungary, which inspires them to clutch hands and call each other "neighbor." If working in the Sonderkommando has destroyed the human bonds between the men, their shared act of resistance, however Sisyphean, has reestablished those bonds in their last fleeting moments of life.

George Robinson writes in the *Jewish Week* that "*The Grey Zone* is one Shoah film that doesn't present heroic resistance, a "triumph of the spirit," so to speak. Even the Sonderkommando uprising, in which two of the four crematoria were blown up, is depicted without a sense of bravado or heroics. It is not giving anything away to say that this is a film without a happy ending, without even a faintly optimistic ending."[22] But Robinson's summation seems a bit *too* bleak. If it is possible to be heroic even while taking actions that are obviously doomed, then the Sonderkommando behave heroically. And if what counts is not the degree to which an action succeeds but rather the extent to which one recaptures one's humanity by doing it, then *The Grey Zone* has not a "happy" ending but an affirming one.

Of course, these are redefinitions of "heroism" and "happiness" that radically differ from those customarily understood by Hollywood. Thus redefined, the terms are permeated with tragedy and loss. We are back to that "grey zone." But, again, "grey" is not the same color as "black." As Kerner concludes, "As futile as their fight may have been, *The Grey Zone* casts off the Jew-as-victim, while never resorting to jingoistic sentiments."[23]

Reviewing the movie in the *New York Times*, Stephen Holden writes:

The more realistic *The Grey Zone* pretends to be, the more its unrealistic elements stand out. For one thing, the prisoners are far from emaciated. And although there is talk about the differences between Hungarian and Polish Jews, all the characters except one speak in a stagy variation of Quentin Tarantinoesque argot. The exception is Muhsfeldt, a Nazi officer played by Harvey Keitel with a caricatured German accent. David Arquette and Steve Buscemi give gripping performances as rebellious prisoners, but their characters remain frustratingly sketchy.[24]

The Grey Zone is more interested in themes than in characterizations. Perhaps its dearth of well-rounded characters makes it, ultimately, an ambitious failure. But, on a thematic level, few films try harder to dramatize that moral ambiguity that Levi correctly discerned at the heart of the Holocaust.

No doubt alarmed by the film's moral ambiguity, the studio took pains to advertise it as conventionally heroic, even though this focus clashed with Nelson's expressed insistence that he had not made a heroic movie. On the film's DVD jacket, the movie's best-known actors—Keitel, Sorvino, Arquette, and Buscemi—are grouped in head shots above the tag line "While the world was fighting . . . a secret battle was about to erupt." The narrator of the film's trailer declares, "Their freedom was lost; their hope was shattered, until the sight of one girl inspired a people to rebel."[25] This same advertising tactic was tried with an equally nihilistic film, *Triumph of the Spirit*, with equally poor results; both movies were commercial disasters. Indeed, its moral ambiguity may be precisely the reason *The Grey Zone* was a flop. As Levi wrote, with the Holocaust, people seem to need "to separate good from evil, to take sides." [26]

13

WHITE LIES

Life Is Beautiful and *Jakob the Liar*

Both *Life Is Beautiful* (1997) and *Jakob the Liar* (1999) pivot on a white lie, a benevolent fiction. In *Life Is Beautiful*, an Italian Jew, Guido (Roberto Benigni), imprisoned with his son in a concentration camp, convinces the boy that the camp really is part of an elaborate game. In *Jakob the Liar*, the title character, a ghetto inhabitant, pretends to his fellow Jews that he possesses a contraband radio that provides up-to-date information on the progress of the war, revealing that the Germans are losing an increasing number of battles. Both movies suggest that, in the absence of any possibility of armed retaliation, white lies could give prisoners hope for survival as well as constitute a form of resistance to the Nazis.

After *Schindler's List*, probably the most popular Holocaust film in America was made in Italy by an Italian director: *Life Is Beautiful* (1997). Due to its American success, it makes sense to discuss it here, amid its Hollywood counterparts. Not only did Benigni star in the movie, but he also directed and cowrote it, making the film very much a one-man show. A comic film director and stand-up comedian, Benigni had long been famous in Italy but remained almost entirely unknown in America before *Life Is Beautiful*.

The film divides into two extended stories. In its first hour, Guido (Benigni), a poor but plucky Jewish waiter living in Mussolini's Italy in 1939, falls in love with a lively schoolteacher, Dora (Nicoletta Braschi,

Benigni's actual wife, who costars in many of his films), who comes from a wealthy family. Courting her with every madcap scheme he can devise, Guido eventually wins Dora's heart. Fascist Italy, meanwhile, is showing ominous signs of growing anti-Semitism, but the love-struck Guido remains blithely oblivious of anything but Dora—even when, in one scene, a horse belonging to Guido's uncle is daubed with anti-Semitic slogans and then left outside the man's restaurant.

In the film's second half, Guido and Dora are now married with a young son, Giosue (Giorgio Cantarini), and are owners of a small book-store. When the Germans take over Italy (after Mussolini's assassination precipitates the collapse of the Fascist government, though the film never clarifies this history), Guido and Giosue, along with the rest of the community's Jews, are deported to a concentration camp. Because she's a Gentile, Dora isn't arrested, but she demands to join her family, and so ends up in the camp as well, in the women's section. In order to soothe Giosue, Guido—in the film's central conceit—persuades his son that the hardship they are enduring is all part of an elaborate game, with points awarded to those who can weather the various obstacles placed before them. The ultimate prize, the father says, will be a tank. Despite ever-increasing difficulties, which Guido overcomes through his genius for improvisation, the father manages to keep Giosue inno-cently unaware. At the end, as the Germans are hastily trying to vacate the camp before the Allies arrive, a guard takes Guido off and shoots him, but not before the father manages to hide his son. When Giosue leaves his hiding place, the first thing he sees is an American tank rolling into the camp, which persuades him not only that his father was telling the truth all along but also that he is the grand-prize winner. The American soldier driving the tank reunites Giosue with Dora, who has also survived. As the boy leaps into his mother's outstretched arms, he cries, "We won!"

When *Life Is Beautiful* first appeared in Italy in 1997, it was ex-tremely popular, winning eight Donatello awards, the Italian film indus-try's equivalent to the Oscars. At the time, Italians had been paying increasing attention to the Holocaust, through Italian survivor testimo-ny, conferences, and exhibitions. The film capitalized on this interest. *Life Is Beautiful* did have its opponents in the Italian press, however, foreshadowing the attacks that would be launched against it by some American critics and Holocaust scholars. Perhaps because Benigni styles himself as something of a socialist (a political movement more powerful in Italy than in America), several criticisms of the film came from Italy's conservative press. For example, Giuliano Ferrara, editor of the right-wing Roman newspaper *Il foglio*, wrote, "Benigni is very simpatico, but he is self-indulgent and so politically correct. There is this tendency to make the Holocaust banal with easy tears and narcissism."[1] Ferrara felt Benigni had gone beyond the limits of his talent. "It's like Bill Cosby trying to do Off Broadway. Benigni is a good entertainer, and that is what he should stick to."[2]

Ferrara's dislike of *Life Is Beautiful*, however, placed him in a distinct minority. The film continued its European success when it won the 1998 Grand Jury Prize at the Cannes Film Festival. That same year, the movie demonstrated it could also enrapture Jewish audiences when it was awarded the prestigious Mayor's Prize in Jerusalem. The movie was also a hit in Canada, winning audience awards at film festivals in Toronto, Montreal, and Vancouver. But the film's most famous triumph came at the Oscars, where it received an Academy Award for Best Foreign Film, while Benigni won as Best Actor (a prize rarely awarded to actors in foreign-language films). Thanks in good part to an aggressive marketing campaign by Miramax, *Life Is Beautiful* was no less popular with American audiences than it was with Oscar voters. When a slickly dubbed version (which Benigni said he preferred to one using subtitles) appeared in the United States in 1998, the movie went on to become the most successful foreign film ever in America (a distinction the film held until it was surpassed in 2000 by the Chinese martial arts saga *Crouching Tiger, Hidden Dragon*).

Interestingly, when Benigni first conceived the idea for *Life Is Beautiful*, he wasn't thinking in terms of a movie about the Holocaust. "I had this strong desire to put myself, my comic persona, in an extreme situation," the director told *New York Times Magazine* reporter Alessandra Stanley. "I said, 'Well, the ultimate extreme situation is the extermination camp, almost the symbol of our century, the negative one, the worst thing imaginable."[3] Benigni then improvised for his cowriter, Vincenzo Cerami, a scene in which a father calms his son by lampooning the idea that the Nazis could turn the remains of prisoners into buttons or soap (a scene that eventually appeared in the finished film).

Although he himself is not Jewish, Benigni's research was steeped in the works of Yiddish American writer Isaac Bashevis Singer along with those of the Italian memoirist and Holocaust survivor Primo Levi. Benigni also recruited Marcello Pezzetti of the Contemporary Jewish Documentation Center of Milan to serve as historical consultant for the film. Pezzetti had conducted scores of interviews with Italian survivors of Auschwitz and put Benigni in contact with some of them, particularly those who'd been adolescents when they were prisoners. As for the movie's title, originally the movie was called *Boungiorno principessa* (*Good Morning, Princess*), since this was how Guido first greeted Dora when she toppled from a barn loft into his arms. The quote that became the film's final title, however, came from Leon Trotsky. When the former Soviet leader was trapped in a bunker awaiting Stalin's assassins, he wrote in his journal that he still believed that "life is beautiful." Trotsky continued, "Let the future generations cleanse it of all evil, oppression, and violence, and enjoy it to the full."[4] *Life Is Beautiful* also draws on the wartime experiences of Benigni's father. In 1943, while his father was fighting in the Italian army, Mussolini was assassinated. As a result, Italy abruptly changed sides in the war, which led to Benigni's father being imprisoned for three years in a German work camp. On his release from the camp after the war, Benigni's father weighed barely eighty pounds. To console both himself and his children, the senior Benigni turned his camp experiences into comic stories that he shared with his children. "My father laughed with us," Benigni said, "and his nightmares ended." In another interview, Benigni elaborated, "Night and day fellow prisoners were dying all around him. He told us about it, as if to protect me and my sisters, he told it in an almost funny way—saying tragic, painful things, but finally his way of telling them was really very particular. Sometimes we laughed at the stories he told."[5] In *Life Is Beautiful*, when Guido first concocts his fiction to pacify Giosue, Guido says, "My pop planned something like this for me, too, when I was little"—a deliberate nod to the director's father's experiences.[6]

The single greatest cinematic debt *Life Is Beautiful* owes is, by Benigni's own admission, to *The Great Dictator*. Benigni told Annette Insdorf in Cannes that, in homage to Chaplin's movie, he'd made Guido's prison number the same as that worn by Chaplin's barber when he's imprisoned in a Tomanian concentration camp. The two films have other notable similarities as well. When the Germans are tracking down Guido in the camp just before they shoot him, a spotlight captures Guido hanging upside down from a building wall—a shtick that recalls

Figure 13.1. *Life Is Beautiful* (1997). Guido (Roberto Benigni) "explains" to his son that the camp in which they're imprisoned is really just part of an elaborate game. [Screen grab]

Chaplin's physical comedy. Benigni confided to a *New York Times* reporter, however, that he was troubled by Chaplin's remark, made after the war, that had he known the full scope of Nazi barbarism, he'd never have made *The Great Dictator*: "I quote this a lot of times," Benigni said. "I worried about it a lot . . . This is my first thought. Nobody can make a gag about the Nazis; because humor must be detached, and here it can't be."[7]

Life Is Beautiful has some marvelous aspects. The cinematography is generally superb; Benigni uses a bluish-grey filter to film the concentration camp scenes, which creates an eerie, Gothic mood.[8] In general, the first half of the movie works better than the second, even though it goes on too long, because Guido's frantic wooing of Dora is genuinely amusing and touching. As well, the film's satire of Italian Fascism doesn't ensnare Benigni in the aesthetic and ethical conundrums he will fall prey to once the family enters the concentration camp. Since Italian Fascism was at least comparatively less lethal (and decidedly less anti-Semitic), making fun of it is less offensive. A humorous example of the film's anti-Fascist satire occurs right at the movie's start. Guido and a friend are traveling to the restaurant owned by Guido's uncle and their car's brakes give out, sending them hurtling through the middle of a Fascist rally. As Guido and his pal wave frantically at the crowd to try to get them to help stop the car, onlookers assume that the pair are Fascist leaders giving the Fascist salute, and they respond in kind. This moment recalls not only the scene at the end of *The Great Dictator* when the Jewish barber is mistaken for Adenoid Hynkel but also the famous scene in Chaplin's classic *Modern Times*, in which a flag-waving Chaplin inadvertently becomes the leader of an illegal march by striking workers.

The movie provides an even funnier example of anti-Fascist satire when Guido impersonates a Fascist school inspector arriving for a lecture in order to have a chance to flirt with Dora, a teacher at the school. Delivering his speech on the "scientifically proven" inherent racial superiority of Italians, the distinctly homely actor bounds along a table waggling his earlobes and baring his belly button in order to "prove" to the schoolchildren that he, indeed, represents a superior racial type. It's as sharp a satirical thrust at the absurdity of Aryan racial ideology as the scene in *The Great Dictator* in which Garbitsch advises Hynkel that, as soon as he gets rid of the Jews, he should kill off all the brunettes.

Even in *Life Is Beautiful*'s second half, set in the concentration camp, there are a few, less slapstick, moments that work quite well. For example, before his imprisonment, while employed as a waiter at his uncle's restaurant, Guido befriends one of the establishment's regular customers, a German doctor named Lessing (Horst Bucholz). Dr. Lessing is obsessed with riddles, and every time he sees Guido, Lessing recites some new riddle he's puzzling over and requests Guido's assistance. Later, it turns out that Lessing is one of the Nazi doctors working at the camp where Guido is held. When Lessing takes Guido aside and asks to speak with him privately, Guido assumes that the doctor will offer to use his influence to free his friend from the camp. But, in fact, Lessing only wants to solicit Guido's aid in solving a new riddle. Thus, in a pointed irony, Lessing doesn't even consider helping Guido but instead requests *his* help with a meaningless mental exercise. Insdorf writes that Lessing's "inability to see things in balance suggests the myopia that allowed educated Germans to become Nazi doctors."[9] Aaron Kerner also admires this scene and discusses it at some length:

Critics and scholars frequently compare Lessing to Mengele, a physician who conducts his medical duties with the utmost professional care, but without an ounce of humanity. . . . While Lessing cannot sleep, plagued by a riddle he cannot solve, he is not in the least bit disturbed by his role in conducting mass murder. . . . Lessing is a clinical sadist who is not a cold-blooded beast but rather a character enamored with the instrument of reason, divorced of ethics or any sense of human sentimentality—a true sadist. [10]

Life Is Beautiful's comic take on the Holocaust elicited the same kind of controversy that befell two other Holocaust comedies we've explored: *The Great Dictator* and *To Be or Not to Be*. "Benigni's ironic counter-reality undermines this movie, not the Nazis," wrote the *New Yorker*'s David Denby, "who were beyond ridicule for the same reason that they were beyond rationality." [11] Another Holocaust comedy several critics mentioned in the context of *Life Is Beautiful* is *The Day the Clown Cried*, made in 1972 and starring Jerry Lewis. In the film, Lewis plays a clown at Auschwitz who's hired by the Nazis to entertain and so placate children en route to the gas chambers. The movie was never released, and today it's rumored that the only extant copy is locked away in a vault on Lewis's estate. Based on the dreadful buzz it received from those who had a chance to see the rough cut, *The Day the Clown Cried* is apparently a textbook case of how horribly wrong a Holocaust comedy can go. That Benigni himself worried about how audiences might react to his comic approach to the Holocaust is suggested by his opaque remark to interviewer Lee Marshall: "This isn't a comedy about the Holocaust, it's a film about the Holocaust made by a comedian, which is different." [12]

Lawrence Baron explains the film's comic approach by noting that "the surfeit rather than paucity of images about the Holocaust in the 1990s motivated some directors to experiment with genres like comedy to represent the event." [13] At the time of its release, several critics defended the comedy in *Life Is Beautiful*. Insdorf points out that what links the apparently disparate parts of the movie is that, in both, Benigni plays the "clever clown." In the first half, he employs his comic ingenuity to win Dora's heart, while in the second he employs these same skills to protect his son. Michael Berenbaum, a Holocaust scholar and director of Steven Spielberg's Shoah Foundation, told a *USA Today* reporter, "Like many inmates in concentration camps and ghettos, Benigni

uses humor as a weapon of the oppressed, and he does so masterful-
ly."[14] In a similar vein, in a *New York Times* column, Edward Rothstein
defends the film's laughs by arguing that "humor may be, in its essence,
anti-fascistic: It takes what is most self-important, most unyielding and
most unforgiving, and dissolves it into absurdity." Even so, the colum-
nist admits that "the risk . . . is that in the midst of dissolving fascism in
farce, it also dissolves the suffering of its victims."[15]

In discussing the comedy of *The Great Dictator* and *To Be or Not to
Be*, I have referred to the concept of satire as an act of "laughing at the
Devil"—an attempt to diminish the power of evil through ridicule. Certainly, there's a lot of "laughing at the Devil" in *Life Is Beautiful*. The
satire of Italian Fascism in the film's first half, as noted, clearly qualifies
as such. In the second half, a good example of "laughing at the Devil" is
a scene that takes place immediately on Guido and Giosue's arrival at
the camp. A Nazi guard appears in the doorway of the barracks and asks
if there are any German-speaking prisoners who can translate his address. Although he can't speak a word of German, Guido volunteers.
The guard then launches into a long list of all the draconian prohibitions
that dictate the lives of the prisoners—the disobeying of any of which is
punishable by death. Meanwhile, Guido translates the guard's words as
explanations of the rules of the "game" that Guido has told his son is the
real reason they're in the camp. This recitation gets increasingly absurd,
until Guido's "translation" has the guard saying that prisoners shouldn't
ask for any lollipops, because he's already eaten them all. Thus, through
Guido's comic intervention, this terrifying personage, the guard, is reduced to a figure of fun.

However, there is a crucial distinction to be made between sentimental comedy and black comedy in approaching the Holocaust.
Adopting a mocking, cynical tone, black comedy focuses on the chilling-
ly absurd, the horribly outrageous—all of which the Holocaust abun-
dantly provides. Sentimental comedy, in contrast, is a much lighter,
even saccharine kind of humor that never questions the societal truisms
that black comedy upends. Since the Holocaust *itself* demolishes societal truisms, exposing their meretriciousness, sentimental comedy risks
falsifying the essence of the Shoah.

Life Is Beautiful is, taken as a whole, a sentimental Holocaust comedy. Take the "translation" scene with Guido and the Nazi guard just
described. Yes, it's funny. But it's also sentimental, because it dilutes

the horror that prisoners in real concentration camps experienced on arrival. It also fails to address the reality that if the prisoners don't know the camp's rules, they risk being executed. Moreover, because he is such an easy dupe for Guido's charade, the guard comes off as a harmless rube, a cartoon Nazi straight out of *Hogan's Heroes*. From the very first camp scene, we are led to believe that Guido and Giosue can't have arrived in *that* dangerous a place, since the men in charge can be so easily duped.

One might retort that *The Great Dictator* is also a sentimental Holocaust comedy. Without doubt, *The Great Dictator* has its sentimental moments, in particular Chaplin's melodramatic speech at the film's end. However, it's an important distinction that the sentimental scenes in *The Great Dictator* are rarely comic; the film has sentimental moments and comic moments, but Chaplin rarely mixes the two. When Chaplin launches into his didactic final speech, he firmly sets comedy aside. The film's best comic scenes, such as the one in which Hynkel, alone in his study, waltzes to Wagner with a globe of the world turned balloon, are free of even a whiff of sentimentality.

To the reader who thinks I'm splitting hairs, let me make a second point: *The Great Dictator* appeared in 1940, before the worst atrocities of the Holocaust had happened, and when few in the Allied countries knew fully what Hitler had planned for the Jews. Therefore, if a Holocaust comedy like *The Great Dictator* includes a few sentimental moments, a few scenes that reflect Chaplin's ignorance about the true depth of Nazi evil (such as the light-hearted episode in the Tomanian concentration camp), they are representative of the era in which the film was made. But no such allowances can be made for a Holocaust comedy made in 1997, by which time the horrors of the Shoah had been voluminously documented.

By way of contrast, there are some comparisons that can be made: *Seven Beauties* (1976) and *The Producers* (1968) are both black comedies made after the Holocaust. *Seven Beauties* is an Italian film by Lina Wertmüller also produced in this era. It's the story of Pasqualino (Giancarlo Giannini), a homely sad sack who has screwed up every aspect of his life except for the fact that, inexplicably, he is irresistible to women. Pasqualino winds up in a German concentration camp presided over by a sadistic, obese, cigar-smoking female commandant (Shirley Stoler). Since the only talent he possesses is as a Casanova, Pasqualino decides

that the one way he can get out of the camp is by seducing the commandant. This leads to a harrowingly funny scene in which, during one of
the camp roll calls, an emaciated Pasqualino whistles and bats his eyes
at the commandant as she strides in front of the rows of prisoners.
"Who are you?" Pasqualino croaks. "An enchantress? A magician? Because you have put a spell on me." In response, the commandant takes
Pasqualino back to her office, places a plate of Wiener schnitzel on the
desk, and tells him, "If you fuck, you eat." Grunting and sweating atop
the pale, mountainous flesh of the bored-looking commandant, Pasqualino eventually manages an erection. The scene (and the film in general)
was, not surprisingly, highly controversial, but here we see an example
of the essence of Holocaust black comedy, since the scene satirically
makes a point that the testimony of many Holocaust survivors has cor-
roborated: under extreme conditions, human beings will do just about
anything to survive. (Admittedly, if the genders were reversed in this
scene, with a male commandant and a female prisoner, the movie
would probably be criticized as exploitive, if not one step away from
"torture porn.")

Similarly, Mel Brooks's *The Producers*—set on Broadway rather
than in a concentration camp—depicts a crooked theater producer,
Max Bialystock (Zero Mostel), who convinces a milquetoast accountant,
Leopold Bloom (Gene Wilder), to collaborate with him in an elaborate
get-rich-quick scheme to grossly oversell shares in a play so dreadful it's
bound to flop. The play, composed by an ex-Nazi who still adores the
Führer, is a musical titled, unforgettably, *Springtime for Hitler*. Despite
what some critics claimed, Brooks was hardly oblivious to the seriousness of the Holocaust. As Jewish American novelist Thane Rosenbaum
notes in a *Forward* piece on *Life Is Beautiful*, "The whole point of [*The
Producers*] was that nothing could be more distasteful than a musical
about Hitler."[16] Rothstein agrees, writing "When the musical becomes
a comic hit . . . it is not just fascism that is dissolved into farce but
solemn pieties about fascism."[17] *Life Is Beautiful*, in contrast, *reinforces*
"solemn pieties" about the indefatigability of romantic and parental
love, even under the harshest conditions.

The sentimentality in *Life Is Beautiful* is inseparable from an even
larger issue: the cavalier dismissal of realism in the film's portrayal of
the Holocaust. Benigni, however, never claimed to be making a realistic
film about the Shoah. "Once they are deported to the unidentified

camp," Insdorf writes, "Benigni makes it obvious that his film is far from documentary" but rather is "a stylized representation" in which "the horror is muted."[18] In an effort to find out whether his take on the Holocaust would upset Jewish sensibilities, Benigni showed a draft of the script to members of the Roman rabbinate. "I didn't want them to tell me, 'But it was nothing like that,'" Benigni related to *Sky Magazine* interviewer Lee Marshall, "because I knew that it was nothing like that. I just wanted them to tell me if they felt offended by the movie. Anyway, I got the green light."[19] Benigni defended his decision to leave the worst horrors of the Holocaust out of his movie by posing a paradox: "Anything you can see directly will never have the same impact as something you cannot see."[20]

Insdorf calls *Life is Beautiful* "a fable . . . about love."[21] This defense of the film as "fable" was adopted by other supporters. Michael Berenbaum called the movie "a fable, but it is imitating the truth."[22] To the contention of critics that the camp in the film looks nothing like Auschwitz, Insdorf retorts that the film "is not set in Auschwitz" and that "the Nazis created a spectrum of camps, from labor, to concentration, to extermination."[23] While the movie's detractors insist that, in a real camp, had Guido tried to hide Giosue, the boy would have been soon discovered and killed, Insdorf presents two stories of children who were successfully hidden in the camps. (In fact, Lawrence Baron notes that "Benigni knew the story of a four-year-old child who was smuggled into Buchenwald in a suitcase and protected by the camp's underground."[24])

The more significant issue, however, is the effect Benigni's stylized approach has on muting the horror of the camps. The problem with *Life Is Beautiful* isn't that it's a fable. *Seven Beauties* is also a fable; when the film appeared, some critics objected that the movie was unrealistic because there were, in fact, no female commandants of Nazi concentration camps. But Wertmüller, like Benigni, wasn't aiming for realism. But *Life Is Beautiful* presents a Holocaust fable that consistently downplays the horror of the camps in order to ensure that nothing undermines its message about the imperishability of love. Arguments along these lines were made by many of the film's critics. Writing in the *Forward*, scholar and translator Hillel Halkin insists that no one survived, or could have survived, by the power of love and imagination alone. The Nazi death machine was infinitely stronger than imagination, infinitely stronger even than love. . . . Because [the Holocaust] is the most terrible part of human history that is known to us, and because what it tells us about ourselves is so terrible, too, the temptation to soften it, to mitigate it, to sentimentalize it, to distort its lesson—yes, to lie about it—is overwhelmingly strong. *Life Is Beautiful* gives in to this temptation in a flagrant way.[25]

Rosenbaum echoes Halkin's argument, supporting it with more examples of how the film depicts the Holocaust through rose-colored glasses: "Guido moves about the camp freely as though he has written permission from the commandant. . . . Indeed, the camp guards seem [to be] know-nothing buffoons. . . . Life may be beautiful, but one thing is for certain: There was no beauty in the camps. . . . Guido may have been playing a game, but the Nazis weren't, and no clown, no matter how convincing, could bring a smile to mankind's darkest hour." Rosenbaum astutely notes that "parents rarely succeed in shielding their children from the fears that haunt them. If it can't be done in everyday life, then it's even less likely in the camps. Some horrors are simply not concealable, and during such moments, children won't accept a parent's reassurance that everything is okay. No parent could play the game that Guido devises, and no child is born with enough trust to block out the sensory signs of madness and death."[26]

In a *New York Times* op-ed, Anti-Defamation League head Abraham Foxman remarked that, in *Life Is Beautiful*, "Benigni created something very special and very important."[27] Holocaust scholar Alan Nadler responded to Foxman, noting the moment in the film when Giosue, discovering an American tank, tells his mother, "We won!": "The idea that the Jews defeated the Nazis; the desperate attempt to preserve childhood innocence despite Auschwitz; the urge to snatch redemption, morality and victory from the crematoriums—that is what is so emotionally naive and historically wrong about Benigni's work."[28]

Perhaps the most scathing review of *Life Is Beautiful* is leveled by *New Yorker* film critic David Denby, who calls the film "one of the most unconvincing and self-congratulatory movies ever made." Like Halkin and Rosenbaum, Denby argues that it is precisely *because* Benigni sentimentally distorts the Holocaust that the movie became so popular. "The enormous worldwide success of *Life Is Beautiful* suggests that the audience is exhausted by the Holocaust, that it is sick to death of the subject's unending ability to disturb." Denby concludes that the film "is a benign form of Holocaust-denial. The audience comes away feeling happy and relieved and rewards Benigni for allowing it, at last, to escape."[29]

Denby's review is accompanied by an Art Spiegelman cartoon that vividly amplifies its message. It shows an emaciated, blankly staring prisoner in a striped uniform affixed with a yellow star, slumped against a barracks wall beside a barbed-wire fence and clutching in his lap a golden Oscar statue. The cartoon's caption is a quote from an ad for *Life Is Beautiful*: "Be a Part of History and the Most Successful Foreign Film of All Time." Indeed, as I've collected ads for the film from newspapers and magazines, I've been struck by the fact that none of them make any mention of the Holocaust. An ad in the *New York Times*, for example, reads across its top, "An unforgettable fable about love, family and the power of imagination." And when *Life Is Beautiful* was rereleased in theaters in a dubbed version, another *Times* ad crowed, "Share it with your family, take your friends who didn't want to read subtitles, and see 'Life' in a whole new way."

In light of Denby's assertion that the film amounts to "Holocaust-denial," it's intriguing to read the inane remarks Benigni made in his interview with Alessandra Stanley. "I didn't want to make a movie about the Holocaust; I wanted to make a beautiful film. But if this film has even in a tiny way helped people to get over the subject, to feel the absurdity and the incomprehensible folly . . . and if we can talk about it, not sneeringly, but to naturally make fun of it, to smile at the Holocaust, we will be able to get over it, even though I can't say if it is right or wrong to get over it, but it has to be done somehow."[30] But should the aim of Holocaust cinema really be to enable audiences to "get over" the Shoah?

The complaints of all these critics are comparable to Bruno Bettelheim's objections to the maudlin falsifications of the Shoah in *The Diary of Anne Frank*—namely, that the 1959 film reflected a "profound, and still growing, need to blot this horrific event out of history, to erase it from the collective memory of Western, Judeo-Christian, European-American civilization, thus enabling this civilization to free itself of the guilt of having committed the Holocaust."[31]

However, in damning *Life Is Beautiful*'s sentimentality, am I contradicting myself? My argument in discussing *Schindler's List* was that without some affirmative message Spielberg's audience would have turned off and the director would have lost the chance to educate the general public about the Holocaust. Am I not, then, criticizing *Life Is Beautiful* for the very same things I applaud in *Schindler's List*?

I believe it's a question of degree. Since in order to be successful a popular director cannot depict the Holocaust in all its unadulterated horror, the goal should be to walk some admittedly fine line between nightmarish reality and pure kitsch. Within the frame of a formulaic feel-good picture, Spielberg manages to insert scenes that depict the Holocaust as graphically as any film ever made. There is nothing in *Life Is Beautiful* comparable to the liquidation of the Krakow ghetto. Indeed, there is only one truly tragic moment in Benigni's whole movie, and it may be the film's best. This is when, at the end, Guido is taken away by a Nazi guard and shot. As he's hauled off, Guido turns to Giosue, whom he's just hidden in an alley, and breaks into a mock goose-step—a final act of amusing and soothing his son before Guido dies (and a last instance of "laughing at the Devil"). The moment has exactly that quality of tragicomedy rendered through slapstick that one finds so often in the films of Benigni's idol, Charlie Chaplin. It is slapstick that is, at the same time, utterly heartbreaking.

Jakob the Liar was released in America in 1999, one month after the dubbed version of *Life Is Beautiful*. As noted, both films pivot on a benevolent lie. The title character in *Jakob the Liar* (Robin Williams), a Jewish resident of a Polish ghetto in 1944, pretends he has a radio that relays information about the rapidly advancing Soviet army—a lie Jakob spreads not only to Lina, a small orphaned Jewish girl he's hiding in his apartment, but to the entire ghetto. In both films, the protagonists' improvisational skills are put to the test as each character must devise ever-more-elaborate schemes to sustain his fiction; and in both films, such trickery proves at least temporarily life sustaining.

Jakob's fictitious radio reports raise hope within the ghetto—the suicide rate drops, and a romance blooms—although, ultimately, the Germans deport its inhabitants to a death camp just before the Soviets arrive. Thus, both films present Jews who aren't pure victims and suggest that make-believe can be a form of resistance to Nazi persecution in the absence of more aggressive possibilities—valuable even if illusory. Both films are also distinctly fable-like: both Guido's camp and Jakob's ghetto are left unnamed in order to stress their stories' universality. Finally, both films incorporate comedy into their Holocaust narratives. As always, such an approach inspires controversy, although Robin Williams (also executive producer of *Jakob the Liar*) relates in an interview included on the DVD version that the survivors he met while making the film told him, "Don't be afraid of the humor."

Jakob the Liar is based on the novel of the same name by Jurek Becker, who died in 1997. As a child, Becker was one of the few Jews to survive the Lodz ghetto. He spent the last two years of the war imprisoned, along with his mother, first in Ravensbruck and then in Sachsenhausen. His mother died in Sachsenhausen, but his father managed to survive Auschwitz. After the war, Becker made the decision, rare among German Jewish Holocaust survivors, to return to East Germany to live. His decision was influenced by his father, who feared that Polish Gentiles would attack Jews as a way to vent their anger over the Soviet occupation of their country, whereas the Communists in East Germany opposed anti-Semitism.

Initially, Becker followed the Communist Party line, perceiving World War II as a battle between capitalism and communism. But eventually, Becker grew disillusioned with the Communist regime and became a dissident who was surprisingly tolerated by the government, until he was finally expelled to West Germany in 1977. Becker originally wrote *Jakob the Liar* as a screenplay in 1965, but East German censors rejected the script, on the grounds that it focused too much on Jewish suffering and was too flippant about the Soviet contribution to the liberation of Germany. In response, Becker converted the screenplay into a novel. Published in 1969, it won the prestigious Heinrich Mann Prize for Fiction in Germany, but wasn't translated into English until 1990.[32]

In 1978, *Jakob the Liar* was made into an East German film, based on another script by Becker, who teamed up with Frank Beyer, whom the East German authorities had barred from making movies since 1960. Although the Moscow Film Festival refused to screen the movie, it became the only East German film ever nominated for an Oscar for Best Foreign Language Film. Thus, the story had a long, complex, and distinguished lineage prior to its American incarnation. Shot on location in Poland and Hungary, the film was directed by Peter Kassovitz, another European Jew who, like Becker, was a child survivor of the Nazis. Born in 1938, Kassovitz endured the Nazi occupation of Budapest because his father and mother hid him with a Catholic family before they were deported to the death camps. Both parents survived and were reunited with their son after the war. During the 1956 Hungarian Revolution, which was crushed by a Soviet invasion, Kassovitz sought and received asylum in France. Since then, he has worked primarily in French television. He optioned the film rights to Becker's novel in the early 1990s, and, given the recent success of *Schindler's List* and the fact that Kassovitz had signed Robin Williams to play Jakob, the project looked to Hollywood like a profitable investment. It also received some added traction from *Life Is Beautiful*, which had proven that a Holocaust movie could employ comedy and still be commercially successful.

The movie opens with a joke. As the camera pans across the ghetto, rendered in muted earthen colors, we hear Jakob in voice-over: "Hitler goes to a fortune teller and asks, 'When will I die?' The fortuneteller replies, 'On a Jewish holiday.' 'How do you know that?' Hitler asks. The fortune teller replies, 'Any day you die will be a Jewish holiday.'" The camera then pans to Jakob sitting alone on a tree stump near the ghetto wall. He continues to the audience, "So you ask me, as a Jew, 'How could you tell a joke like that at a time like that?' That's how we survived, and those were some of the things that kept us going." Thus, the film defends from the start its comedic approach to the Holocaust, on the grounds that humor enabled the Jews, powerless to take more aggressive action, to survive the Nazi onslaught. This is one of several standard defenses of Holocaust comedy. As the Romanian director of the internationally made *Train of Life*, another Holocaust comedy, Radu Mihăileanu, told an interviewer, "Laughter after all is another form of crying." He added, "Comedy is tragedy's balm."[33]

While Jakob is alone outside after curfew, he meets Lina, a young girl who has escaped from a concentration camp transport during a stopover at the ghetto. Lina is played by Hannah Taylor Gordon, who, a year later, would give a brilliant performance as Anne Frank in the television miniseries of the same name. Indeed, Gordon bears an uncanny resemblance to Anne Frank, and there are similarities in Lina's and Anne's stories, since both are not only young Jewish girls hidden by others from the Nazis but also possess an intelligence that belies their years.

Jakob only grudgingly agrees to conceal Lina, knowing that by doing so he's risking his life. Jacob's own wife has been shot by the Nazis, so it's no surprise that the widower and the orphan develop a bond, creating their own surrogate family. Soon after, Jakob is again out in the ghetto after curfew, and this time he's caught by a Nazi guard. Interrogated by the SS, Jakob manages to lie his way out of trouble and leave the Nazi compound alive—no small accomplishment. But before he does, he happens to overhear a military report on an office radio, which reveals that the Germans are suffering setbacks against the Soviets in their campaign on the Eastern front. When Jakob shares this news with the residents of the ghetto, the others are all convinced, despite Jakob's protestations to the contrary, that he secretly possesses a radio, providing him with unique access to the outside world. Of course, the irony is that Jakob does have a secret, that he's hiding Lina; it's just not the secret he's credited with by the rest of the ghetto.

As in many scenes in Hollywood Holocaust films, the picture of the ghetto that emerges isn't quite grim enough to be realistic (though it's

Figure 13.2. *Jakob the Liar* (1999). Polish ghetto resident Jakob (Robin Williams) tries to hide a young Jew who has escaped from a camp transport train. [Screen grab]

true that life was at least comparatively less awful in the ghettos than in the camps). Despite the best efforts of the makeup and costume personnel, everyone looks a bit too well fed and well clothed, and the film fails to capture the animalistic battle for survival that often characterized ghetto life—especially by 1944, when most of the ghettos had already been liquidated, conditions were worsening, and the Nazis had grown increasingly erratic as the Allies closed in.[34]

Still, one aspect of the film rings absolutely true: the desperate need among the ghetto residents for good news—a reason to hope—to continue their struggle to survive. When Jakob manages to persuade one of his fellow ghetto dwellers that, in fact, he *doesn't* have a radio, the man ends up taking his life. This, for Jakob, is a turning point. He realizes that, although it's the last thing he wants to do, he has to keep perpetuating his inspirational lie. However, the results of Jakob's lies aren't all benign. For example, when a boxcar full of prisoners bound for the camps stops at the ghetto station, one ghetto Jew, Herschel (Mathieu Kassovitz), feels compelled to tell the passengers that, as Jakob's "radio reports" have been revealing, the Soviet army is rapidly approaching. When Herschel races to the boxcars with the news, he's shot dead by one of the German guards. Reasonably or not, Jakob feels he has Herschel's death on his hands.

Yet the film's tragic moments are often juxtaposed with comic ones. Perhaps the funniest scene is when Jakob finally agrees to satisfy Lina's perpetual curiosity by showing her his vaunted radio. Jakob insists, however, that Lina can only *hear* the radio, not see it, and pretends to keep it hidden behind a curtain. Bustling about behind the scenes, Jakob launches into a hilarious impersonation of a BBC program broadcasting a speech by none other than Winston Churchill. "The whole megillah will soon be over," Jakob-as-Churchill intones stentoriously, "and that *schmendrick* Hitler will be gone." Lawrence Baron criticizes this scene, arguing that "Jakob stages a convincing radio program that verges on becoming the Holocaust equivalent of *Good Morning, Vietnam*. His Churchill imitation is what we would expect from the talented comedian Williams, but not from Jakob."[35] In general, Baron finds Williams's performance over the top in a way that distorts Jakob's character, and places some of the blame for this distortion on Kassovitz's direction: "Many of the jokes in the Kassovitz film seem to be Williams' one-liners and don't arise intrinsically from Jakob's character. . . . In Becker's and

Beyer's version, Jakob is a timid man who tries to avoid drawing attention to himself. Kassovitz's Jakob has a punch line for every occasion."[36] Baron's final assessment of the film is that "Kassovitz tried to rescue Becker's novel and Beyer's movie from obscurity by tailoring the part of Jakob to Williams' comedic talents."[37] The radio scene, however, provides Williams with a chance to unleash his celebrated gift for comic impersonations in a way that arises naturally from the story line; other than this scene, Williams is forced by the personality of his meek and ordinary character to give a notably restrained performance, which he does well. Baron may have been more influenced by Williams's reputation as a comedian than he was by the actual performance the actor delivered on the screen.

One wonders if the bright Lina sees through Jakob's transparent impersonation and is only pretending to be fooled in order to please her protector. But, based on a later scene, it seems that Lina, like Giosue in *Life Is Beautiful*, is fully taken in. Apparently, both *Jakob the Liar* and *Life Is Beautiful* are invested in the sentimental notion of impregnable childhood innocence, although it seems more reasonable to assume that children grew up fast in the conditions of the ghettos and camps, rapidly leaving childhood naiveté behind.

Another scene in *Jakob the Liar*, however, does introduce moral and thematic complexity. One ghetto resident, Kirschbaum (Armin Mueller-Stahl, who also appeared in the original East German version of *Jakob the Liar*), had been, before the war, a distinguished doctor and medical professor who specialized in heart-related illnesses. One evening, the SS arrive at Kirschbaum's apartment. Kirschbaum assumes that he's being dispatched to his death. But, in fact, the Nazis have summoned him because they can find no one else with comparable expertise to treat the ghetto's commandant, who suffers from a chronically weak heart. The commandant offers Kirschbaum a chance to save himself. If he will tend to the Nazi chief, as well as reveal the possessor of the contraband radio (a ghetto informer has clued the Germans in on this alleged development), Kirschbaum will be spared the next day when, as the commandant reveals, the ghetto will be liquidated. Kirschbaum's response is to swallow a cyanide capsule he'd hidden in his clothing when the SS arrived. The scene suggests that suicide, like Jakob's hope-sustaining lies, could be a form of Jewish resistance when armed rebellion was impossible. It recalls the 1942 decision of Adam

Czerniakow, leader of the *Judenrat* in the Warsaw ghetto, to shoot himself rather than obey the Nazi order to turn over the ghetto's children for deportation to Treblinka.

Eventually, the SS identify Jakob as the owner of the secret radio and arrest him. Despite Nazi torture, he refuses to confess. Jakob's interrogation coincides with the liquidation of the last remaining inhabitants of the ghetto. The commandant orders Jakob to admit to his fellow ghetto dwellers, who are assembled in the main square prior to their deportation, that he has no radio—a confession the commandant hopes will break whatever spirit remains among the Jews. A battered Jakob is propped up before the assembled throng. But, despite the commandant's increasingly shrill orders, Jakob refuses to speak. Finally, the frustrated commandant shoots him dead.

Baron criticizes this scene as melodramatic, claiming that "it is here that Kassovitz puts a heroic spin on the story" by depicting "the transformation of Jakob from an improviser of morale-boosting news to a defiant martyr."[38] By refusing to do the commandant's bidding, Jakob behaves heroically, but because Jakob doesn't spout some grandiloquent speech (as, say, Schindler does at the end of *Schindler's List*), we are spared sentimentality. Jakob's silence is more eloquent than words. Like Kirschbaum's suicide, it is a form of passive resistance—the kind of resistance that, unlike armed rebellion, has a chance for at least partial success.

The film's conclusion is bizarre. Speaking from the grave, Jakob tells the audience about the transport of the ghetto residents to the camp. What would have happened, Jakob wonders, if the Soviet army had intercepted the transport en route? We are then treated to a scene in which Jakob's imaginings come true. Indeed, not only do the Soviets, with their troops and tanks, liberate the boxcars, freeing Lina and the others, but an American swing band also appears, complete with a trio of elegantly dressed female singers, who serenade the astounded Jews with a rousing version of "The Beer Barrel Polka," the same Andrews Sisters tune to which Jakob and Lina had danced in his attic earlier in the film. Some critics dislike this surreal conclusion. For example, Insdorf points out that in the original German version of *Jakob the Liar*, the camera merely freeze-frames on the faces of the doomed Jews. Kassovitz's version, in contrast, "invites a kind of revisionist hope, suggesting that Hollywood is Jakob, preferring illusion to the depiction of gritty reality."³⁹

But Insdorf misses the point. The film's final scene *can't* be true. Had Jakob merely imagined the liberation of the transport by Soviet troops, we might conclude that Jakob's optimistic speculations became reality. But what we are seeing on the screen is purely Jakob's wild fantasy, a final "lie" Jakob has delivered from beyond the grave. How, after all, could an American swing band turn up at a train deporting prisoners to the camps? Since we know the scene can't be true, we assume that a far grimmer fate actually awaits the Jews, Lina included. Although his lies about a radio had temporarily sustained the morale of the ghetto, now, with the camps on the horizon, Jakob's fantasies can do no good at all. Ultimately, there's a limit to the degree to which imagination can serve as a viable form of anti-Nazi resistance. I fail to find any "revisionist hope" in the film's ending.

However, Hollywood's ending of *Jakob the Liar* is at least relatively more hopeful (or at least more heroicized) than the version found in Becker's provocative novel. The book's narrator isn't Jakob at all but an unnamed Holocaust survivor who'd met Jakob in the boxcar en route to the camps and during the journey heard from him the story of the radio. The novel's conclusion is rather obscure, but it seems the narrator posits two endings for the story—one real and the other imagined by the narrator. In the actual ending, Jakob is simply taken with the rest of the ghetto inhabitants to his death in the camps. In the imagined ending, in contrast, Jakob escapes from the ghetto before the final liquidation: "He has the daring plan," the narrator says, "of returning to the ghetto some time during the following night; he only wants to get out now so as to obtain some useful information to feed through his radio."⁴⁰ However, as Jakob is slipping back into the ghetto, his mission a success, he is spotted by one of the German guards and shot dead. "Let each reader choose the [ending] that," the narrator concludes, "according to his own experience, he finds the most valid."⁴¹

In other words, the implication is that in the real conclusion, Jakob ends his life unheroically as just another victim in the gas chambers. But in the narrator's imagined ending, Jakob winds up a martyr, killed in the process of trying to sustain the morale of the ghetto. When the narrator lets the reader choose the ending he or she prefers, he is offering a choice between grim truth and a heartening illusion. In the film version, however, Kassovitz takes the novel's imagined ending and makes it the real one, although here Jakob attains his martyrdom by refusing to heed the commandant's order to confess. The novel suggests that we'd prefer Jakob to die a martyr but that it's unlikely; the film makes him a martyr and turns his martyrdom into the climax of the story. If there's any "revisionist hope" inserted as the tale has traveled from page to screen, this is it. But in the very last scene with the swing band, the movie preserves the novel's theme that people will always prefer illusion to dark reality. Rather than condemning this choice, both book and movie suggest that, in times as dark as the Holocaust, reality may be so unbearable that people have almost no choice but to turn to at least temporarily sustaining illusions. In such conditions, lying becomes an act of heroism.

Despite the similarities between the two movies, the vast majority of critics and audiences preferred *Life Is Beautiful* to *Jakob the Liar*. Certainly, *Life Is Beautiful* was the infinitely more commercial film. Yet my own preference is just the opposite, mainly because of the different way the act of lying is dramatized in each film. In *Life Is Beautiful*, Guido's lying succeeds (although at the cost of his own life). Giosue survives the camp; a tank does appear; the film ends with the boy crowing, "We won!" In *Jakob the Liar*, in contrast, while Jakob's lying temporarily sustains the ghetto's fragile capacity for hope, ultimately his illusions spare no one the gas chambers. In other words, Benigni's film makes the patently outrageous claim that the spinning of fictions could defeat the Nazis, whereas Kassovitz acknowledges that such fictions can provide, at best, a temporary respite from inevitable doom.

14

THE NAZIS' SUCCESSORS

Apt Pupil

Life certainly isn't beautiful in *Apt Pupil* (1998), a movie that appeared a year after Benigni's film. Like *The Odessa File*, *Marathon Man*, and *The Boys from Brazil*, *Apt Pupil* uses the Holocaust as an engine to drive a Hollywood thriller, though it's considerably gorier and more Gothic than those earlier films. Based on a novella by Stephen King from the collection *Different Seasons* and directed by Bryan Singer (who also made the thriller *The Usual Suspects*), *Apt Pupil* is basically a two-character film that explores the tortured love/hate relationship between a fresh-faced but Holocaust-obsessed California teenager, Todd Bowden (Brad Renfro), and Kurt Dussander (Ian McKellen), a former SS officer from a fictionalized concentration camp, who, since the war, has been hiding in America. (The names of the main characters are suggestive; in German "tod" means "death" and "dussander" translates as "other.")

The plot of *Apt Pupil* abounds in improbabilities and contrived coincidences. It's implausible enough that an escaped Nazi just happens to live in the same small town as the Holocaust-obsessed Todd. But it really stretches credibility that Todd is able to recognize Dussander immediately when the two end up together on a city bus, even though, before this, Todd has seen Dussander only in grainy, forty-year-old photographs in history books. Since the war, the ex-Nazi, who has successfully eluded American law enforcement authorities for decades, not only has grown a beard but has also aged beyond such easy recognition.

Apt Pupil is also sorely lacking in character development. We are never shown why this apparently ordinary American teenager, with his boyish good looks and doting parents, has grown so morbidly fascinated with the Holocaust. The film's opening scene depicts Todd's history teacher lecturing on the Shoah as he points to a pie chart showing that most of the victims were Jews. The teacher wraps up the class by asking, "Where does evil come from? Are its roots economic, political, or does it just display human nature at its worst?" The fact that Todd's teacher never even attempts to *answer* these questions, so central to study of the Holocaust, suggests that a combination of timidity and superficiality in American public education undermines a full exploration of the most disturbing issues raised by the Holocaust.

Similarly, the movie never explains why, if Todd is so enamored of the Third Reich, he never even considers joining some local band of skinheads or neo-Nazis. Instead, flashy cinematography and a booming soundtrack are substituted for characterization. Thus, in an early scene we see Todd in the public library poring over gory photos of gas chambers and crematoria along with glossy snapshots of Hitler and his henchmen while a shadowy outline of Todd's entranced face is artfully superimposed on the screen.

Narrative implausibility returns when Bowden first turns up at the front door of Dussander's decrepit home. Displaying forensic and investigatory talents that would make a G-man proud, Todd swiftly entraps the old man by explaining that not only has he compiled a detailed dossier on the former Nazi but he's also dusted the knob on the front door for fingerprints, matching them with fingerprints taken when Dussander was in the SS, which the boy has *somehow* unearthed. Unless Dussander agrees to do Todd's bidding, Todd threatens to expose the old man to the Americans or, even worse, the Israelis.

When Dussander asks Todd, reasonably enough, what exactly he wants, Todd replies, "I want to hear about it. The stories . . . everything they're afraid to tell us at school." However, because of Todd's ill-defined character, it's never clear if his wish to hear the most sordid details of the Holocaust stems, ultimately, from a genuine philosophical desire (however twisted) to probe the depths of human evil or is simply the product of a morbid adolescent yen to revel in blood and gore.

Whatever Todd's motives, Dussander proceeds to comply with his demands by graphically describing the most grisly details of the Nazi extermination of the Jews—details that aren't likely to appear in most high school history lectures. Sitting with Todd at Dussander's grubby kitchen table (Todd with a glass of milk and the alcoholic German with his ubiquitous tumbler of brandy), the old man describes how, in sealed gas chambers, victims lost control of their bowels; how they clawed their way atop one another in a desperate quest for air (although the gas was emanating from the ceiling), leaving the children crushed at the bottom; how the victims "died in a mountain of themselves."

Todd is an "apt pupil," absorbing every detail. As a result, he's plagued by waking hallucinations (showering in the locker room in the school gym, Todd suddenly imagines he's surrounded by naked camp inmates) as well as recurrent nightmares, in particular one in which he envisions the looming metal door of the crematorium, with licking flames visible through its small glass window. (Interestingly, the scene in the locker room shower, with its brief shot of naked teenage boys, led the parents of these boys to launch a lawsuit against the filmmakers, arguing that the sight of their nude children appealed to pedophiles.)

To its credit, the film doesn't present Todd and Dussander's relationship *purely* as mutually destructive. On the contrary, there's a sense in which Dussander functions as a surrogate parent for the isolated teen, while Todd serves as a substitute son for the lonely old man. As James Greenberg sums it up in *LA Magazine*, their relationship is "part pathological, part familial."

Familial or not, Dussander's influence ultimately culminates in Todd's moral and spiritual degeneration. For example, one scene shows Todd in his high school gym playing basketball—badly—whereupon his defender knocks him to the floor. Alone after the game, Todd uses his basketball to torture and kill a wounded pigeon, affirming that bullies often feel like losers and therefore scapegoat those weaker than themselves. The scene immediately follows one in which Dussander engages in his own brand of cruelty against helpless animals by attempting to stuff a stray cat into his kitchen oven. The juxtaposition signals—rather blatantly—the way in which Dussander's barbarism has infected Todd.

In a *New York Times* interview published just prior to *Apt Pupil*'s release, director Singer explained that he saw Todd's moral decline as central to the film, which he described as "a gripping examination of the

contagiousness of evil . . . done with the emotions, not the supernatu-
ral." Singer continued, "It is creepy. But it's also an intriguing premise.
A boy plays with a monster and gets eaten. It is a true horror story."[1]
Indeed, Singer confessed that, as a child, he tended to share his protagonist's perspective on the Holocaust, even though Singer is Jewish.
"Growing up in New Jersey, I was appalled, but also fascinated by the
Holocaust," he explained. "I was fascinated by how a society could
become gripped by fear and ultimately hatred. Part of my answer is
Todd, who doesn't even know what he is being taught until it's too
late."[2] But Singer didn't see his early obsession with the Shoah as
unique, remarking, "I think anybody could be fascinated by the Holocaust and the atrocities."[3] In *Frames of Evil: The Holocaust as Horror
in American Film*, Caroline Picart and David Frank comment, "*Apt
Pupil* is Singer's attempt to work through this fascination."[4] Picart and
Frank compare the director's efforts to what "Steven Spielberg did in
linking his direction of *Schindler's List* to the rediscovery of his Jewishness and his attempts to work through the Holocaust."[5]

Unfortunately, since Todd's precise moral state isn't clarified at the
start of the film, we never know how far he has fallen. Since his character is a cipher from the beginning, it's possible to conclude that he
doesn't morally decline at all over the course of the film—that he was
an unmitigated bastard from the start. Perhaps Brad Renfro's mediocre
performance is partly to blame for the murkiness of Todd's characterization. A child star in 1994's *The Client* who resurfaced in 1997's *Telling Lies in America*, the handsome Renfro (who died of a heroin over-
dose in 2008) wasn't much of an actor. In all fairness, Renfro had the
added challenge of having to play alongside the British-born Ian
McKellen. His hammy, zestful tour de force as the demonic Dussander—the world-weariness of his frown competing with the satanic twin-
kle in his eye—is surely a tough act with which to compete.

Todd and Dussander are locked in a deadly power struggle. At first,
Todd seems to have the upper hand, successfully blackmailing Dussander into relating his wartime atrocities. However, eventually Todd's
formerly outstanding grades begin to fail as a consequence of his increasing entanglement in Dussander's nightmarish past. Ostensibly to
help his protégé, the old Nazi impersonates Todd's grandfather during
a meeting with the boy's kind-but-naive school guidance counselor,
Edward French (David Schwimmer). By helping to keep Todd's par-

ents in the dark about his failing grades, Dussander puts Todd in his debt, tilting the balance of power in his own favor. In theory, a battle royal between a cagy old Nazi and a deranged American teen might have provided some wicked fun. However, because Renfro's Todd can't equal the depth of malevolence that McKellen's Dussander exudes, the combat between the two never seems a fair fight, and the possibility of real dramatic tension is lost.

In a potentially intriguing subplot, Todd's unearthing of Dussander's Nazi past seems to revive Dussander's Nazi soul, which had apparently remained dormant during the many years he posed as a harmless German immigrant. In one of the film's best scenes, Todd somehow obtains a replica of an SS uniform and demands that Dussander not only don the uniform but also goose-step around the kitchen. Singer first shows us only a shot of Dussander's polished black boots thumping down the stairs before we see the old man in full Nazi regalia. At first, an anxious Dussander obeys Todd's commands only grudgingly. However, as the old man marches about, he begins to feel his former glory and power return, until, unprompted, he lets fly a stiff-armed "Heil Hitler!" Later, we see Dussander alone at night in his bedroom donning the uniform on his own and preening in front of the mirror. Aaron Kerner sees a sexual tension between Dussander and Todd in this scene: "As if bringing home some sexy new lingerie for his partner, Todd buys a Nazi uniform for Dussander. . . . [Their relationship] is clearly filtered through the lens of a perverse eroticism."[6] As Dussander parades in his Nazi garb, the two characters become increasingly excited, building to what Kerner claims is a near-"orgasmic" pitch.

Later in the film, when a bitterly disillusioned Todd demands that he and Dussander sever all ties, the old man seems to agree and invites the boy to join him in a drink to toast "our lives together, both the start and the end." "Fuck yourself," Todd snaps. Flashing his best satanic smile, Dussander drolly replies, "Dear boy, don't you see we've been fucking each other." Clearly, the old man is referring to metaphorical "fucking," the Darwinian struggle for dominance embroiling both characters. But is Dussander also implying, more sardonically, that a homoerotic tension suffuses their relationship? Kerner sees much significance here, arguing at length that "*Apt Pupil* conflates homosexuality, pedophilia, and sexual perversion with fascism."[7] Picart and Frank agree, arguing that the film uses "the recurring representation of sexual

Figure 14.1. *Apt Pupil* (1998). Kurt Dussander (Ian McKellen), an escaped Nazi hiding in America, befriends Holocaust-obsessed teenager Todd Bowden (Brad Renfro). [Screen grab]

'abnormality' . . . as a series of codes meant to signal Todd's descent into Nazism," while establishing "Dussander as a homoerotic surrogate and as a monster because he threatens heterosexual masculinity."[8] The film's homoerotic themes seem stuck at the level of ideas, however, rather than woven organically into the story.

Another scene meant, it seems, to signal the resurrection of the old man's Nazi essence is his aforementioned attempt to kill the cat. To make sure even the most obtuse viewer catches the analogy to the gas chambers and crematoria, Singer offers a lingering close-up of the oven's jetting blue and yellow flames while suitably dirgelike music swells. Perhaps Singer means also to allude to the Nazi perception of the Jews as animals who could be exterminated with a clear conscience. But the scene represents another failure of narrative credibility: How plausible is it that Dussander's first act after the revival of his "inner Nazi" is to try to shove a cat in an oven? More importantly, the scene's campily Gothic tone undermines any serious exploration of Holocaust-related themes.

The violence inherent in both characters reaches its climax in *Apt Pupil*'s gory final scenes, where whatever thematic significance the film may have displayed is lost in a torrent of stock horror-flick gore. The film's concluding bloodbath is sensationalized and incoherent. This is particularly true of the strange scene in which Dussander inexplicably murders a homeless man, Archie (Elias Koteas), who solicits him for sex. (In King's novella, by now Todd is also a murderer, randomly firing a rifle at cars on the freeway, but Singer chose to omit this scene.) Apparently, Dussander's resurgent Nazism has led him to unleash his murderous rage on the weak and marginal. He seems to gain no tangible reward for the slaying, but Kerner attempts to explain Dussander's muddled motivation:

> While seemingly disavowing his own latent homosexual desire, Dussander apparently views Archie as a "legitimate" target for elimination precisely because he is coded as queer, and by killing Archie, Dussander might "regain" his sense of masculinity, which is tightly wrapped up with his former identity as an SS officer. . . . Furthermore, Archie, like the Gypsies, is a transient, and thus from Dussander's perspective of no consequence, justifying his murder.[9]

Dussander's stabbing of Archie is only the start of the gorefest at the film's finale. After the knifing, Dussander dumps Archie's body in the basement, only to have this exertion trigger a heart attack. The stricken old man telephones Todd, whom he's not seen for a while, and threatens to expose him as a collaborator in Dussander's deception unless the boy agrees to conceal all traces of the murder and then call an ambulance—in that order. When Todd arrives, he discovers that the gravely wounded Archie is still floundering about in Dussander's basement. This turn of events compels Todd to grab a nearby shovel and dispatch the homeless man with a swift blow to the head. We see Todd's face splattered with Archie's blood, his profile glowing in the red light from the basement furnace, looking so demonic that we know his spiritual degeneration has reached its nadir. Indeed, the blood spattering seems a kind of satanic baptism, signaling that whatever faint pangs of conscience might have troubled the boy before have been permanently banished.

After dutifully stowing Archie's corpse in a shallow grave in the basement, Todd calls an ambulance, which saves Dussander's life. At the hospital, in the film's final absurd coincidence, Dussander just happens to share a room with an elderly Jewish Holocaust survivor, Morris Heisel, who turns out to have been imprisoned at the same camp where Dussander was an SS officer. But Heisel remains too minor and purely instrumental a figure to offer an ethical counterweight to Todd and Dussander's villainy. In *Apt Pupil*, the Jewish victims of the Nazis remain abstractions, "stories" Dussander and Todd can relish together.

Eventually, memory dawns for Heisel. Plunging his fist into his mouth to keep from crying out, he staggers down the hospital corridor, collapsing in the arms of a nurse. By informing the authorities of Dussander's true identity, Heisel plays the role Hollywood often thrusts onto its heroicized Holocaust survivors—that of avenging angels who ensure that their former tormentors receive their just desserts. In the next scene, the truth about Dussander is out. When the old man wakens, he finds his hospital bed surrounded by law enforcement officials, including a German Jew named Weiskopf, who sports a Star of David lapel pin. A professor of Judaic Studies who takes breaks from his scholarly labors to help the Israelis capture escaped Nazis, Weiskopf informs Dussander, "You'll be in Jerusalem by the end of the summer." (In King's novella, Weiskopf is a Mossad agent—but Hollywood's era of the lionization of the Israeli military, evident in *The Odessa File*, was, by 1998, a distant memory.)

By this time, rival crowds of rowdy demonstrators have assembled outside. On one side stands a raucous bunch of neo-Nazis waving signs denying the Holocaust's existence while, on the other, American Jews—some Holocaust survivors—are gathered, all equally vociferous. Disturbingly, the scene's staging—equal numbers of chanting demonstrators on either side of the barricades—seems to suggest, no doubt inadvertently, that their two positions (for and against the reality of the Holocaust) are in some sense comparable. At the very least, some less informed viewers might assume that Holocaust-deniers enjoy widespread support, which they presently lack.

Dussander's exposure is crosscut with a scene showing Todd as valedictorian at his high school graduation, regaling his classmates with the myth of Icarus, which apparently serves for Todd as a cautionary tale. Like Icarus, Todd suggests, the Nazis considered themselves omnipotent, intoxicated by a belief in their ability to soar above the rest of humanity. And, as with Icarus, this hubris led to the Nazis' moral and physical destruction.

At the graduation ceremony, when guidance counselor French meets Todd's parents, he discovers that the man claiming to be Todd's grandfather must have been an imposter. Then, after Dussander's true background is publicly revealed, French learns that the imposter was also a hidden Nazi. When French hurries over to Todd's house to confront the boy, Todd threatens to accuse the guidance counselor of sexual advances unless French keeps his mouth shut. J. M. Clark remarks, "Singer plants doubts in us as to whether French is gay and whether his concern carries with it a hidden agenda."[10] Picart and Frank add, "This is a much subtler subtext in the novella, in which French's actions could be read either paternalistically or homoerotically."[11] Personally, I prefer to interpret Todd's threat as a pure fabrication, because it renders his character more purely evil.

Much of the imagery Singer deploys in this scene stresses Todd's highly ironic "all-American-ness." Throughout his exchange with French, a large American flag draped across the front of Todd's house is a prominent backdrop. As he bullies French into silence, Todd clutches a basketball. After French retreats, Todd swishes the ball through the hoop in his driveway—symbolizing his very American "victory" over the counselor. The surfeit of Americana in this scene seems to suggest the profoundly subversive notion that violent neo-Nazism runs deeply through the American grain.

Wily to the last, Dussander eludes justice by committing suicide in his hospital bed before Weiskopf can deport him to Jerusalem. The film's final image is a close-up of the dead Dussander's blanched face, blank eyes open wide. While presumably Singer meant this closing image to symbolize something profound, it comes across as just standard horror-flick fare, with Dussander looking like Count Dracula in his coffin. By crosscutting Dussander's suicide with the scene in which Todd vanquishes French, Singer leaves the impression that Dussander not only has succeeded in eluding earthly justice but also has managed to pass the Nazi torch posthumously to his all-American disciple.

Ultimately, *Apt Pupil*'s attempt to graft a Holocaust theme onto an otherwise fairly conventional horror movie results in exploitation of the Shoah. Is the film trying to teach something about the Shoah, or has it tossed in Holocaust references merely in an attempt to titillate audiences? *Apt Pupil* falls squarely into the latter category, especially as the film degenerates from psychological warfare between Todd and Dussander into a Gothic gore fest.

Had it been better handled, its theme—that an all-American teenager can, if badly influenced, turn into a Nazi—is rife with cinematic potential. Christopher Browning's *Ordinary Men: Reserve Police Battalion 101 and the Final Solution in Poland* makes the controversial but defensible argument that the Holocaust, rather than revealing some unique homicidal anti-Semitism in 1930s Germany, illustrates that a range of ignoble but common human traits (sadism, conformity, insecurity, blind obedience to authority, Darwinian striving for dominance) can predispose the average individual, under the right set of extreme circumstances, toward mass murder. The film's design as a Hollywood blockbuster, however, trumped the film's potential for any meaningful commentary on the Holocaust.

15

MUTANT HOLOCAUST SURVIVORS, OR THE ANTI-AMERICAN SIN OF PESSIMISM

X-Men

The *X-Men* phenomenon has been remarkably popular—first as a long-running series of comic books, which are still being produced, and then as a franchise of lucrative films. Mutants with superpowers, the X-Men live uneasily among the human race. They are divided into two, more or less "good" and "evil" groups, who tend to battle one another when they aren't in conflict with mankind. What is so remarkable, and the reason why *X-Men* is relevant to this book, is that the leader of the "evil" mutants, Magneto, is presented as a Holocaust survivor.

If one considers the history of the *X-Men* comic book series, this seems a less surprising choice than it may at first appear. The comic's original creators were Jack Kirby and Stan Lee, American-born children of Jews who immigrated to the United States before the war. In 1941, Kirby designed the cover page for the first issue of *Captain America*, which featured the patriotic superhero punching Hitler in the face. As for Lee, his first comic book hero was the Destroyer, a superhero committed to defeating the Third Reich.

In the 1970s, Marvel Comics writer Chris Claremont changed the villain Magneto into a Holocaust survivor. In an interview, Claremont explained: "I was trying to figure out what made Magneto tick. . . . And I thought, what was the most transfiguring event of our century that would tie in the super-concept of the X-Men as persecuted outcasts? It *has* to be the Holocaust!"[1] In the comics, Magneto meets and befriends a fellow mutant, Professor X, in Israel, where Magneto is employed at a psychiatric hospital treating Holocaust survivors. In one especially vivid episode, Professor X uses his mutant powers to literally enter the mind of a Holocaust survivor, where he encounters monsters that symbolize the traumas afflicting the survivor as a result of the Shoah. Later, Professor X's Israeli paramour, Gabrielle Haller, a survivor of Dachau, is kidnapped by Baron von Stryker, an SS war crimes fugitive based on a historical figure of the same name. As Cheryl Alexander Malcolm notes, "As Magneto equates mutants with Jews and anti-mutantism with anti-Semitism, the X-Men comics rapidly become an extended Holocaust narrative and meditation on the viability of assimilation in light of the near total destruction of European Jewry."[2]

In other words, the series as a whole draws a parallel between the Nazis' real-life persecution of the Jews and humanity's fictional persecution of the mutants. Most recently, Marvel issued a book-length graphic novel detailing Magneto's experiences before and during the Holocaust, excising his mutant powers (as well as his villainy), portraying him as Jewish (which previous *X-Men* comics and films do not), and placing his character at the center of many of the key events of the Shoah. Remarkably, little attention has been paid to Magneto's status as a Holocaust survivor, though that status is vital for understanding Magneto's animosity toward humanity and though the figure has attained an iconic position in American pop culture.

Directed by Bryan Singer (who also directed *Apt Pupil*), the first *X-Men* movie, which appeared in 2000, opens in an unnamed concentration camp, depicting a scene that seems a deliberate nod to *Schindler's List*. As part of the "selection" process that routinely occurred when prisoners were herded from the boxcars on arrival at the camps, a small boy is separated from his parents. Crying out as he's dragged away by the guards, the boy stretches his arms toward his father and mother as a barbed wire gate slams shut between them. Miraculously, the gate is wrenched apart and the guards flung to the ground. Apparently, the boy, who will grow up to be Magneto, has discovered his supernatural mutant powers.

The movie then shifts to modern times. A campaign is afoot in Washington, led by a devious Senator Kelly (Bruce Davison), to force all mutants to register their alien status so that they can be distinguished from the rest of the population. As long as mutants are allowed to remain hidden among "normal" Americans, Kelly thunders, there's no telling what havoc they may wreak. To Magneto (Ian McKellen), Kelly's registration drive is a replay of the initial steps taken by the Nazis against Holocaust victims such as himself. The lesson Magneto has drawn from his Holocaust experience is that humanity is inherently, irredeemably evil. After Magneto's mutant henchmen kidnap Kelly (and just before Magneto, with poetic justice, turns the senator into a mutant himself), Magneto tells Kelly, "Mankind has always made laws to protect itself from what it doesn't understand. Laws like your Mutant Registration . . . Trust me . . . it is only a matter of time before mutants will be herded into camps."

Historically, of course, the Nazis (who indeed saw the Jews as sub-human "mutants") did force Jews in Germany, and in allied and occupied countries, to register their "racial" status—registration that was a crucial first step in the process of their systematic annihilation. As a preemptive strike against his human foes, Magneto plans to detonate an unnamed but fearsome device during a peace conference on Ellis Island (no doubt a carefully chosen target, since this was the venue by which millions of immigrants entered America) attended by all the world's leaders.

Magneto's nemesis is the wheelchair-bound Professor X (Patrick Stewart)—whom the film and comic books establish as the leader of the "good" mutants. Magneto and Professor X's close friendship has ended as a result of their irreconcilable dispute over how mutants should deal with the human race. Unlike Magneto, Professor X is optimistic about the human potential for good. While acutely aware of the virulent bigotry humans harbor toward mutants, he feels the best response is not violence but rather patient diplomacy. "Don't give up on them," the professor beseeches his former friend, when the two encounter one another following Kelly's harangue, concluding, "I'm looking for hope." At the end of the film, after Professor X has thwarted Magneto's plot to murder the world's leaders, the professor visits Magneto in the mountain fortress in which he's been imprisoned. "You know this is a war," Magneto says as the two play a heavily symbolic game of chess, "and I intend to fight it by any means necessary." Professor X quietly replies, "And I will always be there, old friend." The message isn't hard to discern: a sequel is in the works. Magneto and Professor X have many battles yet to fight. Lawrence Baron observes that Professor X "fits a traditional stereotype of Jewish males whose intellectuality compensates for a lack of physical prowess."[3] If this is true, the stereotype is rendered positively, since Professor X is clearly the primary hero of the series.

Reviewer Chuck Rudolph fumed that "parallels [between mutants and Holocaust victims] are dangerously shallow and exploitive,"[4] but other critics have defended Magneto's Holocaust status. For instance, Roger Ebert remarked, somewhat whimsically, "One could argue that the Holocaust is not appropriate subject matter for an action movie based on a comic book, but having talked to *X-Men* fans, I believe that in their minds the medium is as deep and portentous as say, *Sophie's Choice*."[5] Baron makes the pro-Magneto case more forcefully: "If Art Spiegelman can be acclaimed for presenting the Holocaust as a conflict between Jewish mice and Nazi cats, then why is it inappropriate for a cinematic allegory about the fear and persecution of genetic mutants to draw parallels with the Holocaust?"[6] On the contrary, Baron thinks *X-Men's* mega-popularity enables its Holocaust references to serve as an effective educational tool: "As a stimulus to increase interest in the Holocaust, *X-Men* has a better chance of reaching younger audiences than most movies."[7]

While I doubt that many *X-Men* fans are dashing off to the library to check out Raul Hilberg's *The Destruction of the European Jews*, I tend to agree with Ebert and Baron. The mutants/Holocaust victims parallel is not only clever but also makes an important point about how the masses (and their political leaders) throughout history have feared and persecuted the "Other," at times through genocide. In the differing responses of Magneto and Professor X to humanity's anti-mutant agitation, one can see the clashing reactions of any minority group to persecution (European Jewry being a prime example): Do you try to pacify your attacker, or do you fight back?

Magneto represents a laudable departure from a trend in pop cultural Holocaust representations that seems otherwise omnipresent: namely, the "heroicizing" of Holocaust survivors as plaster saints sanctified by suffering. However well intentioned, such portrayals implicitly demonize all those Holocaust survivors who emerged from the camps, quite understandably, in states of existential despair. Heroicizing survivors reflects the American obsession, faithfully parroted by Hollywood, to

Figure 15.1. *X-Men* (2000). Holocaust survivor Magneto (Ian McKellen) emerges as a mutant super-villain bent on destroying the human race. [Screen grab]

find in even the most tragic human circumstances some uplifting moral message, no matter how desperately contrived. Finally, by sanctifying survivors, Hollywood "Christianizes" the Holocaust, since Christian theology teaches that suffering is redemptive. Such Christianizing is offensive not only because most Holocaust victims were Jews but also because the New Testament's demonizing of Jews as "Christ-killers" laid the foundation for the Holocaust.

However, *X-Men* only *appears* to reject these distortions of the Holocaust elsewhere so rampant in Hollywood. Instead, it merely repackages such distortions in a new and, in some respects, even more disturbing way. The film portrays the misanthropic despair Magneto has drawn from the Holocaust as not only a delusion but one with potentially catastrophic consequences while contrasting it with the nobly indefatigable optimism of Professor X. Admittedly, it's a bit of an overstatement to see the movie as implying that if Holocaust survivors lose their faith in humanity, before long they'll be trying to blow up world leaders. But consider the final words of Frances Goodrich and Albert Hackett's *Diary of Anne Frank*: "In spite of everything, I still believe that people are really good at heart." Wouldn't this line fit perfectly into the mouth of Professor X?

On one level, the film's message is surely valid: contrary to Magneto's assumptions, contemporary America, however flawed, is *not* another Nazi Germany. In this regard, the film serves as a welcome antidote to Hollywood's perennial penchant for Nazi/American parallels. The film also makes an implicit plea for tolerance and empathy toward minorities. At a time when minorities and immigrants are so demonized in American society—slandered as stealers of "real" Americans' jobs and as onerous burdens on the welfare state—the *X-Men* series, given its popularity, may perform an admirable service in challenging such atavistic trends. Moreover, there are moments in the film that present Magneto as a somewhat sympathetic villain, driven to evil less by any intrinsic nastiness than by the traumas of the Holocaust.

Still, it's hard to retain too much sympathy for Magneto when he is portrayed not merely as benightedly misanthropic but also as a proto-Nazi. While Magneto may claim he is only seeking to protect imperiled mutants everywhere, there seems little doubt that his true aim is a distinctly Hitlerian quest for world domination. "Mankind has evolved . . . into us," he tells Professor X, portraying mutants as a kind of *Übermenschen* who have evolved from the pitifully inferior human race. In the novelization of the movie, during the climactic battle between the good and bad mutants atop (in more ponderous symbolism) the Statue of Liberty, Magneto asks one of Professor X's mutant followers, Logan, "Why do you stand in my way? I am doing this for you," to which Logan replies, "All hail Magneto. King of the new race and all-around genocidal maniac." Logan then adds with a sneer, "Hey, that sounds familiar."[8] The film cannot draw the Magneto/Hitler parallel much more clearly than that.

When in popular culture the relentless optimism of the American spirit collides with the intrinsic nihilism of the Shoah, what can emerge is the bizarre message of *X-Men* (whether intentional or not): if Holocaust survivors become so traumatized that they despair of humanity, they will be demonized as villains, which is precisely what happens to Magneto. Just as David Denby complained about the sentimentality of *Life is Beautiful*, this demonization of Magneto seems a kind of Holocaust-denial—denial of a basic message of the genocide: namely, that misanthropic despair is a perfectly understandable, and even reasonable, response to the trauma of the Shoah.

In fairness, subsequent entries in the *X-Men* series allude to the Holocaust in ways that are less offensive. In the second movie of the series, *X2: X-Men United* (2003), a subplot features another member of the "good" mutants, Wolverine (Hugh Jackman). As a young man, Wolverine was selected by the Canadian army to undergo experimental surgery that rendered his bones unbreakable and affixed retractable claws onto his hands. Apparently, the surgery was excruciating, enough so that Wolverine periodically experiences traumatic mental flashbacks. In *X2*, Wolverine returns to the abandoned compound where the procedure took place. As he looks around, the site blurs on the screen into soft focus and then is replaced by exterior shots of German concentration camps. Baron plausibly argues that Wolverine's operation "conjure[s] up images of Nazi medical experiments."[9] Thus, in the second film, the Holocaust is invoked purely to stress its horror, not as a means to demonize misanthropic Holocaust survivors.

The fifth, and at this writing, most recent *X-Men* sequel (or, more precisely, "prequel"), *X-Men: First Class*, also touches on the Holocaust. Like the first movie, it opens in a Nazi concentration camp. In fact, there are many similarities between the films' first scenes. In *First Class*, the young Magneto (at this time named Erik Lehnsherr) is once again separated from his parents in the camp by a metal gate. And, again, Lehnsherr discovers his mutant powers by telepathically opening the gate. But in this version he's then knocked unconscious by a Nazi guard. When he comes to, he finds himself in the office of a tea-sipping Nazi scientist, Sebastian Shaw (Kevin Bacon). Shaw orders Erik to use his magnetic powers to move a coin he's placed on the desk. When the boy, still discovering the extent of his abilities, is unable to do so, Shaw shoots and kills Erik's mother right in front of him—not an uncommon experience for Holocaust victims. It turns out that Shaw is himself a mutant with supernatural capabilities, and the two will battle (with Erik transformed into Magneto) for the rest of the film.

The story then leaps ahead in time from World War II to the Cold War. In Switzerland, Erik, now a young adult, rips metal fillings from the mouth of a banker (which recalls the actions of the Sonderkommando with the corpses of gassed prisoners) in order to force the banker to reveal the whereabouts of a gold bar the Nazis had stolen. Eventually, the banker discloses that the gold is in the possession of Shaw, who, like many escaped Nazis, is hiding in Argentina. Thus, the film at least glances at the ignominy of Swiss bankers safeguarding ill-gotten Nazi wealth.

At this point, the mutants who will become archrivals as Magneto and Professor X are still the best of friends. As in the first film, young Magneto (Michael Fassbender) is playing chess with an equally youthful Professor X, still known as Charles (James McAvoy). Soon after, the pair teams up to capture Emma Frost (January Jones), one of Shaw's confederates. *First Class* then goes on to dramatize the origins of what would become Magneto's and Professor X's lifelong antipathy. Before long, both the "good" and "evil" mutants are plunged headlong into the 1962 Cuban Missile Crisis. Thus, in its own trademark fashion, the *X-Men* series continues its mission to educate its millions of fans about world history.

If there is a disparity between Magneto's characterization in *X-Men: First Class* and in the first *X-Men* movie, it's that the mutant leader is now depicted as far less villainous. Merely by dramatizing the early friendship of Magneto and Professor X, *First Class* generates sympathy for Magneto, who is thus portrayed as an inherently good mutant gone bad. Moreover, supplying Magneto with an evil nemesis—the diabolical Shaw—renders his character far more appealing than he is in the first film, where Magneto's only enemy is the noble Professor X. As the *Oregonian*'s Mike Russell writes in a review, "Fassbender plays Magneto as a supercool assassin with a completely understandable set of beefs."[10] Apparently, the makers of the newer film have decided that a Holocaust survivor's misanthropy is less sinful today than it was back in 2000. Perhaps the catastrophe of 9/11, which transpired between the making of the original *X-Men* and its sequels, has left Hollywood a tad more susceptible to a tragic vision. Moreover, *X-Men: First Class* handles its Holocaust material with a slightly defter touch than was exhibited in the inaugural film. In her *New York Times* review, Manohla Dargis opines, "The weighty themes—post-Holocaust defiance and post-Stonewall pride—are still in play but less laboriously. 'Never again,' vows Erik, raising the freak flag."[11]

16

KIDS BEFRIENDING KIDS
IN THE HOLOCAUST

The Boy in the Striped Pajamas

The Boy in the Striped Pajamas, which appeared in theaters in 2008, is based on Irish writer John Boyne's young adult novel—one widely used in Holocaust curricula in middle and high schools in America and abroad. The movie version, too, seems pitched at children as well as adults. Thus, both book and film raise important questions about how best to introduce the Holocaust to the young.

Appropriately, since it's a story for young adults, *The Boy in the Striped Pajamas* (even more than *Life Is Beautiful*, with which it bears comparison) approaches the Holocaust through the eyes of a child: an eight-year-old German boy, Bruno (Asa Butterfield). Bruno has a doting mother, Elsa (Vera Farmiga), and a precocious older sister, Gretel (Amber Beattie). His father, Ralph (David Thewlis), is an SS officer originally stationed in Berlin. However, early in the film, Bruno's father is transferred in order to serve as commandant at a concentration camp. The camp is unnamed, but Bruno calls it "Out-With," and it seems likely that the boy has mispronounced Auschwitz. (The novel makes clearer that the camp is indeed Auschwitz.)

Lonely and miserable at the camp, Bruno notices out his bedroom window a development that he assumes is a "farm." The "workers" at this establishment appear to be dressed in striped "pajamas." Both of Bruno's parents are terse and evasive when he questions them about this "farm," so against his parents' expressed orders, Bruno sneaks off to find out for himself. Looking in through the barbed-wire fence that rings the establishment, Bruno meets Shmuel (Jack Scanlon), who turns out to be Bruno's age. Initially, Bruno is envious of Shmuel, since he assumes the boy has other children to play with. Gradually, Bruno and Shmuel become friends, and Shmuel informs Bruno that the camp is a prison and that he has been placed there because he is Jewish. Shmuel also relates that his grandparents and mother have disappeared.

Eventually, Shmuel is ordered to work in the house as a servant. When Bruno discovers this, he gives the starving Shmuel some cake. A Nazi lieutenant, Kotler, accuses Shmuel of stealing food. Shmuel defends himself by insisting that Bruno gave him the cake. When Kotler demands that Bruno tell him whether Shmuel is lying, Bruno has his one moment of moral weakness. Terrified, Bruno states that he has never seen Shmuel before. When Bruno returns to the camp to apologize, he discovers that Shmuel has been beaten. Nevertheless, Shmuel accepts Bruno's apology.

When Bruno's mother discovers that Auschwitz is an extermination camp, not just a forced labor camp, as she'd believed, she decides to take her children to live with relatives in Heidelberg, leaving her husband. Just before mother and children are to depart, Shmuel informs Bruno that Shmuel's father has disappeared. Spurred by a desire to help his friend, Bruno asks Shmuel to steal a camp uniform; garbed in camp attire, Bruno tunnels under the fence, and then both boys set off to find Shmuel's father. Before long, Shmuel and the disguised Bruno are herded with a group of other prisoners into the gas chamber, where they are all asphyxiated. Meanwhile, Bruno's parents discover he is missing. Spotting the tunnel under the camp fence beside a heap of Bruno's clothes, his mother falls to her knees. Bruno's father rushes to the outer door of the gas chamber. The film's final shot shows the striped camp uniforms hung on pegs in the deserted antechamber.

Reviewers were sharply divided about *The Boy in the Striped Pajamas*. Many found the movie powerful and insightful about the Holocaust. In the *London Times*, James Christopher wrote, "It is one of the most moving and remarkable films about childhood I've ever seen," concluding that the film "engages with the complexity of the Holocaust in a language that can move children as profoundly as adults."[1] In the *Miami Herald*, Rene Rodriguez observed that "By keeping its child

Figure 16.1. *The Boy in the Striped Pajamas* (2008). Bruno (Asa Butterfield), eight-year-old son of the camp commandant, plays checkers through the fence with Shmuel (Jack Scanlon), a young Jewish prisoner. [Screen grab]

protagonist front and center, [the film] lulls you into a false sense of security, helping its finale . . . achieve its pulverizing power."[2] Comparing the film to *Life is Beautiful* Margaret Burke noted in the *New York Times* that both movies "utilize a child's eyes, but [*The Boy in the Striped Pajamas*] is an altogether different film. It may not use comedy, but nor is it heavy-handed or severe in its story-telling."[3]

Perhaps the most significant figure to speak in favor of the film was Abraham Foxman, head of the Jewish Anti-Defamation League (ADL). A child of survivors who survived the war himself by hiding with a Catholic family, Foxman deemed *The Boy in the Striped Pajamas* to be "a powerful and complex movie" in an op-ed reprinted on the organization's website. The ADL head maintained that the film "demonstrates that hatred is not a natural phenomenon for young people." He felt the movie raised important questions about the Holocaust: "Is it possible to sympathize with individuals in a family of a concentration camp commandant? . . . Is it appropriate to think about moral complexity in the face of the greatest evil imaginable? And is it possible . . . to think not simply of evil Nazis and innocent Jews, but of people simply being people?"[4]

However, critics of *The Boy in the Striped Pajamas* were just as outspoken in their denunciation. In the *New York Times*, Manohla Dargis decried that the film represented "the Holocaust trivialized, glossed over, kitsched up, commercially exploited and hijacked for a tragedy about a Nazi family."[5] A highly substantive attack voiced by Rabbi Benjamin Blech was not of the movie but of the 2006 novel. Regretting that *The Boy in the Striped Pajamas* is used regularly in high schools to teach the Holocaust, Rabbi Blech felt the novel downplayed the horrors of Auschwitz: "The camps certainly weren't that bad if youngsters like Shmuel were able to walk about freely, have clandestine meetings at a fence . . . which even allows for crawling underneath . . . and as for those people in the striped pajamas—why if you only saw them from a distance you would never know these weren't happy masqueraders." The rabbi found implausible Shmuel's very existence in the camp: "There were no eight-year-old Jewish boys in Auschwitz—the Nazis immediately gassed those not old enough to work."[6]

On this last point, Blech is factually incorrect. In fact, there *were* male (though apparently not female) children at Auschwitz. In 1944, for example, according to the Nazis' meticulous records, there were 619 male children at the camp, ranging in age from one month to fourteen years old. Some of the boys were employed by the Nazis as camp messengers, while others were simply kept around as mascots and curiosities. Probably some of these children were sexually abused by the guards. Of course, thousands of other children at Auschwitz (including all the girls who arrived at the camp) were gassed.

Blech's criticism ignores the film's complexities, such as the scene in which Bruno denies knowing Shmuel. Here, Bruno behaves in a manner that is neither saintly nor confused but rather just acts immorally out of a child's fear. Unfortunately, the film's other characters are generally presented as morally one-dimensional—Bruno's mother, his strongly anti-Nazi grandmother, and Shmuel are purely good, while Bruno's father; Bruno's tutor, Herr Liszt; and Lieutenant Kotler are purely bad. Levi's moral "grey zone" is almost entirely absent from the film.

To the film's credit, the end of *The Boy in the Striped Pajamas* is suitably tragic, and audiences are spared a Hollywood happy ending. If Bruno's father had rushed into the gas chamber and plucked his son to safety just as Zyklon B started to seep through the ceiling vents, perceiving the error of his ways, the film would have been ruined. Its existing grim conclusion showed considerable audacity on director Mark Herman's part, especially since the film was partially designed for younger audiences. *The Diary of Anne Frank*, for example, omitted Anne's death in Bergen-Belsen.

It is interesting to note that opposition to the Nazis in the film breaks down along gender lines, with the men backing the Führer, while the women oppose him. It is tempting to think that the qualities normally associated with women, such as gentleness and nurturing, would make them less fervent in their support of the Third Reich than were German men, who might be more drawn to the Nazis' macho ethos. But this view is historically inaccurate. As Gisela Bock concludes in her essay "Ordinary Women in Nazi Germany: Perpetrators, Victims, Followers, and Bystanders," "Most German Gentile women complied with Nazi rule, for all or most of its duration, as bystanders, or, less passively, as followers. . . . A larger and more powerful minority, including women of all walks of life and social classes, actively participated in racist and genocidal policies; their beliefs, motives, and acts were similar to those of comparably ordinary men."[7] That *The Boy in the Striped Pajamas* circulates the myth that German women were more anti-Nazi than German men is one example (among others) of the film's sentimentality.

Aaron Kerner, in contrast, construes the film's view of women very differently, in particular its portrayal of Bruno's mother. He argues that by being a "good wife" to her Nazi husband, Elsa ultimately becomes a "bad mother," despite her loving treatment of Bruno, and that the film punishes her for her transgression by killing off her son. To support his case, Kerner quotes Katharina Von Kellenbach, who maintains that "it is the 'good wife' who ultimately made genocide possible: 'Women's love nourished and condoned the violence, rewarded and soothed the perpetrators, and normalized and sanitized a world that was profoundly disordered and depraved.'"[8] Kerner concludes, "Elsa . . . is subject to the Nazi taint; she is a 'bad mother' because she's a 'good Nazi wife,' and she is tortured for it."[9] As Bock's analysis suggests, Von Kellenbach and Kerner are probably right about the role and behavior practiced by most actual German women in the Third Reich, with the active encouragement of the regime, but they are wrong in their reading of Elsa's character. Elsa plays the role of "good Nazi wife" to her commandant husband only because she is unaware that the camp over which he presides is engaged in mass murder (however implausible her ignorance may seem). The moment she discovers the camp's true purpose, she immediately, and angrily, plans to depart with her children, leaving her husband behind.

The film also deserves credit, as Foxman suggests, for portraying the German response to Hitler as diverse. Although they were very much in the minority, there were indeed "good" Germans who opposed the Nazis, like the brave German students who founded the White Rose (whose nonviolent protests against the regime led to their executions), as well as Germans whose response to Hitler was neutral. Nonetheless, it stretches credibility to depict so many Germans in *The Boy in the Striped Pajamas* as naively ignorant of the Führer's designs regarding Jews—a tradition extending back in Hollywood Holocaust films all the way to the anti-Nazi movies made during World War II, which, as discussed, sharply distinguished between the Nazi elite, who were "evil," and the bulk of the German population, who were "good." In this, Bruno's mother contrasts sharply with Mrs. Rudolph Hoess in *Sophie's Choice*—who clearly knows about and fully supports her husband's genocidal activities.

Equally improbable is Bruno's naiveté. Though only eight, could Bruno really have gone his whole life without hearing the word "Jew"? While attending school during the Nazi era, German children saw their Jewish classmates singled out for opprobrium by teachers and principals. Then the day arrived when Jewish students simply vanished from the classroom, evicted by Nazi edict; wouldn't Bruno have wondered where these classmates had gone and why?

If *The Boy in the Striped Pajamas* absolves too many Germans of support for the Nazi regime, it also downplays the Holocaust's horrors in the way Auschwitz is portrayed, as Rabbi Blech argued. It's absurd that Shmuel can linger at the fence of Auschwitz for extended periods without any guards or *Kapos* at least ordering him back to work, if not punishing him more severely, perhaps with death. It is true that, after Shmuel has been schmoozing with Bruno for who knows how long, a whistle sounds, which snaps Shmuel to attention, but this seems more like the signal children in a schoolyard hear when recess is over rather than the discipline exacted at a place like Auschwitz. In one especially objectionable scene, Bruno and Shmuel actually play checkers, seated cross-legged on either side of the camp fence, with the Jewish boy explaining to his German friend which moves to make on his behalf.

Not only is Shmuel allowed to play checkers, but however haunted he looks, the boy is still far too pink cheeked and well fed to be a believable prisoner in a concentration camp. The same holds true for the other Auschwitz prisoners with whom Bruno and Shmuel are herded toward the gas chambers. At one moment in this scene, we see a prisoner raising his shirt, exposing a shriveled stomach, but since this is the only prisoner who looks emaciated, he comes off as an anomaly at the camp rather than the norm.

Because of all the improbabilities in *The Boy in the Striped Pajamas*—all of which soften the full evil of Auschwitz—Blech's point has merit: neither the novel nor the film are wise choices for teachers looking for ways to introduce their students to the Holocaust. A young adult author seeking to address the Shoah faces many of the same challenges confronted by Hollywood filmmakers. That is, neither author nor film director can present the Holocaust with unadulterated horror. Especially in the case of children, many aspects of the Shoah are simply too grim to be foisted on the young. The issue, then, becomes the same one confronted by Hollywood: How much softening of representation is acceptable before the Holocaust becomes essentially falsified? While it's impossible to draw that line precisely, *The Boy in the Striped Pajamas* clearly rings false.

17

SHAGGING NAZIS AND OTHER POSTWAR GERMAN ADVENTURES

The Reader

In 2008, the same year as *The Boy in the Striped Pajamas* appeared, the film version of *The Reader* made it to theaters. However, unlike *The Boy in the Striped Pajamas*, *The Reader* is a Hollywood Holocaust movie very much made for adults. The film is based on a semiautobiographical 1995 novel of the same name by Bernhard Schlink, a German law professor and practicing judge. Schlink was raised in an anti-Nazi family; his father was a Lutheran pastor (and later professor of theology in Heidelberg after the war) who was a member of the "Confessing Church," Bonhoeffer-like liberals who opposed the Nazi regime.[1] Translated into English in 1997, *The Reader* hit the jackpot when Oprah Winfrey picked it for her vaunted book club. Blessed with the Oprah bump, *The Reader* became the first German novel ever to sit atop the *New York Times* Bestseller List and went on to be translated into over forty languages. The novel was critically as well as commercially successful, picked as the *Los Angeles Times* Book of the Year and a *New York Times* Notable Book of the Year. However, *The Reader* had its often vociferous detractors, especially among Holocaust scholars and survivors, who condemned the book for portraying a Nazi perpetrator sympathetically. Not surprisingly, the film version of *The Reader* raises this same divisive issue.

The main difference between book and film involves narrative structure. Director Stephen Baldry and screenwriter David Hare dropped the book's straightforward chronological format and adopted a flashback technique, with the story's protagonist, Michael Berg (Ralph Fiennes), now middle-aged, recalling events that occurred during his adolescence. The film then shuttles between past and present. Some viewers may find this plot structure confusing, especially since the film doesn't include a clarifying voice-over narration. However, by starting the movie with the protagonist older and then flashing back to his youth, the film, even better than the novel, can explore the ways in which Michael's adulthood has been scarred by his past.

The Reader opens in the adult Michael's apartment the morning after what appears to have been a casual sexual encounter. Michael is polite but chilly with the young woman he's slept with. Thus, right away we infer that Michael has a detached relationship with women, for reasons that are clarified as the story unfolds. After the woman departs, Michael stares out the window at a train rattling past, which inspires a flashback. The action rewinds to 1958, to the middle-sized West German town of Neustadt. Now fifteen, Michael (David Kross) sits aboard a tram, looking nauseated. After vaulting from the train, he vomits in an alley. A thirty-something woman, Hanna Schmitz (Kate Winslet), is passing by, and, in no-nonsense fashion, she cleans up Michael's vomit, takes him to her nearby apartment, and then walks him home. Afflicted with scarlet fever, Michael is confined to bed for several months.

After recovering, Michael goes to thank Hanna, and even though Hanna is twice Michael's age, they soon embark on a torrid affair. If the virginal Michael feels exploited by Hanna, he certainly doesn't show it. On the contrary, Michael seems to find the affair with the attractive older woman incredibly exciting, even transformative. Although Hanna is sexually voracious, she remains aloof with Michael out of bed, referring to him as "kid," thus stressing their age difference and demoting him to subordinate status. As well, Hanna makes an odd but fervent demand; she wants Michael to read books to her. Since Hanna insists that Michael read before they have sex, the reading seems to function as a strange kind of foreplay. The result is an informal "Great Books" tutorial, with Michael whisking through Homer, Chekhov, Mark Twain, and even D. H. Lawrence's *Lady Chatterley's Lover* (which Hanna finds obscene, even as she insists that Michael continue reading).

However, one day when Michael turns up at her flat, Hanna has disappeared. The action then jumps ahead eight years, with Michael now a law student. As part of a seminar on legal ethics, Michael and the rest of the class, along with their professor (Bruno Ganz), attend a Nazi war crimes trial of lower-level perpetrators, part of a general de-Nazification process that Germany underwent in the 1960s. (Although invented, this particular trial is representative.) There, Michael is shocked to discover that his former lover is one of the defendants. It turns out that Hanna had been a guard at Auschwitz, where she and her fellow guards were responsible for choosing prisoners to die in the gas chambers.

Another serious charge is leveled against the defendants when a survivor testifies to what happened when the prisoners were taken on a brutal march into Germany in advance of the Allied forces. The prisoners were forced to spend a night in a church with the doors locked. That night, during a storm, a bolt of lightning set the church ablaze. Even as the trapped prisoners beat frantically against the doors, the guards refused to release them, with the result that everyone save the survivor burned to death. When the judge brandishes a report issued by the Nazis detailing the event, Hanna's codefendants claim that Hanna not only wrote the report but was also in charge at the time, with the others merely following orders.

It is at this point that Michael realizes something the viewer has probably known for some time: Hanna is illiterate and thus couldn't have written the report. Of course, this revelation explains Hanna's

Figure 17.1. *The Reader* (2008). Postwar German teenager Michael Berg (David Kross) reads to Hanna Schmitz (Kate Winslet), a former SS guard. [Screen grab]

demand that Michael read to her during their affair because she herself couldn't read. However, Hanna is apparently so ashamed of her illiteracy that she would rather take the blame for the church atrocity than confess that she can't read and write. In a momentous decision, Michael decides not to share his knowledge of Hanna's illiteracy with the court. While his motives are never clarified, it seems that Michael is partly acquiescing to what he perceives to be Hanna's wishes and is partly fearful of providing information that might lead the court to discover his affair with the defendant. As a result, while Hanna's codefendants receive light punishments, she is given a life sentence.

During Hanna's prison term, Michael (now morphed into Fiennes) begins an epistolary relationship with his former lover, sending her dozens of audiotapes of himself reading the sorts of classic works he'd shared with Hanna before. By comparing the tapes with the actual texts, which she checks out of the prison library, Hanna laboriously teaches herself to read. This process is implicitly presented as a kind of reformation—not exonerating Hanna for her past crimes but representing moral, as well as intellectual, progress. When the now elderly Hanna is about to be paroled, Michael finds her a job and apartment. But Hanna has no intention of trying to start over in the outside world. Instead, in a highly symbolic gesture, she climbs atop a stack of books piled in her cell and hangs herself. As for Michael, his reunion with Hanna seems to have freed him emotionally, a change reflected in his attempt to improve his relationship with his now grown daughter. On this note of muted optimism, the film ends.

Shortly after *The Reader* appeared in theaters, screenwriter Hare, a noted British playwright, gave an interview in which he stated that Schlink's novel is "more about the impact of the Holocaust on succeeding generations. That is where the book's originality lay. How do you live in the shadow of a great ethnic crime?"[2] By focusing on postwar German guilt and on the conflicted relationship between the wartime and postwar German generations, *The Reader* stands out from most other Hollywood Holocaust films. "In that twenty-year period after the war," Hare continued, "there was this strange silence about what happened. It was broken by the Auschwitz trials in the early '60s."[3]

The interview further revealed an intriguing concern on the screenwriter's part. "With the film's graphic depiction of sex, I worried about making the Holocaust seem pornographic," Hare said. "We were very concerned—I think we have to be clear about this—we were worried that if the film became too sexual, we would seem to be equating Nazism and sexuality. There is nothing sexy about the Nazis, and that is not in any way what either the book or the film is about."[4] Instead, Hare said he focused his script on the implicit analogy the novel drew between Michael's infatuation with Hanna and Germany's infatuation with Hitler: "The way that metaphor was sustained over a thirty-year period, I found that pretty wonderful and really an exciting subject for a film."[5]

The metaphor that Hare drew from the novel is provocative. Nonetheless, when Hare flatly insists that "there is nothing sexy about the Nazis," he comes off as uneasy and defensive. The disturbing truth is that there *is* something "sexy" about the Nazis, which is substantiated by the fact that there is a revolting pornographic genre known as "Holocaust porn," which focuses on sadomasochistic sex between prisoners and guards. Concealed behind an ersatz artistic gloss, this sort of pornographic plotline gets foregrounded in the film *The Night Porter* (1974), in which, after the war, a former Nazi guard and a Holocaust survivor, who'd had a sadomasochistic affair in the camp, meet again and waste no time in resuming their erotic games.

Indeed, the Nazis—with their impeccably polished black leather boots and form-fitting uniforms adorned with death's heads and lightning bolts—exerted a potent sexual magnetism over the German people that still has not lost its allure in certain circles. It's an allure also reflected in the plethora of myths, some still in circulation, about the various sexual deviancies with which the Führer was allegedly afflicted. In fact, acknowledging the Nazis' sexiness develops the metaphor that Hare finds at the heart of Schlink's novel—that is, just as Michael is seduced by Hanna's wiles, so the German people were seduced by Hitler's erotically charged charisma, a connection the film implies, whether Hare admits it or not.

In this light, it is interesting to contrast *The Reader* with *Sophie's Choice*. As Aaron Kerner points out, "*The Reader* is *Sophie's Choice* in reverse. Where Stingo, the principal male character in Pakula's film, undergoes a transformative process—namely, a sexual coming of age— via a victim of the Holocaust, Sophie, in *The Reader*, Berg undergoes an analogous transformation via a perpetrator."[6] Moreover, to its credit, *The Reader* rejects the implication found in *The Boy in the Striped*

Pajamas that most German women were anti-Nazi and uninvolved in the process of genocide.

Although *The Reader* tries to explore the nuances of German post-war guilt, and the polarized relationship between Germany's wartime and postwar generations, it ultimately fails, in part because Michael and Hanna's torrid affair overwhelms this comparatively academic subject. As Manohla Dargis wrote in her *New York Times* review, *The Reader*

> is also, very obliquely, about the Holocaust and the generation of Germans who came of age during that catastrophe. This, at any rate, is what the film would have us believe it's about, though mostly it involves Kate Winslet, her taut belly and limbs gleaming under the caressing light, deflowering a very surprised-looking teenage boy who grows up to become a depressed-looking Ralph Fiennes.[7]

The *New York Post*'s Kyle Smith makes a similar point: "Although the script works in a couple of college-level ethical debates about 'the question of German guilt,' what the movie is really interested in is the question of German sex. So think of it as *Schindler's Lust.*"[8]

Dargis and Smith make a significant point. For example, when Michael sits down in the prison cafeteria with Hanna to discuss her upcoming parole, rather than questioning her closely about why she enlisted as a camp guard or how she now feels about her Nazi past, he primarily talks about the details of her release. Had it been inserted, this deeper conversation—which perhaps Michael avoids because he considers it too sensitive—might have lapsed into didacticism, but if handled subtly, it could have been revealing.

The novel handles this scene better. In it, Michael asks Hanna, "'Didn't you ever think about the things that were discussed at the trial, before the trial? I mean, didn't you ever think about them when we were together, when I was reading to you?'" Hanna replies, "'Does that bother you much? . . . I always had the feeling that no one understood me anyway. . . . And you know, when no one understands you, then no one can call you to account. Not even the court could call me to account. But the dead can. They understand. . . . Here in prison they were with me a lot. . . . Before the trial I could chase them away when they wanted to come.'" It's an interesting speech in which Hanna seems, paradoxically, to be both acknowledging and sidestepping her guilt. However, Hare's script retains only Hanna's reference to being haunted by the Holocaust "dead." On the other hand, Schlink himself misses a chance when Michael's response is simply, "She waited to see if I had anything to say, but I couldn't think of anything."[9]

Although the film treats Michael as a representative of Germany's postwar generation, it's surprising that the whole issue of German behavior under the Nazis seems never to have crossed his mind prior to Hanna's trial. As Kirk Honeycutt asks in the *Hollywood Reporter*, "Did [Michael] never question his father—depicted here as a stern, unsympathetic man—about what he did during the war?"[10] Perhaps the film's point is that because the entire German nation colluded after the war in repressing anything to do with their Nazi past, the younger generation was never exposed to information that might have inspired pointed questions. The very fact that Michael attends a trial of Nazi defendants shows that by the 1960s the German government was making an attempt to confront its nation's past through its de-Nazification program, a program that must have received considerable national attention. Why, then, has Michael, a law student no less, remained so oblivious?

Many Holocaust survivors and scholars denounced *The Reader* for allegedly making a Nazi perpetrator sympathetic. True, Hanna is no Nazi caricature, no emblem of pure evil. But her affair with Michael is certainly exploitive, given the difference in their ages and the fact that he is a minor, regardless of how much the young man is enjoying himself. Perhaps the fault lies not with the script but with Baldry's no doubt commercially motivated decision to cast Kate Winslet, a Hollywood darling, as Hanna. It's not easy for audiences to think badly of a character played by Winslet (who won an Oscar for her performance in the film).

Some critics found Hanna's character less sympathetic than simply annoyingly vague. Elizabeth Weitzman writes in the *Daily News* that Hanna's "character remains a frustrating cipher. We never get more than a merest glimpse of her nature, and have no real understanding of her motives at any point. Both she and Kross [the young Michael] spend much of the movie unclothed, but only he comes across as truly exposed."[11]

But Weitzman is wrong that we "have no real understanding of [Hanna's] motives." Instead, explicitly in the novel and more subtly but still distinctly in the movie, the implication is that Hanna became a camp guard because the post didn't require literacy skills. Indeed, almost *all* Hanna's actions are driven by her desperate desire to hide her illiteracy from the world. We eventually discover that the reason she leaves town, ending her affair with Michael, is that she has been promoted from tram conductor to a desk job, which will require her to read and write. Rather than take a job she is incapable of performing, she flees. Hanna's behavior at her trial, where she falsely confesses to having written the report about the church burning, has the same motive. Hanna is more ashamed of being illiterate than of having been a guard at Auschwitz. However, one can see how Hanna's motives might fuel the charge that the film and novel are guilty of making a Holocaust perpetrator too sympathetic. If Hanna is seen as representative of the Nazis as a whole, then the implication seems to be that those Nazis who volunteered to serve as camp guards were driven more by shame than by malice or sadism.

One might retort that Hanna's illiteracy suggests not a condition outside her control but rather a flaw for which she should be held responsible, all of which might imply, if Hanna serves as a symbol of the German people under Hitler, that the nation was comparably flawed. This is the tack taken by Richard Schickel in *Time*: "Hanna's illiteracy symbolizes the willed ignorance of the German people about the genocide that was going on around them during World War II."[12] But this symbolic reading doesn't withstand scrutiny. After all, Hanna *can't* read because she's never learned, whereas the German people *could* have read the signs of Hitler's evil yet chose not to. The first is true ignorance, while the other is feigned.

Clearly, Michael is racked with guilt when he discovers that the woman who was the great love of his life was responsible for crimes against humanity. But is his guilt really appropriate? In her *Slate* review, Dana Stevens thought not: "Maybe I'm lacking in moral complexity . . . but *The Reader's* central problem (which seems reducible to 'I Shagged a Nazi') strikes me as . . . bogus. . . . If Michael can say, truthfully, that he knew nothing about his lover's past, doesn't that effectively absolve him of guilt? . . . Why on earth should a horny teenage boy have to abstain from sex with a willing blonde goddess on the off chance she might be S.S.?"[13] By this logic, *The Reader* would have been more ethically complex had Michael *known* Hanna was an ex-Nazi and slept with her anyway, overwhelmed by her eroticism, which paralyzed his moral sense.

In short, on closer inspection, the deeper meanings in *The Reader* don't really add up. This underlying confusion makes the film deficient as a portrayal of the Holocaust. In a favorable review in the *Seattle Post-Intelligencer*, William Arnold inadvertently makes this very point:

> *The Reader* is significant because . . . it asks us to see not just the Jews but the whole German people as victims of the Holocaust, and to view Nazism as more a product of explicable ignorance than inexplicable evil. This is a message—and a movie trend—that would have been unthinkable a decade ago, and one that still might not go down well with critics and moviegoers who could choose to see [the] film as a whitewash of German guilt for the phenomenon of the Third Reich. But it . . . may represent a whole new stage in our culture's continued efforts to understand, come to terms with and maybe even get past the 20th century's most unthinkable horror story.[14]

Were the German people really "victims of the Holocaust" just like the Jews? To say so redefines the concept of victimhood in a way that renders the term meaningless. And was Nazism "more a product of explicable ignorance than inexplicable evil"? Certainly, the Nazis weren't ignorant of the Final Solution. As for the German people as a whole, while they may not have known all the details of the Holocaust, they surely weren't ignorant of Hitler's virulent anti-Semitism, which the Führer made no attempt to conceal. Finally, should Holocaust films aim to enable viewers to "get past" the Shoah? (As noted, Roberto Benigni claimed to have the same ambition with *Life Is Beautiful*.) Shouldn't these movies do just the opposite and root us in the genocide?

Rather than being "unthinkable a decade ago," such a "trend" of whitewashing German guilt for Nazism has a long history in Hollywood Holocaust films, dating all the way back to such anti-Nazi propaganda as *Hitler's Children* and *Tomorrow the World!* Thus, the exculpation of German guilt is no new message in Hollywood but rather the resurrection of a very old message one might have hoped Hollywood would have left behind as a greater understanding of the Holocaust filtered into public consciousness. If this is a cinematic trend (and given the popularity of both *Life Is Beautiful* and *The Reader*, it might be) it is regressive, not progressive.

18

NO SHEEP TO THE SLAUGHTER
Defiance

At the start of *Defiance*, an on-screen caption informs the audience that what they are about to see is "a true story." Not *based* on a true story but a true story, period. While *Defiance* takes more liberties with the historical record than these words suggest, mainly in order to make it a more commercial film, the movie does stick fairly faithfully to an actual episode from the history of the Holocaust—one little known and worth publicizing. It's the story of three brothers—Tuvia, Zus, and Asael Bielski—who were poor farmers and small-time crooks in Belarussia (today Belarus). When the Nazis invaded, killing the Bielskis' parents and other siblings in the course of a massive pogrom, the brothers escaped to the neighboring woods. Over time, they were joined by hundreds of other Jewish refugees fleeing German persecution. With Tuvia as their leader, the refugees formed a kind of kibbutz—building a school, a hospital, and other facilities. They also banded together as partisans, harassing the German troops at every opportunity. In this way, the community survived for the two remaining years of the war. At war's end, only fifty of their number had been killed, while 1,200 were saved, making it the largest and most successful act of Jewish resistance during the Holocaust. The heroic story remained virtually unknown until 1993, when historian Nechama Tec published a book on the subject, *Defiance: The Bielski Partisans*. With the release of the film in 2008, the Bielskis' story was brought to a much larger audience.

In an interview, director Edward Zwick (who also cowrote the screenplay with Clayton Frohman) said he initially had no interest in pursuing the project. Instead, when offered the film, he said, "I groaned, 'Not another movie about victims.'"[1] But Zwick was ultimately persuaded because he felt the Bielskis' story challenged the traditional Holocaust narrative (presented by historians and filmmakers alike) that the Jews responded passively in the face of the Nazis, meekly plodding into the gas chambers like sheep to the slaughter. Here, in contrast, Zwick concluded, were Jews who fought back. In this respect, *Defiance* differs sharply from *Schindler's List*. In Zwick's film, unlike Spielberg's, Jews do not need a Righteous Gentile to "rescue" them; on the contrary, they are perfectly capable of resisting on their own.

A prolific filmmaker, Zwick's other films include *Glory*, *Courage Under Fire*, *The Siege*, *The Last Samurai*, *Legends of the Fall*, and *Blood Diamond*. This oeuvre demonstrates that Zwick is drawn to historical stories that both foreground action-oriented plots and grapple with ethical issues. In this way, Zwick is something of a latter-day Stanley Kramer, director of *Judgment at Nuremberg*, known in his time as the "king of the message movie." For example, Zwick's most acclaimed film, *Glory*, dramatizes the Civil War tale of an all-black Union regiment, led by a staunchly abolitionist white major, which fights with uncommon valor. And *Blood Diamond* considers civil-war-torn African countries, such as the Congo, where rebel groups use the local population as slaves to mine diamonds, with the profits funding the rebels' warmongering. Zwick generally tells these stories in a traditional, chronological manner, with plenty of stirring speeches and melodramatic moments, and *Defiance* is no exception.

Defiance opens with actual black-and-white documentary footage of German soldiers slaughtering Jews and other civilians during the Nazi invasion of Belarussia, with captions providing historical information about the assault. Thus, from the start, *Defiance* has the feel of a docudrama. Next, we see Tuvia (Daniel Craig) and Zus (Liev Schreiber) returning to their farmhouse to discover the slain bodies of their family. Only one member has survived, their younger brother Asael (Jamie Bell). Shell-shocked and lost, the brothers flee to the nearby Naliboki Forest. The film was shot in Lithuania and Canada by the skilled cinematographer Eduardo Serra, and the forest scenes are lushly green and twinkling with light; with the aid of computer enhancement, they have an almost fairy tale look (which clashes with the movie's interest in documentary realism but enhances the film's suggestion that the forest represents some almost magical escape from the Nazis). Eventually, Tuvia procures a pistol and decides to shoot the Belarussian collaborator who killed his parents. Surprising the man at dinner, he not only murders the collaborator, who's on his knees pleading for his life, but also guns down his two sons. Tuvia never discusses his feelings about the shooting with Zus or anyone else, but an expression on his face as he exits the cottage implies that the cold-blooded killings have pricked his conscience. Zus, on the other hand, is thrilled. "Feels good, doesn't it?" he tells Tuvia, flashing a wolfish grin.

Not long after, Asael discovers in the woods a family of Jewish refugees, whom he brings to the encampment. While Zus grumbles about more mouths to feed, Tuvia lets the family join their contingent. Gradually, increasing numbers of refugees straggle into camp, until the group has swelled into a bona fide community. A natural leader, Tuvia sets strict rules that all must follow—everyone must work, and no women can get pregnant, since the community lacks the ability to care for infants. The group includes a rabbi, Shimon Haretz (Allan Corduner, who gave a riveting performance in *The Grey Zone*), and a socialist intellectual, Isaac Malbin (Mark Feuerstein). Since one man is religious and the other secular, the two engage in endless, relatively genial disagreements, which provide *Defiance*'s only moments of humor. For example, when Malbin says to Haretz, "At least Descartes proved the subjective nature of all experience," the rabbi replies, "Yes, you annoy me, therefore I exist." Both city folk, like many of the refugees, the pair is ill equipped for the harsh, demanding life of the forest, but under Tuvia and Zus's tutelage, they toughen up. Wielding a hammer, Malbin cries, "If the members of the Socialist Club could see me now!"

The forest community represents an inversion of traditional Jewish life, with those customarily elevated, the religious scholars and rabbis, reduced to the low rungs of the social ladder, while those normally marginalized and even despised—farmers, laborers, like the Bielski brothers—occupying leadership roles. Before the war, the real-life Bielskis had been smugglers, though their criminal past is downplayed in the film. While the director's decision seems to stem from a reluctance to tarnish the Bielskis' halo, Zwick need have looked no further than

Figure 18.1. *Defiance* (2008). **Brothers Tuvia and Zus (Daniel Craig and Liev Schreiber) form a unit of Jewish partisans, battling the Germans in the forests of Belarus. [Screen grab]**

Schindler's List to find an example of how a rogue and swindler can be dramatically transformed into a hero in a Holocaust film.

In the alternate universe of the forest camp, the rules for relationships have also been rewritten, with the men of the group procuring what are called "forest wives"—romantic partnerships formed even if the members had other spouses before they fled. Thus, the Bielski brothers are each outfitted with a "forest wife," all of whom are blessed with movie starlet voluptuousness. These relationships lead to some clichéd romantic dialogue; for example, when Tuvia and his forest wife lie together in their shelter, wrapped in furs and bathed in golden sunlight, she murmurs, "You saved my life," and he woodenly replies, "No, you saved mine."

Asael and his forest wife's romance is the most developed, with the pair getting married in the woods in a ceremony performed by Rabbi Haretz. In an arresting juxtaposition, this ceremony is crosscut with a scene of Zus and some other partisans attacking a Nazi convoy. Reviewing *Defiance* in the *New Yorker*, David Denby comments on the symbolic significance of the montage:

Zwick has made an obvious swipe from *The Godfather*: a climactic moment in which a joyful, Chagallesque wedding in the forest is intercut with a bloody attack on the Germans recalls the baptism of Michael Corleone's child, which is intercut with the slaughter of Michael's Mob rivals. But the meaning of the juxtapositions is quite different. The first is sardonic—Corleone is a hypocrite. This one is resolutely existential: if Jews want to marry and produce another generation they must learn to kill, a lesson that's bound to elicit a mixed response.[2]

But all is not well in the forest compound. When winter arrives, the refugees begin to starve, forcing them to steal food from neighboring farms, though they scrupulously take only as much as they need. An even bigger problem is the conflict that erupts between Tuvia and Zus—a rivalry that lies at the heart of the film, assuming an almost biblical quality, a kind of Cain-and-Abel story. Tuvia is the more pacifist of the brothers; his aim is to try to stay away from the Germans while creating a harmonious, sustainable community. Zus, in contrast, is the more bloodthirsty; he is determined to kill Germans and collaborators, a goal about which Tuvia has ethical qualms. To Zus, all those in the community who, for one reason or another, are unable to fight are what he calls "*malbushim*" (a Hebrew word that literally means "clothes" but that Zus uses to signify dead weight).

The tension between the two brothers comes to a head when they rob a local milkman, only to see the milkman lead a band of pro-Nazi Belorussian peasants to the Jews' forest hideout. After the battle, in which the Jews prevail, Zus snaps at Tuvia, "We should've killed the fucking milkman." Eventually, the brothers' argument reaches such a pitch that they physically fight, and Tuvia is about to crush Zus's skull with a rock before he comes to his senses.

Ultimately, Zus abandons the community, taking with him those refugees who are willing to desert, and joins up with a roving band of fierce Soviet partisans, led by a taciturn, no-nonsense commander named Viktor Panchenko (Ravil Isyanov). Earlier, when Tuvia and Zus had introduced themselves to the Soviet soldiers, Panchenko had responded, "Jews don't fight," to which Tuvia had laconically replied, "These Jews do." Now, Panchenko and Zus become friends, with the Soviet leader impressed by Zus's courage and martial skills. But it turns out that the Russians are hardly less anti-Semitic than the Germans.

One of the Jews who joins the Soviets is badly beaten by Panchenko's right-hand man (Rolandas Boravskis) because he has the temerity to defecate in the same latrine the Russians use.

Finally, Tuvia's Jews are forced to flee in the face of the oncoming German army. Slowed by women, children, and those stricken with malnourishment and disease, they stumble through the woods until they reach what seems to be an impassable swamp. All along, the film has implied that Tuvia is a kind of latter-day Moses leading the Jews from enslavement to freedom. When the refugees reach the swamp, the Moses parallel is underscored, rather heavy-handedly, when one of their number tells Tuvia that they can't count on supernatural aid to part *these* waters. Undaunted, Tuvia leads the Jews through the swamp to dry land, even hoisting the rabbi on his back when the latter is too weak to continue.

But no sooner have the Jews apparently reached safety than they are attacked by a German tank. The refugees fight back bravely. Malbin, the intellectual, discovering hitherto unknown reserves of courage, loses his life in a suicide mission, dashing toward the tank clutching a grenade. Just as the tide of battle seems to be turning against the refugees, Zus and the other Jews who'd joined the Soviet partisans show up, like the cavalry coming to the rescue at the climax of a Hollywood Western. With this assistance, the Jews emerge victorious.

San Francisco Chronicle reviewer Mick LaSalle observes that "the Holocaust film has practically become a Hollywood subgenre, and one convention of the drama is to try to end on an upbeat note. It doesn't take more than ten seconds to realize how ridiculous that is."[3] However, other critics, such as Gene Newman in *Premiere*, praise *Defiance's* conclusion: "Unlike most World War II films, this one won't make you depressed. . . . There's a powerful undercurrent of survival, hope and honor in *Defiance*, so you'll leave the theater feeling triumphant."[4] But the question remains: Should one leave a Holocaust movie "feeling triumphant"? Newman seems oblivious to the distortions of a Holocaust "feel-good" flick.

Aaron Kerner also dislikes the film's ending but focuses on the way it dehumanizes the Nazi soldiers as abstract embodiments of pure evil, a message even inscribed in the film's cinematography:

The undeniable adrenaline rush that the spectator experiences while watching the film—especially in the Exodus sequence, when the Germans beset the band of Jews—is rooted in the fact that the representatives of evil are not represented as agents but as pawns sacrificed to the service of the uplifting and action-packed narrative. In the climactic battle sequence the Germans are depicted in medium long shots, or long shots, with very little or no recognizable facial features. They are largely disembodied, merely extensions of their weapons, instead of characters, . . . The climactic sequence is little more than an American Western, where American frontiersmen (Jews) fend off the marauding Indians (Germans). The Jewish characters, on the other hand, are given close-ups; they're fully embodied, and are privileged with subjective shots.[5]

Kerner's objection to this Manichean division between purely evil Nazis and purely good Jews is clear. Once again, we are a long way from Primo Levi's "grey zone."

Defiance also adheres to Hollywood conventions in the screenwriters' penchant for inserting rhetorical, high-flown speeches that stretch credibility. Exhorting his fellow refugees, Tuvia declaims, "We have all chosen this—to live free like human beings for as long as we can." Later, he announces pithily, "Our revenge is to live." That a poorly educated peasant, who in other respects is portrayed as anti-intellectual, is capable of and drawn to such grandiloquence defies belief.

Also at issue is Zwick's decision to cast Daniel Craig (best known for his portrayal of the most recent James Bond) in the lead role of Tuvia. Craig's Aryan good looks—blond hair, blue eyes—simply don't fit in this context. (Admittedly, Craig did play an Israeli Mossad agent in *Munich*, but he didn't look Jewish there either.) Not only are Craig's eyes blue, but, perhaps through some cinematographic trick, they seem to be positively glowing, as if suffused with an inner light, especially in those scenes in which Tuvia makes his most stilted, impassioned speeches. Moreover, Craig's fame hinders the audience's suspension of disbelief in this historically based story. Zwick would have been better off casting a lesser-known actor in the role, even at the risk of riling his financial backers, just as Steven Spielberg did by casting Liam Neeson as the lead in *Schindler's List*. On the other hand, Zwick chose wisely in picking Liev Schreiber to play Zus, since not only is Schreiber Jewish, with grandparents who emigrated from Russia at the turn of the twentieth century, but in 2005 Schreiber directed the Holocaust-oriented film *Everything Is Illuminated*, based on the celebrated novel by Jonathan Safran Foer.

Some critics find the Tuvia/Zus imbroglio lacking in intrinsic drama. LaSalle argues, "Yet whatever the conflict between the brothers, real or dramatized, their struggle is not with each other, and the audience knows it. . . . The Bielskis' fight is with the Germans, and yet aside from a few skirmishes, the Jewish refugees steer clear of the German army."[6]

The Tuvia/Zus conflict is another example of the way *Defiance* falls back on stock Hollywood characterizations, but it's unfair to claim that the clash lacks drama. On the contrary, the struggle between pacifism and warfare is deeply rooted in the Torah, and, as a result, in Jewish tradition. God includes as one of his Ten Commandments, "Thou Shalt Not Murder," but he also repeatedly orders the Israelites to slaughter any number of peoples against whom he holds a grudge. Thus, Tuvia and Zus are enacting a very Jewish conflict. Moreover, the struggle is well balanced. Given the heroic way Tuvia leads the bedraggled refugees, he becomes a figure who commands intense respect—a kind of modern-day Moses. But Zus also makes a powerful argument that the appropriate response to radical Nazi evil must be to fight.

While most reviewers recognize that what sets *Defiance* apart from most other Holocaust films is its depiction of Jews fighting back against the Nazis, others claim that the fighting-Jew theme is presented with insufficient ambiguity. For example, the *A.V. Club*'s Nathan Rubin compares *Defiance* unfavorably to Steven Spielberg's *Munich*, also about tough Jews, in this case the Mossad agents who tracked down the PLO terrorists responsible for killing Israeli athletes at the Munich Olympics: "Where Spielberg used Israel's quest to hunt down and kill the people responsible for the 1972 . . . massacre as a springboard to . . . explore how the lust for revenge poisons and corrupts, Zwick uses the true story of Jewish outlaws who fought [the Nazis] largely as a vehicle for false uplift and a steady stream of big Oscar moments."[7] This view, however, is wrong-headed: there's a lot of moral ambiguity in *Defiance*, reflected most strongly in Tuvia's qualms over Zus's bloodthirstiness. Moreover, both the Israeli government and many critics attacked *Munich* for objectionably equating Palestinian terrorism and Israeli counterterrorism. But, most importantly, the analogy of Jewish partisans during World War II to Israeli Mossad agents is false. After all, one group represented the weaker side in a hopelessly lopsided struggle, while the other worked for a nation with the strongest military in the Middle East.

The most thoughtful and original analysis of *Defiance*'s portrayal of the fighting Jew appears in A. O. Scott's *New York Times* review:

> *Defiance* presents itself as an explicit correction of the cultural record, a counterpoint to all those lachrymose World War II tales of helplessness and victimhood. . . . But the problem is that, in setting to overturn historical stereotypes of Jewish passivity, Mr. Zwick . . . ends up affirming them. His film . . . implies that if only more of the Jews living in Nazi-occupied Europe had been as tough as the Bielskis, more would have survived. This . . . has the effect of making the timidity of the Jews, rather than the barbarity of the Nazis and the vicious opportunism of their allies, a principal cause of the Shoah. What the Bielskis did is treated not as the extraordinary, odds-defying feat it was, but rather as an ideal that those who did not survive failed to live up to. . . . *Defiance* celebrates strong men . . . at the expense of those whose weakness—whose inability to fight back, or stay alive—was not a moral failure but a fact of history.[8]

As Scott suggests, some Jews did resist the Nazis, a fact that must be noted in the historical record, but such resistance was the exception, not the norm. However, the reason for the relative paucity of Jewish resistance was *not*, as is so often assumed, some ingrained Jewish cowardice or passivity but rather the gargantuan imbalance of the struggle. As Rita Steinhardt Botwinick explains in *A History of the Holocaust: From Ideology to Annihilation:*

> The obstacles to establish a viable Jewish resistance movement were compelling. Jews rarely owned weapons and found it nearly impossible to acquire them. In order to fight the Germans from hidden encampments, a supportive native population was essential. Polish Jewry, which suffered the greatest losses, could not rely on much help from their Christian neighbors. The Gestapo held all Jews collectively responsible for defiance by a single man or woman. This left the possible opponent with a terrible choice: Was it morally right to endanger the community in order to kill a few Germans? Communication between Jewish resistance groups was uncertain and dangerous. To keep from starving and freezing, to constantly move from

one hidden location to another, demanded much of the strength of Nazi resisters. The Germans, on the other hand, had every advantage: arms, manpower, economic resources, radios, and telephones.[9]

Defiance fails to sufficiently dramatize just how difficult a successful Jewish resistance against the Nazis actually was, thus leaving the impression, however inadvertently, that nonresisting Jews must have been cowards. This is, in a sense, a comforting misimpression because human beings—particularly Americans—cling fiercely to the notion that we always retain free will, that we can never find ourselves in a situation in which our fate is simply out of our control. However, in almost every instance, such was precisely the fate of the Jews.

There were other important reasons for the comparative absence of Jewish resistance. Viciously persecuted in Christian Europe for centuries, the Jewish community's evolved response, given the near impossibility of active resistance, had been acquiescence and diplomacy. Thus, when Jewish populations formed *Judenraete*, which negotiated with the Nazis and counseled their people against fighting back, they were simply following a time-honored strategy that had historically enabled the Jews to survive against overwhelming odds. It is easy in historical hindsight to see that negotiation with the Nazis was fruitless, but this reality was much more difficult to perceive at the time, especially since the Nazis deliberately tricked the Jews into believing that if only they remained productive workers in the ghettos, their survival was ensured. Reports of exterminations in the camps were trickling into the ghettos from Jews who had escaped, but it's only human nature never to want to believe the worst.

Defiance includes a scene set in a nearby ghetto where Tuvia and Zus try to convince one of the *Judenrat* leaders to advise his people to join their partisan band. In response, the leader makes the sorts of arguments just outlined. But the film stacks the deck, making the *Judenrat* leader look like a deluded fool, rather than a man doing what he sincerely thinks best in a hopeless situation. There is no mention in the film of the reality Botwinick describes—namely, that if any ghetto Jews joined the partisans, the Germans would retaliate against all those who remained behind. We see a contingent of ghetto Jews enlisting with Tuvia and Zus, but we never see what happens to those who don't enlist.

Under the circumstances, Jewish resistance was essentially an act of suicide, a decision to die fighting rather than being led meekly to the gas chambers. As Botwinick says of the fighters in the Warsaw ghetto, "They knew their choices were not between life and death but between death in combat or death in Treblinka."[10] And as the historian writes of the three revolts by prisoners at German concentration camps (Treblinka, Sobibor, and Auschwitz-Birkenau), "Revolts in three of the death camps confirmed the desperation underlying this unequal struggle. As symbolic actions, these efforts merit respect; as battles to save Jewish lives they failed."[11] In almost every case, nearly all the resisters were ultimately killed, and the Nazi machinery of death was scarcely impeded at all. By focusing on one of the rare instances in which Jewish resistance was successful, *Defiance* misleadingly implies that such success was the norm (or *could* have been, if more Jews had resisted).

If *Defiance* had acknowledged these complexities, it would have rendered problematic the heroism of the film's resisters, but it would also have resulted in a more authentic movie. In this respect, *The Grey Zone* is a more nuanced film because when the leader of the female prisoners from Birkenau refuses to reveal to which Sonderkommando members she and her confederates had smuggled explosives, the Nazis execute all the other women in her barrack, driving her to suicide. Thus, *The Grey Zone* questions the morality of Jewish resistance, an issue *Defiance* never dares to consider.

19

CARTOON JEWISH REVENGE

Inglourious Basterds

Quentin Tarantino's *Inglourious Basterds* underwent a long gestation. When Tarantino released his underrated *Jackie Brown* in 1997, the director told interviewers he was interested in making a World War II action flick, so it seems Tarantino may have been contemplating the idea for the film for a decade before it came to fruition. Tarantino, of course, is known for the leisurely pace at which he makes movies—a pace that doesn't, however, always result in accomplished films.

Inglourious Basterds is very loosely based on a 1978 B-grade Italian film of the same name (but spelled correctly)—which, in turn, is a *Dirty Dozen* knockoff about a footloose band of disreputable American GIs killing Nazis in Europe. While he stated in an interview at Cannes that he was "never going to explain" the spelling of the title, when pressed in later interviews, he is noted to have claimed, "That's just the way you say it 'Basterds,'" and also that the spelling was an attempt to give the title a "Basquiat-esque touch."[1]

The movie was shot almost entirely at Babelsberg Studio outside Berlin, with some brief location work in Paris. Babelsberg was famed as the studio used by many of Germany's greatest directors of the Weimar era, such as Fritz Lang and Josef von Sternberg, and was also employed by the Nazis for their propaganda films—background that is all evoked in *Inglourious Basterds*.

The film is divided into chapters with on-screen titles, and the first, a twenty-minute sequence that was almost universally acclaimed by reviewers, is titled "Once Upon a Time . . . In Nazi-Occupied France." This captures the paradox of the film. On the one hand, "once upon a time" implies that the film will have a fairy tale quality, while the title's second part, "Nazi-Occupied France," suggests the movie will have at least some basis in history. (Indeed, the film's blend of fantasy and history is a major problem, with each aspect tending to cancel out the other.) As the camera pans over the idyllic French countryside, we see in the distance a convoy of Nazi trucks approaching a French farmhouse. The farmer is Perrier Lapadite (Denis Menochet), who, we later learn, is hiding Jews under the floorboards of his house. Lapadite is questioned by the Nazi leader, Colonel Hans Landa (played by the previously obscure—at least to American audiences—Austrian actor Christoph Waltz, who won a Best Supporting Actor Oscar for his performance). In almost lackadaisical fashion, Landa questions the increasingly distraught Lapadite and eventually works his way around to mentioning that one Jewish family in the region has so far eluded capture by the Germans. Landa also notes that the French have nicknamed him the "Jew Hunter."

The scene is not only suspenseful but also contains comic moments; for example, when Landa asks if Lapadite minds if he smokes, the Nazi officer extracts an enormous Meerschaum pipe that looks like it had last been puffed by Sherlock Holmes. Reflecting his education and sophistication, Landa effortlessly switches from addressing his soldiers in German to chatting with the farmer in French to, on Landa's request, shifting their discussion into English. Indeed, much of the dialogue in *Inglourious Basterds* is spoken in various foreign languages, with subtitles—a fact that, unsurprisingly, was omitted in American previews for the film, since Hollywood is well aware how much American audiences hate subtitles.

Landa promises the farmer that if he admits to concealing Jews, he and his family will not be punished. Eventually, a sweating Lapadite murmurs that the Jews are under the floorboards, whereupon Landa has his soldiers strafe the floor with bullets. All the Jews are killed, save for one, Shosanna Dreyfus (the French actress Mélanie Laurent), who is seen sprinting for her life away from the farmhouse while Landa observes her from the doorway with a jaundiced eye but, oddly, makes no attempt to stop her. We never learn if Landa keeps his promise to spare Lapadite and his family.

In the film's second chapter, we are reintroduced to Shosanna Dreyfus, who, concealing her Jewish identity, has resurfaced as the owner of a charming Parisian movie theater. Another example of Tarantino's sloppy plotting is the extreme improbability that a Jewish refugee would decide that the best way to hide from the Nazis would be to open a cinema in Paris (or, for that matter, that she'd have the means to do so). In any event, while Dreyfus is putting up signs for the next film, a German officer named Frederick Zoller (the German actor Daniel Bruhl) flirts with her. It turns out that Zoller is a war hero who had single-handedly held off an entire battalion of American soldiers, a feat that has led him to be dubbed the "German Sergeant York." Goebbels, in fact, has sponsored a film celebrating Zoller's heroism called *Nation's Pride*, which is due to premiere in Paris, with all the Nazi brass in attendance, including Hitler himself. Smitten with Dreyfus, Zoller convinces Goebbels to move the premiere's location to her theater. This

Figure 19.1. *Inglourious Basterds* **(2009). Hans Landa (Christoph Waltz), a Nazi colonel known as the "Jew Hunter," converses with a nervous French farmer who is hiding Jews under the floorboards of his home. [Screen grab]**

change of venue inspires Dreyfus to hatch a daring scheme—namely, setting the theater ablaze during the screening and thus wiping out the entire Nazi elite. Learning that Colonel Landa—the man responsible for killing Dreyfus's entire family—will also be in attendance gives her added incentive.

The action then shifts to the title characters: a squadron of Jewish American GIs, led by Tennessee hillbilly Lieutenant Aldo Raine (Brad Pitt), who are dropped into Nazi-occupied France and ordered to kill and terrorize as many German soldiers as possible. Lieutenant Raine commands each of his soldiers to give him "one hundred Nazi scalps"— and Raine means "scalps" literally, since the Basterds do scalp the German soldiers after they kill them, an action Tarantino (never squeamish about on-screen violence) vividly depicts for the audience. (Apparently, Raine has chosen the scalping ritual because he's part Apache.)

The Basterds not only shoot Germans, but one of their number, known as the "Bear Jew" (played by Eli Roth), graphically beats them to death with a baseball bat. Occasionally, the squadron lets a German soldier live so that he can report on their actions to his superiors, but in those cases the Basterds carve a swastika into the soldier's forehead.

Meanwhile, the fact that the top Nazis will be attending the Parisian premiere of *Nation's Pride* comes to the attention of the British government—though they are unaware of Dreyfus's scheme. British General Ed Fenech (a heavily made-up Mike Meyers), in collaboration with Winston Churchill (an almost unrecognizable Rod Taylor), assigns Lieutenant Archie Cox (the Irish German actor Michael Fassbinder, Magneto in *X-Men: First Class*) a top-secret mission—round up the Basterds to infiltrate the film premiere and blow the theater to smithereens. It turns out—in a throwaway detail that is pure Tarantino—that Cox is not only a secret agent but also a noted film critic with expertise on German cinema (which gives added resonance to the movie being filmed at Babelsberg Studio).

Cox and the Basterds rendezvous in the basement of a tavern in the French countryside. The British agents and some of the Basterds gather in the bar, where a group of German soldiers is seated at a neighboring table. The Basterds are soon approached by a German, Major Hellstrom (August Diehl), who has been sitting alone and is struck by Cox's unusual German accent. Precipitously fearing their cover is blown, the agents and the Basterds shoot it out with the Germans. It is unclear how this long scene furthers the action in any discernible way, though, other than killing off a few participants in the secret operation.

The climactic chapter of *Inglourious Basterds* occurs at the premiere of *Nation's Pride*. Raine and two other Basterds are in attendance, posing absurdly as Italian officers even though they barely speak Italian. Seeing through their transparent disguise, Landa arrests the Americans. However, rather than foiling their scheme, Landa agrees to surrender to Raine on the condition that he be allowed to immigrate to America, where he can live out his days incognito and unscathed. There is no pragmatic reason for Landa's surrender, since he has the upper hand with Raine and the Basterds. It seems that Tarantino couldn't allow the Basterds' plot to be foiled and discards narrative plausibility in order to achieve his central end: the death of Hitler and his inner circle.

Meanwhile, manning the projector, Dreyfus begins to ignite the film but is interrupted when Zoller turns up at the booth. To get rid of him, Dreyfus pretends to be interested in sex and then shoots Zoller in the back while he's locking the door. With his dying breath, Zoller shoots and kills Dreyfus. The scene is shot in slow motion, and the soundtrack—a bizarrely anachronistic touch—features David Bowie singing the theme from the film *Cat People*.

But, even in death, Dreyfus gets the last laugh when, as fire engulfs the theater, a film she's secretly shot is superimposed on *Nation's Pride*, showing a gigantic shot of Dreyfus's head brazenly intoning, "This is the face of Jewish vengeance." As Hitler leaps up in sputtering indignation, the crowd of German officers begins fleeing for the exits. At this moment, two Basterds, who have positioned themselves in the balcony of the theater, spray the audience with machine-gun fire, which succeeds, in a wild rewriting of history, in killing Goebbels, Goering, and Hitler himself, whose bullet-ridden body is lingeringly displayed on screen.

The movie's final scene shows Landa in the woods with Raine, with the Nazi colonel preparing to surrender to the Allies. Raine then explains that he can't kill Landa due to the terms of their agreement, but he wants to do something to ensure that Landa won't lead a comfortable life in America. So, in accordance with standard Basterds' practice, he carves a swastika into the forehead of a shrieking Landa. Grinning with relish, Raine calls this action, in the film's last words, "my masterpiece."

The killing of Hitler and his associates is an example of "alternate history," a subgenre of science fiction that has produced some fascinating works. At the time of its release, critics were divided as to whether the alternate-history ending of *Inglourious Basterds* succeeded. According to Scott Tobias on National Public Radio:

> There's hardly a sober moment in this alternate-history cartoon about Jews having their revenge on Nazis even as the Reich pursues its Final Solution. To the contrary, the film stands as a vulgar kiss-off to the august trappings of World War II movies and for that alone it's a refreshing and sometimes empowering wish-fulfillment fantasy. Leave the real history to be fussed over in the halls of academe: Tarantino's version more closely approximates one that might be invented by thirteen-year-olds playing with action figures in the backyard.[2]

It's unclear why Tobias thinks that "thirteen-year-olds playing with action figures in the backyard" are the ideal people to be hatching ideas for a movie. But other critics took Tarantino to task for his conclusion. In the *Oregonian*, reviewer Shawn Levy wrote, "The film's final act is so wildly different from what has come before—on the level of sincerity, history, artistic ethics, and empirical logic—that the film unravels," concluding that "it's possible to get so caught up in the audacity of *Basterds . . .* that you're converted to Tarantino's point-of-view, and find pleasure in the preposterous turn of the finale. But to do so is, I fear, to approach the film in the throes of a fanboy crush and not with the sort of rigor that an artist of Tarantino's stripe deserves."[3]

The ending of *Inglourious Basterds* is indeed a disaster. At its best, alternate history helps us better understand actual history by contemplating how events might have turned out differently. In Robert Harris's *Fatherland*, for example, the novel's alternate history twist is that the victorious Nazis have successfully concealed knowledge of the Holocaust, which provocatively suggests that our awareness of the Final Solution was contingent on the Allied victory. And in Philip Roth's equally compelling *The Plot against America*, the anti-Semitic aviation hero Charles Lindberg defeats Roosevelt in the presidential election, whereupon Lindberg not only immediately signs a peace treaty with Hitler but also inaugurates a sinister program relocating urban American Jews to the countryside in order to expose them to "real"

America, an action that may be a prelude to genocide—all of which informs readers of the anti-Semitic nature of the isolationist movement in 1930s America. But what historical insight is offered by an alternate ending that bumps off Hitler, Goering, and Goebbels? As Tobias admits, it's a comforting "wish-fulfillment fantasy." In this respect, *Inglourious Basterds* ends up a perverse example of a Hollywood feel-good movie.

Kerner sees the climax of *Inglourious Basterds* as possessing significant moral complexity:

> That the spectacle of violence also takes place in a movie theater begins to point back at the spectator. We might feel a rush of adrenaline as the Bear Jew stands over Hitler's prone body, pumping it full of lead, but our own giddy euphoria is made uneasy in relation to *Nation's Pride*. . . . More so than any other film he has done in the past, Tarantino seems to hold filmmaker and spectator alike quite accountable, complicit in the fantasies of revenge. This fact is emphasized in the closing moments of the film when Lieutenant Aldo Raine, the commanding officer of the Basterds, carves a swastika on Landa's forehead with a buck-knife. . . . The pleasure we commonly derive from the sadistic voyeuristic gaze is compromised. . . . When Lieutenant Raine carves the swastika on Landa's forehead, this is done in a POV shot; the spectator is literally placed in the Nazis' shoes, branded with the swastika. . . . Indeed, Tarantino might have turned a corner here, and is perhaps asking us to interrogate the pleasure that we derive from spectacles of violence.[4]

Kerner's interpretation seems more clever than plausible. The setting of the film's violent climax in a movie theater seems, merely, more evidence of Tarantino's much-discussed obsession with cinema, his fondness for cluttering his movies with film references both famous and obscure, than it does with any desire "to interrogate the pleasure that we derive from spectacles of violence." Indeed, it would be rather odd, to say the least, if a filmmaker whose entire career has been devoted to celebrating on-screen violence of the most graphic kind would suddenly develop such delicate moral scruples. On the contrary, I think voyeuristic pleasure is precisely what Tarantino means the audience to derive, both from the Basterds' slaughter of the Nazi elite in Dreyfus's movie theater and from the scene in which Raine carves a swastika into Landa's forehead. When, after the completion of this mutilation, Raine chortles, "My masterpiece," his words seem implicitly spoken not only by the lieutenant but by the director as well—that is, mutilating the film's archvillain is a "masterpiece" accomplished by Tarantino as well as Raine, the crowning triumph of his "masterpiece" of a movie.

Central to Tarantino's intentions is the thrill of having Hitler defeated in a movie theater. As Tarantino crowed in an interview at the Cannes Film Festival, "The power of cinema is going to bring down the Third Reich. . . . I get a kick out of that!"[5] There is an undeniable potency to the image of Dreyfus's huge head on the screen (reminiscent of the similarly disembodied head of the Wizard of Oz) chastising the Nazis. Moreover, we should never underestimate the power of movies. *The Great Dictator*, for example, probably did some real good in alerting the world to the danger of Hitler and preparing America to enter the war. It's also likely that those anti-Nazi propaganda movies discussed earlier helped boost the public's morale during the war itself. Of course, the Nazis, as *Inglourious Basterds* suggests, were profoundly aware of the ability of mass media to shape public opinion.[6] But taking Tarantino's statement literally would be taking the power of film too far. We must also make distinctions between anti-Nazi films made during the war—which at least had some remote chance of altering history— and movies made decades after the Nazi era, like *Inglourious Basterds*, which simply replace history with a more palatable fiction.

Like *Defiance*, *Inglourious Basterds* features "tough Jews" who fight back against the Nazis. As Tarantino told the *Atlantic Monthly*, "Holocaust movies are always having Jews as victims. . . . We've seen that story before. I want to see something different. Let's see Germans that are scared of Jews. Let's not have everything build up to a big misery, let's actually take the fun of action movies and apply it to this situation."[7] In another interview, published in the *Austin Chronicle*, Marjorie Baumgarten remarked, "The Holocaust is so sacrosanct; you're treading into some tricky territory by the historic leaps you make in this movie." Tarantino responded, "Doing research, I found it was not uncommon for American soldiers to capture Germans and interrogate them the way Aldo did and say: 'Look, here's the deal. If you don't tell us what we want to know, we're going to give you to our Jew. You *don't* want that. You're gonna want to talk to me.'"[8]

Few reviewers, however, were impressed by Tarantino's attempt to "take the fun of action movies and apply it" to the theme of anti-Nazi

Jewish revenge. *Slate*'s Dana Stevens, for example, caustically asked, "Is the best way to work through the atrocities of the twentieth century really to dream up ironically apt punishments for the long-dead torturers? . . . The death camps are never directly mentioned, perhaps because Tarantino sensed that acknowledging their existence would shatter the movie's carefully maintained half-mocking tone. . . . The queasiness comes in when the movie unproblematically offers up sadistic voyeurism as a satisfying form of payback."[9] Another insightful analysis of the failure of Tarantino's "revenge fantasy" appeared in the *Christian Science Monitor* in a review by Francois Duhamel:

> Doesn't [Tarantino] realize that making a righteous fantasy about the Jewish incineration of the Nazi brass only reinforces the sad reality that, tragically, this never happened? . . . Tarantino's fantasy implies that if only there had been Jews like the Basterds, there would not have been an Auschwitz. This ahistoric revisionism is pure malarkey, but it may seep into the moviegoing consciousness of audiences, including young Jewish audiences, who might come to believe that a few roving bands of renegade Jewish scalpers might have terminated the whole Holocaust thing.[10]

Finally, noting the film's constant self-referential allusions to movies, both German and American, cinema historian Thomas Doherty concurs that the picture is ahistorical, concluding that "nowhere do the real images of Nazism crash the party and wrench the spectator back into history."[11]

Tough Jews decimating Nazis is an extremely potent fantasy, especially for Jews themselves. As Tom Segev documents in *The Seventh Million*, postwar Holocaust survivors were often unwelcome guests in Israel because many Israelis had accepted the notion of Jewish passivity in the face of genocide, which was contrasted with alleged Zionist toughness.[12] It was only with the nationwide televising of the Eichmann trial that Israelis finally began to feel sympathy for Holocaust victims. In America, survivors were at first similarly shunned (though with less ideological vehemence than the Israelis displayed), which was why most opted to keep their stories secret.[13] Also not widely reported were examples of Jewish resistance—from the Warsaw ghetto uprising to the rebellions at Sobibor and Treblinka to the Jewish partisans celebrated in *Defiance*. Nonetheless, despite evidence to the contrary and despite all the necessary qualifications, the "sheep to the slaughter" myth still survives, fueled by widespread anti-Semitic stereotypes about alleged Jewish cowardice in battle (stereotypes, of course, that the Nazis themselves propagated). All this gives the image of the Nazi-fighting Jew tremendous cachet—a cachet *Inglourious Basterds* exploits without ever acknowledging the painful history that inspires it.

However, as Duhamel implies, because the Jewish revenge theme in *Inglourious Basterds* is so obviously one of wish fulfillment, divorced from historical reality, only the shallowest viewers will be satisfied by images of Jewish American GIs scalping German soldiers and beating them to death with baseball bats. Instead, astute viewers will reflect only on how different the historical record actually was. In this respect, *Defiance*, for all its aesthetic failures, is a far superior film, in that its tale of Jewish partisans battling the Germans is based on a true story, however distorted in the telling. Moreover, unlike the Basterds, the Jews in *Defiance* (especially Tuvia) have moral qualms about killing, particularly when civilians are targeted, based on their understanding of Jewish ethics.

But the cartoonish Jewish American GIs in *Inglourious Basterds* are simply murder machines. In his *Austin Chronicle* interview, Tarantino said, "I like the idea that, on first glance, you would think that [Aldo's] a redneck, that he would be a racist. Actually, he's the opposite of racist. He's been fighting racism in the South. He's been fighting the Klan before he ever started fighting Nazis . . . and because he's a big student of history, the reason he wants to lead Jewish soldiers is not just for the greater glory of Jews, but because he knows he can take these guys and turn it into a holy war."[14] All this is fine and good, but the problem is that *none* of this characterization of Raine makes it into the actual movie. There is never a moment when Raine seems human. Instead, abetted by Pitt's over-the-top performance, he comes across as a stock redneck—albeit one who has puzzlingly been put in charge of a band of Jews. (By putting a non-Jew in charge of a Jewish regiment, Tarantino resurrects the problematic stereotype of the Righteous Gentile who is necessary to Jewish success.) According to insider reports, the other Basterds also had backstories in the original script, as did Shosanna Dreyfus, but none of this material turned up in the final film.[15]

Why did Tarantino cut back stories that might have turned his characters into genuine people? Perhaps because *Inglourious Basterds*, at two and a half hours, was already so long. But surely much of the film could have been trimmed to make room for the characterization of key figures. One suspects that a truer explanation for this superficiality is that, as a director, Tarantino is committed to cinematic in-jokes, on-screen violence, and technically polished filmmaking, but not to creating three-dimensional characters. His previous two films, the paired *Kill Bill I* and *II* (also orgies of on-screen bloodshed), are inhabited by similar caricatures. Perhaps the only Tarantino film in which the characters seem human is *Jackie Brown* (1997).

Some reviewers singled out one character in *Inglourious Basterds* who *wasn't* a caricature—namely, the main villain, Colonel Hans Landa. In *Entertainment Weekly*, Lisa Schwarzbaum noted, "In Tarantino's besotted historical reverie, real-life villains Adolph Hitler and Joseph Goebbels are played as grotesque jokes. The Basterds are played as exaggeratedly tough Jews. The women are femme fatales. In such a cartoon world, the appearance of one stereotype-resistant protagonist—a Nazi, no less—counts as something glorious indeed."[16] Kerner similarly opines that "in Tarantino's film our gaze is aligned with Landa, who, despite his cruelty, is nevertheless a seductive character."[17]

What separates Landa from the film's other characters is not that they're all cartoons and he's human but simply that he's a more *interesting* cartoon—more detailed, more eccentric, funnier, and hence more memorable. But, in truth, Landa does fit into a hoary Hollywood stereotype—the urbane, sophisticated, slightly effete, highly intelligent, demonically evil Nazi officer. That type dates all the way back to the portrayal of Heydrich in the World War II flick *Hitler's Madman*. This stock figure then reappears constantly in Hollywood Holocaust films: the escaped Nazi dentist in *Marathon Man*, the hidden Nazi turned industrialist in *The Odessa File*, the Hitler-cloning Josef Mengele in *The Boys from Brazil*. Even Oskar Schindler fits that stereotype at the start of *Schindler's List* when he's suavely wooing his Nazi colleagues for financial gain. Susan Sontag was delineating this type when, in her profile of the Nazi filmmaker Leni Riefenstahl, she coined the term "fascinating fascism": the mesmerizing effect of Nazism's combination of hauteur and amorality.[18] We are naturally attracted to a lifestyle in which all the annoying ethical niceties mandated by our superegos, which frustrate our naked desires, have been banished forever. In some strange way, then, the Nazis succeeded in persuading the rest of the world that they *were* the "Master Race."

In no respect does Colonel Landa depart from this stereotype. As with all the other characters in *Inglourious Basterds*, he is given no backstory—no information about his upbringing, his life before the war, why he decided to join the Nazi Party. We're never even sure if he's a Nazi due to sincere conviction or amoral pragmatism. His decision to surrender to Raine might suggest the latter—that is, that he's a mere careerist—but this is one of the least plausible moments in the entire implausible film. All we know about him is that he has a gift for hunting Jews—which verges on a dictionary definition of an SS officer. Many reviewers were deluded into believing that Landa had depth simply because Waltz's performance was brilliant. In this respect, Landa bears comparison to Olivier's sadistic Nazi dentist in *Marathon Man*, another character who gave the illusion of depth because the actor's performance was superlative. In short, *Inglourious Basterds* is a shallow movie in which *all* the characters are cartoons.

Conclusion

WHERE DO WE GO FROM HERE?

What is the future of Hollywood Holocaust films? As we have seen, there has been a gradual, sporadic, but continuous movement forward toward a more honest, realistic engagement with the Shoah. Will this trend continue? Or will the cynics be proven right: after *Schindler's List*, will Hollywood complacently conclude that it has "done" the Holocaust and so can return to churning out mindless entertainment?

Certainly, as this book has demonstrated, one discerns in the Hollywood Holocaust films from the postwar era to the present a growing willingness to clarify that Jews were the primary targets of the Holocaust rather than merely part of a wider and equal set of victim groups. One also sees a gradual disinclination to uproot the Holocaust from history and transform it into some universalized morality play in which abstract good is pitted against abstract evil. Instead, the historicity of the Holocaust has slowly come to the fore in Hollywood films. At the same time, filmmakers have shown a burgeoning willingness to plunge their cameras into the lowest levels of that Dantean inferno that was the Shoah, realms that earlier moviemakers had timorously shunned— namely, the ghettos, the camps, the gas chambers. Surely, we've come a long way from *Hitler's Children* to *Schindler's List*.

On the other hand, the fact that an epitome of "Holocaust kitsch" like *Life Is Beautiful* can be a mega-hit just a few years after the appearance of Spielberg's film shows that the general public has not really caught on when it comes to the Holocaust and that the desire for sentimental distortion remains strong. Moreover, it's noteworthy that the last four Hollywood Holocaust films under discussion, all appearing within the last several years—*The Boy in the Striped Pajamas*, *The Reader*, *Defiance*, and *Inglourious Basterds*—are significantly flawed. *The Boy in the Striped Pajamas* is only slightly less kitschy than *Life Is Beautiful*; *The Reader* has a confused view of the relationship between Nazi perpetrators and the German generation that succeeded them; *Defiance*, for all its good intentions, ends up a Hollywood melodrama; and *Inglourious Basterds*, while exhibiting great technical skill, is a soulless film that exploits the Shoah for the sake of in-jokes about movies and graphic on-screen violence. Thus, it would appear that while Hollywood continues to make Holocaust films, too many of them are artistic and thematic failures. Certainly, the pinnacle reached by *Schindler's List* has so far not been even remotely glimpsed again.

In an essay titled "Lest We Remember," which appeared in a 2011 issue of *Tablet Magazine*, *Nation* film critic Stuart Klawans makes what at first appears an outrageous demand: Hollywood should issue a moratorium on Holocaust movies. Klawans begins by noting that, in the movie season that had just concluded, there had been no less than *six* movies about the Holocaust: *Defiance*, *Valkyrie*, *The Boy in the Striped Pajamas*, *The Reader*, *Adam Resurrected*, and *Good*. The result, Klawans concludes, is just the opposite from what one might hope—namely, that movie audiences are becoming better informed about the Holocaust. On the contrary, he argues, "by continually replaying and reframing and reinventing the past, these movies are starting to cloud the very history they claim to commemorate. . . . Very soon, with Holocaust movies, we'll need to forget if we want to remember."[1] Klawans concludes, "For the most part . . . the mounting volume of the material seems merely to have allowed people to think of the Holocaust as another choice on the entertainment menu, another imaginative world to inhabit at will and then abandon."[2]

Several critics of *Defiance* echo Klawans in deploring what the overstuffed genre of Hollywood Holocaust films has become. *Time's* Richard Corliss bemoans, "The Holocaust has become not just a topic but a genre, one that, at its most reductive, exploits the awful events to badger viewers, intimidate critics, elicit easy tears and serve as a backpatting machine for serioso directors. The excesses of the genre have spawned derisive nicknames: 'Holo-kitsch' (Art Spiegelman's term) and 'Holocaust porn.'"[3] Likewise, in his *Entertainment Weekly* review,

Owen Gleiberman argues, "To this season of grimly hokey Third Reich parables, it's hard to shake the feeling that the Holocaust has turned from the ultimate furrowed-brow movie theme into a *genre*, with its own built in flowers-of-evil mystique. Rarely has genocide been put to the service of so much unabashed . . . entertainment."[4] Several critics note a scene in *Extras*, the HBO comedy series lampooning the movie industry, in which a self-parodic Kate Winslet, playing a nun in a Holocaust drama, tells Ricky Gervais that the only reason she took the role was to snare an Oscar, which is more or less guaranteed for actors in Holocaust films. When, only a couple of years later, Winslet received a Best Actress Oscar for *The Reader*, one can't help but imagine that she recognized a certain irony as she approached the podium.

Is Klawans right that Hollywood should issue a moratorium on Holocaust films? Has the Holocaust movie devolved into just another variant of Hollywood entertainment, clouding rather than illuminating the public's awareness of the Shoah? It seems that, by the lights of the critical establishment, Hollywood is damned if it does and damned if it doesn't. In the postwar era, after all, critics bemoaned the fact that there were too *few* Holocaust films, that Hollywood was too timid to tackle the subject, a silence that was ultimately shattered by movies like *The Diary of Anne Frank* and *Judgment at Nuremberg*. Today's critics are raising the opposite complaint—that there are too *many* Holocaust movies. Still, there is surely validity to the argument that, ever since the success of *Schindler's List*, we've seen a glut of Holocaust films, and that, as a result, there's a danger that audiences perceive the Shoah as just another source of blockbuster entertainment.

But the real problem is not that we have too many Hollywood Holocaust films but rather that we have too few *good* ones. If the last four movies discussed in this book had all been on the level of *Schindler's List*, no critic would be complaining about Holo-kitsch. I have argued that Hollywood has come a long way since the war years in terms of depicting the Holocaust authentically. But the opposite may also be true—namely, that the problems that have inhibited Hollywood all along from honestly confronting the Shoah still remain. That is, we still feel the need to give the Holocaust, perhaps modern history's most tragic event, a thoroughly implausible happy ending, as seen in *Defiance*; we still feel the need to appeal to the lowest common denominator in the audience by inserting into our Holocaust dramas the requisite quotient of sex and violence, à la *The Reader* and *Inglourious Basterds*; we still feel the compulsion to downplay the full horror of the camps, as evinced in *The Boy in the Striped Pajamas* .

In a sense, everything has changed, and yet nothing has changed at all. Perhaps, then, what we need is not a moratorium on Holocaust films but instead an upgrade of the genre. Directors of Hollywood Holocaust movies need to learn from independent and foreign Holocaust films such as *Shoah*; *Europa, Europa*; *Au Revoir, Les Enfants*; *The Pianist*; *The Nasty Girl*; *The Garden of the Finzi-Continis*; *Mephisto*; *Night and Fog*; *Seven Beauties*; *The Sorrow and the Pity*; and *The Tin Drum*, to provide only a partial list—all movies that treat the genocide with a far greater accuracy (while also displaying aesthetic superiority) than anything emanating from our nation's movie capital. Of course, one might argue that European cinema portrays the Holocaust better than Hollywood does, since the Shoah happened on European soil and since Europe, while no utopia, at least isn't burdened by the cult of optimism that seems endemic to American society. As well, European cinema, often state funded, is less enslaved by the commercial pressures that so often force Hollywood to resort to melodrama and sentimentality.

Still, is it too much to ask that the American public might start preferring reality to kitsch, and might make that preference known at the box office? Yes, this may seem a quixotic hope. Yet the American public has, over time, demonstrated increasing willingness to sanction realism in Holocaust films. Had *Schindler's List* appeared in theaters at the same time as *The Diary of Anne Frank*, surely it would have flopped. So maybe there's cause for qualified optimism.

On the other hand, if Hollywood stopped producing quite so many Holocaust movies, this would not be a disaster, especially if it began displaying a parallel interest in making films about *other* historical genocides. Especially given the plethora of Holocaust films, Hollywood has shown a marked lack of interest in dealing with other atrocities. *The Killing Fields* (1984), a British production, is the only film widely distributed in America about the Cambodian genocide, in which the radical Communist group, the Khmer Rouge, killed 1.5 million people in four years. The only film that comes to mind about the 1915 Armenian genocide, when Turks slaughtered Armenians en masse (and have claimed ever since that the massacre was simply a regrettable byproduct of World War I), is 2002's disappointing *Ararat*, and that film was made by an independent, joint Canadian/American film company. There has been just one major film about the Rwandan Hutus' 1994 butchering of the Tutsis, which killed more people in a shorter space of time (800,000 in three months) than any other genocide: *Hotel Rwanda*, which was a relative hit in this country but was only partly American made. Amazing as it may seem, Hollywood seems to have ignored Stalin's genocide against his own people, even though historians estimate that the number of its victims—factoring in deliberate starvation, the repopulation of peoples, the massacre of the kulaks, the show trials and the Gulag—may run as high as fifty million. The same is true of Mao Zedong's murder of millions of Chinese via the forced collectivization of agriculture and other ideologically driven follies that occurred during the Cultural Revolution in the 1950s and 1960s. The Serbian genocide against the Bosnian Muslims in the 1990s inspired one major film, 1997's *Welcome to Sarajevo*, but this movie, like the rest, was made not in Hollywood but by a joint British and American company. Clearly, there is a gross imbalance between the plenitude of Hollywood Holocaust films and the extreme dearth of portrayals of other genocides.

How does one account for this imbalance? Director Oliver Stone blamed the plethora of Holocaust films on "the Jewish domination of the media."[5] This theory seems unlikely, however, given that Hollywood has always been largely a Jewish industry,[6] and yet, as we've seen in this book, Jewish studio heads such as Adolph Zukor and Louis B. Mayer, during and immediately after World War II, were loath to calling attention in their films to Nazi persecution of their coreligionists in Europe—a box-office-driven aversion that doubtlessly persists in varying forms today.

A better explanation for the absence of films about other genocides is that Hollywood is allergic to "feel-bad" movies, deeming them sure-fire commercial disasters, and nothing makes audiences feel quite so bad as a movie about genocide. In picking between the latest *Iron Man* installment and a film about the Turkish slaughter of the Armenians, which is your average moviegoer likely to choose?

But if Hollywood considers movies about genocide to be box office poison, why have they produced so many films about the Holocaust? This book's introduction suggests some possibilities—namely, that contemporary America fosters a "culture of victimization," and twentieth-century European Jewry has been deemed the consummate victim group. A second explanation is that World War II was a conflict in which America was indispensably involved, so the Holocaust seems less foreign, more like a part of our own history. Finally, there's the oft-heard argument that the Holocaust is "unique" and therefore, presumably, uniquely deserving of Hollywood portrayals.

The question of the Holocaust's alleged "uniqueness" is exceedingly complex, but let me touch on the issue. There is some truth to the argument. With almost all the other genocides discussed previously, the victim group posed some tangible danger to the victimizing group so that the genocide was not justifiable, certainly, but was rationally explicable. For example, when Yugoslavia imploded with the fall of communism, the new Bosnian state, ruled by Muslims, hastily declared independence, which left the Bosnian Serbs a disenfranchised minority within their own country; thus, it's no surprise that the Bosnian Serbs banded together with their ethnic brethren in Serbia to attack the Bosnian Muslims. In the case of the Armenian genocide, Bernard Lewis has argued that the slaughter also took place within the framework of genuine political conflict: "It was a struggle, however unequal, about real issues; it was never associated with demonic beliefs or the almost physical hatred which inspired and directed anti-Semitism in Europe and sometimes elsewhere."[7] The Jews, however, posed absolutely no threat to the Nazis, except in the fevered fantasies of Hitler and his henchmen. On the contrary, German Jewry had made a substantial contribution to German society in a range of cultural, economic, social, and political arenas. It was precisely because German Jewry was so positively interwoven into the fabric of German society that German Jews were often so reluctant to flee when Hitler came to power.

A second argument frequently presented to bolster the "uniqueness" thesis is that, in contrast to previous massacres, the Holocaust was an attempt at total annihilation, with every last Jew on earth slated for extermination. That's why Hitler called the genocide the *Final* Solution.

While the Nazis massacred countless members of other groups, such as gypsies, Jehovah's Witnesses, homosexuals, Poles, Ukrainians, political prisoners, prisoners-of-war, and so forth, Nazi ideology didn't demand that these groups suffer complete annihilation. But complete annihilation was exactly the fate mandated for the Jews. As Michael Marrus maintains, "Unlike the case with any other group, and unlike the massacres before or since, *every single one* of the millions of targeted Jews was to be murdered. Eradication was to be total."[8] When Hitler was holed up in the bunker under Berlin, with the Allies closing in and the war clearly lost, one of the Fuhrer's principle complaints was that he'd failed in his attempt to wipe the Jews off the face of the earth.

For reasons I've already described, however, I'm uncomfortable with the idea that the Holocaust was unique. For one thing, such a thesis seems to remove the Holocaust from history, which makes it almost impossible to discuss meaningfully. History is, after all, best understood by way of comparison. As Franklin H. Littell has emphasized, "The one who seeks to understand the Holocaust must risk entering the ground of comparison and analysis."[9] And one of the leading historians of the Holocaust, Yehuda Baur, has written that "the worst massacres perpetrated by the Nazis have exact precedents, given the level of technical development, from ancient times to modernity."[10] Moreover, to insist too strenuously on the Holocaust's pristine uniqueness seems to downgrade, deliberately or not, the atrocities perpetrated against other groups. Of course, upholders of the uniqueness theory argue just the opposite—namely, that it trivializes the Holocaust ("relativizes" is the common term) to compare it to other genocides.[11] But how is the Holocaust trivialized, exactly, by comparing Hitler's crimes to those of monsters like Stalin or Mao?

Some years ago, I met an Israeli who worked for a chapter of the Simon Wiesenthal Center in Jerusalem, where he specialized in tracking down living Nazis and their collaborators. This was not long after the Rwandan genocide, and the Israeli, because of his expertise on the Holocaust, had been summoned by the Rwandan government that had toppled the murderous Hutu leaders to help them figure out how to deal with the thousands of perpetrators of genocide who remained in the country. "I used to think the Holocaust was unique," this man told me, "but after seeing what happened in Rwanda, I'm not so sure." This brief conversation has haunted me ever since.

However, whether the uniqueness argument is persuasive or not, Hollywood may find it sufficiently credible to justify a focus almost exclusively on the Shoah. But even if, for the sake of argument, one grants that the Holocaust is unique, that's no excuse for focusing on it *at the expense of* other genocides. Especially since we've seen such a welter of Hollywood Holocaust movies that critics are lamenting that the Shoah has been turned into just another "entertaining" movie genre, it's surely time to give other genocides a place in the Hollywood spotlight. While Hollywood continues to teach us to "never forget" the Holocaust, it can also teach us to remember what was done to the Cambodians, the Armenians, the Rwandan Tutsi, the Russians, the Chinese, the Bosnian Muslims, and all the other abused peoples of the world.

Meanwhile, despite the continued outpouring of Hollywood Holocaust films, we seem to be just at the beginning of a true cinematic engagement with the Shoah. Perhaps it's Levi's "grey zone," a focus on the moral ambiguity of the Holocaust, that best points the direction for Holocaust films to follow. While Hollywood needs to expose other genocides, with the Holocaust we have reached a point where we can transcend mere exposure and explore complexities. The intricate human complications such a process might uncover could not only make for great cinema but deepen public understanding of the Holocaust as well.

NOTES

INTRODUCTION. CAN HOLLYWOOD GET IT RIGHT?

1. Judith Miller, *One, by One, by One: Facing the Holocaust* (New York: Touchstone Books, 1990), 232.

2. Aaron Kerner, *Film and the Holocaust: New Perspectives on Dramas, Documentaries, and Experimental Films* (New York: Continuum Books, 2011), 15.

3. Ibid., 16.

4. Frederic Spotts, *Hitler and the Power of Aesthetics* (Woodstock, NY: Overlook, 2002), xi–xii.

5. Saul Friedlander, *Reflections on Nazism: An Essay on Kitsch and Death* (Bloomington: Indiana University Press, 1993), 14.

6. Robert Hughes, *Culture of Complaint: The Fraying of* America (Oxford: Oxford University Press, 1993), 9.

7. Peter Novick, *The Holocaust in American Life* (Boston: Houghton Mifflin, 1999), 8.

8. Dan Amira, "Mike Godwin on Godwin's Law," *New York Magazine*, March 8, 2013. http://nymag.com/daily/intelligencer/2013/03/godwins-law-mike-godwin-hitler-nazi-comparisons.html

9. Larry Kramer, *Reports from the Holocaust: The Story of an AIDS Activist* (New York: St. Martin's, 1994).

10. Rush H. Limbaugh, *The Way Things Ought to Be* (New York: Pocket Books, 1992), 193.

11. Mary Elizabeth Williams, "Why You Should Never Engage with an Abortion Protester," *Salon*, March 14, 2014, http://www.salon.com/2014/03/14/why_you_should_never_engage_with_an_abortion_protester/

12. Adam Shah, "Fox News Turns to LaPierre, Who Once Called ATF Agents 'Jack-Booted Government Thugs,'" *Media Matters for America*, March 10, 2011, http://mediamatters.org/blog/2011/03/10/fox-news-turns-to-lapierre-who-once-called-atf/177439

13. "Hank Williams Jr. Compares Obama to Hitler, Gets Pulled from *Monday Night Football*," *Huffington Post*, October 3, 2011, http://www.huffingtonpost.com/2011/10/03/hank-williams-compares-obama-to-hitler_n_992513.html

14. Kevin Weston, "Why Would Anyone Laugh at *Schindler's List*? Hollywood Hasn't Taught History to Blacks," *Los Angeles Times*, February 28, 1994.

15. Kerner, *Film and the Holocaust*, 154.

16. Quoted in J. Hoberman, "When the Nazis Became Nudniks," *New York Times*, April 15, 2001, 13.

17. Kerner, *Film and the Holocaust*, 80.

18. Quoted ibid.

19. Ibid.

I. THE LITTLE TRAMP BATTLES HITLER

1. Quoted in Eric L. Flom, *Chaplin in the Sound Era: An Analysis of the Seven Talkies* (Jefferson, NC: McFarland, 1997), 122.

2. Cited in Michael Hanisch, "The Chaplin Reception in Germany," in *Charlie Chaplin: His Reflection in Modern Times*, ed. Adolphe Nysenholc (Berlin: Mouton de Gruyter, 1991), 30–31.

3. Bill Krohn, "Hollywood and the Shoah, 1933–1945," in *Cinema and the Shoah: Art Confronts the Tragedy of the Twentieth Century*, ed. Jean-Michel Frodon (Albany: State University of New York Press, 2010), 151.

4. Ibid.

5. Ibid., 153.

6. Judith E. Doneson, *The Holocaust in American Film*, 2nd ed. (Syracuse, NY: Syracuse University Press, 2002), 31.

7. Ilan Avisar, *Screening the Holocaust: Cinema's Images of the Unimaginable* (Bloomington: Indiana University Press, 1988), 138.

8. Kenneth S. Lynn, *Charlie Chaplin and His Times* (New York: Simon and Schuster, 1997), 395.

9. Flom, *Chaplin in the Sound Era*, 122.

10. Annette Insdorf, *Indelible Shadows: Film and the Holocaust*, 2nd ed. (Cambridge: Cambridge University Press, 1989), 61.

11. Doneson, *Holocaust in American Film*, 31, 33.

12. Lynn, *Charlie Chaplin and His Times*, 404.

13. Avisar, *Screening the Holocaust*, 145.

14. Flom, *Chaplin in the Sound Era*, 135.

15. Lynn, *Charlie Chaplin and His Times*, 410.

16. Flom, *Chaplin in the Sound Era*, 39.

17. Doneson, *Holocaust in American Film*, 42–43.

18. Michael D. Richardson, "'Heil Myself!': Impersonation and Identity in Comedic Representations of Hitler," in *Visualizing the Holocaust: Documents, Aesthetics, Memory*, ed. David Bathrick, Brad Pagar, and Michael D. Richardson, (Rochester, NY: Camden House, 2008), 281.

19. Ibid., 282.

20. Insdorf, *Indelible Shadows*, 61.

21. Quoted in David Bathrick, "Introduction: Seeing against the Grain," in *Visualizing the Holocaust: Documents, Aesthetics, Memory*, ed. David Bathrick, Brad Pagar, and Michael D. Richardson (Rochester, NY: Camden House, 2008), 14.

22. Doneson, *Holocaust in American Film*, 40.

23. Avisar, *Screening the Holocaust*, 141.

24. Richardson, "'Heil Myself!,'" 282.

25. Quoted in Kerner, *Film and the Holocaust*, 82.

26. Ibid., 83.

27. Ibid., 84.

28. Ibid., 85.

29. Richardson, "'Heil Myself!,'" 282.

30. Kerner, *Film and the Holocaust*, 83.

31. Richardson, "'Heil Myself!,'" 282.

32. Lynn, *Charlie Chaplin and His Times*, 405.

33. Insdorf, *Indelible Shadows*, 62–63.

34. Gottfried Wagner, *Twilight of the Wagners: The Unveiling of a Family's Legacy* (New York: St. Martin's Press, 1997), 39–40.

35. Krohn, "Hollywood and the Shoah," 160.

36. Ron Rosenbaum, *Explaining Hitler: The Search for the Origins of His Evil* (New York: Random House, 1998), 369.

37. Quoted in Doneson, *Holocaust in American Film*, 39.

38. Quoted in Avisar, *Screening the Holocaust*, 148.

39. Quoted ibid., 143.

40. Ibid.

41. Ibid.

42. Richardson, "'Heil Myself!,'" 283.

43. Krohn, "Hollywood and the Shoah," 160.

44. Quoted in Avisar, *Screening the Holocaust*, 143.

45. Lynn, *Charlie Chaplin and His Times*, 400.

46. Ibid., 402.

2. ACTORS VERSUS NAZIS

1. Thomas Doherty, *Hollywood and Hitler, 1933–1939* (New York: Columbia University Press, 2013), 15.

2. Judith E. Doneson, *The Holocaust in American Film*, 2nd ed. (Syracuse, NY: Syracuse University Press, 2002), 44–45.

3. William Paul, *Ernst Lubitsch's American Comedy* (New York: Columbia University Press, 1983), 227.

4. Quoted in Annette Insdorf, *Indelible Shadows: Film and the Holocaust*, 2nd ed. (Cambridge: Cambridge University Press, 1989), 67.

5. Quoted ibid.

6. Quoted in Paul, *Ernst Lubitsch's American Comedy*, 227.

7. Ibid., 229.

8. Ibid., 230–231.

9. Insdorf, *Indelible Shadows*, 67.

10. Michael D. Richardson, "'Heil Myself!': Impersonation and Identity in Comedic Representations of Hitler," in *Visualizing the Holocaust: Documents, Aesthetics, Memory*, ed. David Bathrick, Brad Pagar, and Michael D. Richardson (Rochester, NY: Camden House, 2008), 285.

11. Ibid., 286.

12. Irving A. Fein, *Jack Benny: An Intimate Biography* (New York: Putnam, 1976), 72.

13. Richardson, "'Heil Myself!,'" 284.

14. Quoted in Richardson, "'Heil Myself!,'" 285.

15. Paul, *Ernst Lubitsch's American Comedy*, 250.

16. Insdorf, *Indelible Shadows*, 71.

17. Ron Rosenbaum, *Explaining Hitler: The Search for the Origins of His Evil* (New York: Random House, 1998), 105.

18. Ibid., 105–106.

19. Insdorf, *Indelible Shadows*, 68.

20. Richardson, "'Heil Myself!,'" 290.

21. Bill Krohn, "Hollywood and the Shoah, 1933–1945," in *Cinema and the Shoah: Art Confronts the Tragedy of the Twentieth Century*, ed. Jean-Michel Frodon (Albany: State University of New York Press, 2010), 161.

22. Ibid., 162.

23. Deborah E. Lipstadt, *Beyond Belief: The American Press and the Coming of the Holocaust 1933–1945* (New York: Free Press, 1986); David S. Wy-

man, *The Abandonment of the Jews: America and the Holocaust, 1941–1945* (New York: Pantheon Books, 1984).

3. HOLLYWOOD FIGHTS WORLD WAR II

1. The other Lidice film was made by another émigré in Hollywood, Fritz Lang's *Hangmen Also Die*, which focused more on the plight of Heydrich's assassin, played by Brian Donlevy, and featured a script cowritten by Lang and Bertolt Brecht.

2. Bill Krohn, "Hollywood and the Shoah, 1933–1945," in *Cinema and the Shoah: Art Confronts the Tragedy of the Twentieth Century*, ed. Jean-Michel Frodon (Albany: State University of New York Press, 2010), 165.

3. Ibid., 168–169.

4. Quoted in Ilan Avisar, *Screening the Holocaust: Cinema's Images of the Unimaginable* (Bloomington: Indiana University Press, 1988), 97.

5. Such as the dissenting Reverend Martin Niemoeller,

6. Thomas Doherty, *Hollywood and Hitler: 1933–1939* (New York: Columbia University Press, 2013), 71.

7. Hans Mommsen, "German Society and the Resistance against Hitler," in *The Third Reich: The Essential Readings*, ed. Christian Leitz (London: Blackwell, 1999).

8. Keren G. McGinity, "Intermarriage: Twenty-First-Century United States," in *The Cambridge Dictionary of Judaism and Jewish Culture*, ed. Judith R. Baskin (Cambridge: Cambridge University Press, 2011), 278.

9. Samuel G. Freedman, *Jew versus Jew: The Struggle for the Soul of American Jewry* (New York: Simon and Schuster, 2000), 73.

10. Quoted in Eric A. Goldman, *The American Jewish Story through Cinema* (Austin: University of Texas Press, 2013), 147.

11. David S. Wyman, *The Abandonment of the Jews: America and the Holocaust, 1941–1945* (New York: Pantheon Books, 1984), 14.

12. Ibid., 97.

4. HOLLYWOOD DISCOVERS THE HOLOCAUST

1. During the war, Robinson, who was Jewish (his original name was Emmanuel Goldberg), had been one of the staunchest members of the Hollywood Anti-Nazi League, often holding meetings of the organization at his home.

Thomas Doherty, *Hollywood and Hitler, 1933–1939* (New York: Columbia University Press, 2013), 119.

2. Bill Krohn, "Hollywood and the Shoah, 1933–1945," in *Cinema and the Shoah: Art Confronts the Tragedy of the Twentieth Century*, ed. Jean-Michel Frodon (Albany: State University of New York Press, 2010), 149.

3. Ibid., 149–150.

4. Lawrence Baron, *Projecting the Holocaust into the Present: The Changing Focus of Contemporary Holocaust Cinema* (Lanham, MD: Rowman and Littlefield, 2005), 30.

5. Ibid., 33.

6. Ibid.

7. Ibid., 16

8. Stephen J. Whitfield, *In Search of American Jewish Culture* (Hanover: Brandeis University Press, 1999), 172.

9. McCullers expressed interest, though the deal ultimately fell through.

10. Lawrence Graver, *An Obsession with Anne Frank: Meyer Levin and the Diary* (Berkeley: University of California Press, 1995), 54.

11. Ibid.

12. Melissa Müller, *Anne Frank: The Biography*, trans. Rita Kimber and Robert Kimber (New York: Metropolitan Books, 1998), 305.

13. Whitfield, *In Search of American Jewish Culture*, 177–178.

14. Ibid., 178.

15. Peter Novick, *Holocaust in American Life* (Boston: Houghton Mifflin, 1999), 119.

16. Ibid., 120.

17. Ibid.

18. Quoted in Graver, *An Obsession with Anne Frank*, 59–60.

19. Ibid., 89.

20. Ibid.

21. Ibid.

22. Ibid., 97.

23. Judith E. Doneson, *Holocaust in American Film*, 2nd ed. (Syracuse, NY: Syracuse University Press, 2002), 73.

24. Ibid., 72.

25. Graver, *An Obsession with Anne Frank*, 138.

26. Annette Insdorf, *Indelible Shadows: Film and the Holocaust*, 2nd ed. (Cambridge: Cambridge University Press, 1989), 7.

27. Baron, *Projecting the Holocaust into the Present*, 36.

28. Whitfield, *In Search of American Jewish Culture*, 178.

29. Ibid., 14.

30. Ibid., 57.

31. Ibid.

32. Baron, *Projecting the Holocaust into the Present*, 37.

33. Ibid., 37–38.

34. Whitfield, *In Search of American Jewish Culture*, 41–42.

35. Ibid., 57.

36. Neal Gabler, *An Empire of Their Own: How the Jews Invented Hollywood* (New York: Crown, 1988), 278.

37. Doneson, *Holocaust in American Film*, 65.

38. Ibid., 92.

39. Baron, *Projecting the Holocaust into the Present*, 38.

40. Whitfield, *In Search of American Jewish Culture*, 177.

41. Ibid., 97.

42. Bruno Bettelheim, "The Informed Heart," in Albert H. Friedlander, ed., *Out of the Whirlwind: A Reader of Holocaust Literature* (New York: Schocken Books, 1976), 40.

43. Ilan Avisar, *Screening the Holocaust: Cinema's Images of the Unimaginable* (Bloomington: Indiana University Press, 1988), 116.

44. Quoted in Graver, *An Obsession with Anne Frank*, 95.

45. Quoted in Avisar, *Screening the Holocaust*, 116.

46. Frances Goodrich and Albert Hackett, *Diary of Anne Frank* (New York: Dramatists Play Service, 1954), 99.

47. Ibid., 101.

48. Müller, *Anne Frank: The Biography*, 258.

49. Alvin H. Rosenfeld, "Anne Frank—and Us: Finding the Right Words," *Reconstruction* 2.2 (1993), 88.

50. Aaron Kerner, *Film and the Holocaust: New Perspectives on Dramas, Documentaries, and Experimental Films* (New York: Continuum Books, 2011), 136.

51. Ibid., 137.

52. Ibid.

53. Whitfield, *In Search of American Jewish Culture*, 174.

54. Quoted ibid., 181.

55. Ibid., 184.

56. Mervyn Rothstein, "In Three Revivals the Goose-Stepping is Louder," *New York Times*, March 8, 1998, 23.

5. HOLLYWOOD JUDGES THE GERMANS

1. Bradley F. Smith, *Reaching Judgment at Nuremberg: The Untold Story of How the Nazi Criminals Were Judged* (New York: Basic Books, 1977), xvi.

2. Gavin Lambert, "Review of *Judgment at Nuremberg* by Stanley Kramer," *Film Quarterly* 15, no. 2 (Winter 1961–1962), 52.

3. Annette Insdorf, *Indelible Shadows: Film and the Holocaust*, 3rd ed. (Cambridge: Cambridge University Press, 1989), 3.

4. Quoted in Alan Mintz, *Popular Culture and the Shaping of Holocaust Memory* (Seattle: University of Washington Press, 2001), 93.

5. Judith E. Doneson, *The Holocaust in American Film*, 2nd ed. (Syracuse, NY: Syracuse University Press, 2002), 97.

6. Ibid., 97.

7. Lambert, "Review of *Judgment at Nuremberg* by Stanley Kramer," 52.

8. Ibid., 204–205

9. Quoted ibid., 96.

10. Quoted ibid.

11. Ibid., 103–104.

12. Ibid., 94.

13. Ibid., 104–105.

14. Ibid., 106.

15. Ibid.

16. Ibid.

17. Quoted in Mintz, *Popular Culture and the Shaping of Holocaust Memory*, 97–98.

18. Quoted ibid., 98.

19. Ibid., 97.

20. Lawrence L. Langer, *Admitting the Holocaust: Collected Essays* (Oxford: Oxford University Press, 1995), 170.

21. Ibid., 173.

22. Daniel Jonah Goldhagen, *Hitler's Willing Executioners: Ordinary Germans and the Holocaust* (New York: Alfred A. Knopf, 1996), 9.

23. Michael Dobbs, "Ford and GM Scrutinized for Alleged Nazi Collaboration," *Washington Post*, November 30, 1998, http://www.washingtonpost.com/wp-srv/national/daily/nov98/nazicars30.htm

24. Corey Adwar, "Here's Why Some Nazis Enjoyed Their Freedom in the US after World War II," *Business Insider*, June 24, 2014, http://www.businessinsider.com/heres-how-nazis-have-escaped-charges-in-the-us-2014-6

25. Kirsten Fermaglich, *American Dreams and Nazi Nightmares: Early Holocaust Consciousness and Liberal America, 1957–1965* (Lebanon, NH: Brandeis University Press, 2006), 2.

26. Quoted in Mintz, *Popular Culture and the Shaping of Holocaust Memory*, 102.

27. Ibid.

28. Henry Ford's campaign against the Jews began on May 22, 1920, with a front-page article in Ford's international weekly, the *Dearborn Independent*, titled "The International Jew: The World's Problem" and vigorously continued well into the 1930s after the Nazis had come to power. Neil Baldwin, *Henry Ford and the Jews: The Mass Production of Hate* (New York: Public Affairs, 2001), 102. See also Edwin Black, *IBM and the Holocaust: The Strategic Alliance between Nazi Germany and America's Most Powerful Corporation* (New York: Crown, 2001).

29. An image gleefully perpetuated by the Nazis—for example, in the 1940 Nazi propaganda film, *Jud Suss*.

30. Doneson, *Holocaust in American Film*, 102.

31. *Hitler: Beast of Berlin* (1939) did include some archival footage of Hitler himself but not of the concentration camps.

32. Doneson, *Holocaust in American Film*, 102.

33. Mintz, *Popular Culture and the Shaping of Holocaust Memory*, 100.

34. Quoted ibid., 101.

35. Ibid., 104.

36. Quoted ibid., 106.

6. HOLLYWOOD'S HOLOCAUST SURVIVOR

1. Alan Mintz, *Popular Culture and the Shaping of Holocaust Memory* (Seattle: University of Washington Press, 2001), 110–111.

2. Joshua Hirsch, *After Image: Film, Trauma, and the Holocaust* (Philadelphia: Temple University Press, 2004), 109.

3. Ibid., 107.

4. Ibid., 108.

5. Quoted in Mintz, *Popular Culture and the Shaping of Holocaust Memory*, 115.

6. Quoted in Hirsch, *After Image*, 104.

7. Ibid., 109.

8. Annette Insdorf, *Indelible Shadows: Film and the Holocaust*, 2nd ed. (Cambridge: Cambridge University Press, 1989), 28.

9. Haskel Lookstein, *Were We Our Brothers' Keepers? The Public Response of American Jews to the Holocaust* (New York: Vintage Books, 1985), 22.

10. Insdorf, *Indelible Shadows*, 28.

11. Quoted in Judith E. Doneson, *The Holocaust in American Film*, 2nd ed. (Syracuse, NY: Syracuse University Press, 2002), 110.

12. Quoted ibid., 110.

13. Quoted in Mintz, *Popular Culture and the Shaping of Holocaust Memory*, 117–118.

14. Elie Wiesel, *Night* (New York: Hill and Wang, 1972, 1985).

15. Raul Hilberg, *The Destruction of the European Jews* (New York: Holmes and Meier, 1985), 14.

16. Rita Steinhardt Botwinick, *A History of the Holocaust: From Ideology to Annihilation*, 2nd ed. (Upper Saddle River, NJ: Prentice Hall, 2001), 18.

17. Tom Segev, *The Seventh Million: The Israelis and the Holocaust* (New York: Hill and Wang, 1993), 117–118.

18. Ilan Avisar, *Screening the Holocaust: Cinema's Images of the Unimaginable* (Bloomington: Indiana University Press, 1988), 125.

19. Quoted ibid., 124.

20. Quoted ibid.

21. Quoted ibid.

22. Jonathan Kaufman, *Broken Alliance: The Turbulent Times between Blacks and Jews in America* (New York: Simon and Schuster, 1988), 86.

23. Quoted in Mintz, *Popular Culture and the Shaping of Holocaust Memory*, 116.

24. Quoted ibid.

25. Lawrence Langer, *Art from the Ashes: A Holocaust Anthology* (Oxford: Oxford University Press, 1995), 5–6.

7. THE HOLOCAUST ON THE HORIZON

1. Michiko Kakutani, "Window of the World," *New York Times Magazine*, April 26, 1998, 15.

2. Quoted in Thomas Doherty, *Hollywood and Hitler, 1933–1939* (New York: Columbia University Press, 2013), 32.

3. Rita Steinhardt Botwinick, *A History of the Holocaust: From Ideology to Annihilation*, 2nd ed. (Upper Saddle River, NJ: Prentice Hall, 2001), 65.

4. Judith E. Doneson, *The Holocaust in American Film*, 2nd ed. (Syracuse, NY: Syracuse University Press, 2002), 127.

5. Ibid., 123.

6. Quoted ibid., 125.

7. Kakutani, "Window of the World," 15.

8. John Podhoretz, "The Great White (Nazi) Way: A Brilliant Production of a Classic Raises Disturbing Questions," *New York Post*, March 26, 1998, 35.

9. Linda Winer, "The Down-and-Dirty Party That Hitler Ended," *Newsday*, March 20, 1998, n.p.

10. Podhoretz, "Great White (Nazi) Way," 35.

11. Ibid.

12. Ibid.

13. Ben Brantley, "Desperate Dance at Oblivion's Brink," *New York Times*, March 20, 1998, http://www.nytimes.com/1998/03/20/movies/theater-review-desperate-dance-at-oblivion-s-brink.html

14. Winer, "Down-and-Dirty Party," n.p.

8. HOLLYWOOD HOLOCAUST THRILLERS

1. Tom Segev, *Simon Wiesenthal: The Life and Legends* (New York: Doubleday, 2010), 257.

2. Paul Breines, *Tough Jews: Political Fantasies and the Moral Dilemma of American Jewry* (New York: Basic Books, 1990), 173.

3. Frederick Forsyth, *The Odessa File* (New York: Bantam Books, 1972), viii.

4. Ibid., 27.

5. Segev, *Simon Wiesenthal*, 260.

6. Ibid., 347.

7. Aaron Kerner, *Film and the Holocaust: New Perspectives on Dramas, Documentaries, and Experimental Films* (New York: Continuum Books, 2011), 169–170.

8. Ibid., 170.

9. Ibid.

10. Segev, *Simon Wiesenthal*, 332.

11. Ibid., 333.

12. Ibid., 334.

13. Quoted in Annette Insdorf, *Indelible Shadows: Film and the Holocaust*, 2nd ed. (Cambridge: Cambridge University Press, 1989), 11.

9. THE HOLOCAUST'S NON-JEWISH VICTIMS

1. Interesting to note, however, is that, when I screened the film for my Polish students, they complained that Streep's Polish is actually rather amateurish, immediately recognizable to a Pole as coming from a nonnative speaker—a flaw that was naturally lost on American audiences.

2. Quoted in Annette Insdorf, *Indelible Shadows: Film and the Holocaust*, 2nd ed. (Cambridge: Cambridge University Press, 1989), 36.

3. Quoted in Ilan Avisar, *Screening the Holocaust: Cinema's Images of the Unimaginable* (Bloomington: Indiana University Press, 1988), 125–126.

4. Quoted ibid., 126.

5. Hannah Arendt, *Eichmann in Jerusalem: A Report on the Banality of Evil* (New York: Penguin Books, 1963), 49.

6. Insdorf, *Indelible Shadows*, 35.

7. Alvin H. Rosenfeld, *A Double Dying: Reflections on Holocaust Literature* (Bloomington: Indiana University Press, 1980), 106.

8. Ibid., 51.

9. Rosenfeld, *A Double Dying: Reflections on Holocaust Literature*, 164.

10. Avisar, *Screening the Holocaust*, 126–127.

11. Kerner, *Film and the Holocaust*, 127.

12. Ibid., 130.

13. Although a Polish Gentile, Borowski was arrested for, of all things, publishing a book of poems the Germans deemed subversive. He arrived in Auschwitz one day after the Nazis stopped executing non-Jews. He may have served in the camp as a *Kapo*. After his liberation, he worked as a hack writer in the Polish Communist government and committed suicide by sticking his head in an oven. At the time, his wife was pregnant with their first child.

14. Lawrence L. Langer, *Holocaust Testimonies: The Ruins of Memory* (New Haven, CT: Yale University Press, 1991), 6.

15. Kerner, *Film and the Holocaust*, 130.

16. Ibid., 122–123.

10. CHOICELESS CHOICE

1. Lawrence L. Langer, *Art from the Ashes: A Holocaust Anthology* (Oxford: Oxford University Press, 1995), 154.

2. John Tagliabue, "Fighting for Life in a Nazi Boxing Ring," *New York Times*, 5/14/89, http://www.nytimes.com/1989/05/14/movies/film-fighting-for-life-itself-in-a-nazi-boxing-ring.html, n.p.

3. Ibid., n.p.

4. Paul H. Broesky, "Filming in a Killing Ground: 'Triumph of the Spirit is the first film to be shot almost entirely at Auschwitz death camps," *Los Angeles Times*, 5/23/89, http://articles.latimes.com/1989-04-23/entertainment/ca-1909_1_auschwitz-death-death-camp-ss-officers, n.p.

5. Lawrence Baron, *Projecting the Holocaust into the Present: The Changing Focus of Contemporary Holocaust Cinema* (Lanham, MD: Rowman and Littlefield, 2005), 91–92.

6. Ibid., 91.

7. Ibid., 89–90.

8. Annette Insdorf, *Indelible Shadows: Film and the Holocaust*, 2nd ed. (Cambridge: Cambridge University Press, 1989), 349.

9. Baron, *Projecting the Holocaust into the Present*, 93.

10. Leonard Maltin, *Leonard Maltin's 2005 Movie Guide* (New York: Signet, 2006), 1455.

11. Quoted in Baron, *Projecting the Holocaust into the Present*, 92.

12. Insdorf, *Indelible Shadows*, 349.

13. Baron, *Projecting the Holocaust into the Present*, 90.

11. SPIELBERG REINVENTS THE HOLOCAUST

1. Alan Mintz, *Popular Culture and the Shaping of Holocaust Memory* (Seattle: University of Washington Press, 2001), 126.

2. Thomas Keneally's 1982 novel, on which the movie is based, is more historically accurate.

3. Herbert Steinhouse, "The Man Who Saved a Thousand Lives," Thomas Fensch, ed., *Oskar Schindler and His List: The Man, the Book, the Film, the Holocaust and Its Survivors* (Forest Dale, VT: Paul S. Eriksson, 1995), 35.

4. Although many viewers and some more populist critics liked it, with Roger Ebert, for example, calling it "the year's best film."

5. Edward Guthman, "Spielberg's List: Director Rediscovers His Jewishness while Filming Nazi Story," Fensch, ed., *Oskar Schindler and His List*, 54.

6. Ibid.

7. Ibid., 59.

8. Ibid., 52.

9. Ibid., 62.

10. Ibid., 51.

11. Ibid., 54.

12. Ibid.

13. Ibid., 61.

14. Ibid., 60.

15. Ibid., 64.

16. Ibid., 148.

17. Ibid.

18. Ibid., 84.

19. Ibid., 68.

20. Ibid.

21. Lawrence Baron, *Projecting the Holocaust into the Present: The Changing Focus of Contemporary Holocaust Cinema* (Lanham, MD: Rowman and Littlefield, 2005), 212.

22. Anne Thompson, "Making History: How Steven Spielberg Brought 'Schindler's List' to Life," Fensch, ed., *Oskar Schindler and His List*, 69.

23. Tim Cole, *Selling the Holocaust: From Auschwitz to Schindler, How History Is Bought, Packaged, and Sold* (New York: Routledge, 1999), 94.

24. Michael R. Kagay, "Poll on Doubt of Holocaust is Corrected," Fensch, ed., *Oskar Schindler and His List*, 207. Admittedly, the accuracy of the Roper poll was challenged at the time by critics who argued that the polls use of double negatives in the questions posed to respondents and other examples of linguistic obfuscation had skewed the results. A second Roper poll, also commissioned by the American Jewish Committee, found that only 2 percent or less of the American public were consistent Holocaust-deniers.

25. Quoted in Mintz, *Popular Culture and the Shaping of Holocaust Memory*, 131.

26. Quoted ibid.

27. Stephen Schiff, "Seriously Spielberg," Fensch, ed., *Oskar Schindler and His List*, 146.

28. Quoted in Mintz, *Popular Culture and the Shaping of Holocaust Memory*, 135

29. Baron, *Projecting the Holocaust into the Present*, 210, 214.

30. Terrence Rafferty, "A Man of Transactions," Fensch, ed., *Oskar Schindler and His List*, 84.

31. Thomas Keneally, *Schindler's List* (New York: Simon and Schuster, 1982), 87.

32. Omer Bartov, "Spielberg's Oskar: Hollywood Tries Evil," *Yosefa Loshitzky, Spielberg's Holocaust: Critical Perspectives on* Schindler's List (Bloomington: Indiana University Press, 1997), 43.

33. Quoted in Baron, *Projecting the Holocaust into the Present*, 214.

34. Keneally, *Schindler's List*, 113.

35. Stanley Kauffmann, "Spielberg Revisited," Fensch, ed., *Oskar Schindler and His List*, 113.

36. Annette Insdorf, *Indelible Shadows: Film and the Holocaust*, 2nd ed. (Cambridge: Cambridge University Press, 1989), 36.

37. Stephen Schiff, "Seriously Spielberg," Fensch, ed., *Oskar Schindler and His List*, 143.

38. Ibid., 228.

39. Ibid., 141.

40. Ibid., 169–170.

41. Ibid., 187.

42. Cole, *Selling the Holocaust*, 82.

43. Judith E. Doneson, *The Holocaust in American Film*, 2nd ed. (Syracuse, NY: Syracuse University Press, 2002), 146.

44. Frank Rich, "Extras in the Shadows," Fensch, ed., *Oskar Schindler and His List*, 187.

45. Ibid.

46. Ibid.

47. Ibid., 138.

48. Baron, *Projecting the Holocaust into the Present*, 213.

49. Thomas Doherty, "Schindler's List," Fensch, ed., *Oskar Schindler and His List*, 122.

50. Ibid., 236.

51. Baron, *Projecting the Holocaust into the Present*, 213.

52. Thomas Doherty, "Schindler's List," Fensch, ed., *Oskar Schindler and His List*, 122–123.

53. Ibid., 180–181.

54. Quoted in Aaron Kerner, *Film and the Holocaust: New Perspectives on Dramas, Documentaries, and Experimental Films* (New York: Continuum Books, 2011), 47.

55. Cole, *Selling the Holocaust*, 177.

56. Ibid., 91.

57. Omer Bartov, "Spielberg's Oskar: Hollywood Tries Evil," Loshitzky, ed., *Spielberg's Holocaust*, 49.

58. Kerner, *Film and the Holocaust*, 42.

59. Loshitzky, *Spielberg's Holocaust*, 45.

60. Ibid., 164.

61. Ibid.

62. Mintz, *Popular Culture and the Shaping of Holocaust Memory*, 153.

63. Simon Louvish, "Witness: Is Spielberg's 'Schindler's List' More than a Ride in a Holocaust Theme Park? And How Has the Film Imagined the Unimaginable?," Fensch, ed., *Oskar Schindler and His List*, 79.

64. Berel Lang, *Holocaust Representations: Art within the Limits of History and Ethics* (Baltimore: John Hopkins University Press, 2000), 14.

12. MORAL AMBIGUITY IN THE HOLOCAUST

1. Morris Dickstein, *Gates of Eden : American Culture in the Sixties* (New York: Penguin, 1989), 111.

2. Ibid., 112.

3. Levi's memoir, *The Reawakening*, about his attempts to return to his native Italy after being liberated from Auschwitz, was turned in 1996 into a worthwhile if uneven film called *The Truce*, starring John Turturro as Levi.

4. Primo Levi, *The Drowned and the Saved* (London: Michael Joseph, 1988), 23.

5. Ibid., 227.

6. Lawrence Baron, *Projecting the Holocaust into the Present : The Changing Focus of Contemporary Holocaust Cinema* (Lanham, MD: Rowman and Littlefield, 2005), 255.

7. Aaron Kerner, *Film and the Holocaust : New Perspectives on Dramas, Documentaries, and Experimental Films* (New York: Continuum Books, 2011), 66.

8. Kristin Hohenadel, "A Holocaust Story without a Schindler," *New York Times*, January 7, 2001, 22.

9. Ibid.

10. George Robinson, "The Real Auschwitz," *Jewish Week*, September 13, 2002, 40.

11. Daniel Menaker, "A Holocaust Story That Has Roots in His Own," *New York Times*, October 20, 2002, 13.

12. Ibid.

13. Hohenadel, "A Holocaust Story without a Schindler," 22.

14. Stephen Holden, "An Uprising at Auschwitz with Emphasis on Realism," *New York Times*, September 17, 2002, 24.

15. Hohenadel, "A Holocaust Story without a Schindler," 22.

16. Kerner, *Film and the Holocaust*, 65.

17. Baron, *Projecting the Holocaust into the Present*, 257.

18. Hohenadel, "A Holocaust Story without a Schindler," 22.

19. Baron, *Projecting the Holocaust into the* Present, 256.

20. Ibid., 252.

21. Ibid., 256.

22. Robinson, "The Real Auschwitz," 40.

23. Kerner, *Film and the Holocaust*, 66.

24. Holden, "An Uprising at Auschwitz," 24.

25. Baron, *Projecting the Holocaust into the Present*, 258.

26. Primo Levi, *The Drowned and the Saved*, 23.

13. WHITE LIES

1. Quoted in Allessandra Stanley, "The Funniest Italian You've Probably Never Heard Of," *New York Times Magazine*, October 11, 1998, http://www.

nytimes.com/1998/10/11/magazine/the-funniest-italian-you-ve-probably-never-heard-of.html, 42.

2. Quoted ibid., 43.

3. Ibid.

4. Lawrence Baron, *Projecting the Holocaust into the Present: The Changing Focus of Contemporary Holocaust Cinema* (Lanham, MD: Rowman and Littlefield, 2005), 145.

5. Ibid., 144.

6. Stanley, "Funniest Italian," 44.

7. Annette Insdorf, *Indelible Shadows: Film and the Holocaust*, 3rd ed. (Cambridge: Cambridge University Press, 2003), 224.

8. Baron, *Projecting the Holocaust*, 146.

9. Annette Insdorf, *Indelible Shadows: Film and the Holocaust*, 2nd ed. (Cambridge: Cambridge University Press, 1989), 288.

10. Aaron Kerner, *Film and the Holocaust: New Perspectives on Dramas, Documentaries, and Experimental Films* (New York: Continuum Books, 2011), 100.

11. David Denby, "In the Eye of the Beholder," *New Yorker*, March 15, 1999, http://www.newyorker.com/magazine/1999/03/15/in-the-eye-of-the-beholder, 96.

12. Lee Marshall, "His *Life Is Beautiful*," *Sky*, March 1999, 65.

13. Baron, *Projecting the Holocaust*, 149.

14. Mike Clark, "*Life Is Beautiful*: Brave Humor Amid Holocaust," *USA Today*, October 23, 1998, 16.

15. Edward Rothstein, "Using Farce to Break the Dark Spell of Fascism," *New York Times*, October 18, 1998, 28.

16. Thane Rosenbaum, "With the Shoah, Can Tragedy Become Farce?" *Forward*, October 23, 1998, 11.

17. Rothstein, "Using Farce to Break the Dark Spell of Fascism," 28.

18. Insdorf, *Indelible Shadows*, 287.

19. Marshall, "His *Life Is Beautiful*," 66.

20. Baron, *Projecting the Holocaust*, 147.

21. Insdorf, *Indelible Shadows*, 286.

22. Quoted in Clark, "*Life Is Beautiful*," 16.

23. Insdorf, *Indelible Shadows*, 289.

24. Baron, *Projecting the Holocaust*, 144.

25. Hillel Halkin, "The Temptation of Roberto Benigni," *Forward*, March 27, 1998, 18.

26. Rosenbaum, "Using Farce to Break the Dark Spell of Fascism," 11.

27. Abraham H. Foxman, "The Holocaust Meets Popular Culture," *New York Times*, October 31, 1998, 15.

28. Allan Nadler, "Holocaust Film Offends History," *New York Times*, November 1, 1998, 12.

29. Denby, "In the Eye of the Beholder," 97.

30. Stanley, "Funniest Italian," 43.

31. Quoted in Baron, *Projecting the Holocaust*, 149.

32. That translation, by Leila Vennewitz, received the Helen and Kurt Wolff Translator's Prize in 1997.

33. Michael D. Richardson, "'Heil Myself!': Impersonation and Identity in Comedic Representations of Hitler," in *Visualizing the Holocaust: Documents, Aesthetics, Memory*, ed. David Bathrick, Brad Pagar, and Michael D. Richardson (Rochester, NY: Camden House, 2008), 267.

34. Rita Steinhardt Botwinick, *A History of the Holocaust: From Ideology to Annihilation*, 2nd ed. (Upper Saddle River, NJ: Prentice Hall, 2001), 208.

35. Baron, *Projecting the Holocaust*, 157.

36. Ibid., 156.

37. Ibid., 160.

38. Ibid., 159.

39. Insdorf, *Indelible Shadows*, 292.

40. Jurek Becker, *Jakob the Liar*, trans. Leila Vennewitz (New York: Plume, 1990), 232.

41. Ibid.

14. THE NAZIS' SUCCESSORS

1. Quoted in Aaron Kerner, *Film and the Holocaust: New Perspectives on Dramas, Documentaries, and Experimental Films* (New York: Continuum Books, 2011), 53.

2. Janet Maslin, *"Apt Pupil," New York Times*, October 23, 1998, http://www.nytimes.com/movies/movie/158801/Apt-Pupil/overview

3. Caroline Joan (Kay) S. Picart and David A. Frank, *Frames of Evil: The Holocaust as Horror in American Film* (Carbondale: Southern Illinois University Press, 2006), 100.

4. Ibid.

5. Ibid.

6. Kerner, *Film and the Holocaust*, 54.

7. Ibid., 58.

8. Picart and Frank, *Frames of Evil*, 121.

9. Kerner, *Film and the Holocaust*, 57.

10. Picart and Frank, *Frames of Evil*, 121.

11. Ibid.

15. MUTANT HOLOCAUST SURVIVORS, OR THE ANTI-AMERICAN SIN OF PESSIMISM

1. Samantha Baskind and Ranen Omer-Sherman, eds. *Jewish Graphic Novel: Critical Approaches* (New Brunswick, NJ: Rutgers University Press, 2008), 144.
2. Ibid.
3. Lawrence Baron, *Projecting the Holocaust into the Present: The Changing Focus of Contemporary Holocaust Cinema* (Lanham, MD: Rowman and Littlefield, 2005), 259.
4. Ibid., 260.
5. Quoted ibid., 258.
6. Ibid., 261–262.
7. Ibid., 262.
8. Lara Mike That Way, and Proud of It.,them (for extracts vs. run-in)please changes these to the individual chapter author and title, (Bergen, *X-Men* (New York: Dell Yearling, 2000), 168.
9. Baron, *Projecting the Holocaust into the Present*, 260.
10. Mike Russell, "*X-Men*: Mutant Mania Returns to Form in *First Class*," *Oregonian*, June 2, 2011, http://www.oregonlive.com/movies/2011/06/x-men_mutant_mania_returns_to.html
11. Manohla Dargis, "Born That Way, and Proud of It," *New York Times*, June 2, 2011. http://www.nytimes.com/2011/06/03/movies/x-men-first-class-review.html?_r=0

16. KIDS BEFRIENDING KIDS IN THE HOLOCAUST

1. James Christopher, "*The Boy in the Striped Pajamas*," *London Times*, September 11, 2008, http://www.entertainment.timesonline.co.uk/tol/arts_and_entertainment/films/film_reviews/article4725128
2. Rene Rodriguez, "*The Boy in the Striped Pajamas*," *Miami Herald*, September 2008, http://www.miami.com/the-boy-in-the-striped-pajamas-pg-13-article
3. Manohla Dargis, "Horror through a Child's Eyes," *New York Times*, November 6, 2008, http://www.nytimes.com/2008/11/07/movies/07paja.html
4. Abraham H. Foxman, "*The Boy in the Striped Pajamas*," ADL, December 9, 2008, http://archive.adl.org/nr/exeres/a21b4cf5-e638-4b09-afa5-2e8a00d7b1d2,213018c9-567c-418c-bdea-1cbda8f58810,frameless.html

5. Dargis, "Horror through a Child's Eyes."

6. Benjamin Blech, *The Boy in the Striped Pajamas*," AISH, October 23, 2008. http://www.aish.com/j/as/48965671.html

7. Gisela Bock, "Ordinary Women in Nazi Germany: Perpetrators, Victims, Followers, and Bystanders," in *Women in the Holocaust*, ed. Dalia Ofer and Lenore J. Weitzman (New Haven, CT: Yale University Press, 1998), 91.

8. Quoted in Aaron Kerner, *Film and the Holocaust: New Perspectives on Dramas, Documentaries, and Experimental Films* (New York: Continuum Books, 2011), 131.

9. Ibid., 132.

17. SHAGGING NAZIS AND OTHER POSTWAR GERMAN ADVENTURES

1. Rita Steinhardt Botwinick, *A History of the Holocaust: From Ideology to Annihilation*, 2nd ed. (Upper Saddle River, NJ: Prentice Hall, 2001), 109–110.

2. Kelly, "Writing *The Reader*," *Austin Chronicle*, December 26, 2008. http://www.austinchronicle.com/screens/2008-12-26/718932/

3. Ibid.

4. Ibid.

5. Ibid.

6. Aaron Kerner, *Film and the Holocaust: New Perspectives on Dramas, Documentaries, and Experimental Films* (New York: Continuum Books, 2011), 285.

7. Manohla Dargis, "*The Reader*," *New York Times*, December 9, 2008. http://www.nytimes.com/2008/12/10/movies/10read.html

8. Kyle Smith, "Death Camp for Cutie," *New York Post*, December 10, 2008. http://nypost.com/2008/12/10/death-camp-for-cutie/

9. Bernhard Schlink, *The Reader*, trans. Carol Brown Janeway (New York: Vintage Books, 1997), 198–199.

10. Kirk Honeycutt, "Film Review: *The Reader*," *Hollywood Reporter*. November 30, 2008. http://www.hollywoodreporter.com/review/film-review-reader-125129

11. Elizabeth Weitzman, "*The Reader*: Worth Seeing, Leaves You Wanting More." *Daily News*, December 10, 2008. http://www.nydailynews.com/entertainment/tv-movies/reader-worth-leaves-wanting-article-1.354592

12. Richard Schickel, "*The Reader*: Love and the Banality of Evil," *Time Magazine*, December 10, 2008. http://content.time.com/time/arts/article/0,8599,1865533,00.html

13. Dana Stevens, "Must Love Nazis," *Slate*, December 11, 2008, http://www.slate.com /articles/arts/movies/2008/12/must_love_nazis.html

14. William Arnold, *"The Reader* Oozes Quality in Every Way," *Seattle Post-Intelligencer*, December 24, 2008, http://www.seattlepi.com/ae/movies/article/The-Reader-oozes-quality-in-every-way-1295674.php

18. NO SHEEP TO THE SLAUGHTER

1. Gene Newman, *"Defiance," Premiere*, January 2009, cited at FilmAffinity, http://www.filmaffinity.com/en/film886922.html

2. David Denby, "Survivors: *Defiance* and *The Secret of the Grain*," *New Yorker*, January 19, 2009, http://www.newyorker.com/magazine/2009/01/12/survivors-8

3. Mick LaSalle, "Real Holocaust Story Gripping and Heroic, but the Movie Isn't," *San Francisco Chronicle*, January 16, 2009, http://www.sfgate.com/movies/article/Real-Holocaust-story-gripping-and-heroic-but-the-3254321.php

4. Newman, *"Defiance."*

5. Aaron Kerner, *Film and the Holocaust: New Perspectives on Dramas, Documentaries, and Experimental Films* (New York: Continuum Books, 2011), 66–67.

6. LaSalle, "Real Holocaust Story Gripping and Heroic."

7. Nathan Rabin, *"Defiance," A.V. Club*, December 31, 2008, http://www.avclub.com/review/defiance-17073

8. A. O. Scott, "Society in the Forest, Banding Together to Escape Persecution," *New York Times*, December 30, 2008, http://www.nytimes.com/2008/12/31/movies/31defi.html?_r=0

9. Rita Steinhardt Botwinick, *History of the Holocaust: From Ideology to Annihilation*, 2nd ed. (Upper Saddle River, NJ: Prentice Hall, 2001), 210–211.

10. Ibid., 212.

11. Ibid., 216.

19. CARTOON JEWISH REVENGE

1. Damon Wise, *"Inglourious Basterds* Guide," *Guardian*, August 15, 2009. http://www.guardian.co.uk/film/2009/aug/15/inglourious-basterds-guide

2. Scott Tobias, "Off to War, Brandishing Weapons and Words," *National Public Radio*, August 20, 2009, http://www.unz.org/Pub/NPR-2009aug-00866

3. Shawn Levy, "A Fever Dream of World War II: *Inglourious Basterds*," *Oregonian*, August 20, 2009, http://blog.oregonlive.com/madaboutmovies/2009/08/a_fever_dream_of_world_war_ii.html

4. Aaron Kerner, *Film and the Holocaust: New Perspectives on Dramas, Documentaries, and Experimental Films* (New York: Continuum Books, 2011), 76–77.

5. E. J. Hoberman, "Quentin Tarantino's *Inglourious Basterds* Makes Holocaust Revisionism Fun," *Village Voice*, August 18, 2009, http://www.villagevoice.com/2009-08-18/film/quentin-tarantino-s-inglourious-basterds-makes-holocaust-revisionism-fun/

6. See, for instance, Jeffrey Herf, *The Jewish Enemy: Nazi Ideology and Propaganda during World War II and the Holocaust* (Cambridge: Harvard University Press, 2006).

7. Jeffrey Goldberg, "Hollywood's Jewish Avenger," *Atlantic Monthly*, September, 2009. http://www.theatlantic.com/magazine/archive/2009/09/hollywoods-jewish-avenger/307619/

8. Marjorie Baumgarten, "Once Upon a War Story," *Austin Chronicle*, March 19, 2009, 13.

9. Dana Stevens, "The Good, the Bad and the Nazis," *Slate*, August 20, 2009, http://www.slate.com/articles/arts/movies/2009/08/the_good_the_bad_and_the_nazis.html

10. Francois Duhamel, "Review: *Inglourious Basterds*," *Christian Science Monitor*, August 21, 2009, 19.

11. Thomas Doherty, *Hollywood and Hitler 1933–1939* (New York: Columbia University Press, 2013), 373.

12. Tom Segev, *The Seventh Million: The Israelis and the Holocaust* (New York: Hill and Wang, 1993).

13. Peter Novick, *The Holocaust in American Life* (Boston: Houghton Mifflin, 1999), 98.

14. Marjorie Baumgarten, "Once Upon a War Story," *Austin Chronicle*, March 19, 2009, 13.

15. Ibid.

16. Lisa Schwarzbaum, "*Inglourious Basterds*," *Entertainment Weekly*, August 21, 2009. http://www.ew.com/article/2009/08/21/inglourious-basterds

17. Kerner, *Film and the Holocaust*, 77.

18. Susan Sontag, "Fascinating Fascism," in *Under the Sign of Saturn: Essays* (New York: Picador, 1972), 73.

CONCLUSION. WHERE DO WE GO FROM HERE?

1. Stuart Klawans, "Lest We Remember," *Tablet Magazine*, December 5, 2008, http://tabletmag.com/jewish-arts-and-culture/1258/lest-we-remember

2. Ibid.

3. Richard Corliss, "*Defiance*: Beyond Holo-kitsch," *Time*, January 1, 2009, http://content.time.com/time/arts/article/0,8599,1869229,00.html

4. Owen Gleiberman, "*Defiance*," *Entertainment Weekly*, January 14, 2009, http://www.ew.com/article/2009/01/14/defiance

5. "Oliver Stone: Jewish Control of the Media is Preventing Free Holocaust Debate," *Haaretz*, July 26, 2010. http://www.haaretz.com/jewish-world/oliver-stone-jewish-control-of-the-media-is-preventing-free-holocaust-debate-1.304108

6. As Neal Gabler documents in *An Empire of Their Own: How the Jews Invented Hollywood* (New York: Crown, 1988).

7. Quoted in Michael R. Marrus, *The Holocaust in History* (New York: Meridian, 1987), 22.

8. Ibid., 24.

9. Quoted in Eric Markusen and David Kopf, *Holocaust and Strategic Bombing: Genocide and Total War in the Twentieth Century* (Boulder, CO: Westview Press, 1995), 12.

10. Quoted ibid.

11. Lucy S. Dawidowicz, *The Holocaust and the Historians* (Cambridge, MA: Harvard University Press, 1981), 13–16.

BIBLIOGRAPHY

Adwar, Corey. "Here's Why Some Nazis Enjoyed Their Freedom in the US after World War II." BusinessInsider.com, June 24, 2014. http://www.businessinsider.com/heres-how-nazis-have-escaped-charges-in-the-us-2014-6

Amira, Dan. "Mike Godwin on Godwin's Law." *New York Magazine*, March 8, 2013. http://nymag.com/daily/intelligencer/2013/03/godwins-law-mike-godwin-hitler-nazi-comparisons.html

Arendt, Hannah. *Eichmann in Jerusalem: A Report on the Banality of Evil*. New York: Penguin Books, 1963.

Arnold, William. "*The Reader* Oozes Quality in Every Way." *Seattle Post Intelligencer*, December 24, 2008. http://www.seattlepi.com/ae/movies/article/The-Reader-oozes-quality-in-every-way-1295674.php

Avisar, Ilan. *Screening the Holocaust: Cinema's Images of the Unimaginable*. Bloomington: Indiana University Press, 1988.

Baldwin, Neil. *Henry Ford and the Jews: The Mass Production of Hate*. New York: Public Affairs, 2001.

Baron, Lawrence. *Projecting the Holocaust into the Present: The Changing Focus of Contemporary Holocaust Cinema*. Lanham, MD: Rowman and Littlefield, 2005.

Baskind, Samantha, and Ranen Omer-Sherman, eds. *The Jewish Graphic Novel: Critical Approaches*. New Brunswick, NJ: Rutgers University Press, 2008.

Bathrick, David. "Introduction: Seeing against the Grain." In *Visualizing the Holocaust: Documents, Aesthetics, Memory*, edited by David Bathrick, Brad Pagar, and Michael D. Richardson, 1–18. Rochester, NY: Camden House, 2008.

Bathrick, David, Brad Prager, Michael D. Richardson, eds. *Visualizing the Holocaust: Documents, Aesthetics, Memory*. Rochester, NY: Camden House, 2008.

Baumgarten, Marjorie. "Once Upon a War Story." *Austin Chronicle*, March 19, 2009, 13.

Becker, Jurek. *Jakob the Liar*. Translated by Leila Vennewitz. New York: Plume, 1990.

Bergen, Lara. *X-Men*. New York: Dell Yearling, 2000.

Black, Edwin. *IBM and the Holocaust: The Strategic Alliance between Nazi Germany and America's Most Powerful Corporation*. New York: Crown, 2001.

Blech, Benjamin. "*The Boy in the Striped Pajamas*." AISH, October 23, 2008. http://www.aish.com/j/as/48965671.html

Bock, Gisela. "Ordinary Women in Nazi Germany: Perpetrators, Victims, Followers, and Bystanders." In *Women in the Holocaust*, edited by Dalia Ofer and Lenore J. Weitzman. New Haven, CT: Yale University Press, 1998, 89–99.

Borowski, Tadeusz, *This Way for the Gas, Ladies and Gentlemen* (New York: Penguin Books, 1976).

Botwinick, Rita Steinhardt. *A History of the Holocaust: From Ideology to Annihilation*, 2nd edition. Upper Saddle River, NJ: Prentice Hall, 2001.

Brantley, Ben. "Desperate Dance at Oblivion's Brink." *New York Times*, March 20, 1998. http://www.nytimes.com/1998/03/20/movies/theater-review-desperate-dance-at-oblivions-brink.html

Breines, Paul. *Tough Jews: Political Fantasies and the Moral Dilemma of American Jewry*. New York: Basic Books, 1990.

Christopher, James. "The Boy in the Striped Pyjamas." *London Times*, September 11, 2008. http://www.entertainment.timesonline.co.uk/tol/arts_and_entertainment/films/film_reviews/article4725128

Clark, Mike. "*Life Is Beautiful*: Brave Humor Amid Holocaust." *USA Today*, October 23, 1998, 16.

Cole, Tim. *Selling the Holocaust: From Auschwitz to Schindler, How History Is Bought, Packaged, and Sold*. New York: Routledge, 1999.

Corliss, Richard. "Defiance: Beyond Holo-kitsch." *Time*, January 1, 2009. http://content.time.com/time/arts/article/0,8599,1869229,00.html

Dargis, Manohla. "Born That Way, and Proud of It." *New York Times*, June 2, 2011. http://www.nytimes.com/2011/06/03/movies/x-men-first-class-review.html?_r=0

———. "Horror through a Child's Eyes." *New York Times*, November 6, 2008. http://www.nytimes.com/2008/11/07/movies/07paja.html

———. "The Reader." *New York Times*, December 9, 2008. http://www.nytimes.com/2008/12/10/movies/10read.html

Dawidowicz, Lucy S. *The Holocaust and the Historians*. Cambridge, MA: Harvard University Press, 1981.

Denby, David. "In the Eye of the Beholder." *New Yorker*, March 15, 1999. http://www.newyorker.com/magazine/1999/03/15/in-the-eye-of-the-beholder

———. "Survivors: *Defiance* and *The Secret of the Grain*." *New Yorker*, January 19, 2009. http://www.newyorker.com/magazine/2009/01/12/survivors-8

Dickstein, Morris. *Gates of Eden: American Culture in the Sixties*. New York: Penguin, 1989.

Dobbs, Michael. "Ford and GM Scrutinized for Alleged Nazi Collaboration." *Washington Post*, November 30, 1998. http://www.washingtonpost.com/wp-srv/national/daily/nov98/nazicars30.htm

Doherty, Thomas. *Hollywood and Hitler, 1933–1939*. New York: Columbia University Press, 2013.

Doneson, Judith E., *The Holocaust in American Film*, 2nd edition. Syracuse, NY: Syracuse University Press, 2002.

Duhamel, Francois. "Review: *Inglourious Basterds*." *Christian Science Monitor*, August 21, 2009, 19.

Fein, Irving A. *Jack Benny: An Intimate Biography*. New York: Putnam, 1976.

Fensch, Thomas, ed. *Oskar Schindler and His List: The Man, the Book, the Film, the Holocaust and Its Survivors*. Forest Dale, VT: Paul S. Eriksson, 1995.

Fermaglich, Kirsten. *American Dreams and Nazi Nightmares: Early Holocaust Consciousness and Liberal America, 1957–1965*. Lebanon, NH: Brandeis University Press, 2006.

Flom, Eric L. *Chaplin in the Sound Era: An Analysis of the Seven Talkies*. Jefferson, NC: McFarland, 1997.

Forsyth, Frederick. *The Odessa File*. New York: Bantam Books, 1972.

Foxman, Abraham H. "The Boy in the Striped Pajamas." *ADL*, December 9, 2008. http://archive.adl.org/nr/exeres/a21b4cf5-e638-4b09-afa5-2e8a00d7b1d2,213018c9-567c-418c-bdea-1cbda8f58810,frameless.html

———. "The Holocaust Meets Popular Culture." *New York Times*, October 31, 1998, 15.

Freedman, Samuel G. *Jew versus Jew: The Struggle for the Soul of American Jewry*. New York: Simon and Schuster, 2000.

Friedlander, Albert H., ed. *Out of the Whirlwind: A Reader of Holocaust Literature*. New York: Schocken Books, 1976.

Friedlander, Saul. *Reflections on Nazism: An Essay on Kitsch and Death*. Bloomington: Indiana University Press, 1993.

Gabler, Neal. *An Empire of Their Own: How the Jews Invented Hollywood*. New York: Crown, 1988.

Gavin Lambert, "Review of *Judgment at Nuremberg* by Stanley Kramer." *Film Quarterly* 15, no. 2 (Winter 1961–1962).

Gleiberman, Owen. "*Defiance*." *Entertainment Weekly*, January 14, 2009. http://www.ew.com/article/2009/01/14/defiance

Goldberg, Jeffrey. "Hollywood's Jewish Avenger." *Atlantic Monthly*, September, 2009. http://www.theatlantic.com/magazine/archive/2009/09/hollywoods-jewish-avenger/307619/

Goldhagen, Daniel Jonah. *Hitler's Willing Executioners: Ordinary Germans and the Holocaust*. New York: Alfred A. Knopf, 1996.

Goldman, Eric A. *The American Jewish Story through Cinema*. Austin: University of Texas Press, 2013.

Goodrich, Frances, and Albert Hackett. *The Diary of Anne Frank*. New York: Dramatists Play Service, 1954.

Graver, Lawrence. *An Obsession with Anne Frank: Meyer Levin and the Diary*. Berkeley: University of California Press, 1995.

Halkin, Hillel. "The Temptation of Roberto Benigni." *Forward*, March 27, 1998, 18.

Hanisch, Michael. "The Chaplin Reception in Germany." In *Charlie Chaplin: His Reflection in Modern Times*, edited by Adolphe Nysenholc, 25–34. Berlin: Mouton de Gruyter, 1991.

"Hank Williams Jr. Compares Obama to Hitler, Gets Pulled from *Monday Night Football*." *Huffington Post*, October 3, 2011. http://www.huffingtonpost.com/2011/10/03/hank-williams-compares-obama-to-hitler_n_992513.html

Herf, Jeffrey. *The Jewish Enemy: Nazi Ideology and Propaganda during World War II and the Holocaust*. Cambridge, MA: Harvard University Press, 2006.

Hilberg, Raul. *The Destruction of the European Jews*. New York: Holmes and Meier, 1985.

Hirsch, Joshua. *After Image: Film, Trauma, and the Holocaust*. Philadelphia: Temple University Press, 2004.

Hoberman, E. J. "Quentin Tarantino's *Inglourious Basterds* Makes Holocaust Revisionism Fun." *Village Voice*, August 18, 2009. http://www.villagevoice.com/2009-08-18/film/quentin-tarantino-s-inglourious-basterds-makes-holocaust-revisionism-fun/

Hoberman, J. "When the Nazis Became Nudniks." *New York Times*, April 15, 2001, 13.

Hohenadel, Kristin. "A Holocaust Story without a Schindler." *New York Times*, January 7, 2001, 22.

Holden, Stephen. "An Uprising at Auschwitz, with Emphasis on Realism." *New York Times*, September 17, 2002, 24.

Honeycutt, Kirk. "Film Review: *The Reader*." *Hollywood Reporter*. November 30, 2008. http://www.hollywoodreporter.com/review/film-review-reader-125129

Hughes, Robert. *Culture of Complaint: The Fraying of America*. Oxford: Oxford University Press, 1993.

"*Inglourious Basterds* Has One Tricky Title." MSNBC. http://www.today.com/id / 32588484#.VO9rR81pB80;

Insdorf, Annette. *Indelible Shadows: Film and the Holocaust*, 2nd edition. Cambridge: Cambridge University Press, 1989.

Kakutani, Michiko. "Culture Zone; Window on the World." *New York Times Magazine*, April 26, 1998. http://www.nytimes.com/1998/04/26/magazine/culture-zone-window-on-the-world.html

Kaufman, Jonathan. *Broken Alliance: The Turbulent Times between Blacks and Jews in America*. New York: Simon and Schuster, 1988.

Kelly, Kevin. "Writing *The Reader*," *Austin Chronicle*, December 26, 2008. http://www.austinchronicle.com/screens/2008-12-26/718932/

Keneally, Thomas. *Schindler's List*. New York: Simon and Schuster, 1982.

Kerner, Aaron. *Film and the Holocaust: New Perspectives on Dramas, Documentaries, and Experimental Films*. New York: Continuum Books, 2011.

Klawans, Stuart. "Lest We Remember." *Tablet Magazine*, December 5, 2008. http://tablet-mag.com/jewish-arts-and-culture/1258/lest-we-remember

Kramer, Larry. *Reports from the Holocaust: The Story of an AIDS Activist*. New York: St. Martin's Press, 1994.

Krohn, Bill. "Hollywood and the Shoah, 1933–1945." In *Cinema and the Shoah: Art Confronts the Tragedy of the Twentieth Century*, edited by Jean-Michel Frodon, 141–164. Albany: State University of New York Press, 2010.

Lambert, Gavin. "Review of *Judgment at Nuremberg* by Stanley Kramer," *Film Quarterly* 15, no. 2 (Winter 1961–1962) 51–55.

Lang, Berel. *Holocaust Representations: Art within the Limits of History and Ethics*. Baltimore: John Hopkins University Press, 2000.

Langer, Lawrence L. *Admitting the Holocaust: Collected Essays*. Oxford: Oxford University Press, 1995.

———. *Art from the Ashes: A Holocaust Anthology*. Oxford: Oxford University Press, 1995.

———. *Holocaust Testimonies: The Ruins of Memory*. New Haven, CT: Yale University Press, 1991.

LaSalle, Mick. "Real Holocaust Story Gripping and Heroic, but the Movie Isn't." *San Francisco Chronicle*, January 16, 2009. http://www.sfgate.com/movies/article/Real-Holocaust-story-gripping-and-heroic-but-the-3254321.php

Levy, Shawn "A Fever Dream of World War II: *Inglourious Basterds*." *Oregonian*, August 20, 2009. http://blog.oregonlive.com/madaboutmovies/2009/08/a_fever_dream_of_world_war_ii.html

Limbaugh, Rush H. *The Way Things Ought to Be*. New York: Pocket Books, 1992.

Lipstadt, Deborah E. *Beyond Belief: The American Press and the Coming of the Holocaust 1933–1945*. New York: Free Press, 1986.

Lookstein, Haskel. *Were We Our Brothers' Keepers? The Public Response of American Jews to the Holocaust*. New York: Vintage Books, 1985.

Loshitzky, Yosefa, ed. *Spielberg's Holocaust: Critical Perspectives on* Schindler's List. Bloomington: Indiana University Press, 1997.

Lynn, Kenneth S. *Charlie Chaplin and His Times*. New York: Simon and Schuster, 1997.

Maltin, Leonard. *Leonard Maltin's 2005 Movie Guide*. New York: Signet, 2006.

Markusen, Eric, and David Kopf. *The Holocaust and Strategic Bombing: Genocide and Total War in the Twentieth Century*. Boulder, CO: Westview Press, 1995.

Marrus, Michael R. *The Holocaust in History*. New York: Meridian, 1987.

Marshall, Lee. "His *Life Is Beautiful*." *Sky*, March 1999, 65.

Maslin, Janet. "*Apt Pupil*." *New York Times*, October 23, 1998. http://www.nytimes.com/movies/movie/158801/Apt-Pupil/overview

McGinity, Keren G. "Intermarriage: Twenty-First-Century United States." In *The Cambridge Dictionary of Judaism and Jewish Culture*, edited by Judith R. Baskin, 278. Cambridge: Cambridge University Press, 2011.

Menaker, Daniel. "A Holocaust Story That Has Roots in His Own." *New York Times*, October 20, 2002, 13.

Miller, Judith. *One, by One, by One: Facing the Holocaust*. New York: Touchstone Books, 1990.

Mintz, Alan. *Popular Culture and the Shaping of Holocaust Memory*. Seattle: University of Washington Press, 2001.

Mommsen, Hans. "German Society and the Resistance against Hitler." In *The Third Reich: The Essential Readings*, edited by Christian Leitz, 255-273. London: Blackwell, 1999.

Müller, Melissa. *Anne Frank: The Biography*. Translated by Rita Kimber and Robert Kimber. New York: Metropolitan Books, 1998.

Nadler, Allan. "Holocaust Film Offends History." *New York Times*, November 1, 1998, 12.

Newman, Gene. "*Defiance*." *Premiere*, January 2009. Cited at FilmAffinity. http://www.filmaffinity.com/en/film886922.html

Nicoletti, L. J. "No Child Left Behind: Anne Frank Exhibits, American Abduction Narratives, and Nazi Bogeymen." In *Visualizing the Holocaust: Documents, Aesthetics, Memory*, edited by David Bathrick, Brad Prager, and Michael D. Richardson, 86–113. Rochester, NY: Camden House, 2008.

Novick, Peter, *The Holocaust in American Life*. Boston: Houghton Mifflin, 1999.

Ofer, Dalia, and Lenore J. Weitzman, eds. *Women in the Holocaust.* New Haven, CT: Yale University Press, 1998.

"Oliver Stone: Jewish Control of the Media is Preventing Free Holocaust Debate." *Haaretz,* July 26, 2010. http://www.haaretz.com/jewish-world/oliver-stone-jewish-control-of-the-media-is-preventing-free-holocaust-debate-1.304108

Paul, William. *Ernst Lubitsch's American Comedy.* New York: Columbia University Press, 1983.

Picart, Caroline Joan (Kay) S., and David A. Frank. *Frames of Evil: The Holocaust as Horror in American Film.* Carbondale: Southern Illinois University Press, 2006.

Podhoretz, John. "The Great White (Nazi) Way: A Brilliant Production of a Classic Raises Disturbing Questions." *New York Post,* March 26, 1998, 35.

"Quentin Tarantino on the *Inglourious Basterds* Trailer." *Empire.* http://www.empireonline.com /features/tarantino-talks-inglourious-basterds-trailer/

Rabin, Nathan. "*Defiance.*" *A.V. Club,* December 31, 2008. http://www.avclub.com/review/defiance-17073

Richardson, Michael D. "'Heil Myself!': Impersonation and Identity in Comedic Representations of Hitler." In *Visualizing the Holocaust: Documents, Aesthetics, Memory,* edited by David Bathrick, Brad Pagar, and Michael D. Richardson, 277–297. Rochester, NY: Camden House, 2008.

Robinson, George. "The Real Auschwitz." *Jewish Week,* September 13, 2002, 40.

Rodriguez, Rene. "*The Boy in the Striped Pajamas.*" *Miami Herald,* September 2008. http://www.miami.com/the-boy-in-the-striped-pajamas-pg-13-article

Rosenbaum, Ron, *Explaining Hitler: The Search for the Origins of His Evil.* New York: Random House, 1998.

Rosenbaum, Thane. "Using Farce to Break the Dark Spell of Fascism." *New York Times,* October 18, 1998. http://www.nytimes.com/1998/10/18/movies/film-using-farce-to-break-the-dark-spell-of-fascism.html

———. "With the Shoah, Can Tragedy Become Farce?" *Forward,* October 23, 1998, 11.

Rosenfeld, Alvin H. *A Double Dying: Reflections on Holocaust Literature.* Bloomington: Indiana University Press, 1980.

Rothstein, Edward. "Using Farce to Break the Dark Spell of Fascism." *New York Times,* October 18, 1998, 28.

Rothstein, Mervyn. "In Three Revivals the Goose-Stepping Is Louder." *New York Times,* March 8, 1998, 23.

Russell, Mike. "*X-Men*: Mutant Mania Returns to Form in *First Class.*" *Oregonian,* June 2, 2011. http://www.oregonlive.com/movies/2011/06/x-men_mutant_mania_returns_to.html

Schickel, Richard. "*The Reader*: Love and the Banality of Evil." *Time Magazine,* December 10, 2008. http://content.time.com/time/arts/article/0,8599,1865533,00.html

Schlink, Bernhard. *The Reader.* Translated by Carol Brown Janeway. New York: Vintage Books, 1997.

Schwarzbaum, Lisa. "*Inglourious Basterds.*" *Entertainment Weekly,* August 21, 2009. http://www.ew.com/article/2009/08/21/inglourious-basterds

Scott, A. O. "A Society in the Forest, Banding Together to Escape Persecution." *New York Times,* December 30, 2008. http://www.nytimes.com/2008/12/31/movies/31defi.html?_r=0

Segev, Tom. *The Seventh Million: The Israelis and the Holocaust.* New York: Hill and Wang, 1993.

———. *Simon Wiesenthal: The Life and Legends.* New York: Doubleday, 2010.

Shah, Adam. "Fox News Turns to LaPierre, Who Once Called ATF Agents 'Jack-Booted Government Thugs.'" *Media Matters for America,* March 10, 2011. http://mediamatters.org/blog/2011/03/10/fox-news-turns-to-lapierre-who-once-called-atf/177439

Smith, Bradley F. *Reaching "Judgment at Nuremberg": The Untold Story of How the Nazi Criminals Were Judged.* New York: Basic Books, 1977.

Smith, Kyle. "Death Camp for Cutie." *New York Post,* December 10, 2008. http://nypost.com/2008/12/10/death-camp-for-cutie/

Sontag, Susan. "Fascinating Fascism." In *Under the Sign of Saturn: Essays*, 73. New York: Picador, 1972.

Spotts, Frederic. *Hitler and the Power of Aesthetics*. Woodstock, NY: Overlook, 2002.

Stanley, Allessandra. "The Funniest Italian You've Probably Never Heard Of." *New York Times Magazine*, October 11, 1998, 42. http://www.nytimes.com/1998/10/11/magazine/the-funniest-italian-you-ve-probably-never-heard-of.html

Stevens, Dana. "The Good, the Bad and the Nazis." *Slate*, August 20, 2009. http://www.slate.com/articles/arts/movies/2009/08/the_good_the_bad_and_the_nazis.html

———. "Must Love Nazis." *Slate*, December 11, 2008. http://www.slate.com /articles/arts/movies/2008/12/must_love_nazis.html

Tobias, Scott. "Off To War, Brandishing Weapons and Words." National Public Radio, August 20, 2009. http://www.unz.org/Pub/NPR-2009aug-00866

Wagner, Gottfried. *Twilight of the Wagners: The Unveiling of a Family's Legacy*. New York: St. Martin's, 1997.

Weitzman, Elizabeth. "*The Reader*: Worth Seeing, Leaves You Wanting More." *Daily News*, December 10, 2008. http://www.nydailynews.com/entertainment/tv-movies/reader-worth-leaves-wanting-article-1.354592

Weston, Kevin. "Why Would Anyone Laugh at *Schindler's List*? Hollywood Hasn't Taught History to Blacks." *Los Angeles Times*, February 28, 1994. http://articles.latimes.com/1994-02-28/entertainment/ca-28145_1_schindler-s-list

Whitfield, Stephen J. *In Search of American Jewish Culture*. Hanover: Brandeis University Press, 1999.

Wiesel, Elie. *Night*. New York: Hill and Wang, 1972, 1985.

Williams, Mary Elizabeth. "Why You Should Never Engage with an Abortion Protester." *Salon*, March 14, 2014. http://www.salon.com/2014/03/14/why_you_should_never_engage_with_an_abortion_protester/

Winer, Linda. "The Down-and-Dirty Party That Hitler Ended." *Newsday*, March 20, 1998, n.p.

Wise, Damon. "*Inglourious Basterds* Guide." *Guardian*, August 15, 2009. http://www.guardian.co.uk/film/2009/aug/15/inglourious-basterds-guide

Wyman, David S. *The Abandonment of the Jews: America and the Holocaust, 1941–1945*. New York: Pantheon Books, 1984.

FURTHER READING

Bartov, Omer. *Murder in Our Midst: The Holocaust, Industrial Killing, and Representation.* Oxford: Oxford University Press, 1996.

Brown, Jean E., et al., eds. *Images from the Holocaust: A Literature Anthology.* Lincolnwood, IL: National Textbook Company, 1997.

Browning, Christopher R. *Ordinary Men: Reserve Police Battalion 101 and the Final Solution in Poland.* New York: Harper Perennial, 1992.

Crowe, David M. *Oskar Schindler: The Untold Account of the Life, Wartime Activities, and the Story behind the List.* Cambridge, MA: Westview, 2004.

Dawidowicz, Lucy S. *The War against the Jews, 1933–1945.* New York: Bantam Books, 1975.

Flanzbaum, Hilene, ed. *The Americanization of the Holocaust.* Baltimore: Johns Hopkins University Press, 1999.

Hartman, Geoffrey H. *The Longest Shadow: In the Aftermath of the Holocaust.* Bloomington: Indiana University Press, 1996.

Langer, Lawrence L. *Preempting the Holocaust.* New Haven, CT: Yale University Press, 1998.

Linethal, Edward T. *Preserving Memory: The Struggle to Create America's Holocaust Museum.* New York: Penguin, 1995.

Plant, Richard. *The Pink Triangle: The Nazi War against Homosexuals.* New York: Henry Holt and Company, 1986.

Rubenstein, Richard L. *The Cunning of History: The Holocaust and the American Future.* New York: Harper Colophon Books, 1975.

Schwarz, Daniel R. *Imagining the Holocaust.* New York: St. Martin's, 1999.

Shandler, Jeffrey. *While America Watches: Televising the Holocaust.* Oxford: Oxford University Press, 1999.

Todorov, Tzvetan. *Facing the Extreme: Moral Life in the Concentration Camps.* New York: Metropolitan Books, 1996.

Yahl, Leni. *The Holocaust: The Fate of European Jewry.* Oxford: Oxford University Press, 1987.

Young, James E. *The Texture of Memory: Holocaust Memorials and Meaning.* New Haven, CT: Yale University Press, 1993.

Zelizer, Barbie, ed. *Visual Culture and the Holocaust.* New Brunswick, NJ: Rutgers University Press, 2001.

INDEX

ABOUT THE AUTHOR

Henry Gonshak is a professor of English at Montana Tech, where he teaches a regular course in Holocaust studies. His writings on the Holocaust, Israel, and Jewish American culture have appeared in two book collections, *New Perspectives on the Holocaust: A Guide for Teachers and Scholars* and *The Burdens of History: Post Holocaust Generations in Dialogue*, as well as in a variety of publications, including *Shofar: An Interdisciplinary Journal of Jewish Studies*, the *American Jewish Congress Monthly*, *Response: A Contemporary Jewish Review*, the *Journal of American Culture*, and *Peace Review: A Journal of Social Justice*. He lives in Butte, Montana, with his wife and daughter.